MORNING RISER

MORNING RISER

Multi-authored Junior Devotional Book

REVIEW AND HERALD® PUBLISHING ASSOCIATION
WASHINGTON, DC 20039-0555
HAGERSTOWN, MD 21740

Typeset: 11 pt. Century Light

Printed in USA

R&H Cataloging Service

Morning riser.

1. Youth—Prayer books and devotions.   2. Devotional calendars.

      248.48673202

ISBN 0-8280-0457-9

Let's get acquainted with the authors

Roselyn Edwards has spent most of her life working with children and youth, and says that she feels much more at home with them than she does with the grown-ups at church. She spent several years on the editorial staff of the *Mother Earth News* and now lives on a North Carolina mountainside where she gets her exercise clearing brush.

Adlai Esteb worked his way through school selling Adventist books and had the habit of asking interested persons if they would like Bible studies. At the end of his second year he and the Lord had 34 people ready for baptism. A pastor and missionary, Elder Esteb is probably best known for his poetry.

Mable Hillock was born in Newfoundland but grew up in China, where her parents were missionaries. She and her pastor husband have one son and twin daughters.

Jay and Eileen Lantry have made a good writing team. Jay has been a teacher and principal of boarding academies as well as a missionary in the Far Eastern Division. He enjoys helping people work together. Eileen has just had her twelfth book accepted for publication. They live in the beautiful mountains of north Idaho and enjoy studying nature, cross-country skiing, and bringing people to Jesus.

Robert Pierson is a former General Conference president and author of 28 books. While editor of his high school paper he began a writing career that has spanned 60 years. Retired now, he and his wife divide their time between North Carolina and Florida.

Lois Randolph was born in 1900 and spent 36 years as a teacher. She has written two Morning Watch books, plus many articles and stories. She has a special love for children and enjoys doing volunteer work.

Virgil Robinson was a great-grandson of Ellen White. After teaching church school, he answered a call to Africa, spending 25 years on that continent. Returning home, he worked with Home Study International, taking time to enjoy his hobby of writing. Elder Robinson passed away in 1985.

Walter Scragg is currently president of the South Pacific Division. A good storyteller, he has authored three books for junior youth.

Key

R.E.	Roselyn Edwards
A.A.E.	Adlai A. Esteb
M.H.	Mable Hillock
E.E.L. and J.H.L.	Eileen E. Lantry and Jay H. Lantry
R.H.P.	Robert H. Pierson
V.E.R.	Virgil E. Robinson
L.C.W.	Lois C. Randolph Woods
W.R.L.S.	Walter R. L. Scragg

YOU MUST STOP!

But as for me, I will look to the Lord, I will wait for the God of my salvation; my God will hear me.   Micah 7:7, RSV.

There it is, God's New Year's promise that when you stop, or wait, and look to Him, He will listen or hear you. Don't be too hurried to stop. You'll find it impossible to see what you're looking at or listen to what you hear unless you take time to stop.

I handed my passport and visa application to the immigration officer at the causeway that connects Singapore to mainland Malaysia. Scanning it, he pointed to my address during my stay. I had written "jungle."

"You mean you are going to stay out in the jungle?"

"That's right," I assured him.

"But why spend several days in the hot, humid jungle?"

"I have many friends there—tigers that leave pug marks after a rain, wild boars who root in the soft earth around camp, chattering gibbon apes to awaken me each morning. I love the colorful butterflies and the intricate spider webs along the trails. I get goose pimples when huge hornbills fly overhead. I listen to the tiny sunbirds that flit on the rhododendron, the nightly concert from the insect orchestra, and the music of the jungle streams. The jungle is exciting! Have you been there?"

"No, I've never taken the time to go. Too busy here." He smiled a queer smile as he handed me the stamped documents. "Tell your jungle friends 'hello' from me," he added.

He thought we were queer, but we felt pity for him. So close to a land of wonder and beauty, and he didn't care enough to go. The jungle held no fascination for him. He wouldn't have been able to see and appreciate its beauties. His ears couldn't have identified the bird calls, the croaks of tree frogs, or the cicadas' shrill cry. The jungle would have been a forbidding green blanket interspersed with stinging insects.

You can't appreciate God's beautiful world until you learn to stop, look, and listen where you are. Each morning this year we hope you'll do just that. As you develop the habit of stopping to wait for God, you'll acquire seeing eyes and listening ears. God will speak to you. You'll know joy you never dreamed possible. Begin today.

E.E.L. and J.H.L.

YOURS, ALL YOURS!

See how much the Father has loved us! His love is so great that we are called God's children—and so, in fact, we are. 1 John 3:1, TEV.

Henry was an orphan. He never knew the love of a father or mother. He never knew a clean, comfortable home with tasty, wholesome food to eat. Finally Henry ended up in an orphanage, where he had only the barest necessities.

One day Mr. and Mrs. Goodrich, a wealthy couple from another part of the city, came to the orphanage.

"We never had children of our own," Mr. Goodrich explained to the superintendent of the orphanage. "We would like to adopt a little boy and take him into our home as our son and give him all the things we would give a son of our own."

After looking around and getting acquainted with some of the children, the Goodriches decided—yes, you are right—they wanted Henry. Some weeks later, after all the legal work had been completed, the Goodriches drove up in their shiny, black limousine to take Henry home with them.

The small boy could hardly believe what he saw and heard. Upon arrival at the Goodrich mansion little Henry wandered wide-eyed and open-mouthed from one room to another. He feasted his eyes on the deep carpets, the breathtaking chandeliers, the rich furniture, the stocks of food in the pantry.

"Do you mean that I am now your little boy? Can I really stay here with you always? Do you love me, and are all of these things mine?" he asked almost unbelievingly of his new parents.

Mrs. Goodrich leaned over, gathered little Henry in her arms, and for a minute held him close to her heart.

"Yes, dear," she assured lovingly, "you are our little boy forever. We love you, and everything in this house is yours always."

This story reminds us of the words of John the Beloved in our text for today. God's love for us is so amazing that the apostle challenged all of us to behold it—to see this matchless love for ourselves.

I am so thankful that God loved us so much He wanted us to be His children—aren't you? Because of this all of the glories of eternal life and heaven are ours. Accept this gift of God today. Don't let anything keep you from it.

R.H.P.

KEEP LOOKING UP!

I will lift up mine eyes unto the hills, from whence cometh my help. My help cometh from the Lord. Psalm 121:1, 2.

Three elderly men sat on a park bench watching as another man, head bent and eyes downcast, hobbled slowly past.

"Here comes old Tom again," one of them whispered. "Just watch; he'll walk right past and never see us."

Sure enough, Tom shuffled along without lifting his head. Before he had gone far, one of the men called to him.

"Morning, Tom. Why don't you greet your friends?"

A bit startled to be addressed like that when he had thought himself alone, Tom glanced up sheepishly, then walked over to the bench and sat down.

"What's wrong, Tom?" one of them asked. "I've watched you for several days, and you just keep looking down. I know it rained yesterday, but this morning the puddles are gone and the sky is blue."

Tom looked even more abashed.

"Well, to tell the truth, I picked up a quarter here on this path last week, and ever since I've been hoping I'd find another."

So poor Tom walked around all day with his eyes to the ground, never noticing the blue sky, the birds, trees, or far-off mountains.

Many people, like Tom, never take their eyes off their jobs or their troubles or their struggle to make a living. They never seem to see all the beautiful things God has created to make them happy.

The shepherd-poet David was fortunate. Out with his sheep in the hills of Bethlehem, he had only to look up. What he saw, he described in the book of Psalms.

But even as he gazed upward he was troubled when he remembered that many people chose the hilltops as the best place to worship their idol gods. He saw their temples and the images they worshiped. Some Bible students think that David, when he wrote today's verse, may have been asking a question: Shall I lift up mine eyes unto the hills? From whence cometh my help? My help cometh from the Lord. He knew that help could come only from the God who made those mountains, rivers, and the sea—the Creator of all.

In the city, too, there is beauty. Search for it. Like David, lift up your eyes and behold the things God has created for your enjoyment.

V.E.R.

11

SHADOW TAG

We are strangers before thee, and sojourners, as were all our fathers: our days on the earth are as a shadow, and there is none abiding. 1 Chronicles 29:15.

Jack and Tammy played shadow tag as they walked home from school. Each one tried to step on the head of the other's shadow, and at the same time tried to keep the other from stepping on his own shadow's head.

The game resulted in much ducking, dodging, running, and laughter. The mile of blacktop road between the school and their home seemed much shorter when they played something fun along the way.

Tammy ran ahead and Jack darted after her, trying to catch up with the head of her shadow. Then all at once the sun slid behind a cloud, and the patterns of sunlight and shadow were gone. Jack and Tammy stopped running and laughing.

The next morning when they were ready to start for school, the sun shone brightly again. But this time their shadows walked behind them instead of in front, and they could not play shadow tag and still make progress toward the school.

"Oh, well," said Jack, "we'll play again on the way home."

But when school was out that afternoon, the sun was not shining.

"I wish the shadows weren't so temporary," Jack said. "They're here today and gone tomorrow. I wish we made shadows ahead of us every time we walked along this road."

Our Bible verse this morning compares life on this earth to a shadow. If we could really understand the eternity of time that stretches before those who inherit the earth made new, we could better understand the temporary nature of this life as we know it.

We might also compare the dark spot of our shadow with the colors of reality. There is quite a difference between the colors of our hair and clothing as we stand there in person and that shadow of us stretching out on the ground.

This might remind us of the glory of the new earth that we cannot possibly imagine now, for everything will be so glorious there that we have nothing in our understanding with which to compare it.

Let's not be so caught up with the shadow of this life that we forget the real substance of the life God has planned for us.

R.E.

12

IT'S HARD GROWING UP

They drew and lifted up Joseph out of the pit, and sold Joseph to the Ishmaelites for twenty pieces of silver: and they brought Joseph into Egypt. Genesis 37:28.

As the caravan journeyed southward Joseph saw the hills of home. Filled with uncontrolled grief and terror, he cried bitterly at the thought of leaving his father. Alone and friendless, this tenderly cherished son was now despised.

God turned this experience into a blessing. Joseph learned in a few hours what might have taken years if he had remained the pampered son at home. Do you find growing up hard? Take courage. Even animals and birds have a difficult time.

Especially do adolescents of the wild have trouble leaving the constant care of their parents. Most young animals depart with much agony. The time had come for a mother groundhog to send her first litter of youngsters from the den, for new babies would soon be born. All left but one shy youngster. When he circled back, she headed him off. He lay on his belly, trying to sneak under her. She slashed at him with her teeth, driving him into the woods, until he finally left.

Wild youngsters making their first decisions often get into trouble. A young fox fell into a cistern, a bat landed in a teapot, a young grouse crashed against a window. A few yards from his nest, a young deer mouse stumbled into a bumblebee's lair. Spinning in pain, he slipped and fell into a creek. After he had licked himself dry, he ran into a live trap. Released, he rushed into the home of a strange male mouse, got bit on the ear and fled back to the trap. But he learned fast. Constructing a permanent home for himself, he was soon able to make wise adult mouse decisions.

Growing away from home is nature's way of preventing inbreeding, and averting diseases and tensions that would occur in the wild if the population of birds and animals were too concentrated.

God, too, allows young people to have experiences where they can't lean on parents. To help you to become truly mature, God permits you to go where you won't be pampered or indulged. Though you may make mistakes, trust God to lead you through. As with Joseph, God can use disappointment as a great blessing as you learn real wisdom from Him.

E.E.L. and J.H.L.

WHEN GLOOM CHANGED TO REJOICING

Say among the heathen that the Lord reigneth: the world also shall be established that it shall not be moved: he shall judge the people righteously. Psalm 96:10.

In 1815 the communication system was still dependent upon the old semaphore signal system. There was no telegraph or telephone or radio in those days. So, after the Battle of Waterloo, from the beach across the Straits to the towers and hilltops and on to London was signaled the news that all of England awaited breathlessly. The words were carefully spelled out: WELLINGTON DEFEATED ... At that moment a typical London fog settled down and the full message could not be relayed until the next morning.

Imagine the gloom that settled over England as that tragic message of defeat was repeated from home to home.

However, the next morning the fog lifted and the semaphore message was completed: WELLINGTON DEFEATED THE ENEMY. What rejoicing then thrilled the British people!

There is a solemn message in this for all Christians. When Christ died on the cross, darkness settled down and the disciples misunderstood the message. They thought it was CHRIST DEFEATED. And there was gloom and discouragement. Two men were walking to Emmaus. They were sad, dejected, and discouraged. Unrecognized, Jesus joined them, and asked, "What are you so concerned about?"

One of them, Cleopas, replied, "You must be the only person in Jerusalem who hasn't heard about the terrible things that happened there last week."

"What things?" Jesus asked. Cleopas told the sad news and added, "We had thought He was the glorious Messiah and that He had come to rescue Israel." But he used the *past tense.* Jesus was now dead—*Christ defeated.* Then Jesus lifted the fog from their minds and completed the message that changed their gloom to glory —CHRIST DEFEATED DEATH. Christ was triumphant over death and the grave and could say, "Because I live ye shall live also"! This is the good news!

A.A.E.

COUNTING TROUBLE OR STUMBLING TROUBLE?

Blessed be the Lord, who daily loadeth us with benefits. Psalm 68:19.

Father was in a hurry to get home one winter night, and Bonnie was racing to keep up with him. But even though she was almost running, she could not help noticing the beautiful stars sparkling in the crisp heavens above her head.

"Daddy," she announced, slowing down a little, "I'm going to count the stars."

"All right," said Daddy, "go on."

And Bonnie started. After a while her father heard her saying, "Two hundred and twenty-three, two hundred and twenty-four, two hundred and twenty-five. Oh, dear!" she exclaimed. "I didn't have any idea there were so many!"

Did you ever try to count all the blessings God has given you? If you did, you probably had counting trouble just as Bonnie did. But the funny thing is that some people can't seem to see their blessings. They stumble over them every day and don't even notice them. They are like people in the gold-mining town of Sonora, California, some years ago. Every day they tripped over the rocks in one of the main streets on their way to the mines to search for gold. They never dreamed of the wealth that lay beneath their feet until one day, after a storm, a man led his mule, pulling a cart, up the steep road.

"Whoa!" he cried, reining his mule to a halt. Grimacing with pain, he looked disgustedly at the stone over which he had just stumbled. "Wish they wouldn't use such big rocks in the roads. With rains like the one we just had they get washed loose and can be dangerous. Guess I'd better move this one, anyway," and he bent down to hoist it aside.

"Just a minute!" he whistled to himself as he stopped to take a second look. "This is no ordinary rock." Lifting it into the cart, he examined it more carefully. "Gold if ever I saw it!" he exclaimed, staring in awe at the rock he had just found. And it was. Solid gold. Twenty-five pounds of it.

"Blessed be the Lord, who daily *loadeth* us with benefits."

Are you having counting trouble or stumbling trouble?

M.H.

15

MAGNET

And I, if I be lifted up from the earth, will draw all men unto me. John 12:32.

The woman talked on past closing time, but no one in the audience moved to leave. They sat spellbound, faces upturned, listening.

Something about the speaker drew the people. When she finished talking they surged forward, eager to shake her hand. Many wanted to speak personally with the woman whose story had so stirred them.

"What is it about her that magnetizes people?" Fran wondered.

Fran went to hear the speaker again and again. Each time the people responded in the same manner. She still didn't realize the secret.

Then one day as Fran read a book by Eugenia Price she came across these words: "If (Christ) is in control of you, then He is the most prominent part of your personality. And He has said, 'I, if I be lifted up . . . , will draw . . .'"

Then Fran knew what it had been about that speaker that drew people. It was God's love shining through her personality!

Have you ever felt a magnet of God's love drawing you through a human personality? God gives us experiences like this so that we can better understand His great personality.

You know what the light from the moon is, don't you? It is a reflection of light from the sun. A human personality that draws people like a magnet and points them toward God is a reflection of God's great love. This is one of the special capacities God gave us that He didn't give to other creatures.

The sun is many times bigger than the moon. But when we look at the moon at night, it doesn't seem so small. The reason we do not see the size in real comparison is that the moon is much closer to us. Things always look bigger in proportion as we are closer to them.

Just as the sun is many times bigger and brighter than the moon, so is God's personality many times bigger and brighter than any human personality. But until we learn to know Him better, we sometimes begin to understand His great love if we look at people who reflect that love in their lives.

Let us ask Him today to help us reflect His love in our lives too.

R.E.

FOLLOW A PORPOISE?

The meek will he guide in judgment: and the meek will he teach his way. Psalm 25:9.

Is it difficult for you to make decisions? You know right from wrong, but it is much harder to make good decisions in the "gray" areas. Hardest of all are those in which you must decide between two good alternatives. Jesus promises guidance if you meet one important requirement. What is it? Meekness; humility.

Sailors in the 1800s dreaded the dangerous French pass off the coast of New Zealand. Here the Pelorus Sound was full of treacherous currents and jagged rocks that were concealed just below the surface. Many ships were lost in this region.

One stormy morning in 1871 the *Brindle,* sailing from Boston to Sydney, was having trouble going through the pass when a porpoise leaped out of the water. The men wanted to harpoon it, but the captain's wife suggested they follow it. Experienced sailors, these men didn't want to listen to a woman, let alone follow a marine animal. Still, they knew that the porpoise had spent his lifetime in these treacherous waters. For years he had plied swiftly through the open channels, avoiding the rocks. Yes, he knew a lot more about Pelorus Sound than they did. So putting aside selfish pride and human judgment, they humbly followed him and made a safe passage!

From that time on Pelorus Jack, as they called him, stayed around the Sound. Sailors watched for him. As soon as the porpoise saw a ship he leaped out of the water and was always greeted by a cheer from those on board. For the forty years from 1871 to 1912 Pelorus Jack guided ships through those dangerous waters, saving thousands of lives.

During those years only one ship struck the jagged rocks and sank. Why? In 1903 a drunken passenger shot at the porpoise, nicking him. For two weeks the animal disappeared, and when he returned to work he refused to guide that one ship, which soon struck the rocks and was lost.

Jesus promises to teach you His way, give you good judgment, and guide you in making decisions. Your part? You must be humble and meek enough to follow. You'll get through life safely if you trust Him completely and follow His leading, just as those sailors trusted Pelorus Jack.

E.E.L. and J.H.L.

DASH FOR DIAMONDS

The law of the Lord is perfect, converting the soul: the testimony of the Lord is sure, making wise the simple. The statutes of the Lord are right, rejoicing the heart: the commandment of the Lord is pure, enlightening the eyes. Psalm 19:7, 8.

The psalmist continues his description with these words: "The fear of the Lord is clean, enduring for ever: the judgments of the Lord are true and righteous altogether. More to be desired are they than gold, yea, than much fine gold: sweeter also than honey and the honeycomb. Moreover by them is thy servant warned: and in keeping of them there is great reward" (Ps. 19:9-11).

Years ago in the Orange Free State, South Africa, a new section was to be opened for diamond prospectors. Arrangements were made for all who wished to hunt for diamonds to line up on the boundary of the territory and at the signal of an authority they were to dash in and stake claims.

Among those who made a dash for diamonds that day was young John Cooks—later to become one of the Trans-Africa Division's stalwart leaders. When the signal was given, John dashed in and staked his claim. For some weeks the young man worked his claim and found some diamonds. Down about six or seven feet John struck hard rock. Since the youth lacked the necessary equipment to go through the hard rock, he disposed of his claim.

The man who staked a claim next to John's went down deep. He struck a vein of diamonds that ran back under John's land. Thousands of diamonds were mined, and the new owner became very wealthy. Brother Cooks had stopped digging too soon!

God has given us a mine filled with the most precious ore in the world—the Bible, God's Word. Ellen White says, "There is a rich mine of truth and beauty in this Holy Book."—*Testimonies*, vol. 5, p. 322. "More to be desired are they than gold, yea, than much fine gold: sweeter also than honey and the honeycomb."

How do you study your Bible? Do you just read a few verses every now and then, or do you really study it? Remember, John Cooks lost a fortune because he stopped digging too soon. Don't make the same mistake!

R.H.P.

NAME AND FAME

Wherefore God also hath highly exalted him, and given him a name which is above every name: that at the name of Jesus every knee should bow. Philippians 2:9, 10.

John Harvard was thirty-one years old when he died in the year 1638. You might think that was too young to have accomplished anything that would be remembered, but Harvard University is named after him, and that school is well known around the world. Many men celebrated in history have been students at Harvard.

John Harvard was a bachelor minister. He had no descendants to carry on his name. But he became interested in the small college just then getting started, and he gave one half of his small estate to the college along with 400 books from his library. This was enough to enable the school to organize, so it was named Harvard College in honor of the one who helped.

Alexander the Great died at thirty-three, having conquered the then-known world. He wept because there were no more worlds to conquer. But in his conquest he had brought death, sorrow, destruction, even slavery, to countless thousands of persons. So Alexander is perhaps remembered more with revulsion than with admiration.

Jesus died at thirty-three. He came to do the will of His Father in heaven, and He completed the work He came to do. He brought health, happiness, new life, and freedom to countless individuals while He lived on earth and through His life on earth those of all ages are blessed. His name is remembered with adoration and worship.

On the wall of an ancient Roman schoolroom are an inscription and a drawing that date back to the first century. They must have been scrawled upon that wall by a schoolboy who traced there a rude cross with an outstretched figure upon it and wrote beneath the cross, "Alexminos worships Christ."

We don't know who Alexminos was, but the name of Christ is familiar to us all, because the acts of no man can be compared with what Christ has done for mankind. There is no other name that can be compared with His.

R.E.

ARISE AND GO

*I will arise and go to my father, and will say unto him, Father,
I have sinned. Luke 15-18.*

It was a sad day for Betsy Moody when she returned from the
village store and read the note Edwin had left lying on the kitchen
table. Her first-born son, only seventeen years old, had gone away to
make his fortune. Someday, the note said, he would come back and
take care of her. The poor widow wept. She had depended on
Edwin to help her provide for the six younger children.

"He will come back, I know he will," she told people. To help him
find his way, she placed a lighted lamp in the window every night.
Each morning she expected a letter from him, but no letter ever
came.

Years passed, but Mother Moody never stopped hoping that her
boy would return. One hot day a bearded stranger stopped at her
gate and asked for a drink of water. As she handed it to him, she
noticed that he was gazing earnestly into her face. He seemed
strangely familiar. Then tears began to trickle down his cheeks into
his beard. Suddenly she recognized him.

"Edwin! Oh, Edwin! Come in!"

The man replied.

"No, Mother, I can't come in until I know you have forgiven me for
running away."

Betsy rushed out and threw her arms around him.

"Oh, Edwin," she sobbed, "you were forgiven years ago."

Jesus told a beautiful story about a son who left home, wasted all
his money, and finally "found himself" while tending pigs. He began
thinking of all the good things he had left behind. He remembered
his father's mansion, especially its bountiful kitchen. He resolved to
return home and offer to work as a hired servant.

When he met his father he cried, "I have sinned." There were no
excuses such as "I was foolish" or even "I made a mistake." He had
sinned and he freely admitted it.

"Make me a servant," he began. He could say no more. Arms of
love were around him. Father and son wept for joy.

The Bible says, "All we like sheep have gone astray." God calls for
us to return to Him. His Lamp, the Bible, lights us on our way. But
He leaves one thing for us to do. We must say of our own free will,
"I will arise and go to my Father."

V.E.R.

TASTE AND SEE

O taste and see that the Lord is good! Happy is the man who takes refuge in him! Psalm 34:8, RSV.

After your first sip of well-flavored, piping hot, French onion soup, you may say, "That tastes good!" But that's not the whole picture. Your soup not only tastes good, it smells good! Your taste only tells you that what you eat is sweet, sour, salty, or bitter. Only your sense of smell can give you the true flavor of that delicious soup.

Then why does the psalmist invite you to taste and see that the Lord is good? To find out the flavor of anything, you must experience it personally. There is no way to describe a new taste to someone who has never experienced it. How can I tell those of you who live in temperate climates the exotic flavors of tropical fruits such as mangoes, mangosteens, rambutans, or durian?

What really happens when you taste something? If you hold your nose or have a head cold, flavor almost vanishes. The onion soup becomes just hot, salty liquid. As you eat, the flavors travel from your mouth down your throat, and up again along air passages that lead to your nasal cavities. You smell when you inhale, but you sense the flavors when you exhale. The area with which you smell is about the size of a postage stamp, filled with many nerves high in your nasal passages. Moderate breathing doesn't produce these pleasures; it must be deep inhaling. That's why you sniff when you smell a rose.

You can't taste a blend of good flavors unless it is in your mouth. True, the taste buds on your tongue will tell you whether the substance is sweet, sour, salty, or bitter, but the blended flavors must reach that part in your nasal passages where smell indicates whether the berry you are eating is raspberry or strawberry. Similarly, you can't understand the good qualities of the Lord until He becomes a part of you. Only then will you be sensitive to those gentler elements of God's character, His graciousness, kindliness, and friendliness. When Jesus' love is within you the fragrance will fill you with an enjoyment much greater than that which comes from pleasant odors of gardenias, or of bread baking in the oven. Don't depend on another. Taste for yourself. Take time to have a personal relationship with God. Only then can you taste and see His goodness for yourself.

E.E.L. and J.H.L.

BE KIND

And be ye kind one to another, tenderhearted, forgiving one another, even as God for Christ's sake hath forgiven you. Ephesians 4:32.

Our Morning Watch verse for today says we should be kind and forgiving. Now notice the words, "even as God for Christ's sake hath forgiven you." That is a very good reason to govern the actions of every Christian.

When you bought and paid for your bicycle, it belonged to you. How proud you were of it! Do you remember how much you paid for it? How long did it take you to save up your nickels and dimes and dollars until you had enough money to buy it? You then purchased it and it belonged to you. What a wonderful day that was! It is like that with a car, a boat, a home, or anything you buy.

How long did Jesus work to purchase you and me? He lived on this earth a good many years and worked hard and finally died on a cross to pay the price of our redemption. In one of His wonderful parables He told a story about a merchantman who found a valuable pearl. He quickly sold everything he had to purchase that pearl. So it was called the Pearl of Great Price. Well, Jesus was the heavenly merchantman who left everything in heaven to come and buy what He called precious pearls—pearls of great price. He came to seek and to save what was lost. While seeking, He found this precious pearl—think of it—it was *you.* It was every boy and girl, every man and woman, on this earth. He found it and He gave up everything—even life itself on the cross—to buy the "Pearl of Great Price."

So we are His. We belong to Him. I can't do as I please with myself. You can't do as you please with yourself, unless you please to please Him! Your bicycle or your car are yours. They can't do as they please. They go where you want them to go. They do what you want them to do. But they are mere machines. We are not machines. We are not automatons. We may choose to do everything to please Him. We belong to Him. And so we forgive others because we belong to Him and He has forgiven us. We love others and we are kind because He was kind to us.

A.A.E.

STEPS TO FAITH

Fight the good fight of faith, lay hold on eternal life. 1 Timothy 6:12.

Jerry and Peter stood on the bank of a creek.

"Do you think we can get to the other side?" asked Peter.

Jerry sized up the distance and looked behind him. There was no clear place where he could run and jump the stream to the other bank. He shook his head. "Nope, I don't see how we can do it without getting wet."

They were still discussing the best way to cross, and even had begun to look for a log they could lay between the two banks, when suddenly Jerry shouted, "Look at that!"

Just downstream they could see two girls obviously going from one side of the stream to the other. The boys ran toward the two figures, and then stopped in their tracks and shook their heads in chagrin. Just a few yards from where they had been frantically trying to devise a way across the stream, someone had thoughtfully placed seven large steppingstones. In a matter of moments they were on the other side.

There are more ways of crossing a creek than jumping it. That seemed to be about the only lesson they could learn from that experience, until they told the story to their father.

"Sometimes we think that the only way to win the battle of faith is to go out and fight," he said. "But we fight the good fight of faith best when we take it one small step at a time. Then, when something really big comes up, we know from experience that God will be with us."

"Do you think Daniel could have gone into the lions' den if he had not first won the smaller battle about the food offered to idols?" Mr. Johnson continued.

"I guess not," agreed Peter.

If you want to get to the other side, take the steps placed for you in the pathway of life. Win one battle at a time.

W.R.L.S.

CAREFUL WHAT I SAY

I will take heed to my ways, that I sin not with my tongue: I will keep my mouth with a bridle. Psalm 39:1.

One day I met a friend out walking his dog. I was surprised to see the animal wearing a muzzle.

"Does he bite?" I asked. The man laughed.

"No, he isn't dangerous. But he loves to bark. I got so tired of hearing his voice that I bought this muzzle. I only put it on him when I want peace and quiet."

David faced a similar problem. He had an unruly tongue. He spoke of his determination to keep his mouth shut as if he were wearing a bridle, or muzzle, as the word could be better translated.

In one of his poems, Will Carleton tells of a young couple who struggled to start a ranch in Indiana. One day the man came home and discovered that the cows had strayed away. Angrily he asked his wife why she hadn't watched them, and accused her of sitting around all day, leaving him with the work. Before going after the cows, he saw by her face that his cruel words had wounded her feelings. Only his pride kept him from saying, "I'm sorry."

A few days later he came home again and found the cows out of the corral. On the kitchen table lay a note from his wife saying she had gone to find them, and asking forgiveness if she had failed to do her part.

While reading the note the man heard a distant rumble of thunder. A severe storm was coming. After putting on heavy boots and raincoat, he lighted the lantern and hurried into the night to find his wife. Rain fell in torrents as he walked, frantically calling her name. Toward morning the storm passed, and the rancher returned to his cabin. To his horror he found his wife lying dead on the doorstep and the cows in the corral. He never knew how she had gotten them back.

Many years later the rancher expressed his feelings in these words:

"Boys flying kites haul in their white-winged birds,
You can't do that when you're flying words. . . .
Thoughts unexpressed sometimes fall back dead,
But God Himself can't kill them once they're said."

Let us, like David, ask the Lord to help us control our tongues.

V.E.R.

24

WHERE NO WATER IS

O God, thou art my God, I seek thee, my soul thirsts for thee; my flesh faints for thee, as in a dry and weary land where no water is. Psalm 63:1, RSV.

Not long ago I flew in a jet over Saudi Arabia. Looking down on the vast desert, I saw a dry and weary land where no water is. Arid wasteland covers most of this vast desert peninsula. Rain never falls in part of the large island deserts. Not one river in all of Arabia has water the year round. Because temperatures often rise to 130° F few plants and animals exist except in irrigated spots. Most of the people live in the highlands or at oases along the coast where dates, limes, pomegranates, and coconuts are produced. Except for the modern cities of Judah, Mecca, and Riyadh most of the people live in tents or drab, flat-roofed houses of mud and stone.

On the southeastern tip near the Arabian Sea is the small country of Muscat and Oman. It has little industry, no railroad, few roads, and one important airport at the seaport town of Muscat. A big, dirty, hot city, Muscat has little drinking water, though the ocean is nearby.

How do people obtain fresh water? Recently deep wells have been dug, but previously the only drinkable water was obtained by divers from the salty depths of the Gulf of Oman near Muscat Bay. Carrying bags made from the skins of goats, they dived to the bottom of Muscat Bay where there are springs of fresh water. Pressing the mouths of their bags into the bubbling springs, the divers filled them with pure, fresh water. Quickly closing the top so no salt water could enter, they, with their precious bags, were hauled to the surface by ropes.

Do you search and long for God with the same urgency and intensity as those Arabs dive for water? Do you long to be in the presence of Jesus and feel at home with Him? When His promises flow into your heart your happiness and peace will be like rivers of water. Wave after wave of glory will roll into your soul. No language can describe the joy of just resting in His love. You can be filled with Jesus.

Don't be content to live in a dry and weary land where no waters are. If you will seek for it there is an abundant supply of living water that God longs to give to you.

E.E.L. and J.H.L.

THE SEEING EYE

The hearing ear, and the seeing eye, the Lord hath made even both of them. Proverbs 20:12.

The story is told—perhaps it is only a fable—of a fakir, or holy man, who was wandering across the desert. In his travels he met two men who looked as if they were searching for something. They were about to pass when the fakir spoke.

"Did you lose a camel with a lame left hind leg?" he asked.

"Yes. Have you seen it?"

"No, I never saw it; but tell me, was it blind in the left eye?"

"Yes, yes. You must have seen it. Tell us where it is!"

"I tell you, I never saw it, but does it have two front teeth missing?"

At this the men became angry. "Of course, you have seen the camel! How else would you know so much about it? Tell us where it is or we will take you to the caliph and accuse you of stealing it."

But the fakir only smiled and assured them that he had not seen it. So the camel owners grabbed the fakir and took him to the caliph, where they told of their missing camel, which this man knew so much about.

"All right," the caliph said, turning to the fakir, "we have heard these men's side of the story, now what is yours?"

"Sir," replied the man, "I know nothing of where their camel is. I just know all these things by observation. I saw a camel's footprints in the sand and there were no man's footprints with it, so I decided it must be lost. The left hind footprint was lighter than the rest, so it must be lame. It ate the grass on only the right side of the path where it was walking, so I concluded it must be blind on the left, and each mouthful of grass left tufts sticking up in the middle, so I knew it has some teeth missing. It was all observation, sir."

Do you use your eyes to see the wonderful things God has made for your enjoyment? What are you looking for in your friends? Their bad points or their good ones? Why not today make a list of all the good things you can find? God wants you to use your eyes. That is why "the hearing ear, and the seeing eye, the Lord hath made even both of them."

M.H.

THE DEAF VIOLIN MAKER

Our light affliction, which is but for a moment, worketh for us a far more exceeding and eternal weight of glory. 2 Corinthians 4:17.

Many years ago prospectors passed by the desolate place where Helena, the capital of Montana, is now located. One day a desperate miner began to dig near there in a forsaken gulch. He found what other fortune seekers had missed—more than eight million dollars' worth of gold.

It takes vigorous digging to get results in life. Some men find difficulty a challenge, and relish a task in proportion to its hardness. They face danger with a fierce joy. It takes character to surmount handicaps. For example, take Ben Harrison, of Detroit, Michigan, who has been totally deaf for twenty-seven years. He has given himself to building unusual violins, thus rising above his limitation. His instruments vary in price from $500 to $1,500. One year he won the top prize for tone at the International Violin Makers Festival.

His instruments aren't made in a hurry. It takes him eight months to build a violin. So far he has produced about eighty, usually working on two or three instruments at a time. He explains, "My interest in violins dates back to my boyhood days in Tennessee when I was only 13. I knew a boy who played a violin. He told me that the man who had made his fiddle lived near us. After a visit to his shop I was completely intrigued with violin construction. Before I was seventeen I had made three myself."

When Ben was twenty, he woke up one morning to find that he had completely lost his hearing. Specialists have never found either the cause or the cure. He made a visit back to his boyhood home in Tennessee, and found in his parents' attic one of the violins he had made when he was a teen-ager.

His wife urged him to read up on violin-making and build them again. Soon he set up a shop near his home. He can tune his violins by using a tuning fork and his fingers. He feels the vibrations of the fork with his fingers. He can also determine how thick the wood for the new violin should be through the vibrations of the fork.

You too can use your handicaps to build a more noble character. By taking the right attitude toward our "light affliction" we may begin here on earth to enjoy the "eternal weight of glory" promised to the overcomer.

L.C.W.

EVERGREENS DON'T BREAK

Don't worry about anything, but in all your prayers ask God for what you need, always asking him with a thankful heart. And God's peace, which is far beyond human understanding, will keep your hearts and minds safe, in union with Christ Jesus. Philippians 4:6, 7, TEV.

Don't think that only older people worry. Unfortunately, many children and youth are chronic worriers too. As with those who are older, most of the things that trouble them are not worth worrying about, even from a human evaluation. God says, "Don't worry about anything."

In a new place, do you worry that you'll get lost? Are you worried that your hair isn't just right, or your clothes aren't what the rest of the kids are wearing? Do you worry that others will laugh at you, or not accept you, or that your teacher may be cross? Roy, a constant worrier, learned how to lay aside his troubled thoughts.

One winter after a very heavy snowstorm he and his mother decided to go for a walk to enjoy the winter beauty. Many inches of snow were piled artistically on each house, car, post, or other object. The trees looked the prettiest. Walking down the path between a row of elm trees, they noticed that many of the branches were broken from the heavy snow that had piled on them.

"Some of those trees are hurt so badly they may die," remarked mother. "The elm holds its branches stiff without bending, until finally the weight is too much and they break. How much better if they were like those evergreens. When they get more snow than they can hold, they just let go. The branches get lower and lower, bending down until the heavy snow slips away. The next morning the evergreens are as good as ever."

Roy, noticing that not a single branch was broken, said, "Mother, elms would be smarter if they weren't so stubborn and unbending."

"You're right, son. Be a pine tree. Bear what you can. Then let the rest of the load slide off without worrying. That's what Jesus is for—to do what you can't. You'll be happier and live a lot longer."

E.E.L. and J.H.L.

BEAUTIFUL BOULDERS

Man looketh on the outward appearance, but the Lord looketh on the heart. 1 Samuel 16:7.

Some time ago there was a man who purchased for himself and his family an English home and garden. In the center of the garden was a huge boulder. It was an ugly rock that spoiled the beauty of his otherwise lovely garden. He tried to think of the best way to have it removed. It was too heavy to dig out, so he got some dynamite, thinking that he would blast off parts of it at a time.

But his blasting attempt was not very successful. All he succeeded in doing was breaking all the windows on that side of the house. The great boulder was still there. He then sought the advice of experts about the removal of the huge rock, but there was no one who could come up with any practical solution to his problem.

He did some serious thinking about it and finally decided that if he could not remove it, he would beautify it. He worked diligently adding smaller rocks here and there until the mass was somewhat symmetrical. He added soil and then planted vines and flowers. He was so successful this time that his rock garden became a real beauty spot. So he transformed the ugly boulder into a thing of beauty that caused his home and garden to become the most admired in the community.

If we have disadvantages in our lives that stand out like ugly rocks, God can help us to take advantage of them if we will let Him.

Fanny Crosby became blind when she was six weeks old. As a young child she was often despondent about her handicap. But then it seemed to her that she heard a voice from heaven saying, "I can use you!" This brought great encouragement to her, and she became a happy child. She even wrote little verses to tell of her happiness.

As she grew older she wrote many hymns—more than 6,000 of them! What had been a great boulder of discouragement in her life became a garden of beauty. Through her talent spiritual strength has come to millions of people around the world.

It is not appearances, talents, or handicaps that make the difference in our lives. The Lord, who sees our hearts, knows what each one of us can best do for Him. If we are willing to listen and to do, He wants to tell us. Ask Him today.

R.E.

THE DOVE OF PEACE

Though they stay among the sheepfolds—the wings of a dove covered with silver, its pinions with green gold. Psalm 68:13, RSV.

The homes in Palestine are built with flat roofs. Mounting the outside stairs, the family often enjoys the cool evening air from the rooftop. In many homes the roof is also a place of storage. Broken pieces of earthenware, black with soot and dust, are piled against the wall. Inside these disorderly piles of broken pots are many spaces that make ideal roosting places for pigeons and doves. Though the broken pottery collects dirt, the doves inside remain clean and beautiful. The filthy environment doesn't spoil their spotless beauty.

When the doves fly from their unsightly roosts into the sunshine, their wings reflect the light, shining like silver and yellow gold. Emerging from junk and filth, only their loveliness is seen.

When you invite the Holy Spirit to dwell in your heart, no matter how dirty you are before He enters, He'll come in and transform you. Your character will be made beautiful by the same God who made the beautiful doves of Palestine.

Some young people worry that the Holy Spirit won't find their soiled hearts. If they knew the habits of the dove they would realize their concern is needless. When the Spirit of God rested like a dove of burnished gold over the head of Christ at His baptism, it was a most fitting emblem. The dove, like all members of the pigeon family, has a strong homing instinct. It will fly swiftly through all kinds of stormy weather, darkness, and mountain barriers directly to its roost. In like manner, nothing will prevent the Holy Spirit from reaching anyone who longs to have Him make His home in his heart.

The dove that Noah sent from the ark after the Flood could find no safe place to rest. So it returned to the ark. Just so, the Spirit will not abide in a heart that is disturbed with passion and conflict. The heavenly Dove will only live where there is peace and quiet assurance, a heart stayed on Christ. If you want the Spirit to live in your heart you must let go of all the disturbing elements in your life. Prepared to accept Him, you can pray with the unknown poet,

"Heavenly Dove, within my bosom
Make Thy home and find Thy rest."

E.E.L. and J.H.L.

SIX MORE REASONS

Let all bitterness, and wrath, and anger, and clamour, and evil speaking, be put away from you, with all malice. Ephesians 4:31.

There are many good reasons why we should be kind. First, because it is a command of Christ. How often Jesus mentioned that we should love people, and even love our enemies instead of hating them.

Second, we have a divine Example, even the example of Jesus. "How God anointed Jesus of Nazareth with the Holy Ghost and with power: who went about doing good, and healing all that were oppressed of the devil; for God was with him" (Acts 10:38). Let us, old and young, follow in His steps!

Third, we have a divine indictment against us. God points His finger at us when He says, "The inhumanity of man toward man is our greatest sin."—*The Ministry of Healing*, p. 163.

Fourth, we have been given a divine promise through the Spirit of Prophecy. Listen to it: "If we would humble ourselves before God, and be kind and courteous and tenderhearted and pitiful, there would be one hundred conversions to the truth where now there is only one."—*Testimonies*, vol. 9, p. 189. What a promise! Notice the language. It doesn't say that if we were kind there *might be*, or *could be*, or *should be* one hundred times more conversions than before. No, it says, "there *would* be." That is a promise.

Fifth, we have been given a divine philosophy to be kind! In the parable of the good Samaritan we are taught Christ's divine philosophy of being kind to our neighbor. And we learn that our neighbor is anyone in need, regardless of color, caste, or creed. Christianity is love in action—it is being kind!

Sixth, we have been given a divine prophecy. Here it is: "Before the final visitation of God's judgments upon the earth there will be among the people of the Lord such a revival of primitive godliness as has not been witnessed since apostolic times."—*The Great Controversy*, p. 464. God is love and when this revival of love is a reality, we will then be kind. Haste the day!

A.A.E.

WHY THE INDIANS DIDN'T KILL THEM

Cast they bread upon the waters: for thou shalt find it after many days. Ecclesiastes 11:1.

Years ago Jake Wallock and his wife, Sarah, set up housekeeping in the sparsely settled West where Indians roamed the plains and often fought fierce battles with the white frontiersmen. Jake was a miller, and settlers from miles around brought him their grain to be ground into flour. Indians too found their way to the little settlement, and they were always kindly received by Jake and Sarah.

One cold night there was a knock at the door. When Jake opened it a tall, red man stood shivering on the doorstep.

"Evening, red man, what can white man do for you?" the settler asked cheerily.

"Indian hungry—cold out here!" was the reply.

"Come right in, red man, plenty of food here for you!"

Chief Thundercloud—for that was his name—entered and was given a chair by the fire. Turning to his wife, Jake Wallock asked her to quickly prepare some food for the chief. When the good food was served and Chief Thundercloud had eaten, he was given a warm blanket and a place to curl up for the night.

Many times such deeds of kindness were performed on behalf of Indians who came through the settlement. They were always treated with respect and compassion in the Wallock home.

Then, trouble came. The Indians were cheated, ill-treated, and often killed. One night a band of hostile red men came in the darkness; when they left, the settler families were dead, their houses in flames.

Only one family escaped—the Wallocks. Their home was untouched, Jake and Sarah were unharmed. Kind deeds saved their lives in a crisis. Kindness paid.

Ellen White once wrote, "Under the influence of meekness, kindness, and gentleness, an atmosphere is created that will heal and not destroy."—*My Life Today*, p. 152.

Kindness may cost nothing more than a little thoughtfulness and acts of compassion. But it surely *pays!* Not often does it save a person's life, as it did in the case of Jake Wallock and his wife, but it surely reveals that Jesus is in our hearts and lives.

R.H.P.

READY TO GO

Lord, I am ready to go with thee, both into prison, and to death. Luke 22:33.

When Bill Clapper filled in his application form for college he came to the question "What is your purpose in life?" He wrote, "To be a foreign missionary." That had been his goal for years.

After graduation there was no immediate opening for him overseas, so he accepted a position as an academy teacher. His young wife was kept busy at home caring for their two little boys and baby girl. Their home was filled with gladness.

Bill was a good teacher. When he was called to work in a junior college he bought a beautiful house. The family was now able to enjoy summer vacation trips together. Then one day Bill received two long envelopes in the same mail. The first was from his conference president, inviting him to take the position of conference educational secretary. The second was from the secretary of the General Conference. At last Bill had his overseas call. He was needed in Africa to teach in a large mission training school.

Nine years earlier, this invitation would have thrilled him. Now he began asking questions. There was no academy nearby for his boys. They would have to go to boarding school hundreds of miles from home. His missionary wage would be much less than his present salary. His wife's parents strongly objected to having their child so far away. Bill turned the call down.

The disciple Peter also made a promise he was unable to keep. In the garden of Gethsemane facing the mob, he learned it was one thing to hear about danger, but a very different thing to experience it.

Peter had been thrilled to hear the Master's invitation "Follow me." Jesus was popular, and thousands of people were thronging about Him.

Jesus expected Peter to follow not only to the mountaintop of transfiguration but also to the summit of Calvary. In the judgment hall, when his witness was most needed, Peter failed his Master.

After he was truly converted Peter was able to fulfill his promise. Then he feared neither imprisonment nor death on a cruel cross. He considered it an honor to follow Jesus anywhere.

Will you promise to go *anywhere* for Jesus?

V.E.R.

SUN AND SHIELD

For the Lord God is a sun and shield: the Lord will give grace and glory: no good thing will he withhold from them that walk uprightly. Psalm 84:11.

As we climbed the jungle trails of Sabah (North Borneo) that Sabbath morning, the hot tropical sun beat down on us. Certain facts I'd learned in science class impressed me. That sun was about 93 million miles away, yet I felt we were getting more than our share of the 11,000° F. surface temperature it was sending out into space.

My clothes were dripping wet from sweat, no way to appear in Sabbath school. If I drank too much of the precious water in my canteen it wouldn't last all day. Why, I wondered, do the people of Borneo almost always build their churches on the hilltops and so far from the end of the jeep roads?

Maybe thinking cool thoughts about when we lived in North Dakota would help. I remembered January days when that same sun shone down from a blue sky, and yet in that northland the temperature didn't even rise to zero. But mental visions of snow-banks didn't cool me off as I panted up that steep mountain directly under the sun's hot rays.

Just as I thought I'd collapse, a cloud covered the sun. Suddenly I was cool. Looking up into the open sky, I thanked God for that small cloud. No wonder the Lord chose to lead His people of Israel by a cloud. What a welcome shield from the piercing heat!

God was teaching me that precious lesson that sunshine is not always glorious, nor clouds always dreary. Sometimes God, even as the sun, has to smite us fiercely. That may be the only way He can get our attention. When the heat is on we are forced to stop and turn to Him for relief.

In His love He knows just how much of the hot sun we can stand. When we've had enough to make us start thinking as He wants us to think, then out comes the shield—cooling—of His grace and glory.

I love a God like that. He has promised He will never withhold any good thing from us if we walk along His pathways. Your God is both your sun and your shield. You can trust Him to give you just the right amount of each.

E.E.L. and J.H.L.

THE PLUM-PEACH-APRICOT TREE

In the midst of the street of it, and on either side of the river, was there the tree of life. Revelation 22:2.

Yes, it had plums, peaches, and apricots on it, plus nectarines! How did it get that way? Well, there was a plum tree in the back yard of my grandfather's home. It was strong and vigorous but its plums were sour.

But that was no reason why the tree should not produce good fruit. To start with, my grandfather cut off most of one branch, then took a twig from a peach tree and grafted it on. With the strong sap of the plum pushing through it, it was not long before that peach twig had become a branch and was bearing luscious peaches. Next it was apricots, then some better varieties of plums, and finally nectarines.

By the time several summers had passed, the tree was famous in the neighborhood, and people would come just to look at it. In all, there were eight different varieties of fruit growing on it. In the spring you could see the blossoms coming out at different times.

Have you ever wondered what the twelve different fruits will be on the tree of life? Some of you might wish for peaches or cherries or apples. If you live in the tropics you might think of bananas, mangoes, or papayas. And those who live in drier areas may think of oranges, apricots, or grapes. Perhaps they will be like the *monstera deliciosa*, or fruit salad tree, with its fruit of many different flavors.

How glad we are that our faithfulness will one day give us the right to approach that tree again and eat its fruit.

The Bible says that the leaves of the tree of life are for the healing of the nations. Even in the new earth we shall depend on God for our health and strength and immortality. Each month as we enter the New Jerusalem there will be a new fruit waiting for us.

Obedience to God is one of the fruits of a new life in Jesus Christ. By bearing that fruit in our lives now we shall one day eat the fruit of the tree of life.

W.R.L.S.

RESIST!

Resist the devil, and he will flee from you. James 4:7.

Paul was only three when he learned that memory verse for Sabbath school. He liked the sound of it, and he went around the house solemnly intoning, "Resist the devil."

What a good motto for us to take today. As we resist the devil, we resist sin, for Satan is the author of sin.

The very next verse in the Bible tells us *how* to resist. "Draw nigh to God," it says, "and he will draw nigh to you." That means get closer to Him. The way to do that is through prayer.

We have been told that if we make it a habit to talk things over with God, the power of the devil is broken, for he cannot stay near us when we draw near to God.

We don't have to wait until we have a chance to kneel beside our beds to talk things over with God, either. We can talk to Him at any time, right where we are, and then listen for His answer. He knows all about the problems and temptations that boys and girls meet at school and in all situations.

A boy named Ralph used to be bothered by a temptation to cheat on tests. He sat right where he had a good view of the desk of Caroline, an A student. Right at his desk in the middle of a busy school day, Ralph silently told Jesus of this temptation and asked for help to write the test to the best of his own ability without cheating. By resisting the devil that way, Ralph overcame the temptation.

Kathy broke a lovely glass jar her mother kept in the living room. She didn't mean to break it, and she felt bad about it. She was sorry about it not only because she knew her mother was fond of that jar but also because she feared a punishment for her carelessness. She was tempted to pretend she didn't know anything about it. But as she picked up the broken pieces, she asked for help to admit what had happened instead of trying to cover up. She faced her mother and told the truth. Mother was sorry about the jar, of course, but she was so glad for Kathy's courage that she didn't even scold.

Draw near to God today. When you need His help during the day, simply ask Him for it, and He will help you resist the devil.

R.E.

THE WHY OF TROUBLES

Truly this is a grief, and I must bear it. Jeremiah 10:19.

Have you wondered why many worldly people seem to have so little trouble? Many of them own beautiful homes. They drink and smoke and seem to be very happy. Then there are good people who are poor, ill, and deprived of all the beauties of life. WHY?

During the days of slavery in the United States there lived a rich but godless plantation owner. One of his many slaves had been with him for forty years. Knowing that old Peter was an earnest Christian, his master decided to have some fun at the old man's expense.

"Peter," he said one day, "I want to ask you a question and I want you to give me an answer."

"I'll do my best, Massa."

"All right. I am not a Christian. I never ask God for anything. Yet look at what I have—a mansion, a beautiful wife and four children, of whom I'm proud. Then there's this large plantation of which I am master, and all you slaves to work my land. I have money in the bank and good health. Now take yourself. You are nothing but a slave. You have no way of getting any money. Two of your children died of smallpox. I sold your wife down the river, and you will never see her again. You are bent over and stiff from rheumatism.

"Now tell me, Peter, what's the matter with this God of yours who is so good to me even when I don't believe in Him, and who sends you so much trouble in spite of your faith? Can you explain it?"

The old slave thought for a moment. It was evident that he had given the problem considerable thought.

"Massa, when you goes duck hunting, you fires into the flock. One duck falls dead, while another is only wounded. Which duck do you go after?"

"The wounded one, of course."

"That's how it is with us. The devil knows he has you sure, you're a dead duck. But this poor fellow he ain't sure about. So he chases me all the time, 'cause I struggle to get away from him."

Peter had given Massa something to think about.

If you never have temptations or trials and there are no clouds in your sky, ask yourself:

"Am I a dead duck?"

V.E.R.

EASY DOES IT

They that go down to the sea in ships, that do business in great waters; these see the works of the Lord, and his wonders in the deep. Psalm 107:23, 24.

Years ago a bridge was to be built across New York harbor. The engineers were having considerable difficulty in finding a solid foundation for one of the buttresses. Right where they wanted to put the support they found an old boat whose flat rectangular hull was filled with brick and stones. The old scow was nearly buried in mud. Divers went down and put great heavy chains under the clumsy boat. They tried every modern method of salvaging and raising such sunken craft, but all their effort failed.

Nearing the point of desperation, the experienced engineers were approached by a young engineer who was just beginning his career.

"I think I have a plan that will succeed. May I try?"

They listened, were convinced, and told him to proceed.

Two large barges were towed to the spot. Again chains were placed under the scow. These were attached to the two barges and cinched up tightly during low tide. Now came the test. Anxiously the engineers stopped everything as they waited for the tide to come in. They noticed that the barges began to slowly rise. The old boat so heavily loaded with bricks and stones and stuck fast in the mud could not resist this mighty power. Gradually it was raised by the tide that lifted the two barges.

What human genius couldn't do, God's mighty power manifested in nature did just as simply as a child might pick up a fallen toy. The power that is displayed in the ocean can be in your life too.

If you are trying to solve your problems by your own skill and wisdom you are meeting with failure just as those older engineers did. Like them, you need a power outside of yourself. First, you must rely completely on God's power. When you've turned everything over to Him, your part is to stop and wait for Him to act. God's power in your life can be as great as the power in the tidal waters. He who can do such "wonders in the deep" can easily lift you out of the mud of selfishness into His love.

E.E.L. and J.H.L.

SECURE BECAUSE YOU LISTENED

He who listens to me will dwell secure and will be at ease without dread of evil. Proverbs 1:33, RSV.

What is listening? It's paying attention and then obeying what you have heard. Listening is an art that few practice.

Friendships develop when we begin to pay attention to someone else, to listen to what they say. Gradually we become secure in their presence. We feel at ease with them, losing all fear or dread of them.

It was that way with Spot and Blackie. Living together on a farm in California, they formed a strange friendship because they paid attention to each other and really listened to the other's desires.

This odd pair resembled each other only in color. Spot was a black fox terrier. Blackie, a huge, beautiful, shiny black rooster, stood taller than Spot. Possessing a large red comb and strong, sharp, wicked-looking spurs, Blackie had no fear of any creature. But Spot, a trained hunter, knew well how to use his strong, sharp teeth, and could move quick as a flash. Each chose the other to be his friend.

When Blackie wanted to play, he hunted for Spot. If he found him lying down, he hopped around with wings outstretched, pecking at him but never touching him. If Spot joined him, a lively game began. But if Spot walked away, Blackie got the message and returned to eating.

Often Spot approached Blackie. His signal for fun was to yap loudly and snap at Blackie's legs, never touching him. If Blackie kept eating, Spot understood, and courteously walked away. Neither insisted on having his own way by pestering the other to do what he didn't want to do.

Most of the time, however, each responded when the other wanted to play. Their rough-and-tumble fun almost looked like a fight, but not once did any feather fly nor was any blood drawn by the spurs. Though so different, they felt secure and at ease together. Having learned to listen to and understand each other, all fear vanished.

When you really listen to Jesus your heart will unite with His, and He'll control your mind and thoughts so that you will live securely and relaxed in His sweet presence.

E.E.L. and J.H.L.

GIVE UP

They surrounded me like bees, they blazed like a fire of thorns; in the name of the Lord I cut them off! Psalm 118:12, R.S.V.

He eats his weight several times a week. And what a menu! Almost anything will do. Grasshoppers, crickets, bugs, field mice, worms—all these pests find a place in the diet of this beautiful animal with the lovely broad tail that resembles a feathery plume. This valuable pest destroyer, who carries the fiery spray you've smelled as an acrid, choking odor, is reluctant to use his gas warfare. He'd rather waddle about in the evening coolness, looking for grass snakes or bees and honey.

When the skunk finds a hive he routs the bees out, just as a bear does, by scratching the outside with huge strokes. The bees, hearing the scratching, fill themselves with honey and come out the little hole that is the entrance to the hive. Mr. Skunk is waiting for them. Catching as many as he can gobble up, he thoroughly enjoys the treat of both bees and honey. Some swarm angrily around his furry head, but he beats them to the ground with his strong forefeet. True, they sting him on the lips, the inside of his mouth and gullet, but he doesn't feel the stings at all. The skunk has the good fortune to be totally immune to bee poison.

When temptation swarms around you like bees, or blazes against you like a brilliant, fierce fire of thorns, you can count on today's promise. You may be immune like the skunk. The thorn fire of temptation burns only for a short time and dies as rapidly as it blazed. Since Jesus has already won the victory for you over sin, all you have to do is receive His victory. Don't waste time and effort fighting your sinful desires and bad habits alone, just trying hard to be good, when all you have to do is give up your sins to Jesus. Jesus only asks that you give Him your heart. Then He will help you overcome sin. His part is to supply the will and the strength to make all these difficult changes for you. Your part is to let Him work through you to do it. Just give all the mess to Him. He not only knows how to straighten it out, He is able to do more than you could ask or think.

No matter how much the bees of sin surround you or temptation blazes up, you'll be immune. Jesus has already won the victory over all sin for you. Let Him give you victory too.

E.E.L. and J.H.L.

TESTIFYING FOR JESUS

Come and hear, all ye that fear God, and I will declare what he hath done for my soul. Psalm 66:16.

At the age of twenty-one, Eugene Farnsworth left his father's home in Washington, New Hampshire. He had completed eight grades at the one-room school on the hillside. Years of work on his father's farm had given him great strength. Now he was going to get an education.

Eventually he enrolled as a student at Union College. Being very short of money, he bought a barrel of apples and a barrel of corn meal. On these he lived during his first winter at college. By applying himself to his books, he finished his education in record time.

For more than fifty years Eugene was a preacher of righteousness. He traveled to far countries, including Europe and Australia. He became president of the California Conference and then of the Pacific Union Conference.

At the age of seventy-seven, Elder Farnsworth became very ill. His friends took him to the Glendale Sanitarium, where the doctors operated on this man of God. They found that he was suffering from incurable cancer. In spite of their wisdom, they could do nothing to help him get well.

When he awoke, they told him the sad news. He took it calmly.

"How long do I have to live?"

"Perhaps two or three months."

"Very well, I shall appeal my case to the Great Physician."

So he and his friends prayed and the doctors prayed also. God heard and answered, and after a few weeks Elder Farnsworth was well again. The story was told everywhere. The next year, at the General Conference in Minneapolis, he met old friends from many countries. They were amazed to see him well and strong.

On Sabbath morning he preached to thousands, taking today's text for his sermon. He wasn't there, he said, to tell what the Lord had done for his body, wonderful as that was. They knew all about that. But He had dome much more than that. He had filled Elder Farnsworth's soul with all the blessings of Heaven. So he stood there and testified to the loving kindness of his God.

It is a joy to tell what God is doing for you.

V.E.R.

WITH ALL HER MIGHT

Whatsoever thy hand findeth to do, do it with thy might.
Ecclesiastes 9:10.

Sitting before the fireplace one stormy February night, Martha Berry heard a knock at the front door. She opened it and faced a small and dirty boy who led a muddy pig tied to a rope. The grubby boy looked up at her anxiously.

"Please, ma'am, I'm Willie Jackson, and this is my own pig. We-uns is come to school. I done carried the pig here for my tuition. He's powerful lean now, but he'll pick up tol'able quick."

Pig and Willie were both lean, but were welcomed to the log cabin school for mountain boys.

Martha Berry was the daughter of a wealthy and aristocratic Georgia family. More than seventh years ago as she rode into the hills with her father and saw the hardships of the mountain people, she felt a tormenting desire to help them. When her father died and she inherited the plantation, she opened a school in a log cabin her father had built for her as a child, where she had studied with her tutor.

Her sisters and friends tried to discourage her. They told her she was throwing her life away and that she ought to get married and have children of her own instead of worrying about the education of the mountain children.

It took a lot of time and effort to raise funds and teach, too. Whenever the school needed to expand, she had building plans drawn and got the building started. She went as far as the money on hand would take it, and then raised more money so the building could be finished.

Today Berry College, with an enrollment of approximately 1,200 students, still offers work opportunities for those students who must earn much of their own way. Many scholarships and awards are also offered.

Many young people have been blessed through the life of Martha Berry, whose hand found something to do, and who did it with all of her might.

If we ask God to help us, He will lead each of us to something that our hands can do with all our might.

R.E.

YOUR MANUFACTURING PLANT

For all these mysteries I thank you: for the wonder of myself,
for the wonder of your works. Psalm 139:14, Jerusalem.

When you get to college, some of you will be studying biochemistry, which is a combination of biology and chemistry and their overlapping areas of interest in the study of man, animals, and plants. This science is responsible for many nutritional discoveries that have helped people live healthy lives, and has also aided in the discovery of how the glands affect growth and body activities.

As a chemical manufacturing plant, your body makes dozens of mysterious substances that the best chemists in the best laboratories have never duplicated. Your body is able to produce from the same foods powerful and complicated chemicals that govern your mentality, growth, vitality, speed of movement, and agility when walking or running. By what marvelous process did the beans, potatoes, and other food your mother ate, become the nourishing, delicious milk you drank as a baby?

Can you understand how your body can take spinach, carrots, apples, and bread and convert them into bones, fingernails, teeth, hair, and muscle, or even blood and saliva? How can your stomach know which digestive juices are appropriate for the various foods you eat at a meal, and in what order each should be digested?

Your manufacturing plant is performing miracles every day just as wonderful as the miraculous happenings you read about for your worship from stories in the Bible. Your body is the most complex and efficient processing plant for its size in the world. Take time to understand its mysteries.

No wonder the psalmist said that he was wonderfully made—he must have been thinking of some of these same things. The mystery of it all caused him to be grateful to be alive, for his health day after day, but mostly for the love and wisdom of God as displayed in His creative genius. Have you ever thanked God for your marvelous body? Tell Him about it now in your prayer, for He loves to hear you say it.

E.E.L. and J.H.L.

ARE YOU ASHAMED TO ACKNOWLEDGE HIM?

"If anyone declares publicly that he belongs to me, I will do the same for him before my Father in heaven." Matthew 10:32, T.E.V.

Did you ever eat in a public place and wonder what you should do about asking the blessing? What *did* you do?

In the city of Hilo on the big island of Hawaii young Danny Taka ate his lunch with other crew members of the city waterworks. How should he ask God's blessing with all of these fellows looking at him? First, he somewhat covered his face in a half-hearted yawn, kept his eyes closed, and muttered a few words to himself, thanking the Lord for his sandwiches. At other times Danny just bowed his head and thought his blessing, hoping not to attract too much attention. Then some days he would half bow his head and scratch it, sure the Lord knew from reading his thoughts that he was thankful.

Despite his efforts to be inconspicuous, some of the men with whom Danny worked detected what he was doing. They were impressed.

"Tell us more about this God you talk to before your meals," the men urged. "Thank the Lord for the food all of us are eating," they added.

Now Danny isn't ashamed anymore when he finds himself talking with the Lord in public. In fact, several times he has been invited to pray at company and public functions.

Sometimes we too may find it just a little hard to acknowledge Jesus publicly—when there are a lot of people watching. But it always pays. This is what our text for today is all about.

"If anyone publicly acknowledges me as his friend, I will openly acknowledge him as my friend before my father in heaven" (T.L.B.).

Today Jesus is our high priest, or our attorney, in the courtroom in heaven. He will represent us there when our names come up before God in the judgment. At that time all of our words, thoughts, and actions will be looked over and judged. They have all been carefully recorded.

I want Jesus to acknowledge me in the judgment, so I'm always going to acknowledge Him publicly now. It's the best plan for every one of us.

R.H.P.

THE TOUCH OF LOVE

There is no fear in love, but perfect love casts out fear. 1 John 4:18, R.S.V.

Do you fear someone who loves you? No. His love for you eliminates all dread. If you are afraid, you are not really convinced he loves you. Satan makes you afraid of God. But God loved you first, so you can learn to love and trust Him.

Maybe you are like Butch, the half-grown golden eagle that two boys found on the cliffs near the Snake River in Idaho.

The young eagle hated his cage. He feared and hated his captors. If anyone came near him, he struck furiously with his sharp beak and even sharper talons. In his fear and rage, he refused to eat.

Sadly, the boys realized the eagle would soon die of starvation. It wasn't safe to release him near town. They couldn't return him to the Snake River. Maybe the kindest thing to do was to kill the bird.

When they returned with the gun, 12-year-old Jim, standing in front of the cage, pleaded for Butch's life.

The boy also began to talk affectionately to the young eagle. Butch didn't move. Slowly Jim reached his hand into the cage, and began to stroke the fierce head. Instantly, the eagle changed. That touch of love took away fear, and he was a changed bird. Butch began to eat and drink. He never again slashed with his talons or beak.

With Jesus' touch of love, you too will become a new creature. Fear, sin, and anger will go. Like Butch, who was soon freed from his cage and never confined again, you'll be free from Satan's prison.

Butch became part of the family, as you will become part of God's family. He slept with the dog. He played friendly games with everyone, but he especially loved Jim, whom he followed everywhere.

Their favorite game showed their love and trust for each other. Jim would lie on the grass while Butch would fly to a tremendous height. Circling around as eagles do, he plunged earthward aiming right for Jim with his sharp talons, just as eagles dive to strike their prey. But never once did Jim receive a scratch, for Butch always landed with the gentle touch of love.

Has Jesus touched you? He'll replace your fears with love.

E.E.L. and J.H.L.

HOW TO BE WISE

Whoso is wise, and will observe these things, even they shall understand the lovingkindness of the Lord. Psalm 107:43.

What is there wise about winning souls? How does this show how well educated, clever, and intellectual a person is? Surely it must be because when we win people to God we show that we have learned to work with God in His great plans for mankind.

At the age of sixteen William Cannon went out into the field to practice his first sermon. He knew that on the coming Sunday he would have to stand before a congregation and tell them about the love of God. He chose a field where a number of cows were grazing.

As soon as he began to preach they lifted their heads, looked at him, and finally, with the usual cowish curiosity, ambled over to see what this strange creature was doing. But he did not let this hinder him. Instead, he tried even harder to convey the love of God to his bovine friends.

At the close of his sermon he made his appeal for those who wanted to give their hearts to God to come forward, just as he expected to make his appeal in church.

He was startled when a bedraggled figure staggered up from a hedge and begged him, "Please tell me how God can help me. I have been looking for a way to change my life."

There, surrounded by curious cows, the young man knelt with his new convert and led his first soul to God.

A Christian home, church school, academy, college, should do more than give us a good education. They should make us wise enough to see that the greatest purpose in life, the wisest act that we can perform, is to lead others to a right relationship with God.

And you are never too young to influence someone through your words, your actions, your life. Today, as you go to school, or enjoy yourself at play, why not try for a little heavenly wisdom.

W.R.L.S.

"I WANT MORE OF IT"

"I may give away everything I have, and even give up my body to be burned—but if I have not love, it does me no good."
1 Corinthians 13:3 TEV.

One of the first things a child learns in life is the value of love. He cannot understand all the mysteries and motivations of love, but he soon learns that fondling and food are closely related. A child thrives on love but without genuine love he is being robbed of one of life's necessities.

A little orphan girl was adopted into a lovely family. She was delighted with her beautiful new home, and the dainty dresses that her new mother had made. The woman dressed the child in a pretty dress and then held her on her lap and taught the girl, who had never known a mother's love, to call her "Mamma." Then she drew the child close to her heart and kissed her. The little girl, with wondering eyes, asked, "Mamma, what is this?"

"My dear," said the woman, "this is love!"

"Oh," cried the little girl, "if this is love, I want more of it!"

When our lovely Jesus comes and takes us to our beautiful new home and clothes us in His robe of righteousness, woven by His own nail-pierced hands on the loom of love, and when we taste the precious fruits of the tree of life and bask in His forgiving smiles, doubtless we too will cry out, "If this is heaven, thank God I am here. I'm so happy that it will last forever. No more death, no more tears. Oh glorious thought: I am saved at last and saved forever!"

Such is the value of real love. "No value is attached to a mere profession of faith in Christ; only the love which is shown by works is counted genuine. Yet it is love alone which in the sight of Heaven makes any act of value. Whatever is done from love, however small it may appear in the estimation of men, is accepted and rewarded of God."—*The Great Controversy*, p. 487.

By showing kindness and consideration to those they meet, juniors, by God's grace, may develop this priceless commodity and share it with others along life's road.

A.A.E.

AIR LIFT FOR ELIJAH

*I tell you solemnly, if he find it, it gives him more joy than do
the ninety-nine that did not stray at all. Matthew 18:13, Jerusalem.*

In February, Wallace Powell spotted two horses hemmed in by
snowdrifts on a 12,800-foot ridge in the Colorado Rockies, far above
timber line. Flying back to his Gunnison base, he told his boss, Mr.
Warren. They informed the mayor, who decided to feed the
stranded horses.

"If you fly them the hay, I'll pay for it myself," he said.

When Warren dropped the bale, only one horse was left, and it
was in a pitiful condition. Warren and Powell took turns making two
trips a week. Sometimes wind and weather were so bad it was
difficult to drop the hay close, but often they could fly just twenty
feet above the ground. The horse, hearing the motors, was waiting.
They called him Elijah since he was fed from the sky like the
prophet.

In April a news reporter featured the horse in the Denver *Post*,
starting a fund called "Hay for Elijah." The response was terrific.
Even airline pilots flew over the ridge to point out the horse to their
passengers. Once, while flying a TV crew over the site, Warren saw
a pack of wolves stalking Elijah. They hurried back to Gunnison for
a shotgun, and chased the wolves away.

Bill and Al Turner, who had lost two pack horses in November on
a trip into those mountains, thought it might be "Bugs" who had
disappeared. Using snowshoes they made the seven-mile climb to
Elijah's windswept ridge. They called; he came. Yes, he was their
lost horse. It was still impossible to take him across the snowdrifts,
and seeing he was in good shape, they left him. Returning later
when more snow had melted, they cut through twenty-foot drifts to
get him through to the road.

When Elijah's trailer rolled into the town of Buena Vista, more
than a thousand people watched the parade of floats and the high
school band that welcomed him.

Such rejoicing over a rescued, lost horse reminds us of the joy in
heaven when a sinner returns to God. You can know this greatest of
all joys when you introduce a friend to Jesus or lead one who has
lost his love for God back to real happiness in Jesus.

E.E.L. and J.H.L.

GOD WEIGHS YOUR ACTIONS

The Lord is a God of knowledge, and by him actions are weighed. 1 Samuel 2:3.

Today scientists have precision weighing so delicate that they can weigh the footprints of a fly walking across their balance pan. They even can weigh a period or a comma from a sheet of paper. This precision weighing is important in making of modern printing presses, caterpillars for the farm, automobiles, and jet planes.

But precision weighing is as old as eternity. God has made accurate timing of His suns, stars, and planets so that millions and millions of them follow their assigned course without colliding with one another. The only upset in God's universe has been that caused by sin.

What is it that "weighs" most in the sight of God? For an answer, let us in imagination sit down with Jesus in the Temple and watch the people as they put in their offerings. The wealthy, who bring in large gifts, take care that the people see them drop their money into the treasury. But Jesus has no words of praise for those who give without any sacrifice.

He smiles when He sees a poor widow hurry up to the treasury and put in two small coins, hoping no one will see her. As she leaves, her eyes meet the eyes of Jesus, who calls His disciples to Him for a wonderful lesson on giving.

"Of a truth I say unto you, that this poor widow hath cast in more than they all" (Luke 21:3).

With tears of happiness coursing down her cheeks the widow leaves the Temple, knowing that her two mites have been appreciated by Him who weighs our motives. "It is the motive that gives character to our acts. . . . Not the great things which every eye sees and every tongue praises does God account most precious. The little duties cheerfully done, the little gifts which make no show, and which to human eyes may appear worthless, often stand highest in His sight. A heart of faith and love is dearer to God than the most costly gift."—*The Desire of Ages*, p. 615.

Another gift that Jesus appreciated was the alabaster box of costly ointment brought by Mary to the feast at Simon's house. She did not intend others to know about it, but the fragrance filled the room. Jesus knew that love had prompted her gift and that Mary appreciated what Jesus had done for her.

L.C.W.

49

I WILL SEEK THE LORD

My heart said unto thee, Thy face, Lord, will I seek. Psalm 27:8.

Margaret was a German housewife, one of thousands whose husbands were captured by the Russians during World War II. After the fighting ended, nothing was heard of the prisoners for more than two years. Then the German radio suddenly announced that, on the following day, trains would roll into Berlin bringing thousands of prisoners home. Many people were so excited that they lay awake all night wondering, Will my loved one be on one of those trains?

Before daybreak thousands of women were hurrying toward the station. Margaret placed herself near a gate through which each soldier would pass. The first train steamed slowly up to the platform and stopped. Everyone watched as weary soldiers climbed stiffly out of the coaches. Joyful cries could be heard as husbands and wives were reunited. All day Margaret waited, patiently scanning every face. Finally, toward evening, she had her reward. Her husband looked thin and pale as he hobbled toward her on crutches. One leg was missing. But the hardships he had endured were forgotten as she looked once more into her husband's face.

Sin results in separation from God. When God punished Cain for killing Abel, Cain recognized this as part of his punishment, for he said, "From thy face shall I be hid" (Genesis 4:14).

Although George was born blind, he had forced himself to live as normal a life as possible. His wife, Mildred, was not blind, and there were four perfectly normal children, two boys and two girls.

At the age of thirty-eight George decided to undergo eye surgery, since the doctor held out the hope that he might obtain his sight. The day came when his bandages were removed. The anxious doctor was by his bed. His wife stood there, holding him tenderly by the hand. Silently the children watched also.

The bandages were removed. Suddenly George realized that the operation had been a success. He could see his wife's face. "Oh, Mildred!" he exclaimed. "You are more beautiful than I ever imagined!"

When sin is no more and we look into the face of Jesus, we will find it more lovely than we had ever imagined. That face will be more beautiful than any earthly artist has ever painted it.

V.E.R.

WHY LINCOLN WAS LOVED

May the Lord now show you kindness and faithfulness, and I too will show you the same favor because you have done this. 2 Samuel 2:6, NIV.

Abraham Lincoln, one of our most-loved presidents, showed kindness to many. When a woman came to him at the White House because her husband had been sentenced to be shot, President Lincoln asked, "Is he unkind to you and the children? Does he beat you?"

"No, he is an ideal husband and father, loving me and the children. What would we ever do without him!"

"Then I shall pardon him and let him go home with you," replied Lincoln, who was a friend to the poor and the friendless.

A soldier sleeping on guard duty had been court-martialed and sentenced to be shot. The officer said, "He has no friend to intercede for him."

"If he has no friend, I'll be his friend," said the great President and signed the pardon with this remark, "I think this boy will do us more good above the ground than below it."

No wonder that a soldier who had been saved from the firing squad by Lincoln's intercession had in his pocket a photograph of his earthly savior with the words written, "God bless President Lincoln." After he had died on the battlefield, the picture was found in his pocket.

During the four dark years of the war between the States, Lincoln had many critics and many enemies. After peace had been signed between the North and the South, he hoped his life would be more quiet. But then it was that he was shot by the actor John Wilkes Booth. Some hours after the assassin's bullet had struck him, his heart stopped. Edwin Stanton, secretary of war, declared, "Now he belongs to the ages."

Strangely enough, Mrs. Lincoln said that his last statement was, "There's no place I want to see as much as Jerusalem, where Jesus walked." To this glorious city Abraham, Isaac, and Jacob looked. We read of Abraham, "He looked for a city which hath foundations, whose builder and maker is God" (Heb. 11:10).

During this day let us remember our text and be kind and tenderhearted to all.

L.C.W.

LINCOLN'S MOTHER

Her children arise up, and call her blessed. Proverbs 31:28.

Many of the world's great men have been blessed with godly mothers. When Lincoln was only a small boy he promised his mother on her deathbed that he would never use alcohol or tobacco, a promise he never broke. She also taught him how to pray and encouraged him to memorize much of the Bible and to read it faithfully. Capt. Gilbert J. Greene tells how Lincoln's religious background proved a blessing to him and to others.

"One day while practicing law in Springfield, Mr. Lincoln said to me, 'Gilbert, there is a woman dangerously ill about fifteen miles in the country, who has sent for me to write her will. I should like to have you go with me.' I cheerfully accepted the invitation. When we arrived, we could see that the woman had but a few hours to live. After the will had been written, witnessed, and signed, the dying woman said to Mr. Lincoln, 'Now I have my affairs of this world in order, and I have also made preparation for the life to come. I do not fear death.'

"Mr. Lincoln replied, 'Your faith is wise and strong. Your hope of a future life is a blessed one.' She asked him then if he would read a few verses from the Bible. They offered him the Book, but he laid it aside, and began reciting from memory the twenty-third psalm. Then he quoted the first part of the fourteenth chapter of John 'In my Father's house are many mansions: if it were not so I would have told you. I go to prepare a place for you.'"

After he had given these and other verses from the Bible, he recited several hymns, closing with "Rock of Ages, cleft for me." Soon the woman passed away. As they rode home in the buggy Gilbert expressed surprise that he could act as a pastor as well as an attorney. Lincoln added, "God and eternity were very near us today."

From his mother Lincoln learned lessons of patience, honesty, and kindness. He declared, "All that I am, or hope to be, I owe to my angel mother." In his respect for his mother Lincoln imitated the example of Jesus. "In childhood He could only do the work of an obedient child, fulfilling the wishes of His parents, in doing such duties as would correspond to His ability as a child."—*The Adventist Home,* p. 290.

L.C.W.

"I LIKE LOVE"

This is my commandment, That ye love one another, as I have loved you. John 15:12.

Little, loveless orphan Arnie found himself in the hospital. The cool, white sheets, the good food, were almost heavenly, compared with the rags, the hovel, and the bread crusts he was used to. Here a friendly nurse in a white, starched uniform brought him milk and fruit and all of the other luxuries he had only seen in supermarkets before. He loved every minute of it.

One night as the nurse leaned over the bed to tuck him in for the night, little Arnie mustered up the courage to say something he had wanted to say ever since he had been admitted to the hospital.

"I *like* you," the little fellow gasped.

The Christian nurse paused, looking down at the pale little form. "I *love* you!" she replied.

Big brown eyes looked eagerly up from the pillow. He had never heard those words before.

"What is love?" Arnie asked seriously.

In answer, the nurse gathered the frail form in her arms, hugged him tight, then laying him back on the pillow, she kissed him on the forehead.

Breathless, little Arnie looked up into the kind face bending over him. "I like love!" he exclaimed.

Every one of us likes love. What would this world of ours be like if there weren't any love? If there were no love, there would be no hospitals—if no one cared about the well-being of others, what great suffering there would be in the world. If there were no love, there would be no churches, no beautiful parks, no lush flower gardens. All of these things that cheer people's lives and make the world brighter exist because someone loved, someone cared for, someone else.

In our text today, Jesus tells us the measure of love each one of us should have in his heart. We are to love others as He loved us! That is a big requirement. Jesus loved us enough to leave His heavenly Father and come down to this sinful world to live and die for us. Do you love this much? Would you give your life for someone in your family or in your community? Would you do this for someone you didn't know or even someone who hated you? Do you love to love people? Jesus did.

R.H.P.

ACRES OF BONES

And God shall wipe away all tears from their eyes; and there shall be no more death, neither sorrow, nor crying, neither shall there be any more pain: for the former things are passed away. Revelation 21:4.

Old-time photographs of the Western plains show acres and acres of bones—white bones as far as the eye could see. Whose bones? Once they belonged to the biggest animal on the American continent, now seldom seen.

Great herds of bison, sometimes called the American buffalo, roamed over North America. About 125 years ago around 20 million of these huge animals thundered across the plains. Less than thirty years later, in 1889, only 551 bison could be found alive in the United States. Why did this magnificent animal, the bull often weighing more than a ton, have to die? It wasn't because he was weak or defenseless. His tremendous strength could rip up the tough prairie sod, toss aside a whole wolf pack, or carry a horse and rider a hundred yards before he hurled them to the ground.

Before the white man came herds numbering probably 50 million roamed the continent. Then greedy men began slaughtering until the stench of rotting bodies made vast areas uninhabitable for a time. Imagine killing the huge animals just to eat the "delicious tongue"—leaving the rest to rot! Huge piles of hides were stacked high by the railroad for miles. Because the buffalo stopped trains or blocked river traffic, hunters with Colonel William Cody ("Buffalo Bill"), who killed as many as 69 in a day, boasted they had killed 4,280 in a year and a half.

Because a few friends of this vanishing animal protected them by starting new herds on their ranches, the American Buffalo is not extinct. Today about 10,000 live in game reserves in the United States and another 15,000 roam in Canada.

Soon Jesus will rescue you from all death, sorrow, and pain. Not only will animals be safe, but you, also, will never again need to cry. Jesus will give you joy forever in the earth made new, and take away all death. Oh, if only He'd come today to wipe away all our heartaches and tears!

E.E.L. and J.H.L.

A JOYFUL NOISE

I will sing unto the Lord as long as I live. Psalm 104:33.

Two boys were arguing out in the yard. One yelled, "You did!" while the other retorted, "I didn't!" Back and forth they shouted at each other until their mother decided it was high time to stop the argument.

"Boys," she called from an upstairs window, "why don't you sing it?"

Both boys stopped and stared in amazement. What did she mean? Then their mother started to sing. Using a popular tune, she began chanting, "You did. I didn't. You did. I didn't," until the boys burst out laughing. It did sound funny to hear her singing like that.

"Just try it, boys," Mother advised. "Every time you start to fight, sing the words instead. You can't fight and sing at the same time."

How right she was! Who ever heard an angry person singing? Anger and singing just don't go together. There are a lot of other things that disappear with song, too-such as fear and discouragement.

Perhaps you think you can't sing. Then you should learn another text to go with the one for today. It is found in Ephesians 5:19: "Singing and making melody in your heart to the Lord." There you are! You don't have to sing out loud; just sing in your heart.

However, don't feel embarrassed if you feel like singing aloud but can't manage to be a Del Delker or a King's Herald. Did you know the Bible tells us seven times to make a "joyful noise" to God? So if you can't sing, make a happy noise!

When we get to heaven God will give us each a lovely voice and we are all going to sing. We are going to sing a "new song."

I doubt very much if that new song will be comparable to a hit tune down here. It probably wouldn't even rate in the top ten or twenty down here, but up there I think it will be our theme song and our favorite.

So don't you think we ought to start practicing now, and chase away all those feelings that won't belong in heaven anyway? And let's be careful of the type of music we use for practicing! It would be too bad if our repertoire were the wrong kind for singing with the angels!

M.H.

I WILL REPENT

I will be sorry for my sin. Psalm 38:18.

It was Nancy's duty to wipe the breakfast and supper dishes. To her it wasn't hard work, because she pretended she was building skyscrapers. The big dishes went on the bottom and the smaller ones on top of the pile. Sometimes she had twelve, fourteen, or even sixteen stories.

"Be careful, Nancy," her mother warned more than once. "Those dishes will fall and break sometime."

"Oh, I'll be careful," she always replied.

Of course, one day something did happen. On top of a pile of dishes, Nancy placed her mother's favorite candy dish. It was made of crystal and was quite heavy.

"That's a helicopter landing field," she declared. But suddenly the beautiful dish slid, fell with a crash to the floor, and broke into a hundred pieces. Nancy gazed in horror for a moment, then rushed off in search of her mother.

"Mamma, I'm sorry. I broke your lovely candy dish," she wept.

Mother had heard the crash. But she only said, "Tell me, just why are you sorry?" She led Nancy to the sofa, where they sat down together.

"I'm sorry because that was one of your favorite dishes. And I'm sorry because I didn't listen when you told me to be careful."

"Are you sorry enough so you won't make that mistake again?"

"Oh, yes. I'm so sorry that I'm going to take the dimes you give me for taking care of the baby and buy you another dish just as pretty as the one I broke."

Nancy's sorrow was the right kind. She was sorry because her mistake had hurt someone she loved. That is the kind of sorrow God wants us to have.

When Peter preached on the day of Pentecost he told the people how wicked they had been to put Jesus to death. They saw how terrible had been their sin and cried out, "What shall we do?"

That is the question we must ask when we do wrong. If we feel sorry enough to make things right with the person we have wronged, and if we ask God's pardon, then He will forgive and we can forget it.

Like David, we must be sorry for our sin—sorry enough to quit it.

V.E.R.

SVEA LEARNED TO OBEY

If you are willing and obedient, you shall eat the good of the land. Isaiah 1:19, RSV.

This, like all of God's promises, is conditional. Until you are willing to follow God's ways, which is the path of true obedience, you can never know the joys of the really good life Christ alone can give.

Svea, a cow moose born in Denmark, loved people. As a baby she had been found with a broken leg and had been nursed back to health. Turned loose in the woods, she longed for human companionship. One morning she thumped on the ranger's door. Kirsten, his daughter answered. Svea stood still, hanging her head, as Kirsten timidly scratched the top.

From then on Svea came to the house at the edge of the forest every morning and waited for Kirsten. Dashing up to the girl, she would skid to a stop, and listen as Kirsten talked.

Some time later Svea discovered the nearby town of Helsinge. She delighted the children as she pranced down main street. The forest ranger couldn't persuade her to leave. Only Kirsten's command could cause her to willingly obey and go back to the woods.

But she would always return to town. Her nose took her to the bakery. Poking her head through the doorway, she looked in. The baker gave her fresh bread, and from then on, she came each day. She learned to get pastry by shoving someone from the crowd inside. Always they returned with sweets. She was banished to a game reserve, but in a few days her familiar face was again pressed against the bakery window. Loving people so much, Svea just didn't know she was a wild animal. So she was sent to the zoo.

Meekly she descended from the truck, inspected her new home for an hour, then with a flying leap she cleared the nine-foot ditch surrounding it. With dignity she poked into parked cars, sniffed at people, and nuzzled children. Then she willingly returned to her ditch, leaped across with ease, and settled down, obedient to those who brought her there. She never left her Copenhagen zoo home again.

Svea learned to be willing and obedient. Surely you, as God's child, can also learn that surrender to God's will is the happy way. Then only will you enjoy the good things He has planned for you.

E.E.L. and J.H.L.

POLLUTION

Whatsoever things are pure, . . . think on these things. Philippians 4:8.

Tom Aldrich attended a public high school where his speaking ability landed him a position on the debating team.

The high school debating teams all across the State were assigned the same subject to prepare for the State tournament. The debate winners from each participating high school would go on to the district contest, and debate against the other winners in their area. Then the district winners would be awarded a trip to the State capital to debate there against other district winners.

The subject that year was: Resolved, that pollution regulations should be set and enforced by the Federal Government.

Tom wanted very much to win the debate—not only in his own school, but he wanted to make it all the way to the finals. He wanted that trip to the State capital. He decided to become an expert on the problems of pollution. He went to the library and read all the current magazine articles on the subject. He studied the newspapers for mention of the subject. When listening to the radio or watching television, Tom made note of any mention of pollution. His vocabulary grew as he became more familiar with the subject.

But the pollution that Tom Aldrich became an expert on in order to win his trip to the State capital was air pollution and water pollution, the things we think about when we study ecology. Tom didn't even think of studying another pollution problem that is even more common: mind pollution.

You might think of your subconscious mind as a basket. Into that basket go the things that pass through your conscious mind. The things you look at, the things you read, the things you listen to, the thoughts you think, those are the things that are put into your "basket."

And just as you don't want your drinking water polluted with oil sludge, detergent suds, and bacteria, neither do you want to throw sludgy words, soap-opera dramas, or sick pictures into your mind. You want the air you breathe to be fresh and pure. Your mind deserves that kind of care too.

Ask God to help you avoid mind pollution by guarding your mind as carefully as you do your air and water.

R.E.

HOW I HATED DISCIPLINE

How have I hated instruction, and my heart despised reproof; and have not obeyed the voice of my teachers, nor inclined mine ear to them that instructed me! Proverbs 5:12, 13.

Denny Dorfmann didn't get along well in school. It wasn't that the lessons were hard for him. Studies came easy. Perhaps that was part of the trouble. Denny had too much time and energy left over for other things. He teased the girls, plugged up the drinking fountains, made noise during classes. He kept a commotion going in the classroom all the time.

Yet he couldn't understand why it was that the teacher, whenever anything went wrong, asked him about it first. Denny resented that and would sass the teacher.

Sometimes things got to such a state that the teacher found it necessary to punish Denny. But he would never admit that he had been in the wrong. He often went home from school and told his mother that the teacher was mean and had it in for him.

Even though Denny was impertinent at home also, his mother sympathized with him when he had disagreements with the teacher. She wondered why the teacher would pick on her poor little boy.

Denny finished church school and went on to the academy. He didn't stay long, for he got into all sorts of trouble there. The teachers at the academy picked on him just as his church school teacher had, and when he stole a teacher's car, he was expelled from school. A couple of years later Denny landed in another sort of school—reform school.

The Revised Standard Version of the Bible gives verse 12 like this: "How I hated discipline."

Verses 22 and 23 of Proverbs 5 tell what happens in the end to one who hates to take reproof: "His own iniquities shall take the wicked himself, and he shall be holden with the cords of his sins. He shall die without instruction; and in the greatness of his folly he shall go astray."

Most of us think that we do hate discipline—even self-discipline—until we begin to understand that it is for our own good.

R.E.

TURNIP HILL

By their fruits ye shall know them. Matthew 7:20.

"Take this pound of turnip seeds and drop them evenly along these rows until you have used them all up."

This was Bob's first task at the first job he had ever had. And it seemed a fairly easy one. He watched carefully as the farmer showed him how far apart to sprinkle the seeds in the row.

Taking the packet of seeds, he tried carefully to follow instructions, working slowly and surely down the first row. It was about halfway back on the second row, as he was working downhill, that he first discovered he had back muscles. Protesting against the continuous bending, they were sending urgent "straighten up" messages to his brain.

Bob kept doggedly at the task, finishing the second and third rows. He looked at the packet of seeds. It seemed that he had hardly used any. Perhaps he was not sowing them thickly enough. Back he went to the first row and compared it with the third one. If anything, he was planting a little thicker than the farmer had shown him.

He took a hoe and began to cover the first three rows. This at least was a break from the continuous stooping.

It was just before lunch that he hit on a scheme that would find him an easier job. As he came to the end of the row down near the creek, he took his hoe and scooped out a depression. Then he took a handful of those hated seeds and threw them into the hole.

"Finished so soon?" was all the farmer said. And then he sent the boy to pick peas!

Less than a week later a serious farmer and a worried Bob were looking down at a huge patch of turnip plants so close together that they looked like a lawn. There was nothing Bob could say. He bought another half pound of seed and planted them on his own time. But he did learn a lesson he never forgot: Whatever you plant you reap. And that's true with temper as well as with turnips, and with love as well as with lettuce.

W.R.L.S.

GEORGE WASHINGTON

I am the first, and I am the last; and beside me there is no God.
Isaiah 44:6.

Have you ever been to Mount Vernon in Virginia, the home of George Washington? It is a very interesting place to visit. After looking at the kitchen, I knew I much preferred to be a modern housewife in the twentieth century!

Born on February 22, 1732, just 240 years ago today, George Washington grew up to become the first President of the United States. He was elected for the second term, also, and would have made President for the third time if he had not refused to do so.

What made him so popular? He was not always a brilliant general, but he was courageous and used good sense. He believed in being one with his men, too, when he was leading them through the Revolution.

Once one of his soldiers complained because the going was rough. "The officers don't have it as tough as we do," he griped. "You won't find them hungry and with no shoes for their feet. They are in nice warm houses too. They don't sit around out here in the snow with only a tent to sleep in. I think I'll desert the army."

"Oh," answered a companion, "that just shows all you know about it. General Washington happens to be down in a tent at the far end of this field right now writing letters to try to get some more supplies for us. He says he can't live in a warm house while his men are cold."

"Are you sure?" asked the first soldier.

"Just as sure as I'm standing here."

"Then I guess I'll fight for him some more."

George Washington was like that. He inspired loyalty in his fellow-men. Someone has said of him:

"First in war, first in peace, and first in the hearts of his countrymen."

I'm not saying it is wrong for George Washington to have first place in your heart as a man, but I wonder today who has the *real* first place in your heart.

God says, "I am the first, and I am the last; and beside me there is no God." Have you given God the first place in your heart?

M.H.

YOUR FADED BOUQUETS

The grass withers, the flower fades; but the word of our God will stand for ever. Isaiah 40:8, RSV.

The doorbell rang. When I opened the door the florist handed me a large box with my name on it. Excited, I laid it on the dining room table. Inside I found eighteen beautiful white rosebuds. Their fragrance filled the room. Never before had I received such an exquisite gift of loveliness. As I carefully arranged the blossoms in a vase, my thoughts were on the friend who had sent them. Each day as I changed the water and trimmed the ends of the stems, I marveled at the beauty of the opening roses.

But as the days went by, brown streaks appeared on the edges of the pure-white petals. The stems, no longer firm, allowed the roses to droop. Even though I tried to make them last as long as possible, the day finally came when my bouquet, once so freshly beautiful and fragrant, was just a dead, faded, ugly, smelly mess.

Not long ago our neighbors brought a birthday surprise of seventeen pink roses beautifully arranged in a dainty basket. Only a few days went by before the brilliant color faded and the bright petals curled. Soon all that was left to admire was the basket.

As I threw them away, the putrid odor of decaying vegetable matter in the water contrasted strongly with my memory of the rose scent. How quickly the living flowers faded! Each time this experience is repeated my faith and hope in the word of God grows stronger because of Isaiah's promise, "It will stand for ever." Through the ages men have tried to destroy the Bible, but its words are more precious with each passing day. Countless martyrs have died because they read and treasured God's words, shared them, or translated them into another language. Jesus emphasized the permanent value of God's words, saying they would be accomplished even if heaven and earth would pass away.

As you dispose of your next bouquet of wilted flowers, stop to thank God that the glories of heaven will never fade, that His promises are sure and will stand throughout all eternity.

E.E.L. and J.H.L.

SHADOWS OR SUNLIGHT

Looking unto Jesus the author and finisher of our faith; who for the joy that was set before him endured the cross, despising the shame, and is set down at the right hand of the throne of God. Hebrews 12:2.

This text suggests there is a difference in what you see when you look. Do you see light or shadows? Have you noticed that you cannot make a shadow without light? Made by an opaque object through which light cannot pass, the shadow is the darkness behind the object in the light. Shadows exist around us whenever there is light.

When I was a girl my dad would sit by the kitchen table and play shadows with my brother and me. We seldom played this game except when the electricity went off and we were forced temporarily to use the spare candles Mother kept in the drawer. How I loved those evenings when Daddy couldn't read the paper. He used his hands to make all kinds of clever shadow objects. On our kitchen wall danced shadows that resembled horses, cows, swans, roosters, and other objects.

But most shadows don't produce happiness. They are created by people who dwell on gloomy, unhappy things. Our text tells us Jesus didn't do that. Instead of living in the shadow of the cross, dwelling on the shame, He focused on the precious life-giving rays shining from that cross promising life to all.

How foolish to walk, talk, and think as if you lived in the shadows. The cross points upward to a living Saviour who is already waiting for you at God's throne. When you feel depressed or despondent, it is because Satan has gotten himself between you and the bright rays from the Sun of Righteousness. You've allowed your emotions to become stronger than your faith in Jesus.

How do you get out of the shadows into the light? Look to Jesus. Talk of His love and goodness. Trust Him with your problems. Praise Him even when you don't feel like it. Talk faith, not doubt. Believe each promise is for you personally. Never complain of your sorrows, for that only deepens your troubles.

Turn from your shadows and live in the sunlight of the cross. In the light of Christ's love you may live in the perpetual comfort of His presence.

E.E.L. and J.H.L.

TRUE TO THE LAST

By this shall all men know that ye are my disciples, if ye have love one to another. John 13:35.

Nine-year-old Tom Carter was one of the heroes of the San Francisco earthquake of 1906. His widowed mother had to work hard to support Tom and two-year-old Elizabeth. After school Tom took care of his little sister, although the pupils teased him about his brotherly devotion. He even washed all her clothes. Frecklefaced Tom ignored his friends' remarks. Soon their teasing turned to admiration when the children noticed that when they gave Tom some goodies he always took them home—an apple, a cooky, or a sandwich. The school friends began bringing him toys for Betty.

On April 18 just after five o'clock in the morning the three Carters were awakened by shaking walls and crashing dishes and furniture. The chimney collapsed on the mother's bed so that she could not move. "Tom—an earthquake. Grab Betty and run outside. Don't bother about me."

Tom wrapped a quilt around his small sister and hurried down the swaying steps from the fourth floor. Then he heard "Fire! Fire!" Tom followed the panic-stricken mob as fast as he could carry his precious bundle. Finally exhausted he sat down by a wall to rest. His head, his arms, and his legs ached. Someone was trying to take away his sister. "Don't you dare touch her." Although his arms were hurting badly, he was fighting like a tiger to hold on to Elizabeth. "My dear boy, let us help you," said a physician. At this point the boy lost consciousness. When he came to, he found himself in a clean white hospital bed with a nurse bending over him.

"Where's Elizabeth?" he asked. "I promised mother not to leave her."

"We'll bring her to you." The child cried with delight when she saw her brother. Then he fell back on the bed and aroused himself just enough to ask, "Would it be wrong if I let the nurse take care of Elizabeth while I sleep? I am so tired." Tom never spoke again. He died of fatal injuries.

With tear-filled eyes the nurses looked at one another and said, "Now Betty has no brother or mother. She will be *our* responsibility."

L.C.W.

EASY TO LOVE

He that loveth not knoweth not God; for God is love. 1 John 4:8.

When we have felt God's love in our lives, the next thing for us to do is to show this love to others.

It is easy to love someone that appeals to us—the new girl with the beautiful long hair and the expensive-looking clothes, the boy who excels in athletics, the teacher who is everyone else's favorite teacher too. But if the people easy to love are the only ones we love, that means we do not yet understand the principle of love.

All around us in this world are people who are in particular need of Christian love, the kind that we can give. Ellen White speaks of it as "disinterested love." She means the kind of love that does not come from some selfish interest, but Christlike love that wants the best for others and does not hope for something in return.

In our school life we might take this to mean that we don't show attention only to the kids who are with the "in" crowd. We treat everyone alike. On our home street, we don't just do things with the kids, we also do things for the old lady who can't get to the store or mailbox, for the man who is ill and would appreciate someone to come in and read to him.

In our family we don't grumble about the tasks we are asked to do, or help more quickly if a reward is offered than when one is not. We lighten the burdens of Mom and Dad all we can. This is love in action.

Disinterested love also means loving the teacher—not polishing the apple in order to get a better grade, but doing what we can to be kind and helpful simply to make the teacher happier. And by the way, this is one of the most effective ways of getting along well in school, because when we do this, we are not so apt to do things that annoy the teacher. (Those things, incidentally, are the same things that get us into trouble.)

Perhaps the key thought to remember is that love is not something we feel; it is something that we do.

When we have this kind of love in our hearts, others will see God's love shining through our lives, and we ourselves will be easier to love.

R.E.

PETTING A RATTLESNAKE

The infant plays over the cobra's hole; into the viper's lair the young child puts his hand. Isaiah 11:8, Jerusalem.

Imagine a world without fear! Because of sin we must have fear of evil. No mother would allow her baby to play with a poisonous snake. From the very beginning of consciousness children learn fear. Young animals, perfectly happy playing with other animals normally their enemies, have no fear until it is taught to them. In the new earth, with nothing of which to be afraid, children will never know fear. Gone forever will be the horrible emotions of anger, enmity, and fright.

Three young boys lived in the mountains of North Carolina. One July day they decided to go berry picking. With them was their baby brother, who was about 9 months old.

Putting the baby on the cool, short grass near the berry bushes, the boys went to work. He was within sight of them, and they often peered through the bushes to see whether all was well.

Busy chatting, eating berries, and putting a few in their buckets, the boys heard the baby talking happily, "da, da, da." Hearing him laugh, they peered through bushes. He was petting something.

A huge rattlesnake lay across their little brother's legs. His tiny hands were stroking the snake's smooth skin. Its ugly face was very close to the baby's, but the child felt no fear at a sight that would have sent terror into a more mature person.

The boys watched with alarm. What should they do? They decided to do nothing, realizing that to disturb the snake could be fatal. The baby kept talking in soft tones; patting the sleek body. Finally, after what seemed like a long time to the watching boys, the snake slithered away into the tall grass.

What was there about the soft baby touch that calmed the poisonous snake, whose nature was to sink its poisonous fangs into man? Could it have been the absence of fear and the presence of love? Perhaps snakes, which may again be loved in the new earth, enjoy the feeling of approval and joy just as you and I do.

Life in that glorious land is not far away now. Are you taking time each day to let Jesus make you ready to live with Him?

E.E.L. and J.H.L.

WAX OR CLAY?

Wherefore then do you harden your hearts, as the Egyptians and Pharaoh hardened their hearts? 1 Samuel 6:6.

The soil contained a great deal of clay. Heavy rains had turned it into a slippery, sticky mass of mud. Because the extremely fine particles of clay held too much water on the surface, the moisture couldn't be absorbed below. Then the weather changed. The hot sun beat down on the ground day after day. The clay became stiff and hard, almost impossible to plow. Large, ugly cracks formed. The ground seemed useless for crops.

But if you place a pan of wax under the same sun, it soon becomes soft and pliable. You may shape it as you wish. As it melts you can pour it into a mold to form any shape of candle or object you desire. The same sun shone on these two substances. But how differently each reacted. One became hard and difficult. The other softened and melted.

Tragedy strikes two persons. Faced with sickness, pain, disappointed hopes and plans, or death, one becomes hard and cold, complains, and blames God and others. Gradually he withers up, and cracks mentally, physically, and spiritually. The other suffers too, but he turns to God. Even though he doesn't understand he submits, saying, "The Lord gave, and the Lord hath taken away" (Job 1:21). His heart, melted by God's love, is filled with sympathy, compassion, and kindness for others. Into his life comes a quiet joy and peace, an inner strength and nobility.

Have you been wronged? or treated unjustly? Did you allow your feelings to be hurt and retaliate by defending your reputation? Did you talk about your problem, trying to get sympathy? If you did, friendships cracked and hearts became hard. But maybe you let God help you do everything in your power to make peace with the ones who wronged you. After that you kept silent, refusing to discuss your problem. You left it in God's hands and turned your thoughts to pleasant things.

Can clay become wax? No. But hearts of stone can become flesh. Blind eyes can open. People who walk in their sleep can wake up. Jesus can soften and melt hard hearts. If you've been acting like clay let Him make you into wax. He specializes in melting hard hearts.

E.E.L. and J.H.L.

THE BLEACHING AGENT

Come now, and let us reason together, saith the Lord: though your sins be as scarlet, they shall be as white as snow; though they be red like crimson, they shall be as wool. Isaiah 1:18.

As usual on washing day I put the white clothes into the machine first. When I took out the shirts, T-shirts, shorts, dish towels, et cetera, to hang them up to dry, I groaned.

Everything that had been white when I put them in was now pink. Carefully I hunted for the reason. Hidden inside one of the T-shirts was a red sock. Knowing my family of boys didn't enjoy wearing pink clothes, I knew there was nothing to do but change the color back to white. With so many it wouldn't be an easy job. Throwing aside the offending red sock, I hunted for the bleach bottle.

The directions went something like this: "For nylons, dacron, et cetera, use 2 tablespoons bleach to 1 gallon warm water." Guessing at the amount of water that would cover the clothes, I carefully poured in the bleach and started the agitator of the washing machine. The color slowly began to fade. The pink got fainter and fainter and finally the clothes were white again. Yet a strange thing happened, for even though I soaked them a long while, the water remained clear through the entire process. When I took the now-white clothes out to hang them up, I noticed the water was clear, with not a tinge of pink.

That bleach, whether it was chlorine or hydrogen peroxide, produced a chemical reaction that changed the red dye into a colorless molecule. Thus both the clothes and the water were free from the red.

When we sin and truly repent, God forgives us. We cannot see the purifying agent that cleanses us, but by faith we know a change has come into our hearts. The guilt is gone. Our whole being is transformed by the peace of forgiveness.

Today Jesus is offering you forgiveness. He longs to give it to you, but He will not force your will to accept it. Only you can choose to be free from sin. Jesus waits as a mighty bleaching agent to change your scarlet past into a white more beautiful than fresh snow. He'll take away all the crimson dye of sin and make your life like the whitest wool. Don't keep the heavy burden of sin. Ask for forgiveness now.

E.E.L. and J.H.L.

LOVE HELPS US GROW

When I was a child, I talked like a child, I thought like a child, I argued like a child; now that I am a man, I am done with childish ways. 1 Corinthians 13:11, Moffatt.

Here the apostle Paul paints a picture of a child. But it is also a beautiful word picture of growth, maturity, and victory. And he could add: "Now that I am a man, I am done with childish ways." Every adult must admit that he was once a child. Can he say with Paul, "Now that I am a man, I am done with childish ways"? That is the ideal.

Some people grow up. They are still manifesting "childish ways." They still want to argue. Many people, whether 6, 16, or 60, have not given up this desire to argue! They have not put aside their childish ways. This indicates that we need the victory of love. Paul permitted love to rule in his life and it brought him a glorious victory.

Paul loved God and His precious work so much that he could say: "And now I am going to Jerusalem, drawn there irresistibly by the Holy Spirit, not knowing what awaits me, except that the Holy Spirit has told me in city after city that jail and suffering lie ahead. But life is worth nothing unless I use it for doing the work assigned me by the Lord Jesus—the work of telling others the Good News about God's mighty kindness and love" (Acts 20:22-24, TLB). This is one example of love's victory.

What a man! He gladly gave up his own plans, his own ideas, and was even glad to give up life itself if it could glorify his Lord. He was so sincere, so childlike in his simple trust, but not childish. He didn't argue with God. He had "put away childish things."

Yes, what a man! But remember, he was not always a man. He was first a boy. "When I was a child," he said. And he, like all boys, seemed to think and talk like a child. He probably did many things that boys seem naturally to want to do, for "he thought like a child."

But the important lesson for every junior is that a child can grow up! A boy can become a man. He can achieve maturity and develop mature thinking by the grace of God. Paul could say: "The love of Christ constraineth me" (2 Cor. 5:14).

A.A.E.

COVERLET OF FEATHERS

He shall cover thee with his feathers, and under his wings shalt thou trust. Psalm 91:4.

By collecting and studying bird feathers, I have begun to understand why David, under inspiration, chose the safety of feathered wings to be a symbol of God's strength and love.

One cold night in Germany we discovered the warmth of feathers. Welcomed into a rented room that contained a feather bed and quilt, we were enveloped in a cozy warmth. Then again, while camping in the cold mountains of Colorado, even though the outside temperature often dropped below zero, the warmth of a down sleeping bag, made from feathers with no quills, was marvelous.

God's love is very strong, yet it never crushes. That's why He chose the most appropriate of all nature objects to represent that in which we can put our trust. The feather is the strongest structure for its size and weight known in nature.

Get a feather and examine its three parts. Notice the stiff center which gives it strength. From this shaft come off barbs which, toward the outer end, join together in a smooth web. Did you note the soft, downy part next to the bird's body?

Observing through a magnifying glass, you'll see branching from the center of each barb little barbules with tinier baricels coming from them. Each tiny hook grasps another, making the feather appear to be a solid structure. The hooks on one barb hold to the ridges of the next, locking them together like tiny zippers. If these split apart the bird can easily zip them together again with his bill.

Birds stay dry in wet weather because God arranged feathers to overlap. Squeezing the oil gland near his tail he rubs oil through the feathers. Thus, the under feathers stay dry, and the bird is warm with his downy cover, as the rain runs off the oily outer feathers.

Knowing these beautiful facts about feathers takes away all fear for the times of trouble ahead. If you choose to abide in Christ He surrounds you with His presence. How foolish for us to fear the time of trouble! You only have to trust Him, for Christ is your defense. As long as you are covered with God's strong feathers and His protecting wings, nothing can happen to you that is not for your good.

E.E.L. and J.H.L.

WHAT'S YOUR COURTESY QUOTIENT?

Having compassion one of another, love as brethren, be pitiful, be courteous. 1 Peter 3:8.

With his baskets full of produce Kevin waited for the bus. Then he took the last empty seat on it. When an elderly woman got on the bus Kevin offered his seat. She forgot to thank him. When the bus gave a quick lurch a man fell against Kevin, upsetting his basket so that apples and pears rolled everywhere.

"That's too bad," muttered the man, but made no effort to retrieve the fruit. Kevin picked up what he could, glad his egg basket was still intact. Soon a lady in her finery entered the bus, knocked against the egg basket so that one egg broke, and its contents streamed down her dress. The lad was profuse in his apologies.

"Boys like you should not be permitted on our city buses. There should be some special arrangement for folks who come heavily loaded with stuff."

"I heartily agree," responded Kevin. "I'm sorry for the mishap, but usually I'm not so careless. I'm really sorry about the accident with your dress."

A little girl on her way to school sobbed because she had forgotten her bus pass and had no money. Kevin calmed her and gave the driver a coin for her fare.

One gentleman had been a silent witness to Kevin's behavior. Now he touched the young man's arm and asked his name and his occupation. "Do you like being a delivery boy?"

"No, sir, not especially, but I'm grateful for a part-time job while I finish high school. When I'm ready I want to be an office worker."

"Will your classes permit you to stop a few minutes at my office this morning?" The man handed Kevin his business card.

Then he turned to his nephew after they had left the bus and remarked, "Today I have found a young man for whom I've been searching two years. As I was observing the delivery lad, I noticed his patience under trying circumstances, his thoughtfulness, his courtesy. That's a young man one can depend upon. I want to train him in our business from the ground up."

Neither Kevin nor his friends understood why he was given employment in a large wholesale house, one paying higher wages and offering more fringe benefits than any other business house in the city.

L.C.W.

WHO SENT THE DOLPHINS?

Fear not, for I have redeemed you; I have called you by name,
you are mine. When you pass through the waters I will be with
you; and through the rivers, they shall not overwhelm you.
Isaiah 43:1, 2, RSV.

These precious promises saved young Yvonne Vladislavich in the waters off the East African coast in September, 1972. She and seven other persons were traveling by boat, and had planned to reach their destination in three hours. But the inboard motor suddenly stopped. Failing to find the trouble, they tried the spare outboard motor. When it wouldn't start, they radioed a friend for help. Unfortunately, the radio batteries were wet from the rough sea and the radio was silenced soon after they made contact.

The height of the waves increased to six meters. Those who weren't too seasick bailed water constantly. All day through storm and rain they struggled. At about nine o'clock that night they saw lights of boats. Their flares had been lost, but using their last match, they poured gasoline on clothes and held the makeshift flares high with a fishing rod. One boat signaled, but never found them.

About three-thirty the next morning three huge waves more than nine meters high came one after another. The boat, already half full of water, began to go down.

"Get out, we're sinking," someone yelled. The third wave sank the boat. When, after five hours in the water, the first person died, Yvonne, a strong swimmer, decided to go for help. Claiming God's promises, she started out. Her feet, cut when the boat sank, were bleeding constantly. After about six and a half hours of swimming she noticed black shadows around her—sharks! "O God," she prayed, "if I must die, let it be quick. Not an arm and then a leg. May they do it quickly."

But God had a different plan. Two fins glided toward her. Thinking this was the end, Yvonne watched with amazement as a dolphin bumped the oncoming shark and drove it away. Later she fainted, but became conscious as she was lifted out of the water on the nose of a dolphin.

Two dolphins guarded her for twelve and a half hours until she was picked up by a passing ship sixty-seven kilometers away from the rest of the group. Yvonne knows Jesus sent the dolphins in answer to His promise.

E.E.L. and J.H.L.

BECAUSE HE LOVES US

Beloved, if God so loved us, we ought also to love one another.
1 John 4:11.

Many boys, reaching their teens, don't want a bunch of little kids tagging after them. Who wants to bother with a small cousin, for instance, when he could be going off swimming with boys his own age? Who wants to sit down and talk with a little girl who might just make a nuisance of herself afterwards, following a fellow around?

But James was different. He had several small cousins, much younger than himself, who visited his home quite often, and James went out of his way to see that they had a good time when they came. In the kitchen cupboard was a cup James had used as a small boy. It had a nursery design printed on it, and the littlest cousins liked it. In fact, the two smallest cousins often fought over which would drink from that special cup. So James went out and with his own money bought two unbreakable tumblers with nursery designs. Each had a lid with a hole in it, and through each hole protruded a striped drinking straw. He put those in the cupboard to be used especially by the youngest cousins when they came to visit.

He never was too busy to take a little cousin on his lap. He always had time to admire roads and castles in the sandbox or explain the workings of toys from his own childhood days.

His thoughtfulness was not only for little ones. When his grand-mother was ill, James gave up seeing a special program at the academy to go with his folks to see her. He took along the musical instrument he was learning to play so Grandma could see it.

When James was getting married, his young cousin Laura decided she wanted to give him a gift all by herself. One big present from the whole family was not enough for such a special cousin. She wrapped the package and printed the card herself, "To James from Laura."

Her mother asked her one day afterward, "Why do you children all love James so much?" It didn't take long to get an answer.

"Why, because he loves us so much."

When someone loves us a lot, we want to respond by showing love ourselves. God has shown us love so great we can't understand it. Let's respond to that love by showing love to others.

R.E.

PRESERVED IN ICE OR STONE

We were buried therefore with him by baptism into death, so that as Christ was raised from the dead by the glory of the Father, we too might walk in newness of life. Romans 6:4, RSV.

The earth, a vast burial ground, yields a record of plant and animal life that lived in the past. A fossil may be a whole animal preserved in ice or just a bone or a tooth hardened by minerals. Remains of plants or animals turned to stone are petrified fossils. Giant logs of petrified wood are found in Arizona's petrified forest.

Sometimes living things are buried in mud, clay, or other material that hardens around them. A whole rhinoceros, buried in an ancient lava flow, left a mold of its body. Petrified pitch or amber has perfectly preserved delicate insects. Through this transparent medium even the finest hairs and bristles may be studied under a microscope.

Often prints of leaves, feathers, tracks, or footprints are preserved when the soft mud in which they are made hardens into stone. You may see minute details such as veins of leaves, fish fins, or flying reptile wings.

Most interesting fossils of mummified men, considered to be 2,000 years old, were found in peat in Denmark. One corpse with a rope around his neck, wore a peaceful expression on his face in spite of his probably unwilling entry into the bog. It was evident that he hadn't shaved for several days before his death.

Though all fossils have died and been buried, a few will live again eternally at the first resurrection. Others will rise only to be destroyed after the second resurrection.

You may let Jesus bury eternally all the ugly traits of character in your life. When self dies God will gladly bury all evidence of it, never to be dug up again, as fossils are unearthed by scientists. As a new person you live again in Jesus. Baptized into the death of Christ you signify that you and Jesus have become one. Your old life has died. You are now living a new life in Him.

If you haven't been baptized by immersion, prepare for it now.

E.E.L. and J.H.L.

THE VOICE OF JESUS

When he putteth forth his own sheep, he goeth before them,
and the sheep follow him: for they know his voice. John 10:4.

How important that we always recognize the voice of Jesus and
follow when He calls us. This assures us victory over sin. We may
hear His voice in various ways. Sometimes He speaks in the still
small voice of conscience. At other times by the Holy Spirit He
flashes a word of Scripture into our minds to turn aside the power
of the tempter. Knowing the Bible is one of the best safeguards
against being overcome by Satan. Jesus, weak from His long
wilderness fast, came off a victory by using "It is written."

It never pays to argue with the devil. Even Jesus Himself did not
stoop to argue with the enemy when the evil one protested the
resurrection of Moses. He said only, "The Lord rebuke thee" (Jude
9). The two ways we can best overcome the devil is to quote
Scripture and then to lift our thoughts in prayer to our mighty
Captain, asking Him for strength to overcome.

Today Jesus speaks to us as to His own disciples just before His
ascension: "All power is given unto me in heaven and in earth. . . .
And, lo, I am with you alway, even unto the end of the world" (Matt.
28:18-20). This sense of the presence of Jesus we need in every
time of temptation and trial.

Once in Pennsylvania a dog stood shivering on a thin cake of ice
floating in a reservoir. His pitiful howls stirred the police, the
firemen, and the town folk to help him. They tried in different ways
to remove the dog from the ice.

Then someone had a bright idea. The dog belonged to a little girl
six years old. They brought the child as close as possible to the dog
so that she could call and wave her hands to show her pet she was
there.

When the dog heard the familiar voice of his mistress, he wagged
his tail, splashed to the bank of the reservoir, and up to safety. The
skill of strangers gave the animal no courage, but the voice of one
whom the dog trusted rescued him.

Today listen to the kind voice of your Saviour. He wants to rescue
you whatever may be your temptation or difficulty. Even today His
promise holds, "I will never leave thee, nor forsake thee" (Heb.
13:5).

L.C.W.

"BOSS JOHNSON"

Examine yourselves, whether ye be in the faith; prove your own selves. 2 Corinthians 13:5.

Often we can help ourselves by looking into our lives. Self-examination, self-evaluation, may sometimes be difficult, but it has its rewards.

Mr. Pettigrew stepped into the shipping clerk's office to check on the detail of an order that had to go out that day. It was not often that the manager found time to be in this particular section of the plant, for it ran smoothly and efficiently.

Suddenly he heard a voice outside the wooden partition say, "Johnson, you sweep that floor properly." All was quiet for a few minutes, then the same voice said, "Johnson, those packages are not stacked straight. You straighten them up." Again after a further wait the same voice commanded, "Johnson, get the oil can and oil the rollers on the big door!"

Mr. Pettigrew began to feel sorry for Johnson, and stepped outside quickly to see which foreman was passing so many orders to one man. But there was only a youth in overalls walking toward the back of the plant with an oilcan in his hand.

"Johnson," called Mr. Pettigrew, "come here. Tell me who it was I heard giving all those orders to you." The embarrassed young man didn't know where to look. Finally he confessed, "That was me you heard talking, sir. I know I'm lazy, and the only way I can get a good job out of myself is to boss Johnson."

Perhaps you need to start bossing Johnson. He won't like the discipline, but you can do it.

Try it first thing in the morning: "Johnson, don't forget your morning watch. Johnson, be early for breakfast." Try it at school: "Johnson, be good to that new schoolmate. Johnson, study your lessons better and pay attention in class."

Get the idea? Try bossing Johnson today. You may be surprised at how much he can get done!

W.R.L.S.

HEAVENLY FLIGHT

But they that wait upon the Lord shall renew their strength; they shall mount up with wings as eagles; they shall run, and not be weary; and they shall walk, and not faint. Isaiah 40:31.

Have you ever watched an eagle fly? He soars to great heights, then drops downward, maneuvering his body so accurately that he can make a pinpoint landing without a runway. Using his broad tail and enormous seven-foot wingspan, the golden eagle's graceful flight enables him to surmount all obstacles.

God has wings for you, too, wings of surrender and trust.

Surrender? What are you to surrender to God? Give Him your wicked heart. Give Him your unstable will; give Him your untrained service. Then—trust. Trust implicitly in His promises. They're true. They're dependable. God cannot lie.

What would happen if an eagle attempted to fly using just one wing? He wouldn't get off the ground. Both wings must work together in perfect harmony for an eagle to fly. Neither can you mount up to heavenly flight unless you use both wings. Earthly sorrows, doubts, and annoyances have no power to hinder your heavenly flight when both wings are active and in constant use.

Why didn't God refer to the chicken's flight instead of the eagle's? Chickens do fly for short distances. But could you say a chicken's flight is heavenly? Not in comparison to that of the eagle's, that's for certain. Many self-deceived Christians think they are flying. They practice using their wings of surrender and trust about as often as a chicken uses its wings, and consequently, they are weak. This weakness is shown in their lack of progress in becoming like Jesus. They fly a little, but not far, nor high, nor with the ability of an eagle.

Do you fly like a chicken or an eagle? God promises power to strengthen your weak wings of trust and surrender. When you stop depending on your efforts, He increases your strength. Even young people become weary and exhausted. But those who wait for the Lord to renew their strength will mount up with wings like eagles. They shall not be weary as they run for Jesus. Faint hearts grow strong when Jesus walks beside them.

E.E.L. and J.H.L.

THE CUP OF SALVATION

I will take the cup of salvation, and call upon the name of the Lord. Psalm 116:13.

A hundred years ago, many great ocean-going ships were dependent on the wind for movement. It must have been a lovely sight to see them scudding along under a fresh breeze, sails puffed out, rudder set to steer them in the desired direction. But when the wind failed, many had no engines to take over. Sails lay slack and lifeless, leaving the ship helpless and becalmed, sometimes for days or even weeks.

This is said to have happened once to a ship sailing off the coast of Brazil, South America. The passengers and crew had plenty of food on board, but water soon became scarce. As windless days followed one another, the captain began to wonder whether they would ever move again. Although he had ordered the water to be strictly rationed, the day came when there was no more. All on board prayed for rain, or for assistance from some passing vessel.

Their prayers were answered. From the north they saw a steamer approaching. As soon as the strange ship was near enough the captain of the sailing ship signaled. "Please, can you supply water?" To his amazement the steamer signaled back:

"Dip down and take it."

"It is not seawater we need," the captain replied, "but drinking water."

Back came the same signal. Puzzled the captain dropped a bucket over the side and brought up fresh water! All the time the passengers had been suffering from thirst, the fresh water of the Amazon had been pouring past the vessel. It had been all around them, but they had not known it.

God does not force salvation on anyone. It is available, and He offers it freely to every person who will accept it.

Jesus stood in the Temple and cried, "If any man thirst, let him come unto me, and drink" (John 7:37). He told the woman of Samaria that if she had recognized Him, she might have asked for and received living water.

Like David, we only need to reach out and accept the cup of salvation, filled to overflowing with the water of life. That life-giving water is for you. Dip down, fill your cup, and drink. It is free.

V.E.R.

HIDDEN TERMITES

He that covereth his sins shall not prosper: but whoso confesseth and forsaketh them shall have mercy. Proverbs 28:13.

This morning I read a sad and tragic story of what hidden termites can do. Hidden termites, of course, are the unconfessed secret sins of the human heart. How true is the Bible statement that "the little foxes" are the ones "that spoil the vines" (S. of Sol. 2:15).

What are these "little foxes," these secret sins, these hidden termites? Are they not the covered sins, the unconfessed sins eating away in the human heart?

The story concerns two little girls who went to the same Sabbath school. They sat next to each other in the church school. When one of them was 15 years old she ran away from home and her life was soon ruined. At 21 she was found in a hospital and her life of promise had been utterly wasted.

Her classmate was not a dropout but went on through with her education and a few years later was serving with her husband in a mission land.

Now what was the cause of this great tragedy involving the life of the 15-year-old girl? While she was in the hospital waiting for death to erase from her memory a life of tragedy she shared the secret. She said it all began with "little sins." "I covered up many of my sins," she confessed. She had started going to worldly amusements and the theater and before long was dating non-Christian boys. "My father and mother and the church people didn't know what I was doing," she revealed. "They all thought I was being good when I wasn't. The worst thing about it all is that when I wanted to change, I couldn't."

The author of this story added a stirring paragraph that I would like to share with all our juniors. It needs to be perpetuated, to live on and save many a boy or girl from such a tragedy from hidden termites.

"A men's magazine a few years ago displayed on its front cover a disrobed girl in a garbage can. It was an illustration for an article concerning the new morality, entitled, 'The New American Woman: Through at 21.' Sin is like that. It can take away everything decent, everything worthwhile." Don't let it hide in your life.

A.A.E.

DRAWN TO JESUS

And I, if I be lifted up from the earth, will draw all men unto me. John 12:32.

The prisoner crouched in the corner of his cell, wondering what all the noise was about. It had gone on all morning. Perhaps they were waiting to see him die.

He heard the rattle of a key. The door creaked open, and a Roman soldier stepped into the dark, filthy cell.

"No! No! Not yet!" screamed the convict, retreating to a far corner.

"What's the matter?" asked the soldier. "I've come to set you free."

With a look of disbelief Barabbas gazed up into the soldier's face. "Did you say I'm free? How can that be?"

"Well, I'll tell you. The Jews have decided to set you free at this feast. It seems they had to choose between you and a man named Jesus. Jesus will die, and you . . ." He motioned toward the light coming through the door.

He unlocked the heavy chains binding Barabbas' hands and feet, and the convict hurried out of the prison, a free man.

Did Barabbas follow the crowd out through the gates of Jerusalem? Did he, with them, climb Calvary's hill and there watch the Saviour die? If anyone ever lived who could truly say, "He died for me," that man was Barabbas.

The cross of Jesus has magnetic power. No one can read the story of the crucifixion of Jesus and not want to worship and love Him.

If all men are drawn, why do they not all go?

Take a magnet and pass it over a nail. When you bring it near, the nail literally leaps into the air to meet the magnet. Now drive the nail into a block of wood. Pass the magnet close to it. The magnet may be pulled toward the nail, but the nail does not leap to meet the magnet. Why? Because it is fastened to the block of wood.

People often feel the pull of Jesus' love, but few surrender their lives to Him, because they are held fast to the material things of this world. Could this be why Christians seldom become wealthy? Perhaps God knows that they might become so attached to the world that they would forget Him.

Jesus was lifted up, and is drawing all men to Him. He is drawing you. Respond to His love today.

V.E.R.

DO YOU NEED COMFORTING?

Like a son comforted by his mother will I comfort you. Isaiah 66:13, Jerusalem.

When you are hurt or disappointed, miserable or sick, when you are in trouble or treated unkindly by someone, what a comfort it is to know that you can go to mother and she will understand. With her arms of love around you, the hurt isn't so hard to bear. Even though mothers do bring much love and comfort to their children, Jesus brings even more. There is no limit to the help that your Saviour is willing to give you, for He can give you what your mother cannot—lasting joy, perfect rest, and peace.

Flood waters overflowed the banks of the Santee River in South Carolina. A fierce-looking razorback hog with her nine babies were huddled together on a log, caught in the crotch of a tree. The mother hog knew that soon the swift, swirling water would sweep the log away. She could easily have saved herself, for wild razorback hogs can swim for miles. But could her babies make it through the swift water to a high point half a mile away?

Grunting to her little ones, she plunged into the water. They watched her as she demonstrated how to swim. Then she climbed back on the log. It seemed as if she were saying comforting words of courage such as, "Be brave, little pigs. You can swim to safety."

Carefully she helped them into the water, making sure they were all there. Then she swam slowly, always keeping her body between the babies and the swift, strong current, constantly reassuring them with comforting grunts. When they all arrived at the safety of land, she gathered them around her. Ugly as she was, that old mother pig had beautiful actions. How each little pig must have enjoyed the comfort of snuggling against her warm body and enjoying her milk after such a trying ordeal.

God doesn't promise that Christians will be exempt from sorrow and grief. But He does promise to be with us, to comfort us with His compassionate love, to give us strength for today. Remember that underneath you are the everlasting arms of Jesus. His comforting touch will ease your hurts more than that of your mother.

E.E.L. and J.H.L.

WHAT IF GOD HAD A BUZZER AT OUR CHURCH DOOR?

If you do what is right, will you not be accepted? But if you do not do what is right, sin is crouching at your door; it desires to have you, but you must master it. Genesis 4:7, NIV.

When I travel by plane these days, like millions of other air travelers I have to pass through metal detectors. Perhaps you have traveled by air too and know all about these precautions. Because there have been so many planes hijacked in recent years, the authorities are taking no chances. Personally, I'm glad they do this, for I have nothing to hide and nothing to fear, and I have no desire to take a trip to some unplanned destination.

Before I get on the plane my briefcase and any other parcel I may be carrying in my hands are either examined carefully by a law-enforcement officer or passed through an electronic device that reveals the presence of any metals inside. I have heard of some passengers being delayed when a knife or a gun turned up in their hand baggage.

While my handbags are being cleared I pass through a device that looks like a door frame. This is wired so that a buzzer sounds if I am carrying any metal. I have to be careful not to have keys or change or something else in my pockets that triggers the device. I have often had to go through the second time before being permitted to proceed to the airplane, because I had some metal objects in my pockets.

What if God had a sin-detector device set up in each of our churches? What if this device could look into our hearts and lives and when it found some sin there—when it discovered we had taken something that did not belong to us, that we had spoken that which was not true, that we had broken God's Sabbath day, or that we had been ugly, unkind, or disobedient—would sound a buzzer? Would we be afraid to go to church?

God can and does detect sin in our lives. We cannot fool Him. He doesn't need a detector to know whether or not our hearts are pure and clean.

Remember, our friends think we are what they see on the outside. God looks right into our hearts and knows what's on the inside.

"We are what we are at night," someone has said.

R.H.P.

KEEPING UP

Wrath killeth the foolish man, and envy slayeth the silly one.
Job 5:2.

Gracie was a small girl when she began making herself miserable, and she continued the habit all her life. How? She envied those who had more things, or different things, than she did.

As a little girl on a poor, unproductive farm, she envied a family of cousins whose father owned a store in town. When she went away to school she spent miserable hours envying the wardrobes of the girls who had more than she. She made herself so unhappy about it that her whole personality became tinged with melancholy. Then when it seemed to her that she had few friends, she blamed that on her lack of possessions rather than her lack of cheerfulness.

As an adult she worked hard to have the things she had missed as a girl, but she didn't enjoy them much. You see, when her friend bought a new dress that Grace admired, she couldn't bear to compliment her. Instead of being glad for her friend's nice dress, Grace thought only that she didn't have one like it, so she would buy a similar one.

Another friend bought a new refrigerator to replace a wornout one. The friend bubbled with happiness and wanted to share her joy with Grace. But telling Grace made the bubbles go flat.

"How nice," Grace said, her face stiff with envy. Her own refrigerator looked old-fashioned and drab compared to her friend's new one. Not long after, Grace bought a refrigerator a little bigger and better than her friend had purchased.

If she'd only kept up with one friend, it would have been easier. But Grace bought a coat like Mrs. A., a purse like Mrs. B., and a hat the color of the one she admired on Mrs. C.

When Gracie was an old lady and could no longer work, she lived under a cloud of constant money worry, for it had cost a lot to keep up with so many. After she died her children found she had closets full of clothes that were scarcely worn. She had boxes of new things never used.

"Why," they said, "if she'd lived on her money instead of having it tied up in these things, she wouldn't have had to worry."

Today let's ask God to deliver us from envying those who have more and to make us truly grateful for the blessings in our lives.

R.E.

THE YOUNG SAMARITAN

He brought me up also out of an horrible pit, out of the miry clay, and set my feet upon a rock. Psalm 40:2.

On a Sunday afternoon in Charleston, West Virginia, Alan and his father walked into the city post office. Alan saw a stooped old man trying to mail a letter. Noticing that the man was almost blind, the boy opened the letter slot. As they drove off, Alan watched the old man tapping the street with his cane. "Daddy, why don't we pick up that man? He might be hit by a car. We could take him home."

"Where are you going, sir?" asked Father.

"Nowhere, really. I was thinking that maybe if I walked down to the bridge and jumped into the river, it would settle my troubles once and for all"

"Jump into the river! You can't do that," Alan cried.

"Suicide is not the best way out. God will help you to find new meaning in life, if you let Him," his father added. The stranger talked, telling of the mistakes he had made and how his wife had ordered him out of the house.

Alan prodded his father. "Tell him about *Bible Readings*. Sell him a book."

Father obeyed. "This book will help you find your way out of your problems. Pray God to help you." Gladly the old man paid for the book.

"When I was a boy I lived in a town where most of the people were Seventh-day Adventists. I wish I could be back with those people again and do right."

"I'm an Adventist, and I know of an Adventist lady here who would be happy to give you room and board. I'll drive you right over there now." Soon the old man was comfortably settled in a nice bedroom.

"Invite him to Sabbath school and church," pleaded Alan.

To Alan's delight Mr. Johnson came to church. He had read in the book. He requested Bible studies. The man had once been a loved and respected State senator. His mistakes, especially his liquor problem, had made his family, including a famous doctor brother, disown him. But God changed this man. After a few months he was baptized. Before he died, he said to Alan, "Remember, someday I'm going to see you in heaven." A junior boy had helped win a soul for Christ.

L.C.W.

PELICAN WATCHMAN AND A
CHURCH-GOING BOAR

Can the Ethiopian change his skin or the leopard his spots?
Then also you can do good who are accustomed to do evil.
Jeremiah 13:23, RSV.

Living in both temperate and tropical zones, the pelican is a large
water bird with an enormous, elastic pouch on the underside of its
bill and front of its upper neck. Usually about five feet long, it is the
world's largest web-footed bird, with a wingspread of eight to ten
feet. Almost voiceless, this swift swimmer lives in large colonies that
cooperate with one another in gathering fish for food.

Many years ago one of these strong, graceful fliers swooped down
on an African woman carrying a fish. Frightened, she struck it with
a paddle, breaking one leg and crippling its wing. Nearby was Dr.
Albert Schweitzer's jungle hospital. Hearing of the accident, the
kind doctor took the pelican under his care. In a short time the bird
was healed and set free. But this bird, who had always lived in water
as part of a large colony of pelicans, refused to leave the doctor.
Never was there a better night watchman. His bill frightened any
prowler as he faithfully watched and protected his beloved doctor.
Love for the one who aided him changed the pelican's entire nature.
So love for your Lord can change you from one accustomed to do
evil to one who loves to do good.

One of the wildest of animals is the African wild boar. Yet even
this fierce, ugly creature can respond to the strange experience of
being loved. Dr. Schweitzer adopted a savage hog whom he called
Josephine. Treating the animal with much love, Schweitzer gradually saw the fierce, wild nature softening. Before long that wild pig
followed the doctor on his visits through the little African village.
When the mission bell sounded, the boar ran to the chapel with the
doctor.

True, it is impossible for a man to change his skin color or a
leopard to change its spots, but God can change your desires,
values, and attitudes. You can't do it yourself, but when you submit
to Him, He will do the impossible for you. The wild nature of both
the pelican and the boar changed as they responded to the love of
the great medical missionary. Won't you let Jesus do the same for
you today?

E.E.L. and J.H.L.

ON OUR SIDE

I will contend with him that contendeth with thee, and I will save thy children. Isaiah 49:25.

In one of his nature books Ernest Thompson Seton tells of a mother rabbit and her baby who lived in a grassy nest near a large swamp. One morning the mother rabbit left the nest as was her custom, to find food. Rag, the baby, knew that he was supposed to remain hidden. But he felt that he was becoming both older and wiser. So as soon as his mother was out of sight he hopped out of the nest and began investigating the big world around him.

Suddenly there was a swish and little Rag found himself between the jaws of a large and hungry snake. The serpent glided down the path at top speed, with Rag squealing loudly, wriggling and squirming in a frantic attempt to escape. His cries of pain brought the mother, hopping frantically to rescue her baby.

Although rabbits are usually timid animals, she suddenly became fearless. Again and again she leaped over the body of the snake, each time raking his back with her sharp claws. He writhed and twisted, but finally the pain became so great that he dropped the little rabbit and slithered away into the thick grass. A sadder but wiser Rag followed his heroic mother back to the nest.

The most beautiful woman who ever lived once wandered down a forbidden path, away from her husband. In the branches of a tree she saw a serpent, and it tempted her. The serpent did not open its jaws and try to swallow her, but with smooth words it wound her up in lies. She was tempted and fell.

"Fight the good fight of faith," wrote the apostle Paul to Timothy. We face a powerful enemy—a serpent, Satan, the devil—one so strong that he overthrew such stalwarts as Abraham, Jacob, Moses, David, Peter, and many others. He still lies in wait to capture the first weak victim that comes along.

We are God's children, and God has promised to save us. Abraham, Jacob, Moses, David, Samson, and Peter were rescued from the power of Satan by Jesus, the Mighty Deliverer.

Without help from his courageous mother, Rag's short life would have come to a sudden end. We must have divine help so that we can conquer in the battle against sin, and dwell with Jesus forever.

R.H.P.

THE EAGLE AND THE FISH TRAP

Ye therefore, beloved, seeing ye know these things before, beware lest ye also, being led away with the error of the wicked, fall from your own stedfastness. 2 Peter 3:17.

Near the Canadian boundary at the headwaters of the St. John River an eagle came each morning to fish. One day when the great bird circled its usual breakfast spot he spied a large rock beneath him. He eyed the intruder suspiciously, but as it didn't move, he finally alighted on it and proceeded to catch his fill of fish.

The next morning the eagle returned. The rock was still there. This time a strange contraption was lying across it. Wary at first, the big bird circled the spot before finally deciding everything was safe. Down he swooped and was soon fishing as usual. In his careless movements the eagle stepped on a stick. The trap sprang. An Indian hidden in the nearby bushes rushed out and captured his prey.

Did you ever stop to think that Satan is a trap setter too? Of course, he camouflages his snares well to make everything look safe and attractive. He wouldn't want to frighten people away by making sin appear hateful or hurtful. He dresses the trap up beautifully, and sin looks so inviting.

"Surely *this* can't be wrong," the evil one whispers into unsuspecting ears, "and, anyway, you will only do it *just this once*." You know how Lucifer tries to trick us.

Too late we discover there is more than the "large rock" that we landed on. The "strange contraption" so beautifully camouflaged—that sin we yield to—is a trap from which we cannot free ourselves. We are caught! We disobeyed God. We sinned! How bad we feel that we have been fooled.

The wise man warns us, "As righteousness tendeth to life: so he that pursueth evil pursueth it to his own death" (Prov. 11:19). While we follow Satan's enticement in pursuing evil we may be sure that we do so to our own death—and this is not just the death we die naturally; it's the second death from which there is no resurrection.

Little wonder Peter writes, "Beware lest ye also, being led away with the error of the wicked, fall from your own stedfastness."

R.H.P.

MULES AND MINDS

Be ye not as the horse, or as the mule, which have no understanding. Psalm 32:9.

A farmer once went to buy a mule from a neighboring farmer.

"Is it a good mule?" he asked.

"Oh, yes, it is a very good mule. It will work all day without any trouble at all."

"You mean I won't have to beat it to make it go and it will work all day long?"

"That's right. No beating. It will just work on its own."

So the farmer bought the animal and brought it home. Early the next morning he hitched it to the plow, eager to try out his new acquisition. But the mule would not budge. Not one inch. The farmer pulled, he pushed, he coaxed, and finally, sad to say, he swore, but still that stubborn mule would not move.

Just then the man from whom the farmer had bought the mule came down the road beside the field.

"Say," yelled the farmer indignantly, "I thought you said this animal would work all day without any trouble! This beast won't move!"

"He'll go!" called back the former owner. "Here, I'll start him for you!" And he strode over to the balking mule, picking up a small stick on the way. When he reached the animal, he whacked it over the head with the stick. With a lunge the mule started forward and worked hard all day with no more fuss.

"Well," said the farmer when he saw the man again later, "that mule certainly works well once it gets started, but I thought you said I wouldn't have to hit it to make it work."

"You don't," was the answer. "But you must get its attention first!"

How many boys and girls are like that old mule. They have good brains but just don't study. Their teachers push and pull and coax, all to no avail. They have to be "whacked over the head" with a failing grade or a lecture from Dad or some form of punishment—to get their attention.

Be sure you are "not as the horse, or as the mule, which have no understanding."

M.H.

THE NEED FOR THE MORNING WATCH

Come, listen to me, my sons, I will teach you true religion.
Psalm 34:11 (Moffatt).

We have been thrilled by the stories of our student missionaries serving in so many parts of the world. I have talked to many of them and it has been an inspiration to hear our young men and women tell of their wonderful experiences. They began being "missionaries" in school long before they were old enough to go overseas.

I know one such person. She came from a poor family, but her heart was on fire with love for Christ and His cause. One day in school an appeal was made to give an offering for missions. Her heart was touched. She wanted to help but she had no money to give. Finally she arose and walked to the front and said, "I have no other offering to give, but I give myself to the cause of missions." She never forgot her pledge. Years later I met her and her husband in the mission field.

Some years ago a mother of five children attended an important church meeting on foreign missions. She, too, was poor in this world's goods but her heart was stirred to do something for the church. She went home and looked over her furniture, trying to find something that she could sacrifice for the cause of God. She could not find anything that she felt could be of any value or use.

Suddenly she thought of her five children, three girls and two boys. She entered into her room and there, on her knees, consecrated them to missions. Years later I read a report of this family: "Two of her daughters are now in mission lands and the third is preparing to go. Of her sons, one is on his way to India and the other is preparing for the ministry and has been inquiring on the subject of a missionary life." What a marvelous gift to missions!

Going across the ocean doesn't change our character. There is something deeper needed. This is the heart preparation. We can be missionaries in school or in our neighborhoods. But no matter where we serve we must have a loving spirit in our heart. If we do, we may someday be student missionaries, or adult missionaries.

God wants our lives to be Christ-centered rather than self-centered. While you are young, put Christ in the center of your life.

A.A.E.

SMART COON, NOT-SO-SMART DOG

Father, Lord of heaven and earth! I thank you because you have shown to the unlearned what you have hidden from the wise and learned. Matthew 11:25, TEV.

Because God never gives truth to those who will not accept it, much wisdom is hidden from those who choose not to see. Many who make no pretense of learning show greater wisdom than professed wise men. Even in nature wild animals often outsmart men and trained animals.

Brownie, a hunting dog, found an old fat raccoon in a low, swampy area near a pond. With no tree to climb, the raccoon jumped into the water and started to swim from the dog. Brownie, a faster swimmer, reached the coon just as he climbed onto a log in the middle of the pond. The raccoon turned and faced Brownie. With both front paws he pushed the dog's head under water. Brownie frantically waved his tail and hind feet. Finally he got away and swam to shore.

A week later, while his master fished, Brownie watched by the riverbank. The same coon walked right by the dog, which didn't even get up. Unafraid, the racoon waded into the river and fished for a clam. He found a big one and bit at the closed shell. It wouldn't open, so he laid it on a flat stone. Finding another, he bit it also, to no avail. He kept on fishing, but every clam was closed tight. Finally the flat stone was covered with unopened clamshells. The raccoon walked away with no dinner, leaving all the clams behind on the stone.

Brownie and his master were still fishing when the raccoon returned an hour later. The clams still lay on the rock in the hot sun. He picked up one clam, turned it over, pulled a bit, and the shell opened wide. The orange-colored meat disappeared. Every shell opened easily, and the raccoon had a feast. That wise old fisherman knew that when clams get warm, they get lazy and weak. His God-given wildwood wisdom amazed the man who watched him.

No wonder Jesus thanked His Father for hiding heaven's truths from those who think themselves wise, and revealing it to those who have simple, trusting faith like little children. God is pleased to share His wisdom with those who are humble and willing to learn.

E.E.L. and J.H.L.

STEWED GOOSEBERRIES

I will receive you, and will be a Father unto you, and ye shall be my sons and daughters, saith the Lord Almighty. 2 Corinthians 6:17, 18.

Despite all that happened that Sabbath, I still love stewed gooseberries. For some reason I was first home from church that day, and like any thirteen-year-old boy I was ravenously hungry.

Mother had prepared a big bowl of stewed gooseberries, and they sat on the buffet ready to be served for Sabbath lunch. I looked at them, smelled them; and completely overcome, I took a spoon and sampled them. They were perfect. Spoonful followed spoonful until I felt that that was as far as I could go without my sampling being too noticeable.

But the taste was so good, and again spoonful followed spoonful. I will never forget the amazed look on my mother's face when she saw the bowl. "How could you eat nearly two pounds of stewed gooseberries?" I had no answer to that question.

Punishment? Yes, it came. But it was hardly what I expected. Mother explained to our guests that her gooseberries had all been eaten by her son, except for a few, and then she proceeded to serve me what was left. I cannot remember anything that ever embarrassed me more than eating those gooseberries while the rest of my family and the visitors had to eat less tasty fare.

I wonder what would have happened if I had not been punished. As it was I learned that my parents cared that their son be honest, truthful, and considerate.

What they did was treat me as a son. If it had been a visiting child, they might have been annoyed but silent. Had it been an adult they would have been surprised at his rudeness. But I was their son, so I was treated as a son.

When God says, "I will receive you as sons and daughters," it means that He is interested in all that we do. Next time you pray, "Our Father," think what this means and be glad God treats you as His child.

W.R.L.S.

EVERY SECRET THING

God shall bring every work into judgment, with every secret thing, whether it be good, or whether it be evil. Ecclesiastes 12:14.

Laura Ingalls Wilder tells of three boys many years ago who made a sled. They hoped to be done in time to try it out before sundown Saturday afternoon. Their family kept Sunday from sunset Saturday night until sunset Sunday, just as we begin Sabbath at Friday sunset. But the sled was not finished until just at sundown, so the boys didn't get a chance to try it out.

On Sunday afternoon they sat studying their catechisms, but thinking about the sled. The sun was bright on the snow, a perfect day for sliding. Then they heard their father begin to snore.

The temptation was too great. One by one the boys tiptoed from the room. They took their new sled out quietly to the top of the hill. They could slide down just once and Father would never know. They could put the sled away and be back in the house before he awoke.

Zooming down the hill, they were about to pass the house when a large hog stepped into the middle of the road. The sled was going too fast to stop, or even turn off the road. It went right under the hog and picked him up. He began to squeal for all he was worth. Father came to the door to see what the noise was about. The boys could neither stop nor hide. They went to the bottom of the hill with that pig on the front of the sled squealing all the way.

They had thought the sled ride would be a secret from their father. But now, at the end of their Sabbath hours, they faced a punishment.

Even if their father had remained sleeping, God knew. Sometimes we forget that God is everywhere and that He sees not only our actions but also our thoughts.

Mrs. White once had a vision in which an angel seemed to conduct her on a tour of different departments in a sanitarium. She heard frivolous talk, foolish jesting, and meaningless laughter.

"How little did these light, superficial heads and hard hearts realize that an angel of God stood at the door, writing down the manner in which these precious moments were employed." —*Counsels on Health,* p. 412.

From a few rooms came the sound of prayer, and a bright light shone upon her guide as he wrote the petitions.

Let us ask God to take charge of our thoughts and motives.

R.E.

SEEING ONLY THE SUN

And we, with our unveiled faces reflecting like mirrors the brightness of the Lord, all grow brighter and brighter as we are turned into the image we reflect; this is the work of the Lord who is Spirit. 2 Corinthians 3:18, Jerusalem.

If you look for just a moment at the sun, what happens when you turn your eyes away? The sun's image appears on everything. Even if you close your eyes, you still see the sun. For some time that glowing ball of hot gasses whose center temperature is probably 36,000,000° Fahrenheit is before your eyes.

Do you continue to see it because it is so huge? No. Even though it is 109 times the diameter of the earth, many stars are much larger. Betelgeuse in Orion is more than a million times as big as the sun in volume. If the sun were placed in the center of Betelgeuse, the planets Mercury, Venus, Earth, and Mars could revolve well within the surface of that huge star.

Why does the sun's image so penetrate your eyes and mind that you see nothing else? Why does it appear bigger and brighter than any other star? If it were as far away as the stars in the Big Dipper you could not see it without a telescope. Can you guess the reason? Right, it is because the sun is our nearest star, about 92,957,000 miles away.

When we look to Jesus we become so like our Divine Pattern that we are turned into the image we reflect. Slowly, but surely, as we reflect Him, our dispositions and tempers are subdued.

Then others will see the Sun of Righteousness in us. Like Jesus we will be enthusiastic, yet calm and self-possessed. We will be above the common annoyances around us, yet will enjoy people. Jesus was just as happy playing with little children as eating with rich men. He shunned the artificial, but got excited over the beauty of a lily.

By looking at Him you can combine in your life the innocence of a child with manly strength, devotion to God with tender love for everyone else. You'll understand how to combine dignity with humility and unyielding firmness with gentleness. Self will disappear.

When you live in close connection with your Perfect Pattern, you will automatically reflect Him.

E.E.L. and J.H.L.

TWO DREAMS AND A WEDDING

Do not try to work together as equals with unbelievers, for it cannot be done. How can right and wrong be partners? 2 Corinthians 6:14, TEV.

Do you think that Jesus is interested in everything we do in this life? I mean *everything?* Do you think He would help a Christian young man find a good Christian young woman for a wife in a country where there are not large numbers of young people from which to choose?

Let me tell you a very interesting story. It happened in a country a long way from America. In this country the church members help their young people find life companions. If there isn't someone suitable in their church they contact a nearby church to see if there is a good young man or woman there to meet the need.

We will call the hero of our story Henry. This is not his true name, but it will do. Now, young Henry had a dream one night. In the dream he was shown a fine Christian girl, and he was told that she was to be his life's companion. There was no girl in his church who looked like the girl in his dream.

The church members contacted another Adventist church some miles away. The members replied, "We have a fine young woman in our church. Tell Henry to come and meet her."

Henry went. He met Muriel (this is not her real name). He was greatly impressed with her and, what is more, she looked exactly like the girl he had seen in his dream. After some time Henry asked Muriel to marry him, and she responded favorably. He had not told her yet of his dream.

"There is something I must tell you," Muriel said. "Before I met you I had a dream, and in this dream the Lord showed me the young man whom I would someday marry. You were the young man in my dream."

Do you think either Henry or Muriel doubted the Lord had led them to each other? Of course not!

Someday, when you are older, the Lord will help you find a life companion. He may not give you a dream, as He did Henry and Muriel, but He will guide if you pray and ask Him. Be sure your choice is someone who loves and serves Jesus. Don't be joined with an unbeliever if you want to be truly happy.

R.H.P.

PRECISION INSTRUMENTS

It is like a man on his way abroad who summoned his servants. . . . To one he gave five talents, to another two, to a third one; each in proportion to his ability. Matthew 25:14, 15, Jerusalem.

One of the mechanical wonders of the world is the tongue, or proboscis, of a bee, butterfly, moth, wasp, and fly. Unlike ordinary tongues, they can be extended several times longer than the head and retracted with lightning speed. God planned each proboscis differently.

Those of butterflies and moths are practically air-tight half-tubes hooked together by sickle-shaped devices, top and bottom, and covered outside with hinged segments. Extremely flexible, it may be coiled into a tight spiral or, when sucking nectar, thrown out like a rope to penetrate the deepest flowers. They vary in extended length from the three inches in a species of sphinx moth to a tropical species that holds the world's record of ten inches.

The bee's proboscis fold up like a pocketknife under its lower jaw, and can be extended three fourths of an inch beyond its head. Wasps' tongues are also of the jackknife type, though much shorter. Certain kinds of flies have a remarkable tongue that varies in length from one twelfth to one half an inch, built in three segments with a hinge action. God has equipped each insect with a specialized instrument more precise than the works of the finest watch.

Each proboscis is adapted to the shape of certain flowers. God has also planned the arrangement of the flower parts to fit the heads, feet, bodies, and legs of their visitors. Their nectaries, which may be exposed, hidden, or partially concealed, are placed to accommodate the special abilities of each insect visitor. Even the moth with the ten-inch tongue has a flower that corresponds to it.

God has given you special abilities, too, for a special purpose. What is that purpose? Your talents are to proclaim God's glory in helping your fellowmen. However few or many talents you have, your first duty to God is to develop them for service. God planned your life and ability with greater care than the insects and flowers. This plan may be accomplished by His strength. Aim high. Unless you let Him help you cultivate every talent you can never reach His beautiful plan.

E.E.L. and J.H.L.

GOD NEVER FORGETS HIS CHILDREN

*Behold, I have graven thee upon the palms of my hands.
Isaiah 49:16.*

A trash truck moved slowly down the city street, picking up boxes
and bundles of rubbish placed by the curb for collection. When the
men came to a large pile of old newspapers, they bent down to pick
them up. As one of them was preparing to throw his bundle into the
truck, he felt a slight movement inside the bundle. Quickly he laid
it on the grass and unrolled the papers. There lay a tiny baby girl,
dressed in a dainty pink dress and sweater!

"Whoever could have done such a thing?" muttered one of the
men. "Leaving a baby like that!"

"You'll never know, that's for sure," replied one of his companions.
The baby was taken to the nearest hospital. No one ever learned
who the mother was who abandoned her child in this manner.

God has promised that such a tragedy can never happen to His
children. Our names, He says, are graven on the palms of His hands.
When He looks at His hands He thinks of us and of His love for each
one of us.

We are like the five-year-old who had been adopted by a wealthy
family. When the day came for the little girl to leave the orphanage,
the only home she had ever known, she was afraid.

"Don't you want to go home with me and be my little girl?" asked
her new mother.

"I don't know," the child replied.

"But I'll give you lots of nice things—toys and pets, and a pretty
room all your own."

"But what must I do for all this?" asked the child.

That new mother knelt down and put her arms around the child.

"Do?" she exclaimed. "All I want you to do is love me, and be my
little girl."

In the verse preceding our text for today, God asks whether it is
possible for a mother to forget her own child. "Yes," He replies,
"such a thing is possible." He says He will not forget His children.

We have done nothing to deserve the love of our heavenly Father,
or to earn the gift of eternal life He has promised us. All He asks is
that we love Him more than anything else in the world. Our Saviour
can never forget us. Let us never forget Him.

V.E.R.

DECISION MAKING

Multitudes, multitudes in the valley of decision: for the day of the Lord is near in the valley of decision. Joel 3:14.

One of Sarah Jane's favorite habits was making lists. She made lists constantly—lists of people, lists of books, shopping lists, lists of duties to do that day. But now she was making a list of reasons, and the heading was, Reasons for Going to Judy's Party. It looked like this:

1. Some of my best friends will be there.
2. I could wear my new dress.
3. Judy wants me to come.
4. It would be fun.
5. I want to go.

She hadn't dared hope Mother would let her go to the party, for Mother didn't approve of Judy. She had only asked Mother because Judy urged it, and what a surprise Mother's answer was.

"I think you are old enough to decide for yourself this time."

So Sarah Jane's first thought was that of course she would go. It didn't make her feel as good inside as she had expected. For a moment she wished Mother had decided. If Mother had said a firm No, it would be Mother's fault that she couldn't go.

She took out another sheet of paper and across the top she lettered slowly: Reasons for Not Going to Judy's Party. She could think of only one.

1. Mother would rather I didn't go.

Five reasons to go, and only one for staying home. Then in the stillness of her heart a small voice seemed to say, *"Why* would Mother rather you didn't go?" And Sarah Jane had more reasons to write down.

2. The music might be the kind I shouldn't listen to.
3. The food will be the kind I shouldn't eat.
4. It might not be the sort of party I would want to invite my guardian angel to attend.

She picked up the first list again. Five reasons there, but not one of them big enough to outweigh the second list. Her decision was made. Sarah Jane stayed home.

We make decisions each day of our lives. Some are big decisions; some involve only small matters. But as our decisions are recorded in heaven's books, our destinies are being shaped.

Let us ask God today to guide us in everyday decisions.

R.E.

PLUG IN NOW

And Jesus came and spake unto them saying, All power is given unto me in heaven and in earth. Matthew 28:18. But you are to be given power when the Holy Spirit has come to you. Acts 1:8, Phillips.

Imagine what life would be like if suddenly all electric power ceased. Factories would stop; elevators, escalators, air conditioners, furnaces, refrigerators, radios, TV sets, vacuum cleaners, would all be useless. No electric lights or appliances. No telephones for communication. When the power stopped, so would almost everything else.

Electricity, a form of energy that gives us light, heat, and power, results from the mechanical power of large generators. Turbines drive electric generators in power plants. In turn these turbines need power to operate. This power comes from atomic energy, steam, gas, water, or even wind. But always there must be power.

What is power? Power is strength, might, force, the ability to do or act, the capacity to accomplish something. Jesus has all power, and He has promised to give it to you.

Have you ever spilled flour on a rug? You can't pick it up, nor can you sweep it up. It goes down deep into the nap of the rug. You remember the vacuum cleaner, whose suction will clean it easily. You get it and push it over the flour. The mess gets worse as you smear it around. What's wrong? You didn't plug it in—no power.

You're like that vacuum cleaner. Useless. Your sins, like the flour, are everywhere. The more you try, the messier it gets. Taking the plug, you walk over to the socket. Suddenly you realize that when you plug in, you're no longer in control. The power does it all. You are only the simple little machine through which the power flows. Satan makes you think you'll lose your liberty, your independence, if you submit to that power. There's an inward struggle. You can't straighten up the mess by yourself. It's impossible. Finally you are willing to surrender your useless self to the only force that can accomplish anything through you. You plug in to the power. In moments the whole mess is clean. How foolish to try to do it yourself without power! Why do you hesitate when all the power you need for victory is available when you plug in?

E.E.L. and J.H.L.

TAKING GOD'S NAME IN VAIN

Thou shalt not take the name of the Lord thy God in vain.
Exodus 20:7.

I was a number of years old before I discovered that there is more than one way to take the name of the Lord in vain. You are probably smarter than I was, but I thought a person had to swear to take God's name in vain. Now I know better. When a person is baptized he takes Christ's name, and anything he does that is not Christlike and dishonors the name of Christ is, in a sense, taking God's name in vain.

Victor was baptized when he was in church school. He really felt he wanted to follow Jesus.

"So," said the devil, "Victor thinks he's going to be a Christian. We'll see about that. I'll not let him go without a struggle."

Then the devil started to work, and when Victor went to the academy he fell in with the wrong crowd. He thought girls and cars were much more interesting than schoolwork, and it wasn't long before his Christian experience began drifting. Finally, he drifted right out of the academy into public school and there, again, he picked the wrong friends.

"Aw, come on," coaxed his new pals. "Be a sport and try a smoke. And while you are at it, have a drink, too."

Soon smoking and drinking were added to his list of likes. His parents were frantic with worry, but Victor did not seem to care. He no longer thought about his name—Christian. He had taken the name of the Lord his God in vain.

How different it was with Johnny. He, too, was baptized in church school and then went to the academy.

"I'm going to get Johnny too," boasted the devil. But he was wrong.

Johnny was no saint at the academy, mind you. He had his fun and his moments of mischief, but it was good clean fun, and as he grew older he became more dependable until one day the principal said, "If all our boys were like Johnny, we'd have a model school." The devil was defeated.

Johnny had not taken the name of the Lord in vain. He kept the third commandment both in speech and in action.

M.H.

THE WORKING GIRL'S FRIEND

My God shall supply all your need according to his riches in glory by Christ Jesus. Philippians 4:19.

At one time in her life Louisa May Alcott was deeply discouraged. She had been working as a teacher in a private home, teaching an invalid girl. But now the girl became well enough to go to regular school.

To pay her room rent Louisa May began sewing a certain number of hours. But she needed to earn money for other necessities.

All at once she wished she could die. She did not want to go on living in a world where everything was so hard.

Then she went to church. The minister's sermon that day was full of special encouragement for those in the same situation as Louisa—for those looking for employment or working hard just to keep alive. He spoke with assurance of the one place where they could look for help when they seemed to be at the end of their rope.

For Louisa that church service was a turning point in her life. She realized the goodness of God. She carried away courage and faith and set out at once with renewed energy to continue her search for employment.

The sympathetic minister's wife told her of the possibility of a job mending uniforms and sheets and towels at the reform school.

Louisa made up her mind that if nothing else turned up she would take the job, though she would have to live right at the institution and work ten hours a day. She felt an obligation to support herself and to help her hard-pressed family.

Perhaps the job at the reform school was His answer. But at the last moment, as she was about to leave for that job, her former pupil turned out to be unhappy at school. The mother invited Louisa to come back and teach her again. The salary was enough so that she could keep her little room in Boston and continue her writing on the side.

Louisa never lost her faith in God—"the working girl's friend." She turned to Him for comfort in all her discouragements. Let us do the same.

God is able to fill our spiritual needs when we are discouraged. But He knows our physical needs as well, and will help us find solutions to any problem.

R.E.

ROTTEN CORN

For the man who has something will receive more. As for the man who has nothing, even his "nothing" will be taken away. Mark 4:25, Phillips.

That hardly sounds fair, but an old parable may help you understand Christ's words. Just before an Eastern prince left on a long journey, he gave two of his friends each a large sack of corn to keep till he returned. Many months passed. Soon after he came back home, he visited his friends. The first friend took him to the cellar where he had kept the sack of corn.

"Here is your corn, prince. I've kept it safely for you." But when they opened his sack, the grain was soft, rotten, and useless.

The second friend took the prince to a beautiful field of waving corn, ripe, and ready to harvest. He said, "There is your sack of corn. Soon you'll have much more corn than you left with me."

"Oh, no," said the prince, "I only want one sack of corn. The rest is yours."

Old grain dies if it is kept. That which we selfishly hoard is lost. That which we give to others multiplies.

You may have heard of the old German professor who planted seeds that had been buried with Egyptian mummies for 4,000 years. How he hoped that the germ of life was alive and they would sprout. As the days went by his disappointment grew, for there was no sign of life. Not wanting to admit that old seed wouldn't grow, he kept watching.

His small boys, watching him, saw his sadness. They thought of a way to cheer their father's heart. Taking fresh grain, they sowed it exactly where he had put the old grain. Thrilled when it sprouted, the professor immediately wrote an article about his find, which was published.

Some time later one of the boys told his father how they had made him happy. Disturbed, the professor quickly wrote another article explaining that the old grain really didn't grow. Unfortunately, many who read the first story never saw the second, and the false story grew.

God's principle still stands. What we keep we lose; what we give away or sow, we keep. Blessings used are blessings multiplied.

E.E.L. and J.H.L.

HOW MUCH ARE YOU WORTH?

*I will make a man more precious than fine gold; even a man
than the golden wedge of Ophir. Isaiah 13:12.*

Ralph had a part-time job at a supermarket. One afternoon on his
way to work he stopped at a drugstore and asked the manager
whether he might use the telephone on his desk. The owner agreed.
Ralph dialed and was soon talking to someone on the other end of
the line. The druggist couldn't help overhearing Ralph.

"Good afternoon. I'm calling to ask whether you need a boy at
your store—

"You say you have a boy? Is he dependable?—You say you're
pretty well satisfied with him?—All right. I see you don't need
another boy. Thank you anyway. Good-by."

Ralph hung up the receiver, and with a polite "Thank you," turned
to leave. He looked unusually cheerful for a boy who had just been
refused a job.

"Do you need work?" asked the friendly druggist.

"Oh, no. I'll tell you what I was doing," answered Ralph with a grin.
"Once in a while I check up on myself. I call up my boss and I ask
him whether he is satisfied with my work. It's good to know that I'm
worth something to him. So thanks again, sir." And Ralph disappeared out the door.

"Well," meditated the druggist, "I wish that boy would come and
work for me. He must be worth his weight in gold."

Solid gold! Visitors to the world-famous mines near Johannes-
burg, South Africa, are shown a gold brick. Anyone who can lift that
brick with one hand can keep it. Thousands of persons have tried,
but none has ever succeeded. Gold is a heavy metal, and it is
precious.

God declares that His children are worth more to Him than gold.
How much are you worth? Your parents wouldn't sell you for all the
gold stored up in Fort Knox. At school, are you an asset or a liability
to your teachers? Are you trustworthy? Is home a better place
because you are there?

Put a high value upon yourself. God already has! Through Jesus
you can become "more precious than fine gold." You are of greater
value to Him than the fabled "golden wedge of Ophir."

V.E.R.

LEADING THE BLIND

I will bring the blind by a way that they knew not; I will lead them in paths that they have not known. Isaiah 42:16.

Our text is but one of several precious promises for the blind. We have two kinds of blindness—physical and spiritual. In a sense we are all "blind" in regard to the future, but the future is open before the Lord.

I read of a hotel fire in which a blind woman was one of the few who came out of the building unscathed. In that destruction sixty seeing persons perished and two hundred were injured. Miss Anita Blair, a blind lecturer, had her room on the eleventh floor. With her was Fawn, her Seeing Eye dog. She heard the fire engines and sirens screaming and smelled the smoke in the building.

She took a firm hold on the harness of her dog and trusted him to lead her out. He took her through a window, then onto a fire escape and down the stairs until both of them stood in safety on the sidewalk below.

Here is a lesson of faith. Anita trusted her guide, and he led her in the right way. God loves to have us trust Him, clinging tightly to Him in all life's perplexities.

My father told of an Adventist who at the beginning of World War II escaped the bombing of a large hotel in Warsaw, Poland. He was asleep on one of the upper floors when someone awoke him at 1:00 A.M. A voice told him, "You must leave this hotel at once. It is not safe to stay here."

Quickly the man packed up and took the elevator to the lobby. There he met the night clerk and asked him to alert all the guests and tell them to vacate the hotel. The men gathered in the lobby laughed at the warning. There was no sign of impending disaster. They considered the alarmed guest the victim of some delusion. "If no one will go with me, I must leave alone." The man walked with his suitcase many blocks to the outskirts of town to find another room. Soon the bombers rained destruction on the hotel and the surrounding city section. The next day he went back to see the demolished hotel. He heard one rescuer ask another, "Did anyone escape from this hotel alive last night?"

"Just one," came the answer. "A man whose God warned him left an hour before the bombing began."

L.C.W.

PATSY AND THE DOLLAR

Let him labour, working with his hands the thing which is good. Ephesians 4:28.

Kathy walked into Miss Summers' classroom just in time to see Patsy pick a dollar up from the desk and put it into her purse. All sorts of thoughts raced through Kathy's mind. Was Patsy stealing the money? Did Miss Summers know that Patsy was taking the dollar? Should Kathy tell Miss Summers?

Kathy had to ask for some advice about this problem, so she ran at once to Cindy. "Cindy, what do you think I ought to do? I saw Patsy take a dollar from Miss Summers' desk."

Cindy thought that Larry should know about this, so between classes she told him, "Kathy saw Patsy take a dollar from Miss Summers' desk. Do you think Patsy is stealing things?"

Larry had lost a T-shirt a few days before, so he told Peter about it. "Patsy steals money and things. Kathy caught her at it."

By lunchtime just about everyone in the school knew that Patsy was a thief. Then the big freeze began. No one would talk to Patsy. People walked the other way. Purses were gripped more tightly.

But you can't keep this kind of secret for long. Soon Patsy was talking with the principal, Mr. Abbott. "Patsy, some of the students say that you take things. Someone saw you take a dollar from Miss Summers' desk. Is that true?"

Mr. Abbott did not know how to interpret the flood of tears that started down Patsy's face. "So that's why no one would talk to me yesterday. Mr. Abbott, Miss Summers told me to go and get that dollar. I earned it by looking after her dog last weekend."

Miss Summers was called, Kathy was called, and so were Larry and Cindy and Peter. In fact, in the end Mr. Abbott called a general assembly of the school, and Miss Summers told the story, and Kathy apologized and so did the others. It was a sad and sorry day.

If you have some surplus energy don't use it up making your tongue wag. Work with your hands. Put your energy into doing something practical that will help others, and yourself as well.

W.R.L.S.

VACATION FOR A HORSE

"Now come along to some quiet place by yourselves, and rest for a little while," said Jesus. Mark 6:31, Phillips.

Whatever your occupation, you sometimes need a change. Not only will this respite impart a sense of relaxation but it will also give you new vigor for your tasks. Too much concentration and steady application decreases your efficiency. Jesus knows you need to rest awhile.

Mac had pulled Mr. Peters' wagon through the city streets for twelve years. Now the well-cared-for horse and his master were tired. Talking to his horse, Mr. Peters made a decision.

"Mac, I need a rest. Let's both take a vacation at the seashore."

Although Mac didn't know it, the wagon was packed with food for both him and his master as they started out on the usual route a week later. Soon they left the paved streets, turning down a wooded lane. Mac stopped and looked back at Mr. Peters. Something was wrong.

"It's all right, Mac. Go ahead. You're going to have a vacation."

The horse, happy to obey, threw up his head and started off.

When evening came, they stopped. Mr. Peters pitched his tent in a grassy field. After years of walking on paved streets the soft grass felt strange to the horse. He ran in circles, kicked his heels, stopped to eat, then ran again.

The next day they arrived at the seashore. Mac didn't know how to walk on the dry sand that slipped under his feet. The wet sand was too cold. He was so afraid of the water he wouldn't go near it.

Standing back, he watched Mr. Peters splashing about in the water. When the horse saw his master lie flat and float, he couldn't stand it, and jumped in to save his life. Then Mr. Peters stood up. Assured, Mac began to splash. Soon he was running through the sea, water flying everywhere. Mac had so much fun that Mr. Peters could hardly get him out of the water. Both master and horse greatly enjoyed the change and rest.

Take minute vacations each day. Enjoy the beauty around you. Jesus wants you to take time for rest and for Him. Why hurry through life?

E.E.L. and J.H.L.

ADVENTURES IN PRAYER

How happy are those who know what sorrow means, for they will be given courage and comfort! Matthew 5:4 (Phillips).

Sometimes in our problems God brings comfort and courage in extremely strange ways. For example, after the close of World War II our work in Shanghai was reaching a critical stage. Before the foreign missionaries from the interior of China moved to Hong Kong in the autumn of 1948, a large evangelistic effort was held in Shanghai. Fordyce Detamore was invited to hold what was termed an "international" evangelistic effort. Many languages were employed.

The attendance was excellent. In fact, they had to hold a second meeting each evening. The offerings were very good. But though high in amount they were low in purchasing power, for the Chinese dollar was rolling downhill like a ping-pong ball.

Mary Ogle, in her book *Shanghai Wolfe,* tells how the treasurer, Wolfe Ismond, struggled desperately to meet the bills. One night, he and Roger Clausen, one of the helpers in the series, were talking at the back of the hall before the service. A well-dressed Chinese woman approached and handed Clausen a large manila envelope stuffed with money. Later the two men discussed the perplexing financial situation with Detamore. "Have you counted the money in that envelope?" Clausen asked Wolfe.

"No. I forgot all about it."

"What are you talking about?" Detamore asked. "This may be what we've been praying for. Let's go count it."

When the three men opened that envelope, they poured out a large number of five-, ten-, twenty-, fifty-, and one-hundred dollar bills. They were speechless. Quickly they counted the money and it totaled $7,300. Another person had put US$1,000 in the offering basket that same evening.

They turned the envelope over but could find no name or identification. Someone was heard to whisper, "Maybe she was an angel!"

At the close of Detamore's meetings a unique international English-speaking church was organized. They joined in thanking God for His answers to their prayers.

A.A.E.

WANTS AND WISHES

Do all things without murmurings and disputings. Philippians 2:14.

Have you ever grumbled because there are so many things you have to do—such as homework and dishes and mowing the lawn—that you don't have time to do something else you think would be fun, or at least more interesting? And so you murmur and complain.

The other day when I left the office I wasn't really complaining, but I was wishing there had been some letters for me that day. "Nobody wrote to me," I mourned.

"Just think, you won't have to answer the letters," replied someone trying to look on the bright side.

You see, our family is scattered. The children are in two different boarding schools, my husband is away on a trip, and I am home alone. Thinking of this, I answered, "But I have to write anyhow."

My friend grinned mischievously. "You mean you want to," she said.

Her statement made me think of something I read many years ago that made a deep impression on me. It was, that you are so busy doing what you really *want* to do, that you do not have time to do what you *think* you want to do. I honestly believe that is true.

If you would like to go swimming on a hot summer day, but Dad says, "Sorry, son, I need your help today," so you stay home and work, is that doing what you really want to do? Yes. You really would rather please your dad by obeying and helping him than go swimming. Or perhaps you would really rather work than get punished! At any rate, you work because you would rather have the results from work than the results from swimming.

Susan doesn't care much for practicing the piano. It would be much more fun to talk to her friends on the telephone. But Susan really wants to learn to play, and she knows that if she doesn't practice she won't be a pianist. So she practices. She would rather have the results of practicing than the results of telephoning.

Do you see what I mean? The next time you are tempted to grumble, remember that you are so busy doing what you really want to do that you don't have time to do what you think you want to do. Then "do all things without murmurings and disputings."

M.H.

MAKE IT A HABIT

So will I sing praise unto thy name for ever, that I may daily perform my vows. Psalm 61:8.

Every day!

In those two words lie a grand secret of all attainment.

It is not what we do once with all our heart and every ounce of strength that counts, so much as the things we do every day whether we feel like it or not.

The splendid performance of a musician on his instrument looks spontaneous, but it is actually the result of many years of faithful practicing.

Every day! That is the road to perfection. The public speaker, the baseball player—every one who can do anything well—owes that poise and finish to the daily grind of practice, practice.

No matter how gifted an artist, a musician, a writer, an actor, he cannot master his art without practice.

It is hard to realize the cumulative power that lies in time. You can build up tremendous efficiency in whatever means much to you if you dedicate a certain amount of time to it *each day.*

And where do you find that time? It has been said that nearly everyone wastes enough hours in ten years' time to get a doctor's degree in any university!

In ten years, if you would only be faithful every day, you could be an authority upon some subject that fits your ambition.

The most honest man is the man who has been honest every day. The happiest person is the one who has practiced being happy regularly. The person who is calmest and surest in a crisis is the one who has tackled self-discipline every day.

The most important of all the things a young person can do every day is to form the habit of daily Bible study and prayer. If we spend time reading God's Word, singing praises to Him, talking over our problems and actions daily, He will help us form right habits in each thing. And we don't have to confine our moments with God to just morning and evening at a set time, either. Anytime, all day long, every day He waits to help us.

No force is so great in any person as the stored-up power of what he has been doing every day. Let's use that force and make it count for good.

R.E.

TWO THOUGHTFUL BOYS

Thou shalt rise up before the hoary head, and honour the face of the old man, and fear thy God. Leviticus 19:32.

Allen Polok, a twelve-year-old boy in Wisconsin, noticed that Mr. Snook was growing very feeble. He offered to help him cut the grass around his place, shovel snow in winter, and do his shopping. Avidly he listened to his neighbor's stories of the past. Never did he think of being paid for his kindness.

After some months the old man died. Notified by a lawyer that he had inherited the entire estate, $2,500, Allen explained, "I did what I could for him, because he was my friend."

Long ago four boys were making May baskets. Eric displayed the yellow basket with the blue ribbon he was finishing. "Mark, I'm glad your mother gave us this pretty ribbon."

Vernon showed the boys the list of people he had made baskets for. Each boy had made ten baskets. "Now, Eric, let us see your list. We want to know who gets the yellow basket. What's her name? Is she cute? Does she go to our school?"

Mischievously Eric laughed. "Wouldn't you really like to know?" All his friends' pleading did not make him reveal his secret.

Their baskets all finished, the four boys scattered to deliver them. Eric did not see that his three friends were following him. They noticed that he carried the yellow basket especially carefully. Overcome with curiosity the three boys were neglecting to pass out their own baskets.

Eric turned on East Fifth Street. Then his friends saw him go up to the porch of a small house, hang his basket, ring the bell, and run. They ganged up on him. "Who lives there?" the boys insisted.

An old women stood in the open doorway. She took the basket off the doorknob and remarked, "Bless his dear heart. My friend Eric remembered me."

Mark asked, "Is she your aunt or your grandma?"

"No, just a good friend of mine who gets lonesome living by herself. Her only son lives far away. I thought you might tease me, if I told you."

"God has especially enjoined tender respect toward the aged. He says, 'The hoary head is a crown of glory, if it be found in the way of righteousness.'"—*Education,* p. 244.

L.C.W.

DUCKS ARE BRAVE TOO

A man can have no greater love than to lay down his life for his friends. John 15:13, Jerusalem.

Two-year-old Susie was given Waddles, a baby duck, for a pet. Immediately they became inseparable. Waddles was beside her constantly as she built castles in her sandbox. He followed close behind as she chased butterflies.

When baby Carol was born two years later, Waddles, now a large, strong duck, realized he had a new responsibility. Settling down by her cradle with a wild cry, he became her guard. Whenever the baby was taken to the back yard for her sun bath, Waddles was waiting with great excitement. His place was beneath the baby's buggy, watching constantly.

He was a great help to the busy mother, for often Susie and her friends would forget to close the back gate. Nothing, man nor beast, could enter that gate with Waddles around. His strong beak took care of any intruders.

One morning while Waddles was on guard beneath the buggy, a neighbor called mother with the message, "I just saw a mad dog go into your driveway."

Could the children have left the gate open? Before she was able to run through the house to the yard, she heard a high, wild honk. The dog was in the yard! Rushing through the back door, she saw the huge rabid animal just a few feet from the baby. Waddles was flying at him, his beak snapping. Grabbing Carol, Mother ran for the house, slamming the door behind her.

Quickly she called the police, then waited as she listened to the battle outside the door, a mixture of growls, barks, and flapping wings. If only Waddles could fly away out of danger! But that brave duck was fighting an enemy that could hurt his helpless little friend. When the police arrived, the dog was lying, dead, just outside the gate. Waddles' lifeless body blocked the entrance.

Jesus, too, never stopped in His terrible struggle with the enemy until He gained the victory. But it cost His life that we, His friends, might live. There is no greater love.

E.E.L. and J.H.L.

HOLD FAST

*Hold that fast which thou hast, that no man take thy crown.
Revelation 3:11.*

At some time in your life you will ask yourself, "Wouldn't it be easier to just give up, enjoy life, and take what comes?" Satan thrusts that temptation at everyone. Elijah felt like giving up when he heard that, in spite of all that had happened on Mount Carmel, the wicked queen, Jezebel, was planning to take his life.

The first thing you must do when tempted in this manner is to ask, "Is it worth while holding onto?"

A little girl once got her hand caught in a beautiful vase. It had been so easy to slip her arm in, but it was impossible to get it out. Her mother tried to help her, then her father tried, but in vain. In hope of saving the vase, the father made one last suggestion.

"Stretch your fingers straight out," he said. "Put them as close together as you can. Then try once more."

"But I can't!" said the child.

"Why not?"

"Because if I do I will drop my penny."

In her tight fist she was grasping a penny she had seen in the bottom of the vase. When told she could still have the money if she dropped it, she opened her hand and it was free immediately. In her case, it was not worth holding onto.

In this verse Jesus is not talking about pennies, or anything that can be bought with money. He is talking about an eternal crown. We must hold to this, no matter how hard Satan tempts us to give up.

During the Civil War, Federal troops held a fort in northern Georgia. They were attacked by Confederate soldiers. Many men were killed, and many were wounded. They were about to surrender when they saw a message being flashed from a hilltop several miles away.

"Hold on, for I am coming. William T. Sherman."

Help was on the way! Instead of surrendering, the men continued to fight bravely until the arrival of fresh troops drove off the attackers and saved the fort.

So when you are tempted to give up the fight against sin, remember that our Saviour flashes the message in response to your prayer for help: "Hold on. Fight bravely. I will help you to be strong."

V.E.R.

THE MIRACLE OF A TREE

A thousand years in thy sight are but as yesterday when it is past, and as a watch in the night. Psalm 90:4.

Among the oldest living things on the face of the earth are the giant redwoods of California. Single specimens of these trees measuring upward of 380 feet are now the largest trees still standing, and were giants when Christ walked this earth. One of the mysteries of these trees is that there are no evidences of previous stands of them or of any end to the life of a healthy tree. Apparently they are the original redwoods and have lived for thousands of years.

Next time you pass by a large old tree think of the miracle that it is. Tiny leaves at the tips of its branches have helped make the massive trunk and the seeking roots. Water, minerals, and sunshine produce wood that will endure for centuries even after the tree has died and the wood has been milled.

Actually the leaves and the layers next to the bark are the only living parts of the tree. Its heart and its bark are dead. As the cells that transport water and minerals to the tips of the tree die they are filled with resins and other hard plant fibers. Sealed from the outside, such moisture as they contain is preserved, but the only useful purpose these inner portions of the tree serve is to keep it upright and give it strength. When they rot, the tree is in danger of collapsing.

What sort of power is it that will lift to the top of a forest giant hundreds of gallons of water in one summer's day? All kinds of explanations are given, but scientists have still not found the complete answer. Trees are one great evidence of God's creative power. Like all forms of life, they baffle us with their complexity and efficiency.

Those giant redwoods have watched the passing of the centuries. On their growth rings are recorded the weather history of California, and still they live. Perhaps they will be standing when Jesus comes.

Someday you may measure time with God and discover that this life is nothing more than a few moments compared with eternity.

W.R.L.S.

THE BEST ANSWER

The eyes of the Lord are over the righteous, and his ears are open unto their prayers. 1 Peter 3:12.

Jeannie Gray tells of a day filled with sunshine and balmy spring weather that was suddenly marred by an announcement on the car radio. Tornado warnings! The family had set out for a nearby city without realizing that a storm was brewing. All at once the sky filled with black clouds. A strong wind blew.

They quickly changed their course and headed home. They had not gone far when they sighted the tornado funnel in the distance, looking like a pillar of billowing black smoke. The lights were on in a local drugstore, so they stopped to seek shelter there. But the doors were locked and no one was inside. The wind died down and the air became eerily still.

They didn't know what path the funnel was taking or how fast it was moving. They decided that the best thing to do was race for home. They felt certain they would be safe in their own basement. The wind came up again, shaking the car. The family prayed, "Oh, Lord, please help us get home."

As they turned down one street a tree fell in their path, almost hitting the car. They had to detour, losing precious minutes.

At last they turned down their own street. The wreckage of a neighbor's house lay strewn before them. The funnel had just hit that area! They had missed driving right into it by minutes.

Their home was completely destroyed and their basement —where they had been sure they would be safe—had caved in.

They had prayed that they might reach home, but their loving heavenly Father had prevented it.

There are times when we pray for something we think we would like to have, not realizing that it would lead us to disaster. Sometimes we do not understand why God does not answer our prayers right away, or in just the way we would wish to have them answered.

But as we grow in experience we will realize that God, who sees the end from the beginning, answers prayers in the time and manner that is for our best good. Let us thank Him that we can trust Him to send the best answer in every situation.

R.E.

BURY IT!

At the place where he had been crucified there was a garden, and in this garden a new tomb. John 19:41, Jerusalem.

I know now why Jesus was buried in a garden. Every garden is a tomb. Much of our happy visit with our mother in St. Paul, Minnesota, was spent in her lovely garden. We worked together pruning trees, digging weeds, cutting the broad expanse of lawn. But the dead branches had to be shredded into chips; the cut grass and weeds buried. Because mother had buried dead vegetation and garbage throughout, the wild flowers along the winding wooded path were more beautiful. The remains of former life made the soil more fertile and the living flowers, fruits, and vegetables more lovely.

Kneeling there in her bird sanctuary, I buried dead grass and leaves. Why not bury self, too, so that Christ's righteousness could grow in me? If I could make a grave of my pride, maybe others would see the fragrant violets of lowliness, as I now enjoyed the purple blossoms by the path. Never had the gray-white leaves of the Russian olive looked more lovely against the black branches than when we cut away the dead limbs. It was time I let God cut away all my hatred and bitterness, so that His loveliness could become evident to all.

When mother went deep into her garden and trimmed the honeysuckle bushes, it seemed she was merciless. Yet removing the gloomy foliage made way for the sunlight. Right then I determined to let God kill all falsehood in my life so truth could shine through.

Whenever she transplanted a plant or a bush, mother always went to the compost pile and added several generous shovelfuls. She called the manure pile her "treasure of gold nuggets." Even the green, unsightly mold that creeps over the neglected surface of the flower pots she stirred and mixed with the soil.

As I worked beside mother in her beautiful garden, I learned that what I thought was a hindrance was really a help, that that which seemed to be so troublesome was really an opportunity to grow. The weeds in our lives can minister to all that is fair and beautiful if we will bury them.

Your life can be a garden too, but first you must make it a tomb.

E.E.L. and J.H.L.

THE REWARD OF A YOUNG HERO

But you must keep control of yourself in all circumstances. 2 Timothy 4:5 (TEV).

Louis is a good illustration of a person who kept control of himself in all circumstances. As a young boy in France he did not panic when he heard that awful cry, "Mad wolf!"

He had been playing in the yard of his father's tannery when he heard the cry and saw people running as this animal, frothing at the mouth, came staggering down the street, biting everybody he could reach. Louis got into his home in time but he could never forget that day because eight of the people who had been bitten died of rabies.

Many years later in this same mountain district of Jura, six young shepherds saw a mad dog racing down the road. One look was sufficient and they all scattered in every direction. However, there was one young lad, 14 years of age, who turned to fight the dog to give the rest a chance to escape. The dog grabbed the boy's left hand between his teeth. The boy wrestled the dog to the ground and, while kneeling on the dog's back, forced his jaws open and freed his hand. Then with his shepherd's lash, he succeeded in muzzling the dog and was able to put the poor creature out of its misery. After the dog was dead this brave boy went to the village to have his wounds dressed.

The whole village was stirred over the bravery of the boy but they did not think there was one chance in a hundred for his recovery. However, the mayor of the village remembered the news he had heard of a great bacteriologist in Paris and got in touch with him. Within six days the boy was in the laboratory, where the doctor at once began this new treatment.

For a time the case looked hopeless. Then came a definite turn for the better and the boy's life was saved. Later the doctor read a paper on the case before the French Academy of Sciences. The story deeply moved those distinguished men and they voted a rich reward for the boy who had risked his life to save the other children.

The famous doctor was the same boy, Louis Pasteur, who had heard that awful cry "Mad wolf!" many years before. Now in his renowned *Institut Pasteur* he had developed a treatment for rabies.

A.A.E.

CAN YOU BE TRUSTED?

If therefore ye have not been faithful in the unrighteous mammon, who will commit to your trust the true riches? Luke 16:11.

About A.D. 1016 Canute of Denmark became King of England. He was a wise and good king and brought peace and prosperity to his realm in an age of violence and bloodshed.

On one occasion, hastening to meet a crisis in a distant part of his kingdom, he found his way blocked by a large sheet of frozen water. Only by crossing the ice could he make his destination in time. But was the ice strong enough to bear his weight?

"Does anyone know whether this ice will carry my weight?" he asked.

"If there were someone to go in front of you, we would soon know," one of his counselors ventured.

Standing nearby was Bodge, a huge Saxon slave who had served the king for many years. Grasping the situation, he stepped forward. "Sire," he said, "I will run before you and test the ice."

Holding a long pole above his head, Bodge ran for more than a mile in advance of the king, until they were safely on the other side. The pole offered him some hope if the ice broke.

On the other side of the stretch of water the king halted his retinue. "Not one of my nobles or freemen offered to test the ice for me," he said. "It was left for my slave to risk his life. I would command no man to do what he has done. From now on Bodge will be free and a noble of the realm."

What you are doing now, do skillfully and well. Use wisely the money you earn or that is given you as an allowance. "The amount daily spent in needless things, with the thought, 'It is only a nickel,' 'It is only a dime,' seems very little; but multiply these littles by the days of the year, and as the years go by, the array of figures will seem almost incredible."—*Fundamentals of Christian Education,* p. 152.

God wants to give you greater talents, greater responsibilities. What are you doing with what you already have?

W.R.L.S.

MARJORIE'S DISCOVERY

Beauty is vain: but a woman that feareth the Lord, she shall be praised. Proverbs 31:30.

"Let's not invite Marjorie. She's just, well, different."

"Marjorie? Oh, no! She's a wallflower."

"Not Marjorie! She's too plain. She looks like a farmer's daughter from Hick County."

And so it went time after time. When invitations were given out for various parties and activities, poor Marjorie was always left out. She knew why, too, for the girls were not slow to point out her faults.

Her angular frame just didn't seem to fit anything properly. The prettiest dress looked out of place on her bony body. Her eyes were small, her nose too long, and freckles covered her face.

But Marjorie was not the only one who heard some of the girls' cruel remarks. The teacher was not deaf, and as she watched the unhappy victim go about her classwork, always alone, she determined to help her.

One day when there were no other students around, the teacher said, "Marjorie, I've heard what the girls have been saying to you and I feel so bad about the way they've been treating you."

"But it's true," sobbed the heartbroken girl. "I am plain and ugly and don't know how to act in public. I'm just a misfit!"

The teacher held out a black lump. "This is what you think you are like, but take it and plant it."

Curious, Marjorie took the object home and did as the teacher had asked. Every day she watched to see what would happen. In time a shoot appeared above the ground. Then one day the plant burst into bloom. As Marjorie admired the beautiful lily, she understood what her teacher was trying to tell her.

"I don't have to stay an old black lump," she told herself. "I can grow such a beautiful character that people will not notice the ugly me."

And she did. As Marjorie became less shy and more helpful and kind, her classmates grew to love her. Even her features seemed changed by the glow of happiness that shone from her face. Marjorie had discovered that "Beauty is vain: but a woman that feareth the Lord, she shall be praised."

M.H.

PROTECTIVE CLOTHING

Put on all the armour which God provides, so that you may be able to stand firm against the devices of the devil. Ephesians 6:11, NEB.

Stop for a moment and recall the many types of body coverings that God has made for His created works. Did you name skin, hair, wool, feathers, shells, scales, and even grass? God selected the most appropriate for each creature and for the earth itself.

Many animals wear hair. It's warm and light and fitting protection against cold and water. For some it is long, thick, curly, or shaggy. Others have very short hair. Just think of the problems that birds, fish, insects, and animals would have if their styles were constantly changing.

Whales have a two-foot-thick coat of blubber that not only provides warmth but, being soft, more evenly distributes the intense pressure of water when the animal swims deep down in the ocean. This diving suit is just right as a life preserver.

Consider the porcupine—a slow, relatively weak animal. Lacking suitable claws and teeth for fighting, it is armed with quills that are excelled by nothing for defense. Those sharply barbed quills are sufficient to teach almost any aggressive foe an unforgettable lesson.

Did you know that elephant hide is from one to one-and-a-half inches thick in some places? What mosquito will bore through all that? As elephants break through the dense jungle where they live what better protection could God have given them against the sharp thorn trees and bushes that would tear a hide less thick and tough.

Grass is the covering God gave the earth to protect it from erosion. Rain and melting snow would easily wash away far more fertile soil if it were not for this beautiful protective covering.

What is the element that God wants you to be adequately protected against? Sin. What is the armor that He has provided? The robe of Christ's righteousness is most effective against Satan. How do you receive it? It is Jesus' gift to you when you accept Him as your Saviour. Just as medieval knights put on their armor daily, so you need to ask God for this protective coat each morning. The devil is out to get you! The fight is for real. But with God's armor, victory is assured.

E.E.L. and J.H.L.

$300,000 IN THE CHIMNEY!

The Lord shall open unto thee his good treasure. Deuteronomy 28:12.

Imagine finding three hundred thousand dollars in your chimney! That is exactly what happened in France years ago after World War II ended. Two men made just such a discovery: a small suitcase with an equivalent of three hundred thousand dollars in French francs was wedged in their chimney. Authorities to whom the men reported the find decided that this money must have been hidden away for safekeeping during the war years. Probably the family in whose house the money was found had been deported to some faraway land and were never heard from again.

What a find—three hundred thousand dollars! That is a real treasure! And for many years it remained undiscovered—not doing anyone any good!

You have a treasure right in your own home—or you should have! There is much more than mere money in it, too! In the book *Christ's Object Lessons,* Ellen White tells us that the Bible contains treasure—the gospel (p. 104).

Imagine having such a treasure right within your own reach! What are you doing with it?

What are some of those "gold nuggets" of treasure in your Bible? First and greatest, of course, is Jesus. Without Him we can do nothing (John 15:5). With Him we may have eternal life—which is another gold nugget that is of inestimable worth. This treasure is a life that measures with the life of God. Jesus, through His life and death upon earth, makes such a glorious prospect a reality for us if we will permit Him to do so.

Forgiveness of sin is a nugget found in God's Treasure Chest. We sin. "The wages of sin is death" (Rom. 6:23). We deserve to die, but Jesus promises to forgive our sins if we will sincerely confess them. He also promises "to cleanse us from all unrighteousness" (1 John 1:9). What precious promises—what priceless treasure—forgiveness for sin, complete cleansing, life eternal. All this precious treasure we find in God's Word.

Let us search for the nuggets of truth in God's Holy Book every day. He will never disappoint us.

R.H.P.

THE DAY NIAGARA STOPPED

In returning and rest shall ye be saved; in quietness and in confidence shall be your strength. Isaiah 30:15.

On March 29, 1848, the waters of Niagara Falls stopped flowing. The people suffered a nightmare of fear. Many took it to be a sign of the end. Fathers gathered their wives and children for a special reading of God's Word and the next morning hundreds of people hastened to church for special services. To many the dry riverbed became an "omen of doom."

Later the explanation for the cessation of Niagara's flow proved to be simple. As many tons of ice from Lake Erie were swept along by winds of 100 mph, the mammoth pieces of ice jammed together in a tributary from which the river derives its water before rushing to the falls. These huge chunks of ice dammed up the river. Not until the pieces moved to a new position could the torrent begin to flow. Then the frenzied people began to breathe easily again. The world did not come to an end at that time. Never since have the waters failed to reach Niagara Falls.

Sometimes the Lord has to stop our "rat race," the noises we hear day after day. He asks us to "be still, and know that I am God: I will be exalted among the heathen, I will be exalted in the earth" (Ps. 46:10). Often in quietness God can speak to our souls.

When the child Samuel had gone to bed, he heard the voice of God calling to him. When Moses quietly tended his sheep in the desert, he saw and heard the great I AM at the burning bush. After the "great and strong wind" that tore apart the mountains and broke the rocks and after the earthquake and the fire, at last the "still small voice" of God did speak to the prophet Elijah. Quietly he listened while God gave directions for his future work.

Even Jesus needed quiet in which to commune with His Father. To avoid the crowds He had to spend the late evenings and early mornings in prayer, and even sometimes entire nights in communion with His Strength.

If Christ found prayer a necessity—though He was perfect—how much more we need to seek spiritual power through talking with God. For us the noisy Niagara needs to stop falling that in quietness and in confidence we may be strong.

L.C.W.

FORGIVENESS WITH GOD

Let the wicked forsake his way, and the unrighteous man his thoughts: and let him return unto the Lord, and he will have mercy upon him; and to our God, for he will abundantly pardon. Isaiah 55:7.

This is one of the most wonderful promises in the Bible. It is an invitation to sinners to return to God. No matter how far they have wandered from Him, He is waiting to receive them and pardon their sins.

Some may think that it is all right to go into the ways of sin for a time and have what the world calls "a fling." One can always return to God, they say, and at last be forgiven and saved. The dangerous thing about such a plan is that most people who go into sin often lose all desire to return to God.

Sixty-six years ago there was brought into court in Boise, Idaho, a really bad man. Harry Orchard had killed many people. Some he had shot, and others he had blown up with bombs. His crowning crime came one night when he rigged up a bomb by the gate in front of the home of Frank Steunenberg, governor of the State. A few minutes later, as the governor opened the gate he triggered the bomb. It exploded and the governor was killed.

Arrested for this crime, Orchard was locked up. While waiting for his trial, he was given a Bible. As he read it he saw his great sin, but felt he had gone too far to expect mercy from God. Mrs. Steunenberg, widow of the man he had killed, sent him tracts, and four times visited him in the prison. A faithful Seventh-day Adventist, she assured him she forgave him for what he had done to her husband.

His heart broken, Harry Orchard confessed his crimes, made his peace with God, and joined the Seventh-day Adventist Church following baptism in the prison. When brought to trial, he was condemned to death, but his sentence was commuted to life imprisonment. For more than forty-five years he lived in prison, telling fellow prisoners of the loving-kindness of God, who will pardon the worst sinner who repents.

If anyone is lost, it will not be because God could not save him, but because he chose not to be saved. Let us place ourselves in His hands and ask Him to keep us all through our lives.

V.E.R.

PHYSICAL FITNESS

Take time and trouble to keep yourself spiritually fit. Bodily fitness has a certain value, but spiritual fitness is essential, both for this present life and for the life to come. 1 Timothy 4:8 (Phillips).

For several years we have heard a great deal about physical fitness. Many forms of exercise have been introduced. Jogging, push-ups, bicycling, walking, and a hundred other forms and styles have been promoted. And as the Bible says, "bodily fitness has a certain value."

However, a human being is more than a physical body. A boy might be as physically fit and strong as Samson but that is not enough. It was not enough for Samson. He needed something more. He needed spiritual power and self-control.

One illustration of Samson's spiritual weakness is seen in his attitude toward the Philistine girl with whom he had become infatuated. In keeping with the custom of that time, he asked his parents to get her for him for his wife. They pleaded with their son not to marry a Philistine, but he stubbornly held out and said defiantly, "Get her for me; for she pleaseth me well."

There are still sons like Samson who cast longing eyes toward girls of the world. They forget the mental and spiritual requirements. They fall for the physical and seem to think that that is all that is necessary. Samson said, "She pleaseth me well." He acted as though that was all that was needed.

How wrong he was! He apparently did not think about some other important considerations. A young man must consider these questions: Does the girl please God? Is it only her face and physical form and features that please me? Does she please my parents? Can she cook? Can she sew? Does she love flowers? and gardening? Is she healthy? Does she put forth the time and effort to exercise for health? How about her religious life? Does she take time to read good books and especially the Book of books? What are her hobbies? Remember, "bodily fitness has a certain value," but there are other values. Check them out, too! "Spiritual fitness is essential, both for this present life *and* for the life to come."

"Take time and trouble to keep yourself spiritually fit."

A.A.E.

THOSE VITAL ROOTS

You must live your whole life according to the Christ you have received—Jesus the Lord; you must be rooted in him and built on him and held firm by the faith you have been taught. Colossians 2:6, 7, Jerusalem.

Did you know that the fastest growing part of a tree is hidden from sight? Pearly white root hairs, as fine as a spider's web, grow so fast that could you watch with a microscope, you could see them lengthen.

At the end of each tiny root is a tough little cap. It performs like a miniature armored tank pushing its way between small bits of soil and around rocks. Behind this tip is the growing part that keeps moving deep into the soil. Tiny roots, directly behind the lengthening part, reach out for moisture. They soak it up through thin walls, along with dissolved minerals from the soil. Dr. H. J. Dittmer estimated that there are 14 billion root hairs on a single rye grass plant with a total length of 6,600 miles. In a full-grown apple tree these root hairs absorb about one hundred gallons of water a day. The life of the tree depends on this water-lifting power that begins with these tiny roots.

You don't have to be big to do an important work. God has a plan for each of you, a special plan only you can fill right now, when you are young.

You must be growing constantly to have that vital power with Him. To be strong, your roots must continually draw spiritual help from the water of life. Hidden roots nourish the plant. Faith, like those roots, can't be seen, but it grows by feeding on God's Word.

Roots not only absorb food and water from the soil but they also provide an anchor for the plant or tree. Roots make it easy to withstand the force of pressure. If your roots strike down deep you can be certain of an invisible union of your life with Jesus. You can't be moved by circumstances. Through faith in Him, you will grow. Have you gotten your nourishment from Jesus for today? It's there, but you must take time to go to Him personally, constantly, for a fresh supply. Let your roots grow down deep in Jesus. He only can satisfy. With Him there is no limit to your Christian growth.

E.E.L. and J.H.L.

A CALL TO SERVE

This gospel of the kingdom shall be preached in all the world for a witness unto all nations; and then shall the end come. Matthew 24:14.

When David Livingstone was sixteen he read the story of Gutzlaff, a missionary to China. This first awakened him to the needs of the world, and he began to dream of going to China himself as a missionary.

When war broke out between England and China and the door to China was closed, Livingstone wondered what he should do. Along came Robert Moffat who had spent several years as a missionary in South Africa. One part of his story especially gripped young David.

Moffat told how he had often stood on a hill overlooking a vast expanse of mountains and valleys to the north. "I have seen in the morning sun the smoke of a thousand villages where no missionary has ever been."

Through reading a missionary book and hearing a missionary speak, Livingstone felt a call to become a missionary himself.

Hudson Taylor's call to missionary service came a month after he was converted. Always frail of body, one morning he was forced to stay home from church because of a cold. Deprived of attending the house of God, he decided to spend his time praying and reading his Bible.

While in prayer he felt very keenly the physical weakness that hindered him in working for Christ. He told the Lord he would be willing to go anywhere and do anything if only his weakness would be turned into strength.

God calls each one of us to missionary service. But your call to missionary service may not take you to a foreign field. There are people here, often right in our own neighborhood, who don't know of the love of Jesus Christ. Someone must tell them.

Your call to mission service may not wait until you have finished college, or even academy, or even grade school. You may have friends right now who need someone to lead them to Christ. Perhaps God is calling you today to dedicate yourself to mission service right where you are for the time being, and then farther away if He sends you later. He has something for each of us to do if we are willing.

R.E.

HIS DEBT WAS PAID

Evil pursueth sinners: but to the righteous good shall be repayed. Proverbs 13:21.

Have you ever heard of Henry Clay? He was a statesman who lived before the American Civil War. One time Mr. Clay found himself very embarrassed and distressed because of a debt he owed the bank. He knew he would never be able to pay it on the day it was due.

I will go down to the bank, he decided, and explain my problem to the manager.

A few days later Mr. Clay was in the bank manager's office. "I've come to talk with you about the money I owe the bank," Mr. Clay began.

The manager smiled. "You don't owe us any money," he replied.

Taken aback, Clay thought perhaps the manager did not understand him, so he tried again. "I said I have come to talk with you about the money I owe you," he continued.

"But you don't owe us any money," the banker assured him again.

"Yes, I—" Clay tried to explain.

"No, Mr. Clay, you do not owe this bank a single dollar. You see, some friends of yours came and paid every penny of it."

The surprised statesman stammered a few words of appreciation and hastily left the bank. Tears were in his eyes as he made his way homeward. The debt was cared for. Friends had paid it for him.

It is wonderful to have friends like that, isn't it, boys and girls?

Of course, already you have thought of the Friend that I want us to think about this morning—the Friend who paid the biggest debt any of us will ever owe. I am talking about our Friend, Jesus Christ.

When a person breaks the law of the land we say he owes a debt to the state or to society. He has to pay a fine or go to prison, or sometimes the state even takes his life.

When you and I sin we break God's law. We owe a debt—that debt is a big one, for "the wages of sin is death." Unless someone pays it for us we must die. Jesus came from heaven and died upon the cross in our place. Our awful debt is paid. Thank God for such a Friend!

R.H.P.

THE CHILDREN AND THE KING

When the Son of Man comes as King, and all the angels with him, he will sit on his royal throne, and all the earth's people will be gathered before him. Matthew 25:31 (TEV).

One beautiful June morning Frederick William, king of Prussia, went into the woods for a walk. He loved to see the beautiful flowers in the country. He came to a meadow and found a group of children playing. The king stood for some time admiring them at their games.

Finally he called to them and asked them to sit down on the grass so that they could talk together. They did not know who this strange gentleman was, but thought he had a kind face, and they liked him. They had no idea that he was their king, but they could tell that he was a good man.

The king said, "I want to ask you some questions, and the child who gives the best answer shall have a prize." He held up an orange so that all could see it. "You know that we all live in the kingdom of Prussia, but tell me, to what kingdom does this orange belong?"

The children were puzzled for a little while. Then a brave, bright boy spoke, "It belongs to the vegetable kingdom, sir."

"Why do you think so, my boy?"

"Because it is the fruit of a plant and all plants belong to that kingdom."

The king was pleased. "You are right!" And he tossed the orange gaily to the boy.

Then he took a gold piece from his pocket and held it up so that it glistened in the sunlight. "Now, to what kingdom does this belong?"

A little lad spoke up, "To the mineral kingdom, sir."

"Good," said the king. "The gold piece is your prize."

"Now, one more question—to what kingdom do I belong?"

Some thought they should say to the kingdom of Prussia. Another boy wanted to say to the animal kingdom, but was afraid to say it. Then a sweet little girl said softly, "I think to the kingdom of heaven."

The king lifted her in his arms. Tears were in his eyes as he kissed her and said, "So be it, my child. So be it!"

A.A.E.

WHY REST?

*It follows that there still remains a Sabbath-rest for the people
of God. . . . Let it then be our earnest endeavour to be admitted
to that rest, so that no one may perish through following the
same example of unbelief. Hebrews 4:9-11, Weymouth.*

Did you know that a little muscle only five inches long, three and
one-half inches wide, and two and one-half inches thick, and
weighing from nine to eleven ounces does enough work in twelve
hours to lift a sixty-five-ton railroad tank car one foot off the ground.
Your heart pumps five quarts of blood through your body in about
sixty seconds. In a year it may pump more than 1 million gallons of
blood through 100,000 miles of blood vessels, a distance equal to
four trips around the world. That's enough blood to fill 200 tank cars
with 8,000 gallons each.

How can the heart do all this hard work year after year? Only
because it follows the divine plan and example of its Creator. Even
though the heart beats about seventy times a minute, or 4,200 times
an hour, much of that time it is relaxing. Counting the time between
beats, the heart is at rest about fifteen out of every twenty-four
hours each day. That means it beats about four seconds out of every
ten and rests about six. A regular plan of relaxation and rest is the
secret.

When God made this world in six days He followed it with a day
of rest. That precious day, the Sabbath, is one of God's greatest gifts
to man for his health and happiness. The wonderful relaxation,
change, and rest that come from true Sabbathkeeping makes man
healthier and happier mentally, physically, spiritually, and socially.

But if we use the Sabbath for our ceaseless activity and pleasures,
we soon become as useless as does the heart muscle that is
exercised too much and too long. We must choose to enter into the
full complete rest, which comes only through obedience to God's
directions. He lovingly reminds us each week to remember the
Sabbath day to keep it holy.

Your heart is a wonderful example. Following God's divine laws of
health, it accomplishes much. If you truly enter into God's rest as He
has planned, He'll enable you to do wonderful things through His
power.

E.E.L. and J.H.L.

FOUR TIMES IN FIFTEEN MINUTES

As we have therefore opportunity, let us do good unto all men, especially unto them who are of the household of faith. Galatians 6:10.

Bettie stood ready for school fifteen minutes early that lovely spring morning. She had her room in order, and had even wiped the dishes for her mother. Now she grumbled, "What can I do so early? Can't skate, play house, or do much of anything."

As she walked out on the porch, she looked down half a block and shuddered at what she saw—two-year-old Timmy from next door crossing the busy intersection by himself. She rushed down to him, and snatched him off the street, but not one second too soon. A big moving van was approaching and the light was green. When she delivered the toddler to his mother, Mrs. Hastings noticed the scared look on Bettie's face. "How thankful I am that you looked out in time!"

The girl began the two-block walk to school. As she passed a small cottage, she saw Mrs. Rinehart on the porch reading her Bible, using a magnifying glass. Often Bettie had read for her grandma, who had poor eyes. Now she asked, "Mrs. Rinehart, let me read a verse or two for you."

"God bless you, child. I have such bad eyes I can scarcely read my Bible anymore, even with my glass."

Walking on past two or three more houses a few minutes later Bettie saw Grandfather Doane picking up wood in his back yard. He looked as if it was an agonizing task with his bad back. Bettie rushed over and picked up enough to fill a box and carried it into his kitchen. "I must run now. I hear the five minute bell ringing."

At the school crossing a little first-grader was crying, frightened by a big dog. Bettie saw that it was her own dog, Hero. "Go home, Hero," she said, and gave him a friendly push. Then she walked with the little girl across the street to the school.

She came to the marching line for her room on time. Later in her seat she said to herself, "What fun I had the last fifteen minutes by helping at least four different people. I had thought I couldn't do anything in so short a time."

"The man who appreciates time as his working day will fit himself for a mansion and for a life that is immortal. It is well that he was born."—*Christ's Object Lessons,* p. 342.

L.C.W.

WANTED—GOOD SHEEP DOGS!

Who can have compassion on the ignorant, and on them that are out of the way. Hebrews 5:2.

Without a good sheep dog the shepherd couldn't care for his sheep. The dog keeps the flock together, turns the wandering back, and defends the sheep from wild animals. Our text describes the qualities needed by a sheep dog—compassion for those who have strayed through ignorance, and sympathy for the perplexed, weak, or foolish.

Not all dogs have the loving, gentle heart of a sheep dog. Though able to see danger and act quickly, a watchdog that warns with a bark or a snarl would only frighten a sheep. A sheep dog needs more than a quick mind. He must be loyal to his master, quick to follow his commands, and have a gentle, compassionate spirit.

An artist painted a beautiful picture of a collie dog standing guard over a sick lamb that had strayed far from the flock. The hill where he lay was covered with snow; the sheepfold was far in the distance. The lamb had strayed too far and was too sick and cold to move. It could not follow the dog home. Not daring to leave the lamb for fear that in his absence a wild animal might come, the collie stands sheltering the lamb from the cold wind with his warm body, calling loudly to the shepherd for help. Faithful to his responsibility, still he is gentle and kind to the troublesome lamb.

When others do wrong, how do you treat them? Do you shun them, talk unkindly about them, criticize and condemn? True, their faults may be of their own making; they may have wandered willfully from the right path, and now are caught in a sudden storm of passion or anger. Whatever the cause of their trouble, they are outside the fold, and they can't get back without help.

Are you a faithful sheep dog to "them that are out of the way"? Do you show love, kindness, sympathy, and compassion as you urgently call on the Good Shepherd to come with help? "If we would humble ourselves before God, and be kind and courteous and tender-hearted and pitiful, there would be one hundred conversions to the truth where now there is only one."—*Testimonies,* vol. 9, p. 189.

E.E.L. and J.H.L.

THE UNOFFICIAL TRUCE

He died for all. 2 Corinthians 5:15.

During the American Civil War, when brother fought brother and father fought son, a certain field was taken and retaken several times by both the Northern and the Southern armies. Each time more soldiers were wounded, and there were many of both sides dead and dying lying in the hot sun. From all over the field came the piteous plea, "Water! Water!"

Finally a Southern soldier could stand it no longer. "Let me take water to those poor men," he begged his captain.

But the captain refused. "It would be certain death. The fighting is too heavy," he said. "If you get killed what good would it do? No, I cannot allow you to go."

Sadly the soldier turned away, but he could not shut his ears to the haunting calls. Soon he was back. "Captain, above the roar of artillery and the crack of the muskets I hear those cries for water. Let me go!"

The young soldier was so persistent that the captain finally grudgingly agreed. As the private started across the field with a bucket of water and a tin cup, he knelt first at the side of one and then another fallen soldier, Northern and Southern alike. It made no difference to him. To each he gave a drink of cold water while the bullets whistled around him.

"I say," different ones in the Northern army began to remark as they noticed the lone figure out on the battlefield, "I do believe that man's helping our buddies out there!"

"Hold your fire!" others commanded, and gradually all down the line the shooting ceased.

For an hour and a half there was an unofficial truce as both sides waited for the Southerner to finish his errand of mercy. Each wounded soldier, Northern or Southern, received a drink. Then, picking up his empty pail, the soldier went back to his unit. The firing started again and the truce was over.

This world is a battlefield and we are the sin-wounded soldiers. Jesus came to give us each a drink of the water of life, but the enemy did not stop shooting when He came. It cost Him His life.

"He died for all," saint and sinner alike. And that includes you.

M.H.

BIG BROTHER

Lo, I am with you alway, even unto the end of the world.
Matthew 28:20.

Edward was born and reared in beautiful Austria. As a junior and early teenager he was big and strong. The boys his age were jealous of his strength, and some of them wanted to fight with him. As a Christian he sought to avoid such confrontations, although on occasion he demonstrated to several of them that he could protect himself easily.

Finally six of the boys decided to have a showdown with him—not singly, but all six of them against him at once. "Tomorrow we will get you at the bridge," they threatened.

As I heard Edward—now a leader in God's cause—tell the story many years later, he told how fearful he was. While he ate supper that night he thought of the bridge. When he went to sleep that night he was thinking of the bridge. When he awakened in the morning the first thing he thought of was the bridge. He tried to think of some excuse for not going to school that day, because of the bridge and what he could expect on his way to school.

His older brother, who was a big husky fellow, noticed that Edward was bothered about something, and he urged his younger brother to tell him what was worrying him. Edward told him about the threat of the six boys.

"Don't worry!" Reinholdt told him. "I will go with you to school."

He did. When the plotters saw Edward's big brother with him they all ran away and left him alone.

At school Edward met his tormentors. "Why didn't you keep your appointment with me at the bridge this morning?" he asked.

"We did, but you had your big brother with you," they replied sheepishly.

Young people, it is a wonderful thing to have a big brother to help in time of need. I don't mean when we are threatened with beating; I mean, it is wonderful to have a big Brother who is with us always. Ellen White speaks of God as our heavenly Father and of Jesus Christ as our Elder Brother. He is with us at all times, on good days and bad days, when we are sick and when we are well. I'm glad I have a big Brother like Jesus to be with me always—aren't you?

R.H.P.

CLEANSED FROM SIN

The blood of Jesus Christ his Son cleanseth us from all sin.
1 John 1:7.

One bitterly cold winter day a Salvation Army worker was making missionary calls among the poor people living in one of London's worst ghettos. In one tenement building she walked up a flight of stairs, then went from door to door knocking. At some doors she was rudely refused admittance; a few swung open and the occupants permitted her to enter and tell the story of Jesus.

When she knocked on the last of a long line of doors it opened a few inches and a burly man asked gruffly, "What do you want?"

"I am a Christian worker," she answered, "bringing the good news of salvation."

"Go away. We don't need you here."

The missionary turned to leave but stopped on hearing a faint voice speaking.

"Oh, please let her in. I must see her. Don't send her away."

The man could not resist his sick wife's appeal. Reluctantly he opened the door, and the worker stepped inside. She saw a woman, seriously ill, lying on a pile of straw.

"Oh, madam," gasped the woman, "do you know anything of the blood that cleanses from sin?"

The missionary was startled.

"Where did you hear about it?"

"I can't remember well, but once, years ago, I stepped into a chapel and heard someone talking and singing about the blood that cleanses from all sin. I need that blood, for I have been a sinner and I want to be clean."

"Yes, I know that Man whose blood can cleanse," the visitor replied.

She then spoke lovingly of the Man who willingly laid down His life that all sinners might be cleansed. She prayed for the sick woman and for her husband and promised medical help.

By faith the woman accepted the sacrifice made in her behalf. And a look of peace came into her tired eyes.

"I am no longer afraid," she said, patting the visitor's hand. "I am so glad you came. Go quickly and tell the good news to everyone."

V.E.R.

DEPENDABLE ALICE

Jesus Christ the same yesterday, and today, and for ever. Hebrews 13:8.

With everything in this world changing, and very few things remaining stable, you can depend on Jesus, who never changes. His promises are as sure today as yesterday, and as forever enduring as they are now.

Alice, a circus elephant from India, could be depended on. For 110 years this faithful elephant did her circus jobs without being told.

The circus always opened with the big parade. The band played lively music as the performers and animals marched around the arena. The elephants, wearing bright velvet or satin ornaments, each with a pretty girl perched on its head or riding in a saddle, kept time to the music with their slow, measured tread.

In one town, during the pageantry of the big parade, the audience suddenly screamed. A tiny girl had slipped away from her parents into the circus ring. Running right into the path of the huge elephants, it looked as if nothing could save her from being crushed beneath their feet. Suddenly a large elephant reached forward, lifted the little girl with her trunk, and walked to the side of the ring. The frantic mother reached out and the animal laid the little one in her arms.

That was Alice, the smartest, most dependable animal in the circus. The crowd cheered and marveled at what she had done, but the circus manager was not surprised.

As the circus moved from place to place the huge animal cages had to be lifted onto railroad cars. These and the heavy wagons were loaded by the elephants. Alice never had to be told what to do. In fact, she directed the other elephants so they did their jobs correctly. One time the front wheels of a circus wagon rolled off a flatcar. The wagon hung precariously in the air, ready to fall at any moment. Alice, without a word from anyone, saw the problem and quickly lifted that heavy wagon, pushing it back onto the flatcar.

To be in heaven we must be like Jesus—dependable, the same every day. Can you be depended upon to do the right thing at the right time, even when no one is looking or directing you? If Alice could for 110 years, surely you can today with Jesus' help.

E.E.L. and J.H.L.

STRANGE MEDICINE

A merry heart doeth good like a medicine: but a broken spirit drieth the bones. Proverbs 17:22.

All good medicine does not necessarily come in bottles. Apparently, anything that creates a merry heart affects the health.

Oliver Goldsmith believed this. He had studied to be a physician but he did not practice it in the usual manner. He was a writer, and the poem "The Deserted Village" reveals much of his philosophy of life. In this poem his description of the village preacher reflects his own attitude toward helping people with kindness.

One day a poor woman came to Dr. Goldsmith and asked him to call on her husband, who was sick and could not eat. Goldsmith went and found the family was in great need. Because of his illness the man had not had work for a long time. He was in deep distress. As for eating, there was no food in the house.

"Call at my room this evening," said Goldsmith to the woman, "and I will give you some medicine for your husband."

When she called, Goldsmith gave her a small box that was very heavy. "Here is the medicine," he said. "Use it faithfully, and I think it will do your husband a great deal of good. But don't open the box until you reach home."

"What are the directions for taking the medicine?" asked the woman.

"You will find the directions inside the box," he replied

When the woman reached her house, she sat down by her husband's side, and they opened the box. They were amazed and thrilled by what they found in it. The box was full of pieces of money. And on the top they read the directions:

"To be taken as often as necessity requires."

Dr. Goldsmith had given them all the coins and ready money that he had. He thought that would be the finest medicine for that man and his family. They were greatly comforted and cheered. And since a merry heart is a good medicine who can say that Dr. Goldsmith gave the wrong prescription? In such a case it was probably the finest medicine that could have been given.

A.A.E.

A SOUL FOR EVERY YEAR

He that winneth souls is wise. Proverbs 11:30.

At dinner a physician once told his family about David, a boy of eleven who had been brought to the hospital in a critical condition. As the patient seemed eager to talk, the doctor decided to tell him a bit as to the serious nature of his condition.

"David, we are doing all we can to make you well, but I can't promise that we'll make it, son."

"That's OK, Doc. I know I'm not going to get well. But I'll tell you something—I wouldn't trade places with you." His statement surprised the kind doctor.

"You see, Doc, I'm eleven years old," he went on, "and I've got eleven souls to bring to Jesus, one for every year. I'll bet you haven't got one for every year you have lived." The 66-year-old physician admitted that David was right.

"It's like this. Until lately nobody at our house served Jesus, but we listened to a gospel broadcast and liked it. I was the first one to accept Jesus. Then I got my mother, my brother, my dad, my sister, and some of the kids near us. This week when I came to the hospital I had ten souls won.

"I told the Lord, 'You know that I probably won't get out of the hospital, and I'd like to get another soul so that I'll have eleven—one for every year.' And last night I got the night nurse—so I have my eleven. Honest, Doc, wouldn't you have to go some to make it one soul for every year you've lived?"

"David, I wish I did have a soul for Jesus for every year I have lived," the doctor said.

Just as the doctor had told his family about David, the telephone rang. "I'll answer. It might be about David." After he again seated himself at the table, he sighed. "David is gone, but what a reward awaits that little boy."

In church the next week, which was the physician's birthday, Mrs. Miller noticed that her husband put an unusually large roll of bills in the collection plate. On the way home she asked, "I approve, but I'm curious. How much was in that roll?"

The doctor spoke slowly. "Sixty-six dollars, just a shallow substitute for little David's gift."

L.C.W.

CHANGED PLANS

The steps of a good man are ordered by the Lord: and he delighteth in his way. Psalm 37:23.

More than a hundred years ago, when the game of baseball first began, a twelve-year-old boy named Bill lived in Cincinnati. The greatest ball team in the country at that time was called the Cincinnati Red Stockings. In 1869 they had piled up the amazing record of winning fifty-seven games in a row.

No one worshiped the ball players more than young Bill. In his heart lived just one great dream—to become a major league ball player and play for the Cincinnati team.

Bill was big for his age, and had a hard swing. He practiced ball so much that he began to attract the attention of professional players. It began to look as if his dream of being a ball player might come true.

But Bill's father was a judge. He didn't think baseball was a proper career for his son.

When Bill was actually offered a contract to play major league baseball, his father flatly refused to let him sign it. He angrily insisted that Bill must become a lawyer, maybe even a judge.

Bill decided to leave home. He didn't need his father to support him. He could live on his baseball earnings. He'd show him that he could become famous. Then Father would be sorry. But before he could leave town with the major league team Bill had to play one more game with his small local team. He had promised; they couldn't win the game without him. He'd play that game tomorrow, and the day after he could be on his way.

But Bill's plans didn't work out. The very next day he injured his throwing arm. He was in for weeks of pain and doctor's care. His arm never recovered enough to revive his hopes of being a big-league player. There was nothing to do but become a lawyer, just as his father wished.

But he advanced in his profession. He became a judge like his father. In fact, he surpassed his father, for he became the highest judge in the land, the Chief Justice of the United States Supreme Court.

And that's not all. Later he became the twenty-sixth President of the United States, William Howard Taft.

As we plan for our future let us remember that sometimes God may overrule in our plans so that our lives may accomplish more.

R.E.

YOU CAN TRUST HIM

*Throw all your worries on him, because he cares for you.
1 Peter 5:7, TEV.*

You can trust Jesus to care for you just as Dr. Pete trusted his faithful horse, Charlie. The young country doctor lived before there were many cars. Since the country roads weren't good enough for cars to get through, Dr. Pete used a strong buggy and a good horse. Years before this story took place a veterinarian had given him a sickly colt he thought couldn't possibly live. Dr. Pete tenderly cared for the young animal, who thrived under his loving care. Now a fine, strong horse, they were inseparable companions.

Late one night, Dr. Pete received word that a little boy was critically ill far out in the country. He made the trip and stayed with the child almost all night.

Exhausted, he climbed into the buggy. "Home, Charlie. It's my turn to sleep." Though the road was full of holes, grass, and weeds, the tired doctor slept through all the bumps.

Suddenly Charlie stopped. The buggy was too light. Dr. Pete wasn't in it. Turning around, Charlie started back looking for his beloved friend. Finally in the darkness he found the doctor still asleep on the grass. Stamping his feet, he made all kinds of noises until Dr. Pete awakened and climbed back into the buggy.

"Thanks, Charlie, old boy." The doctor patted his friend. "I promise to try to stay in the buggy the rest of the way home."

Another night he and Charlie were driving through heavy rain to see a patient. Melting snow had raised the water level high.

"Sorry, Doc. It's not safe to cross the bridge. The water is rising fast," warned the man stationed at the river.

Driving along the road by the river, the doctor saw a place that seemed to be only about three feet deep. Maybe he could make it.

"Charlie, we are needed over there. Can you do it?"

Charlie had a difficult struggle to stay on his feet through the swift water, but he kept on till they came safely to the opposite bank.

Christ will do much for you, even far more than this horse did for the doctor. But you must trust Him as completely as Dr. Pete did Charlie.

E.E.L. and J.H.L.

ALMOST UNBELIEVABLE

I love you, O Lord, my strength. Psalm 18:1, NIV.

A minister once sat in one isolated cabin telling the story of the cross to a mountaineer family who had never heard it before. "They followed him with rapt attention; and when he had concluded, the mother, leaning toward him, whispered hoarsely,

" 'Stranger, you say all this happened a long time ago?'

" 'Yes,' he said, 'almost two thousand years ago.'

" 'And they nailed Him to that thar tree when He hadn't done nothin' to hurt them—only just loved them?'

" 'Yes.'

"She leaned farther forward and placed her hand impressively upon his knee. 'Well, stranger,' she said, the tears standing in her eyes, 'let's hope 'tain't so.' "

It is no surprise that a poor, uneducated mountaineer woman could fail to grasp the wonder of Jesus and His redeeming love. Long before her day, Clovis, king of the Franks, heard that same story and reacted with anger. His fists clenched tightly and his eyes flashed as he exclaimed, "If I and my valiant Franks had been there, such a thing would never, never, have been allowed to happen!"

Even wiser beings have had difficulty understanding the willingness of Jesus to sacrifice Himself for lost mankind. "The angels had wondered at the glorious plan of redemption," wrote Mrs. White. At the time of Jesus' birth "the holy beings from the world of light are drawn to the earth. The whole world is brighter for His presence. Above the hills of Bethlehem are gathered an innumerable throng of angels."—*The Desire of Ages,* p. 47.

And when He died on the cross, angels were there also. They were amazed to see "the infinite love of Jesus, who, suffering the most intense agony of mind and body, thought only of others, and encouraged the penitent soul to believe. . . .

"With amazement angels witnessed the Saviour's despairing agony. The hosts of heaven veiled their faces from the fearful sight."—*Ibid.,* pp. 752, 753.

Then Jesus was at rest. When He arose, angels were there to greet Him. The story is almost unbelievable. But, thank God, it's true!

V.E.R.

CAUGHT IN A BLIZZARD

My son, keep thy father's commandment, and forsake not the law of thy mother. Proverbs 6:20.

Fern and Freddie loved going backpacking with their dad. Nearly every spring they would take a long hike up into the nearby mountains. This year they urged their father to take them earlier than usual. The weather was bright and sunny, although the air still was fresh and cold.

The three were having a great time high up among the pines, when a blizzard struck suddenly. There were no shelters nearby. They could only dig in and wait. With the little shovel they had brought along they feverishly dug a trench, threw their tarp across it, and fastened it down with their three packs. Dad held the fourth side down.

The storm outside grew worse. The wind howled, the snow drifted.

"Don't leave this shelter," father warned. He knew the situation was becoming serious and that they might not make it out in the blizzard. "We must wait for help. Someone will come. But don't leave the shelter under any circumstances."

Minutes lengthened into hours. The winds shrieked; the shelter was cold. Father lay in the most exposed place. His own body protected the children from the gusts that came in under the tarp.

Then Dad stopped talking. He lay very still. Fern and Freddie prayed. Help did come some hours later, but their father had frozen to death. The children stayed in the protected area as he had told them to, and it was there that a search party found them.

When I read this story I thought of the words of the wise man: "My son, keep thy father's commandment." Fern's and Freddie's lives were saved because they were obedient to their father's counsel.

The Lord's servant says, "Upon obedience depends life and happiness, health and joy, of men, women, and children. Obedience is for their well-being in this life and in the life to come."—*My Life Today,* p. 162.

You and I should be interested in both lives—this life and the life to come. Obedience is for our well-being. It will assure us health and joy here, and it will assure us a place in God's wonderful home of the saved in the hereafter.

R.H.P.

GOD IS THERE

He that cometh to God must believe that he is, and that he is a rewarder of them that diligently seek him. Hebrews 11:6.

Scott knew that his parents would not give him permission to go surfing on Sabbath. But suppose he didn't tell them where he was going? Suppose his surfboard was left by accident in his friend's car, and then he asked permission to go with Todd to his aunt's cabin up in the mountains?

He held his breath as he asked permission for that, but Mother agreed readily—with the condition that the boys be back for sundown worship.

The boys did not have as much fun at the beach as they had anticipated. The knowledge that they had not told the truth about where they were going hung over them all afternoon. Then, when it was time to start back in order to reach Scott's home for sundown worship, they couldn't find the car key!

Frantically they searched through the shifting sand. No key.

"I can't even call my folks to pick me up," Todd said. "They aren't home this afternoon. You'll have to call your dad."

As Scott thought of the unpleasant task of calling his father to pick them up, he thought of the hurt look that would be on Dad's face. He thought how upset Dad and Mom would be that he had broken the Sabbath.

Scott had been brought up to believe in God and to believe in prayer, but religion had seemed to be so restrictive that he had yearned for freedom. Lately he had asked his folks how they even knew that God existed. Yet in this emergency he turned to the God whom he had begun to doubt.

"If You are there," Scott prayed, "let me find that key in such a way that I can see a supernatural power!"

Then he saw it! The tiny silver tip of the buried key stuck out about an eighth of an inch from the vast white stretch of sand. Scott believed that God had answered.

Scott knew that under the circumstances he had no right to expect God to hear his request. But He did! And Scott understood that God was inviting him to be honest and to be true to the best he knew.

R.E.

"DON'T DESTROY WILDLIFE"

You shall not steal. Exodus 20:15, RSV.

Hiking on a trail in Rocky Mountain National Park, we admired the lovely wildflowers. In a grove of aspens grew many blue columbines, the Colorado state flower. Knowing the park rules prohibited destroying wildlife, we admired them and walked on. Farther up the trail many kinds of small flowers grew profusely. I stopped and rationalized that it wouldn't hurt to pick just a few. Moments later, with the flowers in my hand, I met a man wearing a big hat and with a badge on his green shirt.

I learned a lesson about honesty. Stealing is stealing, even if it is just a few wildflowers on a restricted mountain trail.

Mr. Gray also learned about honesty. Driving down a mountain road, he admired the many bushes blooming with red flowers. Thinking of his garden at home, he stopped his car. No one was around. Taking a shovel from the trunk of his car, he began digging around one of the prettiest in the clump.

It was hard work. Before he put it in his car, he stood back to admire its loveliness. "What a beauty," he said aloud.

"Yes, isn't it?" said a voice behind him. Sitting on his horse was the policeman of the forest, the park ranger. "This forest belongs to all of us. Many people would like to see that beautiful bush. I know a place down the road where you could plant it now."

The ground was hard and dry. Mr. Gray had never had to work so hard. The ranger just watched him until he dug a deep hole.

"There's a stream down there," said the ranger as he pointed down the steep hill. "Do you have something to carry water in?" Mr. Gray had only a small pail.

Many times Mr. Gray climbed up that hill before he had sufficient water. Never had he been so tired. Finally the ranger said, "You may plant it now. It's hard work to plant a bush, isn't it?"

Mr. Gray didn't answer, but got into his car and drove home now that the lesson was ended. It is doubtful he will ever steal another bush. What about you? Are you honest in even the smallest things?

E.E.L. and J.H.L.

THROUGH YOUR PRAYERS

I trust that through your prayers I shall be given unto you.
Philemon 22.

Pastor and Mrs. James White never traveled without committing their ways to God. In every age travel has presented dangers and hazards. Today we fear speeding automobiles and drunken drivers. In their day there were other lurking threats.

In 1854 the young couple left their home in Rochester, New York, and visited Michigan. It was a difficult trip and they had to ride over log roads and through deep boggy areas of mud. Feeling that the Lord wanted them to visit Wisconsin, they boarded a train at Jackson quite late at night.

Mrs. White says of this experience, "As we were preparing to take the train, we felt very solemn, and proposed a season of prayer; and as we there committed ourselves to God, we could not refrain from weeping."—*Life Sketches,* p. 153.

The better cars of the train were at the front, so they went straight there hoping to find seats that would enable them to sleep. But all the cars were full and they had to move back through the train to find a seat.

For some reason the Whites were concerned about the journey and did not even put their bags down. Mrs. White kept her bonnet on and spoke with her husband about the feeling of foreboding they each felt.

Suddenly the train crashed and jerked, finally coming to a stop. There were screams and groans. Through some miracle their own car had been separated from the train and did not leave the tracks. The car where they had previously tried to find seats was wrecked. Four people were killed and many injured in the derailment. "God had sent an angel to preserve our lives," Mrs. White commented.

The next day they completed their journey to Wisconsin, where souls were converted as a result of their efforts.

Today, pray not only for your own safety but for that of those who travel doing the work of God.

W.R.L.S.

LEARN TO DECIDE

How long halt ye between two opinions? if the Lord be God, follow him. 1 Kings 18:21.

David's great-aunt Deborah showed him a plate on which lay a small frosted cake with coconut scattered over it and also a gingerbread man. "This noon, David, which will you have for your dessert?"

"Why, Auntie, I just don't know."

"Don't touch them until you have made your choice," warned Aunt Debbie.

David sighed, "I can't decide. I like them both very much." At home where indulgent Aunt Julia was in charge of the boy, she would have said, "Then you just take both of them. Tell me later which you liked best."

But not so Aunt Debbie, who had in her make-up some New England sternness. "Choose now, David. Never shilly-shally."

"Oh, Aunt Debbie, I can't choose. I guess I really want the frosted cake, but the gingerbread man looks so funny. I don't *know* which one."

"Very well, I'll put them both back in the cupboard." With a sinking feeling the young visitor saw the plate disappear. Would he get a second chance?

At suppertime she again took the plate from the shelf. This time without any hesitation David took the gingerbread man. Later he wished he had chosen the frosted cupcake, but one was surely better than none at all.

During that summer-long visit Aunt Debbie constantly confronted the boy with choices. He never forgot her admonitions, "Choose now, David. Don't shilly-shally. Remember old man Lawson, who couldn't decide whether to plant corn or potatoes in his garden. Finally, nothing was planted and the whole garden went to weeds."

David had seen the old man and his neglected field. He learned to weigh things as well as he could, make his choice promptly, and stay by it. Never thereafter could the lad hesitate without thinking of the word "shilly-shally" and his Aunt Deborah. She taught him that indecision is a bad trait to be uprooted, like loose honesty and an uncontrollable temper. Let us make our many choices according to the Ten Commandments, the golden rule, and good judgment.

L.C.W.

DON'T BE AFRAID

I have chosen the way of truth; I have set my heart on your laws. Psalm 119:30, NIV.

Jack didn't mean to break the lamp. He was only tossing his baseball glove around a little bit while on his way through the living room as he headed outdoors for the ball field.

Yet the next thing he knew, the glove had gone farther than he intended. The lamp was on the floor instead of on the table, and broken at the base.

Jack picked up his glove, and then looked at the lamp. It was a clean break. If he picked it up and put it carefully together and set it back on the end table, it was possible that no one would notice.

The lamp balanced perfectly, and the crack hardly showed. Jack shut the door softly behind him and went on out to play ball. Maybe he wouldn't even have to tell Mother the lamp was broken.

But thoughts of that lamp plagued his afternoon. He knew he *ought* to tell Mother. Why didn't he want to? He was afraid.

He was afraid of the sad look on Mother's face when she would learn that her lamp was broken. He was afraid of the words he might hear about his carelessness. Most of all, he was afraid of the punishment, for he had been told many, many times not to toss his glove around in the house.

Yet at the end of the afternoon when he told Mother, she was so glad her boy was truthful that she did not punish him for the broken lamp.

Many of us are afraid of God for the same reasons Jack was afraid of his mother that afternoon. We are afraid that we may hear Him telling us about something we are doing that we should not, or something He wants us to do that we haven't done yet. We often expect God to be like a parent, ready with punishment for the wrong things we have done.

But we don't need to be afraid of God. Taylor puts the verse this way: "We need have no fear of someone who loves us perfectly; his perfect love for us eliminates all dread of what he might do to us. If we are afraid, it is for fear of what he might do to us, and shows that we are not fully convinced that he really loves us" (1 John 4:18, TLB).

R.E.

THE WHITE DONKEY'S TAIL

And be sure your sin will find you out. Numbers 32:23.

As a traveling guest, James Barton joined Sheik Moosa's caravan of ninety camels and nineteen men.

At all times Barton kept with him a leather bag containing eighty pieces of gold. On the morning of the ninth day the bag was gone. He told the sheik of his loss. The sheik sat in silence. Then he declared they wouldn't travel that day, and the gold would be found by evening.

He left the camp alone. Returning by noon, he and his donkey went into the tent, with the command that he must not be disturbed. Toward the evening he appeared in his finest clothes, sat in the center of camp, and in a dignified voice called, "Bring me the men." He stared at them silently for a long time. Then he began to speak.

"A terrible disgrace has come to me. Someone has stolen from my guest, a traveler who has trusted me. Since no one has been in camp, the thief stands before me. My white donkey is not ordinary, but a descendant from the prophet Mohammed's donkey. God will give him wisdom to tell me who stole the gold. I command every man to go alone in my tent and pull the donkey's tail. Close the flap so only God and the donkey can see. When an innocent hand touches it, the donkey will be silent, but he will speak when he feels the guilty hand."

One by one the men entered the tent and closed the flap. Not a sound came from the donkey. When all returned the sheik commanded, "Hold your hands in front of you, palms up." In silence the dignified sheik bent down to each man and laid his face on their palms. As he lifted his face from the twelfth man, he pulled his sword.

"Get that gold, you thief, or else . . ." he shouted. Begging for mercy, the man ran for the hidden gold. He was beaten and released.

The next day Barton asked, "Sheik, how did your donkey tell you?"

"Don't tell my men. I soaked mint in water and put it on my donkey's tail, knowing that all the men would pull his tail but the thief. His hands, alone, had no smell of mint upon them." Be sure your sin will find you out.

E.E.L. and J.H.L.

THE BOY WHO COULD DO WHAT HE WAS TOLD

And they said, Thou hast not defrauded us, nor oppressed us, neither hast thou taken ought of any man's hand. 1 Samuel 12:4.

That was a wonderful testimony to Samuel, who at this time was an old man—wasn't it? He could look back over his long life and with assurance he could say he had never taken anything from the people—he had always dealt fairly with them. Samuel was a man of great honesty and integrity.

Harry Holden was a junior of integrity too. He read an ad in the paper for a boy to work at old Bill Haynes's store. He hurried over to apply.

"What can you do?" the old man asked rather gruffly.

Harry hesitated. There were many things he thought he could do, but he was timid about boasting. "I can do what I'm told," he responded a bit shyly.

"You can do what you're told, can you?" Old Bill was impressed. "Suppose I were to tell you to stand on your head once every hour. Could you do that?"

Harry was both amused and determined: "I could and I would, sir," he replied unhesitatingly.

"What if I told you to go into the grocery store next to my shop and watch your chance to pick up a loaf of bread and run back here with it without paying for it?"

Harry was disappointed. Maybe he shouldn't work here.

"I couldn't do that, sir," he said firmly.

"But I thought you said you could do what you were told!"

"You see, sir," Harry explained, "I was told about that a long time ago. The Bible says, 'Thou shalt not steal,' and I could not do that."

"Do you mean you would put that before what *I* tell you to do?" Mr. Haynes demanded.

"Yes, sir," Harry was firm, "I would have to."

Old Bill reached out his hand to Harry. "Boy," he began, "you are just the one I'm looking for—I want a boy who will put God even before me. You are hired."

God needs boys and girls today like Samuel and Harry—young people of integrity, who are upright and honest, who cannot be bought or sold—who make serving God the first consideration in their lives.

R.H.P.

READ HIS LETTER

Search the scriptures; . . . they are they which testify of me.
John 5:39.

Mrs. Sloane was heartbroken when her husband died shortly after they celebrated their golden wedding anniversary. For days she wandered through the house he had built before they were married and where they had lived so long. She called him by name, but there was no answer.

Preparing to sell the house and move into an apartment, she came across a bundle of letters in a trunk in the attic. They were messages written to her by John before their marriage. As she reread them, it seemed as if he were speaking to her again, and somehow they brought peace to her heart.

In another house in another city a young woman laid down the book she had been reading, remarking to her sister that it was the dullest book she had ever read. About a year later she became engaged to marry a young man. One day she remarked:

"I have a book in my library whose author has the same name as you. Isn't that strange?"

"What is the name of the book?" he asked. She told him and he smiled.

"Not strange at all," he replied. "I wrote it."

That evening she picked up the book and read it through, and found it very interesting. What made the difference? She knew and admired the author.

Jesus left us messages in His Word, the Holy Bible. He wrote that Book by His holy prophets, and in it He tells us how much He loves us. That Book tells us what to do. If you don't find the Bible interesting, perhaps it is because, like the young woman, you do not know the Author. If you want to know Jesus, take out this Book and read it. It not only tells us about Him, but what He is planning for us.

During the Reformation it was a crime in many countries to read the Bible. Men and women read it secretly by night. The authorities often visited their homes, and if the Bible was found, the owners were cast into prison, and were sometimes burned at the stake. Do we value the privilege that is ours of reading and understanding this Book and its Author?

V.E.R.

KEEP ON BEING KIND

Let us not be weary in well doing: for in due season we shall reap, if we faint not. Galatians 6:9.

I have read a story about a very kind woman, the mother of three children. She was also a practicing physician, with many patients. So she was busy.

One of her patients was an elderly woman who had many ailments but who was very poor. There was no welfare aid available in those days but this kind doctor gave her the same attention that her paying patients received. The doctor listened patiently to her troubles and was sympathetic and kind. And the little old lady always left the office feeling better.

After one extremely exhausting day the doctor was tired and eager to get home to her three children. However, as she left her inner office she went through the reception room and saw this little old lady sitting there in the waiting room. Oh, no, not today, she thought. But instead of speaking impatiently or unkindly, she led her into her private office and motioned to a chair. "Now, my dear," she said sweetly, "what can I do for you?"

The patient replied, "Doctor, you have done so much for me. This time I wanted to do something for you. I pieced a quilt top for each of your children in the double wedding ring pattern." She took them out of her shopping bag and gave them to the doctor.

Tears filled the doctor's eyes. She glanced at all those tiny, tiny pieces sewed by hand—three big quilt tops. What a labor of love! How many months it must have taken to finish such a task.

"To think," the doctor later said, "to think I nearly spoke impatiently to her."

The doctor had the tops quilted for her three children. One of the daughters told the story many years later, and remarked: "Many times as I crawled beneath that beautiful comforter at night, I would remember that little woman. And sometimes when I was weary of working, the memory encouraged me to renewed effort."

The story may help us all to remember the words of today's text. "Be not weary in well doing: for in due season we shall reap, if we faint not."

A.A.E.

GATHERING FEATHERS

It is reported among the nations, and Geshem also says it, that you and the Jews intend to rebel; that is why you are building the wall; and you wish to become their king, according to this report. Nehemiah 6:6, RSV.

Circulating rumors has been one of man's favorite occupations since Satan began it in Eden. Gossip, like poisoned arrows, curses the school, church, and home. Through gossip Satan separates friend from friend and man from God. Not only does the gossiper sow discord by closing his eyes to all that is pure, honest, noble, and lovely, but he destroys the hope and courage of the innocent by whispered suggestions.

A young man, having spread a bad story about a good man, asked a kindly old priest what he could do to atone for his wicked words.

"Your punishment will be to take this sack of feathers to each house in town and drop one feather in each yard. Don't miss a single house. Then come back and tell me about it."

Happily the youth took the feathers, glad for this easy way to get rid of his guilt. Soon he was back with his empty sack.

"I'm finished. I dropped a feather in each yard. My job is done."

"Not yet, my boy. You must go back to each yard and collect every feather. You are finished when you bring them all back to me."

"But I can't, not in a hundred years. A breeze was blowing. The feathers have gone far. You are asking me to do the impossible."

Yes, unkind words can never be brought back, but go on and on for eternity. Like those feathers blown by the wind, you can never recover what you have said.

There is a way to get rid of all that is impure. You have often used a strainer or flour sifter. In some, the wires are far apart, but in others they are close and fine. God gave us a "strainer" verse in Philippians 4:8, through which our thoughts and words should pass. Before you speak, put each word through all eight strainers mentioned in the verse. Are they true, honest, just, pure, lovely, gracious (good report), excellent (virtuous), and admirable (praise)?

By the time you have sifted all your words through God's eight strainers, you will no longer be a gossiper.

E.E.L. and J.H.L.

THE DAY OF SALVATION

To day if ye will hear his voice, harden not your hearts. Hebrews 3:7, 8.

Sometimes juniors put off accepting Jesus as their Saviour. They would never say right out that they expect to be lost. They just want to have a "good time," and by and by they will follow Jesus. Of course, it is possible to do this, but the risks become greater every year. How do we know this?

Out of every twenty Christians, nineteen have given their hearts to Jesus before their twentieth birthday. After the age of twenty-five, only one person in ten thousand is converted, and after thirty-five, only one in fifty thousand! In view of these figures, you know why the Lord said, "To day . . . hear his voice."

In the times of your great-grandparents, the city streets were crowded with horse-drawn wagons and carriages. One day a young man driving a pair of spirited horses lost control. They tore madly down the street, straight toward a narrow bridge. A man on the sidewalk saw the danger. At the risk of his life, he leaped and grabbed the reins, and pulling back with all his might, finally brought the team to a standstill. The young man whose life he had saved was most grateful.

Years went by. A white-faced prisoner stood before a Chicago judge. The jury had brought in a verdict of first-degree murder. The judge asked the convict if he had anything to say before sentence was passed.

The prisoner looked at the judge earnestly.

"Judge, don't you recognize me?" he asked. The judge looked carefully, then shook his head.

"No, I don't remember ever seeing you before."

"Don't you remember how a number of years ago you stopped a team of horses and saved a young man's life?"

The judge nodded his head. It came back to him vividly.

"Oh judge, I am that man. You saved my life once; save it again."

"I'm sorry," the judge answered sadly, "but you have asked something I cannot do. Then I was your savior; today I am your judge."

Today, Jesus is our Saviour, pleading in the courts of heaven. But the time is soon coming when He will come to "judge the world with righteousness."

This is the day of salvation. Let us joyfully accept it.

V.E.R.

THE FORSAKEN LAMB

When my father and my mother forsake me, then the Lord will take me up. Psalm 27:10.

One spring a mother sheep had tiny triplets, too big a family for one ewe. One, especially puny and weak, was completely unable to push his stronger brothers aside for his mother's milk. He became weaker and weaker. The mother, busy with the healthier two, seemed unconcerned that this lamb was starving to death. How could the busy shepherd save the rejected one?

Then he found another ewe standing beside her dead lamb bleating as if her heart would break. She wouldn't be comforted, so the shepherd hid its body so the grieving mother couldn't see it. Realizing she would mourn herself sick over her dead lamb, he took the third starving triplet to her, to adopt as her own. The sorrowing mother smelled it, looked it over, and turned her back. When the hungry baby edged up to her, she pushed him away. He wasn't hers.

Something had to be done soon or both would die. Quickly the shepherd skinned the dead lamb, and carefully trimmed away all the meat. Cutting it down to the size of the weak, living lamb, he carefully tied the skin around its neck and legs, and carried it to the mourning mother. As soon as she smelled the skin, she snuggled up to the lamb. Believing it to be her own baby now, she hovered over it constantly. Never did a lamb have such tender, loving care as that tiny weak one. Gradually the little fellow improved. Accepted and no longer an outcast and a stranger, he followed his adopted mother everywhere. Soon he was frisking about with the other lambs. The false skin was discarded.

Do you ever feel forsaken, unloved, or misunderstood by your mother and dad? Ask the Good Shepherd to teach them how to love and understand you better. Maybe you have been unlovely, uncooperative, stubborn, rebellious, or selfish. Your parents need God's help to love you as God would have them. Each of you needs to turn to God. His love in your hearts can help you to listen sympathetically to one another, so that you will remove all that stands in the way of peace and harmony. If an earthly shepherd can bring a forsaken lamb to a grieving mother, surely Jesus can bring you and your parents together today.

E.E.L. and J.H.L.

THE NAME THAT GREW

*In the beginning God created the heaven and the earth.
Genesis 1:1.*

Many years ago in Aberdeen, Scotland, there lived a man who wanted to teach his little son that God had created him. Taking some mustard and cress seed, he went to the garden and wrote his boy's name in the soft dirt with his finger. Then he sprinkled the seed in the lines he had made. About ten days later, the little boy, who had just learned how to read, came running into his father's study.

"Daddy," he cried, "my name is in the garden!"

"Nonsense!" replied his father. "How could your name be in the garden? Don't be so foolish!"

"But Daddy, it is there. Come and see!"

"Well!" exclaimed Daddy when he read the name, "So it is! But really, that isn't so remarkable. It just happened to be there. Those plants just grew like that by chance." And he shrugged his shoulders.

The little fellow started to argue. "But, Daddy, how could my name grow by chance! Seeds don't just grow that way!"

"Oh?" questioned Daddy. "They don't?"

"No," stoutly declared the boy.

"Then do you think somebody put your name here in the garden?"

"Of course!"

Placing his arm around his son, Daddy drew him close. "You don't believe your name is there by chance and neither do I, because I planted it there." Then pointing to the sky and growing things around them he added, "See the beautiful sky and the white clouds? See the trees and flowers and vegetables? Look at old Spot over there. Do you think they just happened anymore than your name did in this garden?"

The lad shook his head.

"Son," Daddy continued, "some people will tell you that everything grew by chance. They believe that nobody made any of these beautiful things. Don't let them fool you. God created them and He made you too. You didn't just happen any more than your name did here in the garden."

Yes, "in the beginning God created the heaven and the earth."

M.H.

ARE WE PETER'S DISCIPLES?

And immediately Jesus stretched forth his hand, and caught him, and said unto him, O thou of little faith, wherefore didst thou doubt? Matthew 14:31.

A young man went away to college. When he returned after the first year, his faith in God and the Bible was gone. "I don't believe in anything I can't understand!" he told his father.

"Son," the father began patiently, "can you tell me how a black cow can eat green grass and give white milk to make yellow butter?"

While you are trying to solve that riddle let me tell you a story. Jesus had been praying on the mount while the disciples got into their boat and set out for the other side of the lake. After attempting to make their way across the tossing billows they looked up and saw Jesus walking toward them on the water.

The disciples could not understand how anyone could walk on water, but Jesus was doing that very thing. They believed the impossible because they saw it with their eyes.

You remember Peter spoke up: "Lord, if it be thou, bid me come unto thee on the water" (Matt. 14:28). Peter wanted to do what he couldn't understand, and he believed Jesus could help him. Jesus did. He bade Peter, "Come."

You know the story: as long as Peter kept his eyes on Jesus everything was great. He was doing the impossible. He could not understand how he could do it, but he was walking on the water.

Then a wave came between the disciple and his Master. Peter began to doubt what he was doing, and he began to sink. "And immediately Jesus stretched forth his hand, and caught him, and said unto him, O thou of little faith, wherefore didst thou doubt?"

Sometimes we find ourselves like Peter—no, not out on a lake walking on the water—but sometimes like Peter we have some questions come into our minds: Why does God let all of the bad luck come to me? Why do I have to have a leg broken just when I am planning for the big game? Doubt creeps into our minds and soon we become discouraged.

Don't be a disciple of Peter. Be Jesus' disciple. We have to trust God for some things that we can't understand.

R.H.P.

WHO WAS TRAPPED?

Trust in the Lord with all your heart, and do not rely on your own insight. Proverbs 3:5, RSV.

For many days Tom had been formulating his plan. Carefully he studied the chicken-wire pigeon house built just under the over-hanging eaves of the roof of the three-story apartment house opposite his home. He could easily shinny up the columns of the apartment house porch and climb over the porch canopy to get on the roof. Inching over the edge of the roof might be a bit tricky, but Tom, a good climber, knew he could do it. Then it would be a small matter to climb into the wire cage, pick out the best pigeon, and take it home for a pet.

Early one morning Tom put his plan into action. No one saw him cling to the roof edge and slowly crawl through the wire opening into the bird cage. It was a tight squeeze for a 15-year-old boy, but he made it. Inside, with the frightened pigeons, he chose the bird he wanted. Tucking it inside his shirt, he began wiggling and pushing through the opening he had entered. The wires bent in and he had been able to push through them; now they prevented his exit. He pushed, he squirmed, he wiggled, but he was helpless. Huddled fifty feet above the street below, surrounded by flapping pigeons, Tom panicked and yelled for help. Someone, hearing him, called the police, who called the fire department. Trapped inside, Tom waited helplessly.

Two companies of fire fighters arrived with the hook and ladder truck. By using the extension ladder, they reached him under the roof. With the fireman's help, Tom was pulled from his wire prison. Humiliated, he darted over the roof and down the porch columns instead of using the ladder. Just as his feet touched the ground, the pigeon inside his shirt found an opening, crawled out and flew into the air before Tom could grab it. He watched it land on the wire cage.

Tom put his trust in his own insight. Instead of trapping the pigeon, he trapped himself. One dishonest act, one little lie, one cigarette, just a taste of beer, one puff of marijuana—they are all traps, traps from which you cannot free yourself. Don't rely on your own insight, thinking you can get out by yourself. There is only one way to stay free—trust in the Lord with all your heart and obey Him.

E.E.L. and J.H.L.

HANDS—UGLY OR BEAUTIFUL?

Therefore now let your hands be strengthened, and be ye valiant. 2 Samuel 2:7.

Kathleen sighed. "I wish I had white dimpled hands like other girls. Just look at my great paws."

"Kathie, let me see the 'great paws,'" suggested her mother. As she carefully studied her daughter's hands, she asked, "What's the matter with them? I call them beautiful hands, just beautiful!"

"Mother, how can you say that?"

"My darling, I can explain all the blemishes on your big hands. That brown comes from the kiss of the sun and the caress of the wind. It tells of outdoor life, of nutting excursions. Your hands are clean and neatly kept, Kathleen."

The young girl persisted, "See all these scars, burns, and needle pricks."

The mother drew the offending hands fondly to her lips. "In my eyes, dear, these blemishes are only beauty spots. I know about those needle pricks. Last night you hemmed the sails for Jack's new boat, though you wanted to finish an interesting book you had started. That burn is the reminder of the night when my helpful daughter got supper. Those scratches? Remember how I longed for some wild blackberries? My dear girl spent her holiday picking them for me. This cut came because your helpfulness was greater than your skill when you helped little Harold transform his shingle into a big ship. I thank God for your beautiful hands that constantly lighten my load."

After that loving explanation Kathleen looked down at her hands with a happy light in her eyes. Unnoticed, her brother Jack had slipped in to eavesdrop on the conversation. "You've got tip-top hands, Kate. Some girls won't go anywhere or do anything because of their manicures. You aren't always afraid of spoiling your hands."

Mother pinned this clipping on a cushion in Kathleen's room: "I saw a pair of hands—small, shapely with nestling dimples. These hands never lifted another's load; never were raised to wipe away the mourner's tear; never were roughened by any work for others; nor were they ever folded in prayer. God said, 'Ugly hands.'

"I saw another pair—hands which wiped away falling tears, which were misshapen with hard work for others. Ugly hands? God and His angels called them 'beautiful hands.'"

L.C.W.

BOND OF PERFECTNESS

Above all these things put on charity, which is the bond of perfectness. Colossians 3:14.

"Mother, please buy me that big picture puzzle." Lynette looked wistfully at the beautiful stack of puzzle boxes.

"You mean that one with 1,200 pieces! Why you would never finish it."

But a few minutes later Lynette emerged from the store with the picture puzzle. It showed a lovely sunrise scene over a harbor, with small ships at the wharf and fishermen arriving to begin their day's work. Later she spread it out on the apartment floor, all 1,200 pieces of the puzzle.

"Where shall we start with it? I think I'll put one of these ships together. That will be easy." That evening Lynette matched about one hundred pieces. But that was the easy part. The next time she worked on it she found that there were hundreds of pieces of blue that could be either ocean or sky.

"Do you mind if I try?" big brother Ned asked. "I think I could do that part of the sunrise where the red is in the sky." By now, mother, father, and the whole family were all trying their hand at the puzzle. Each would add a piece or two. Days stretched into a week and still hundreds of pieces remained to be placed where they belonged.

"I don't think I'll ever pick out a puzzle as large as this again," confessed Lynette as she finally finished the sea and started on the sky.

"I just can't find this piece of wharf. Do you think they could have left any pieces out?" asked Ned. "You didn't pick any up with the vacuum cleaner, did you, Mother?"

But the day came when the race to fit in the last twenty or thirty pieces began. Lynette tucked one piece away so she could have the honor of putting the last piece in. Finally it was finished, each interlocking unit adding to the beauty of the whole.

When God puts the picture of our lives together there are no missing pieces. That is the sort of care that Someone who loves us takes!

W.R.L.S.

UNFAILING LOVE

Charity never faileth. 1 Corinthians 13:8.

Today we would say: "Love never fails," for that is what this verse means. It is a wonderful thought that God loves everyone, the bad, as well as the good.

It would be too bad if God's love were here today and gone tomorrow. A minister was visiting a farmer who belonged to his church. He noticed high up on the weather vane on top of the barn that the farmer had painted a Bible verse—GOD IS LOVE.

"How do you like it?" asked the farmer.

The minister looked at it for a moment, then shook his head.

"I wish you didn't have it there" he replied.

"But why?" asked the surprised farmer. "Isn't that a good motto for us all to remember?"

"Well," replied the pastor, "when the wind comes from the north the motto will point north, and when it blows from the south, it will point south. I'm afraid that people looking at it up there will think that the love of God changes every time the wind does."

This time it was the farmer who shook his head.

"I don't see it that way at all. Even if the motto changes directions, it still teaches a lesson. When the wind blows hot, God is love. When it brings rain, God is love. Whatever way the wind blows, God's love remains."

A schoolteacher once had a problem boy in his room. He was disobedient, noisy, and a real troublemaker. The teacher tried everything he could think of to bring the boy into harmony with the school. He kept him in; assigned punishment work, even used the switch, but nothing seemed to work.

One day when this pupil had been kept after school, the teacher sat down beside him at his desk and put his arm around him.

"Billy," he said softly, "I know what it is to have no mother, for mine died when I was only five years old. But I am sure that both your mother and mine would want us to be kind, obedient, and helpful. I love you, son, and will try to take the place of your mother if you will let me. Try and live as she would want you to live."

That talk meant a great deal to the lonely boy. Somebody cared for him. Soon everyone noticed the change in Billy. There is great power in love.

V.E.R.

DON'T BE A TURTLE

Say to them that are of a fearful heart, Be strong, fear not: behold, your God will come . . . and save you. Isaiah 35:4.

Are you afraid when you enter a room because you think everyone is looking at you? Are you filled with fear when asked to stand before an audience? Do you hesitate to try new games, engage in new sports, or learn new skills? Why do you refuse to share your musical talents with others?

Maybe it's because you are like the turtle. Turtles on the whole are nice creatures, but like many people, they think mostly of themselves. The turtle carries with him a strong fortress against the outside world—his shell. Whenever he is confronted with a new situation or meets an unknown creature, he draws his head, arms, and legs completely inside his shell. Then he closes the lower part tightly against the upper shell. He feels snug—perfectly safe. Turtles live a long time, some even more than a century, because those around them usually tire of trying to find a way to contact the real Mr. Turtle. They go away and leave him alone. But inside that shell it gets lonely. Could that shell represent selfishness?

Have you ever pulled yourself into your shell, only peeking out as far as necessary? If anyone gets too close to you do you pop your head back inside for protection? Do unexpected encounters with trying circumstances bring about the same response?

Could it be that you are fearful because you are selfish? Are you embarrassed because your self-centered thoughts make you act and talk foolishly? Do you hesitate to try new things because you are afraid others will think of you as a failure? Are you constantly thinking up defensive excuses for your actions? Such excuses usually reveal the basic cause of fear—the sin of selfishness.

Don't be a turtle. Throw away your shell and start thinking about others rather than yourself. Let God save you from all your fears. He'll gladly give you strength for your weakness, confidence instead of fear. Instead of crawling into your shell, hide self in Jesus and you'll be free to enjoy a happy life.

E.E.L. and J.H.L.

THE SIGNAL LIGHT

He is your shield and helper and your glorious sword.
Deuteronomy 33:29, NIV.

Many stories are told of things that happened in the early days of railroading. One is about Henry, a fireman, and George, an engineer. They were crew on a passenger train many years ago when the headlights were still gas lamps.

One dark night rain fell so fast that it was hard to see ahead of the train. Henry and George were straining their eyes to scan the tracks ahead of them, as their passenger train moved along through the night.

All at once George thought he saw a signal of flickering lantern light, as if a light had been waved up and down to signal them to stop the train. But it was so faint he wasn't sure. He slowed and asked Henry if he had seen anything.

"I thought I saw a signal light," Henry said. So they brought the train to a halt and looked back along the tracks, but they saw nothing. They got out and walked ahead of the train to see whether there was trouble. And there only a hundred yards ahead of them a rain-swollen river rushed and the bridge was out.

Back along the track they went to try to find the unknown person who had signaled them to stop, saving their lives and the lives of all on the train. But there was no person in sight. There was no sign of any lantern, no indication that anyone had been near the track at all in the spot where they thought they had seen the signal.

Thoroughly drenched, they climbed back into the cab of the train and reached for their dry jackets hanging there. Then Henry noticed the faint signal again, as if it were right beside the cab at that moment.

Mystified, they got out to investigate, and there, caught between the wire grating and the glass of their acetylene lamp was a large moth. As it made another effort to flap its wings and get away, the light of the lamp flickered from the shadow of the huge moth. George got back into the cab and Henry watched to see whether the moth would try again to move its wings. When it did, the shadow made the flicker of light they had thought was the signal to stop the train.

God can use many ways to send us warning messages. Let us watch for His signals each day.

R.E.

AN ANGEL TOOK THE WHEEL

The angel of the Lord encampeth round about them that fear him, and delivereth them. Psalm 34:7.

Betty Summers taught church school in one of the rougher parts of America. In the winter months she had to drive several miles home alone in the dark. Frequently a thoughtful State-patrol officer would follow her in his car to assure that she reached home safely. When she turned off the highway into her driveway the patrolman would wave and drive off.

One wintry evening when the ground was covered with snow and the roads were slick and icy, Betty got into her car and drove cautiously up and down the steep, winding road home. Behind her drove the patrolman, ready to assist if needed.

When Betty turned into the driveway, instead of tooting his horn and driving on, the patrolman drove in behind her car.

"Who was that man in the seat beside you coming home tonight?" he asked with a perplexed look on his face, "and where is he now?"

"There was no man with me," Betty replied.

"Oh, yes, there was," the officer responded confidently. "I could see him with you all the way home. I noticed, too, that several times when your car nearly slipped down the bank he took the wheel to help you."

"It must have been an angel," the young woman exclaimed joyously, "for God knew I needed help tonight."

The officer walked around the car in the snow. There were no footprints. "It must have been!" he agreed, shaking his head in bewilderment as he walked back to his patrol car. "I sure saw someone in the car with you!"

Betty certainly experienced the fulfillment of the Lord's promise: "Angels of God will preserve His people while they walk in the path of duty."—*Evangelism*, p. 607.

She, likewise, can understand what the Lord's servant means when she writes: "From what dangers, seen and unseen, we have been preserved through the interposition of the angels, we shall never know, until in the light of eternity we see the providences of God. Then we shall know that the whole family of heaven was interested in the family here below, and that messengers from the throne of God attended our steps from day to day."—*The Desire of Ages*, p. 240.

R.H.P.

ASK

Ask, and it shall be given you; seek, and ye shall find; knock, and it shall be opened unto you. Matthew 7:7.

Christy wanted a piano, but her family couldn't afford one. She decided to pray about it. Every day she prayed, though Mother told her that was too tall an order for the family budget. Christy kept praying.

Then one day while Christy was in school, a delivery truck stopped before the house. The deliveryman carried in a used piano! Church friends had sent it for Christy.

Mother called them. They said they had no idea that Christy had been praying for a piano; they just wanted her to have one so she could take lessons.

When Christy came home from school the family met her at the driveway. They blindfolded her and carried her to the house and set her on the piano bench. She touched the keys and said, "I *knew* He would send it."

Del asked for something too. When he went away to college he didn't have much money. He wasn't sure how he would be able to work his way through. But he determined to do it with God's help. Each morning he put his needs before the Lord, asking that the day's necessities be supplied.

A day came when Del was getting behind in his bill. He knew that a student's bill was not allowed to run too high, and he was afraid that he would be asked to leave school. He prayed especially hard that morning.

In the middle of the morning someone brought him a note requesting that he come to the office of the financial manager, Mr. Gray.

This is it, Del thought. And he wondered *why* God was answering No. He felt discouraged as the manager asked him to sit down.

"Do you know a Mr. John Hebert?" the manager asked.

"Why, yes," Del said. "He goes to the same church as my folks."

"Well," said the financial manager, "this morning we got a check for three hundred dollars in the mail from Mr. Hebert for application to your account."

God wants us to bring our requests to Him. Let Him supply your needs. Ask Him today.

R.E.

"BE STRONG AND OF A GOOD COURAGE"

Have not I commanded thee? Be strong and of a good courage; be not afraid, neither be thou dismayed: for the Lord thy God is with thee whithersoever thou goest. Joshua 1:9.

Before he became President of the United States, General Dwight D. Eisenhower was president of Columbia University. At that time he uttered these thought-provoking words: "America is exactly as strong as the initiative, courage, understanding, and loyalty of the individual citizen."

Now see how it appeals to you to change the first and last words of that sentence. Here is how it reads: "The church is exactly as strong as the initiative, courage, understanding, and loyalty of the individual member."

Is God's command merely to the ministers or church leaders? Is it not also to every member, young and old? Is not God counting on every member to help finish His work on the earth?

There are two very important words in that sentence—*courage* and *loyalty*. Does not God still speak to every member of the church: "Have not I commanded thee? Be strong and of a good courage!" Soldiers on the battlefield need courage every day. One young soldier back from service tried to get out of telling his harrowing experiences by saying that nothing ever happened to him. But the woman who was questioning him was persistent. She said, *"Something* must have happened. Now tell me, in all your experiences, what was it that struck you most?"

"Well, ma'am," said the soldier after some thought, "the thing that struck me most was the number of bullets that missed me."

It takes courage to face bullets, even if all of them miss you. And it takes courage to be a good soldier for Jesus.

The second word in the sentence that especially impressed me was the word *loyalty*. And that is the idea that Moffatt uses in 2 Timothy 2:3: "Join the ranks of those who bear suffering, *like a loyal soldier* of Christ Jesus."

God spoke to Joshua in his day, urging him to be strong and of a good *courage,* and He also speaks to us today—be strong, courageous, and loyal. Strong, courageous, loyal soldiers of Jesus will *Go on God's Errands!* And they keep going Straight Ahead!

A.A.E.

THE RUNT

Rest in the Lord, and wait patiently for him. Psalm 37:7.

Twelve-year-old Harold was astonished. There before his eyes was a baby Carolina wren tied to its nest with a horsehair! Surely mother birds don't tie their babies up! But Harold knew this one did because he watched her do it. He could hear the rest of the baby birds outside learning to fly, but the smallest one, the runt, was tied up in bed!

Mr. and Mrs. Wren had built their home in the storeroom of an unfinished house and after the owners moved in, the birds decided to stay. To reach their snug little nest they had to fly in an upstairs window, down the stairs, and through the kitchen. And now it was time to teach the little ones to fly. Four of the five baby birds went out for their lessons, but the littlest one was still tied to his nest.

As Harold was watching, the mother bird flew in, settled on the edge of the nest for a moment, fed the baby a fat juicy worm, and flew off again.

Poor little thing, thought Harold. If his mother isn't going to set him free, I'll help him myself. And he broke the horsehair that was apparently tangled around the bird's leg. It was then that he saw the mother bird, on her next trip, tie the baby up again. So he wasn't just accidentally tangled up there. He was tied on purpose. At intervals all through the day the parents would bring food and encouragement to the little runt, then away they would go back to the training of the rest of their brood.

That night Harold found the four bigger fledglings sleeping outside with their father, but the mother slept with the runt.

Early the next morning Harold was down to see what was happening in the nest. It was empty. The thread was broken and the mother was coaxing her baby across the kitchen floor. Except when she went for worms, she was with that baby all day. It took her until noon to get him as far as the stairs. Then one by one he fluttered up the steps. He seemed to be getting stronger all the time, but she let him rest after each step, and sometimes he even went to sleep. At last he reached the window sill and tumbled out to join his brothers and sisters in the bay tree.

Harold decided that if baby birds can wait patiently for their mothers, surely he ought to "rest in the Lord, and wait patiently for him."

M.H.

MOSS PIE

Turn now, every one of you, from his evil way and wrong doings. Jeremiah 25:5, RSV.

What a joy to visit grandfather's farm! Tony, with his brothers and sisters, chose to go there above any other place, for there was so much to see and do. Best of all, Grandfather spent time with them, showing them new discoveries or revealing secrets that only a large farm can have.

Grandma's blueberry pies were another special treat. Before the pies could be made, someone had to pick blueberries. So Grandfather called the children to go with him to the wild bushes that were several feet high, thick with many green leaves, and in late summer were loaded with berries.

The wild berries were small, but delicious. As they picked, the children, as well as Grandpa, soon had blue color around their mouths and on their teeth, for not all the berries went into the pails. The sun was hot, so Tony soon found a place in the shade where he was hidden by the bushes. While the others picked he rested. Soon Grandfather announced, "Time to go." Although Tony had chosen the smallest pail, his was only half full. Beside him was growing a lot of moss. Quickly he dumped the berries in his lap, filled his pail with moss, and put the berries on the top. They were rounded high as he handed them to Grandpa.

"Good boy, Tony," smiled Grandpa. "I'm proud of your hard work."

The next day when Grandma made pies Tony was pleased when she baked a little pie just for him. It looked so good. He could hardly wait for time to eat dessert. But when he began to eat it he found under the top berries nothing but moss.

Grandpa was watching as Tony looked up with a hurt, surprised look. Smiling, he put a loving hand on Tony's shoulder and said, "Tony, when you cheat others, you really cheat yourself."

That was the turning point in Tony's life. He learned that being lazy isn't the happy way of life. Every time Satan tempted him to cheat, even just a little, he thought of the day when everyone else had a large delicious piece of blueberry pie, and he had moss.

If you have been cheating yourself, Jesus says, "Turn, every one."

E.E.L. and J.H.L.

CHANGED BY A LOOK

For the righteous Lord loveth righteousness; his countenance doth behold the upright. Psalm 11:7.

A little girl wandered into an art gallery. On every side beautiful pictures looked down on her. Entranced, she went from one to another, capturing with her eyes the landscapes and portraits.

Suddenly she stopped in her tracks. Before her hung the most beautiful portrait of a gracious and lovely lady. She looked up, feasting on the draping of her clothes and the richness of their embroidery. Such a sweet and beautiful face she had never seen.

Then she glanced at her own ragged dress, dirty feet and hands. She paused a long time studying the picture. Her hand strayed to her untidy hair. Finally she turned and went out into the street.

But the next day she was back looking intently at the picture. An attendant intrigued by her interest in the picture spoke to her. "She's lovely, isn't she?" "Sir, she's not just lovely, she's the most beautiful person I have ever seen. Who is she?" "She is a princess, and a great artist painted her for the king. Don't you wish you could be like her?"

Again the next day the girl returned. This time the attendant noticed that her dress had been mended; her hair shone from a vigorous brushing; her feet had been washed. Again she stared wistfully into the face of the lady in the picture.

As the days went by a change came in her little face. The influence of beauty was changing her life. She was no longer a street urchin but a sweet young lady, tidy and clean.

In the forest, pine trees stretch straight and tall toward the sun. Even on the steepest slope they rise vertically. And below, the roots reach out to the water and minerals that lie hidden in the soil. These upright trees remain that way because they reach for the sun, and because they are anchored securely in the soil.

Jesus Christ is the righteous One. Anchor yourself in the Word of God and reach for the Son. This way you may become like Him.

W.R.L.S.

THE SHEPHERD KNOWS YOU

I am the good shepherd, and know my sheep, and am known of mine. John 10:14.

One afternoon a tourist visiting the Holy Land saw an interesting sight. He saw two shepherds with flocks of sheep come together from opposite directions. In a moment, hundreds of sheep were milling around. Surely, thought the tourist, those sheep will never get sorted out. He was mistaken. After a little confusion, the shepherds separated and walked along the road in opposite directions. First one, then the other would call. Without a moment's hesitation, each sheep turned and walked toward the voice of its shepherd. They knew that voice, and the shepherd knew his sheep.

Do you know the Shepherd? You have heard Him say, "Follow Me." You have a desire to belong to Him, to be one of His sheep, to be near Him. The Good Shepherd knows every sheep by name, and to save even one He would have come to this world and died on Calvary.

It is not enough to know *about* the Shepherd, we must know *Him.* One evening a man stood on the platform of a large lecture hall, giving recitations. He really knew how to use his voice. Toward the end of a most interesting and inspiring program, he asked whether anyone present had a favorite recitation or reading he would particularly like to hear. An old man stood up.

"Please, sir, give us the twenty-third psalm."

"Very well," replied the speaker, "I will do so on one condition. After I have given it, you must give it also." This would demonstrate how much better he could speak than this old man.

The speaker recited the twenty-third psalm. Every tone was perfect, every gesture correct, every word distinct. When he finished there was a storm of applause. He turned to the old man, quietly standing on the platform, and invited him to recite it, which he did. There was a tremble in his voice as he spoke of his Shepherd. There was no applause when he finished, but there were tears in the eyes of many in the audience.

The elocutionist stepped forward, clasped the old man by the hand, and said to the audience, his voice trembling with emotion:

"I know the twenty-third psalm. This man knows the Shepherd."

Let us listen to Jesus' voice today and let Him lead us.

V.E.R.

STRATEGY THAT WORKED

Then said Jesus, Father, forgive them; for they know not what they do. Luke 23:34.

When Lester went back to school after a bout with rheumatic fever, he was no longer the runner he had been. In his absence a new boy had enrolled, and his two best friends, Danny and Lonnie, appeared to have banded together with Gordon to torment him about his lack of strength. Gordon called him Chief Paleface and would shout, "Get off our ball field, Paleface, and let us play ball."

This teasing really got under Lester's skin. One day at home his dad noticed that something was wrong. "Things go badly at school today? It'll take a while to get your old vim and vigor back."

"It's Gordon, the new boy," Lester blurted out. Soon he was telling Dad all about the teasing he had endured during the two weeks he had been back. Dad did not laugh at the problem, but appeared deep in thought.

Finally he spoke. "Why don't you fight him with strategy? Fight that Gordon with words. Meet him in the open and vanquish your enemy. Next time he calls you 'Paleface' or makes some mean remark agree with him as much as you can. Tell how you admire him and hope to be as strong as he is some day. He'll stagger from such a blow. You might even suggest that he coach you."

"O.K., Dad. Sort of heaping coals of fire on his head. I get the idea."

The next morning Gordon and Lester met at the school gate. Scornfully Gordon said, "Let me open the gate for you. That's too much effort for Paleface."

"I'd sure like to be as strong as you are. I have watched your success on the ball field. You can do most everything the best." Gordon's mouth dropped open.

Lester noticed his advantage. "Say, I'm not strong enough yet to ride my scooter. Come over after school and you ride it down our long winding driveway from the garage to the road. How about it?" Gordon's eyes gleamed. "Sure thing. I don't have a scooter. I'd love to come."

Lester felt content and thought to himself, *Wait till I tell Dad. I hit him right between the eyes.*

L.C.W.

WHERE ARE THEY NOW?

Take heed, and beware of all covetousness; for a man's life does not consist in the abundance of his possessions. Luke 12:15, RSV.

About 150 years ago naturalist Alexander Wilson sat all day in a Kentucky woods, watching one of the most spectacular scenes ever beheld. Flying steadily past him at about sixty miles an hour was a mass of migrating passenger pigeons. They flew in closely packed columns on a front more than a mile wide. Wilson estimated that this flock (one of many) was 240 miles long in flight and contained 2 billion pigeons.

With the beat of their wings sounding like a windstorm they cruised over the forest looking for acorns and wild nuts, and would eat enough to fill a warehouse 100 feet high, 100 feet wide, and 25 miles long.

Where are these passenger pigeons now? You'll never see one alive, for although there were billions, not one is living today.

When word came that a flock was coming to an area to roost, mobs of people gathered for mass slaughtering. Blinding the birds with torches, they clubbed them to death, suffocated them with burning sulphur, or cut down the trees in which thousands were roosting. Mangled dead and dying birds lay in heaps, until each person had gotten all he could dispose of through drying, pickling, salting, or eating. Then herds of pigs fattened up on the remainder.

Thousands of people traveled from one nesting site to another just to kill and process the birds. Millions were shipped to distant areas. An equal number were burned, trampled, eaten by hogs, or spoiled. Within seventy years there were no nesting sites. Only a few scattered pigeons remained. Ten years later the only passenger pigeons left were in zoos.

In 1908 the total population was seven. By 1910 only the female bird, Martha, remained. She died at the age of 29 years in 1914, and is now mounted in the Smithsonian Institution in Washington, D.C.

What a sad memorial to the covetousness of man! Are you, too, never satisfied with what you have, always wanting more? Before it's too late, listen to Jesus, "Beware of all covetousness; for a man's life does not consist in the abundance of his possessions."

E.E.L. and J.H.L.

IN THE MORNING

In the morning, rising up a great while before day, he went out, and departed into a solitary place, and there prayed. Mark 1:35.

Jesus in His ministry lived a busier life than any of us are called upon to lead. He had more people problems, too, as He was followed by both well-wishers and those who wanted to get rid of Him. Yet He never was too busy to begin His day by meeting the heavenly Father in prayer. This was the secret of His ability to carry out His mission.

Morning prayer was so important to Daniel that he would rather be cast into the den of lions than to skip that appointment with God.

Beginning the day with prayer gives a person the necessary strength to resist temptation, to do cheerfully and well the duties of the day, to take care of things that don't go according to plan. It makes things go better all day long.

In the book *Alone With God* are listed five advantages of having a prayer time early in the morning.

1. Sure of the time.
2. Economical—other hours are crowded.
3. The quiet hour of the day.
4. Leaves its impress on the entire day.
5. Seems to be our Master's preference.

When Buddy read those reasons, he said, "Wait a minute. The last two sound all right, but I can't go along with the first three. No one has time in the morning—those are the most crowded hours of the day. And with everyone hurrying to get ready for work or school, it is not the quiet hour of the day, either, but the very noisiest."

Buddy missed the point. Our text does not say to lie in bed until the very last minute. The example that Jesus left us was to rise up a great while before day. This means, decide how much time you need for Bible study and prayer in the morning in order to give you the power you need for the day, and then get up that much *earlier* or a little bit more, in order to be sure of the time. And if you do that, you *will* find a quiet hour. Try it.

But most important of all is that we each *do* find—and keep—a quiet time with God. If you haven't yet, why not talk it over with your family or some close friends and see what special time you can set aside for keeping in touch with God.

R.E.

DO YOU HAVE A BACKBONE OR A WISHBONE?

So let us not become tired of doing good; for if we do not give up, the time will come when we will reap the harvest. Galatians 6:9, TEV.

"Abraham Lincoln failed in business in 1831, was defeated for the Legislature in 1832, failed in business again in 1833, was elected to the Legislature in 1834, lost his dearly beloved sweetheart by death in 1835, had a nervous breakdown in 1836, was defeated for speaker of the State Legislature in 1838, was defeated for elector in 1840, was defeated for Congress in 1843, was elected to Congress in 1846, was defeated for re-election in 1848, was defeated for vice-president of the U.S. in 1856, was defeated for the Senate in 1858. But he was elected President of America in 1860."*

Most men would have given up seeking public office and would have turned to some other work for a livelihood—but not Abraham Lincoln. He had a backbone where many people have only wishbones. Lincoln hung right on, refusing to let defeat make him bitter or cause him to quit.

What was the secret of Lincoln's success? Do you suppose we might find the secret stamped on a penny? Get a penny out of your pocket or purse and have a look. Notice the words right over President Lincoln's head—what are they? Look carefully. They read, "In God we trust."

It's easy to give up when the way is rough, when people oppose us, when circumstances are against us—just give up and say it can't be done. Maybe you are finding math or history hard in school. Maybe you have to work after school, although you would much rather be playing with your friends. Maybe you are ill and there doesn't seem much hope of getting well. Perhaps a friend has turned against you.

When you find yourself in a tight spot, be a Lincoln. Hang right in there. Try again. Don't give up!

In our text for today Paul refers to our Christian life. This is even more important than the sort of battles we have been talking about. Perhaps someone makes fun of you because you are a Seventh-day Adventist, and you think of giving up. Read our text over again. With God's help, be a Lincoln—trust in God and don't give up!

---

*The Quiet Hour *Echoes,* Feb., 1976.   **R.H.P.**

"I WAS ONLY TESTING YOU"

But he knows every detail of what is happening to me; and when he has examined me, he will pronounce me completely innocent—as pure as solid gold! Job 23:10 (TLB).

My friend Norman was a very successful colporteur. When he knocked at a certain door a man opened it and said in a friendly manner, "Come in, young man, come in."

Norman entered and began to give his regular canvass as he pointed to some pictures in the book. Suddenly the man held up his hand and said, "That's enough. That's a religious book. I am an infidel. I don't believe in God. I don't believe in Christianity. In fact, I have never met a real Christian in my life."

Norman was shocked. He closed his prospectus, looked straight in the man's eyes and said, "Sir, you are looking at a Christian right now. I am a real Christian."

With that Norman again opened his prospectus and, with utter confidence, continued with his canvass. When he was through, the man spoke up and said, "I'll take the book in the five-dollar binding."

Norman said, "Thank you, sir." After completing the order form, he added, "I will deliver your book three weeks from today."

Three weeks later he returned. The man had seen him through the window and opened the door just as Norman started to tear the wrapper off the book. He said, "Don't tear the wrapper off. I don't want the book."

Norman, very politely, said, "Sir, this is the book you ordered."

The man roared, "I don't want it. You heard me, didn't you?" Then he angrily cursed Norman.

Norman remained calm. He put the book under his arm and said, "Sir, you don't need to be angry. If you don't want the book, you don't have to take it. I'm sorry, though, for this book has done so much for me. I wish every man on earth had this book."

He was walking toward the gate when the man overtook him. He was smiling and had a five-dollar bill in his hand. "Young man," he said, "here is your money. Give me that book! You *are* a Christian. I apologize for cursing you. I was only testing you, and you stood the test."

A.A.E.

ACT AS IF

For a day in thy courts is better than a thousand. I had rather be a doorkeeper in the house of my God, than to dwell in the tents of wickedness. Psalm 84:10.

Carole had never heard of Seventh-day Adventists until she was fourteen years old. Then the welfare department placed her in the Adventist foster home of Don and Mamie Cole.

Everything was very different than it had been in her own home. It wasn't just that the Coles went to church on Saturday instead of Sunday—Carole had never gone to church anyway. It wasn't that they ate other things instead of meat, didn't smoke, or drink alcoholic beverages. It was *everything.*

For instance, at her house the whole family had never sat down at the table all at once, passed food around, and had a meal together except on Christmas or Thanksgiving. The Coles did it every day. The table was set just so, even though no company was coming.

After the meal, dishes were washed immediately. In Carole's home no one bothered to wash dishes until there were none left to eat from.

At the Coles before anyone left for work or school, the family gathered in the living room and formed a prayer circle. Mr. Cole prayed for God to be with each member of the family that day, mentioning each one specifically by name.

In the evening the family gathered for worship again, and after a short, interesting story, some member of the family offered prayer.

Carole liked it. She liked everything about that home. She even enjoyed going to church. Before she had been there a year, she decided that she wanted to be a Seventh-day Adventist too.

She also decided something else. She wanted to be a Christian lady like Mrs. Cole. But she wasn't sure how to go about it. Then she thought of a plan. She would make a list of how a Christian lady would act, how a Christian lady would dress, how a Christian lady would talk, how a Christian lady would look. Then she would try to be as much like that list as she possibly could.

It was hard at first. She fell short of living up to her ideal. But as weeks and months went by, Carole found it easier and easier. By the time she was ready to graduate from high school, she had become so much like the Christian lady of her list that it was no longer an effort to act that way, dress that way, talk that way, look that way. It was second nature. She had become a Christian lady!

R.E.

DON'T BE A CHESTNUT BUR

Strengthened with all might, according to his glorious power, unto all patience and longsuffering with joyfulness. Colossians 1:11.

What kind of strength is Paul talking about? Since he adds "with all might" it must be a special kind of strength. Surely it is not "might" that will hurt and bruise others. It couldn't mean using hasty, harsh words that injure us more than the one to whom we say them. No, it speaks of strength to have patience, to be longsuffering, with joyfulness.

The chestnut is a beautiful tree with spreading branches and grows in parts of North America, Asia, Africa, and Europe. There are many species of chestnuts, but all have one thing in common. Growing among the serrated glossy green leaves is the tasty fruit known as the chestnut. Most are good to eat, although a few species may be poisonous. The hawkers in their little stands on the streets of Asian cities enjoy a thriving business selling the delicious roasted chestnuts.

But getting to the nuts is not pleasant. Whether there is one or several nuts in a cluster, they are always encased in a prickly bur. Sometimes these fruit spikes are less than an inch long, but in other kinds they may be four inches in length. Unless your fingers are well protected you won't enjoy opening the chestnut bur.

Lots of people are like chestnut burs. They prick whenever touched. Instead of cultivating in their lives the precious plant of love, their unkind actions bring discouragement and despair. Unlike their loving Saviour, they do great harm by their prickly, unsympathetic words and acts. God doesn't approve of their narrow, critical, self-righteous attitude, particularly when aimed toward the young and inexperienced.

Jesus understands and patiently lifts up those who make mistakes. It grieves Him to hear harsh, nagging, rasping words of criticism and condemnation. But He loves to give you His glorious power and strength so that you can fill others with joy and hope.

Never be like the chestnut bur and hurt those who touch your life. Jesus offers freely His glorious power to the patient and longsuffering.

E.E.L. and J.H.L.

A REMARKABLE JOURNEY

To you, O Lord, I lift up my soul; in you I trust, O my God. Ps. 25:1.

When his master left to join the Army Dental Corps, Joker made himself a one-dog search party to locate him. Usually he would be gone two or three days, but finally he departed on a 6,000 mile journey that took three months. Mrs. Raye was astonished when her husband wrote: "This morning I was greeted by an old friend of ours, who is now a world traveler—Joker!"

Unfortunately, Joker could not tell all about his odyssey from Pittsburg, California, to the hot little island of Biak off northwestern New Guinea. From various Army men Captain Raye pieced together the following.

His pet had first gone the thirty miles to the Oakland pier from which his master had departed weeks earlier. Carefully Joker scrutinized the soldiers. Either he followed someone or was carried up the gangplank of a troop transport. The dog kept well hidden until the ship was out at sea.

He made friends with two Army medics in the dispensary, and they provided the dog with water and food. Finally Joker ventured on deck and was seized as a stowaway. The commander tried to find Joker's owner, but, of course, he was not on board. A kindly major saved Joker from being put to sleep and cast overboard by promising the commander to take full responsibility for the dog. Later Joker followed the major down a gangplank.

On the humid little island Joker began to search once more. An officer remembered an ad on a bulletin board, offering a reward for a lost black dog. He put Joker on a leash to take him to the camp where he had seen the ad. Suddenly the dog danced at the end of his leash. Near a group of tents he froze, having picked up a faint scent.

"Joker!" a voice cried out from one of the tents, and the pet rushed in, leaped upon the man, licking him joyfully. The little black dog had reached his goal. His love and faith were rewarded. Said the officer, "If you had told me the dog was yours, I wouldn't have believed you, but I have to believe the dog."

Can't we trust the Creator who made a dog with such loyalty and devotion? He who can guide the birds in their migrations and help a dog to find his master thousands of miles from home has promised, "I will guide thee with mine eye" (Ps. 32:8).

L.C.W.

HE CAN DELIVER

The Lord knoweth how to deliver the godly out of temptations.
2 Peter 2:9.

This verse doesn't say that the Lord takes all temptations away from the godly. So long as we live in this world we will be subject to Satan's temptations. When we come face to face with them, God can, and will deliver us from them so we do not have to sin.

Mr. Andrews built his barn, doing most of the carpentry work himself. While sawing boards, he often left a lot of small pieces of wood lying around. His two children, Mary and John, enjoyed nailing these together.

One morning the father discovered he needed some more lumber to finish up the barn doors and decided to go to the nearby town for it. Before leaving he told the children not to use any nails, since he had just enough to finish the barn.

After he left, the children wondered how they were going to finish nailing the blocks together. They talked the matter over and decided that just a few would not be missed, and so they went ahead using them, perhaps taking more than they had intended.

When Mr. Andrews returned he soon discovered what the children had done, and he punished them. Mary felt bad to think she had disobeyed her father. Going into the house, she entered her bedroom and knelt to pray. Her mother, thinking to comfort her child, went to find her. From outside the bedroom door, she heard Mary's prayer.

"Dear Jesus, please chain Satan up so he won't tempt me anymore. I am sorry I did wrong and I don't want to do it again. Amen."

Mrs. Andrews gently entered the room and took her child in her arms.

"You know, Mary, Jesus isn't able to answer your prayer, at least not yet. The time is coming when Satan will be chained. But until then, he is like a roaring lion, walking about. It is meeting temptations and resisting them that makes us strong."

"But what can I do when Satan tempts me?"

"Send up a prayer for help. Paul tells us that with every temptation there is a way of escape. After you have prayed for help, take the next step, and resist. Then the devil will run away."

"Thank you, Mamma. I'll try harder next time."

V.E.R.

175

PENNY'S REWARD

Be ye . . . courteous. 1 Peter 3:8.

Pete awkwardly shifted his ungainly feet, grunted, coughed, then finally rang the doorbell. Now, if the dean came to the door—horrible thought—how could he ask for Penny? Oh, why did he ever let himself get into this? Just as he was about to turn on his heels and flee, the door opened. What a relief! It was not the dean standing there. But the worst was yet to come. Just how did you ask a girl to go to the biggest affair of the whole year with you?

Meanwhile, Penny was having her own troubles. When she learned who wanted her at the front door, her heart took a downward flip. Why Pete, of all people? He was the laughingstock of the whole boys' dormitory. Why did he have to pick on her? Penny hesitated. She *could* send word that she was sorry, but she was busy—and she was. But then . . .

"Penny Harmer!" Penny lectured herself, "You get yourself down to that door and be civil. If Pete wants you for a date, you just be as nice a date as you can. Nobody else is willing to go to the banquet with him, that's for sure, and he certainly won't improve if everybody shuns him!"

Pete hadn't been polished with his invitation, but the gratitude shining from his eyes when Penny accepted was unmistakable!

Still, it took a bit of doing for Penny to remain cheerful after Pete left, and she didn't go out of her way to advertise her date! Some of the girls thought she had been foolish. After all, a person doesn't *have* to spend the most important night of the school year with a creep just because she is kindhearted!

At last the gala night came and Penny did her best to entertain Pete. He surely wasn't much at entertaining her! Even so, when it was all over, Penny had to admit the event hadn't been a complete failure, and she meant it when she thanked him for the pleasant evening.

Several years later as Penny and her husband were talking, he asked, "Penny, do you remember the night Pete took you to the banquet? I sat just behind you at the program and I couldn't help thinking, That's the kind of girl I'd like to have. If she can give up an evening for Pete, she is worth trying to get."

Penny decided it paid to be courteous!

M.H.

SENSITIVE PLANTS AND PEOPLE

My brothers, be careful that no one among you has a heart so bad and unbelieving that he will turn away from the living God. Instead, in order that none of you be deceived by sin and become stubborn, you must help one another every day. Hebrews 3:12, 13, TEV.

"Look at that pretty bush with all the pink balls on it. I'm going to get some." Our 5-year-old son reached out the window to gather a handful of small pink flowers.

Suddenly he cried out in pain. Stopping the car, we glanced back at the bush he had touched. All the oblong leaflets had folded together and the entire branch was drooping as if dead.

"What did you do to that plant?" we asked.

"I only touched it. Look what it did to me!" He sobbed harder.

His hand and entire arm were covered with hundreds of tiny bristles, imbedded in the flesh. We spent the next painful hour extracting them one by one. His arm was sore for days.

That was our first contact with the common tropical sensitive plant. Prickly and bristly, this spreading shrub has doubly compound leaves. Each of the four branches of the leaf has from twelve to twenty pair of small leaflets less than one-half inch long. When a person or animal walks through a field where the sensitive plant grows, the fronds that are touched close together tightly and droop downward. It is some time before the leaves open again.

People are often like the sensitive plant. They can be hurt by rough touches. Unkind words or looks, and stubborn actions often cause others to become discouraged until their spirits droop. But if we approach others carefully, using tact, kindness, and sympathy, we can be of great help. A kind word of genuine praise, a smile of commendation, will bring hope, courage, and happiness.

On the other hand, avoid being a sensitive plant yourself. Don't let others hurt your feelings. Annoyances and grievances from others need not ruin your day. You can live above slights if self is dead and hidden in Jesus. Keep your heart sensitive to God's Word. Jesus will give you peace, in spite of unkind people or unfavorable circumstances.

E.E.L. and J.H.L.

ADVENTURE WITH POLIO

Gad, a troop shall overcome him: but he shall overcome at the last. Genesis 49:19.

Ann Adams had a normal childhood. Through her teen years she developed her talent for painting. She became an art major at Florida State University. Then she became a free-lance artist, illustrating books and pamphlets for the Florida State Board of Health.

Then, at 21, polio hit her. That was just one year before the Salk vaccine was ready to prevent the crippling march of death caused by that dread disease. Ann's beautiful little world crumbled around her. Ann put it this way: "One day you're walking around and the next day you're in an iron lung."

She was taken to a hospital at first and placed in a ward with eighteen other polio victims, many of them screaming in agony. She spent the next five years in her iron lung in various hospitals, but her case seemed hopeless.

Finally after five years of fruitless, hopeless despair, Dr. Frank Anderson, of Augusta, Georgia, brought her a ray of hope. "I'll get you sitting up in a wheel chair," he promised. But Ann couldn't believe it. She didn't want to build up any false hopes. However, Dr. Anderson persuaded her to try. He used equipment to force air into her lungs so she could sit up, first for a moment or two, and later for an hour. And this kind doctor kept assuring her, "Ann, you'll paint again." She felt it was too good to be true, but a spark of hope had been kindled!

When Ann was able to sit in a wheel chair for four hours they brought her some makeshift equipment and a brush she could hold between her teeth, and she went to work, but it seemed hopeless. She wanted to cry. She looked up and said, "God, please, I can't do this alone. You must help me."

It took Ann ten weeks to learn how to make a straight line. It took her ten years to finish her first painting. In five more years Ann was producing her beautiful Christmas cards commercially. Her story is bringing hope to many handicapped people. Her story reminded us of Gad, who was defeated but overcame at last. Don't give up! Look up! God can help you overcome at last.

A.A.E.

HYPOCRITE!

This people draw near me with their mouth, and with their lips do honour me, but have removed their heart far from me. Isaiah 29:13.

Ken stood up in academy vespers meeting and told how much he loved God and wanted to serve Him. When a fifteen-year-old feels that way about his religion it sends a warm glow through you.

From the outside it appeared that this was a genuine wish on his part. His life did follow closer to God's will, or so it seemed. Then reports began to come in that he had been seen in town without permission. Teachers began to say that he made every excuse imaginable for not completing his assignments.

But each time the speaker on Friday night called for consecration, Ken jumped to his feet or raised his hand. Eventually his words became so different from his actions that both students and teachers felt he could not be trusted.

One day as I stepped into the classroom I heard voices. "He's just a hypocrite," one voice said.

Now that seemed pretty strong language to me. But the other person replied, "You couldn't be righter. It makes me sick to hear him say those goody-goody things on Friday when I know some of the mean tricks he has played and the rules he's broken."

"If I were Ken I'd keep my mouth shut and . . ." Just then they saw me standing in the doorway. There is an old saying: You can fool some of the people all of the time, and all of the people some of the time, but you can't fool all the people all of the time.

Ken left academy about the middle of the school year. Both students and faculty wondered why he had not gone sooner. When your performance doesn't match your promise people begin to think you are a phony—a hypocrite.

Of course, no one is perfect, and we do not always attain our high expectations. One mistake spoils the pattern, but it doesn't necessarily make a person a hypocrite. God can help you live according to His will if you will let Him.

W.R.L.S.

RETURN OR PAY

Will a man rob God? Malachi 3:8.

David looked at his paycheck from his summer job. He had been fortunate to find a job at fourteen, and it amazed him how his money had mounted up. But now summer was over and there was so much to do with that money. School fees, or at least part of them, would come out of it. And there would be presents for some of the family, and he wanted badly to buy a new bicycle. The more he thought about it, the more he realized that only one way to balance the budget remained.

"Dad," he asked, "do I really have to pay tithe?"

"No, son, you don't have to *pay* tithe. God doesn't ask us to *pay* tithe."

Now David could see that father had some special point to his story. "What do you mean? You pay tithe, don't you? And you are always telling me to remember my tithe when you give me my allowance."

"I guess it is a matter of the words you use. You see, everything belongs to God in the first place. You don't pay a person with things that already belong to him. It is more correct to speak of *returning* a tithe to the Lord, not *paying* tithe."

"Does that make any difference, Dad?"

"I think it makes a difference inside us. If we think of paying tithe, we are doing no more than we would do in paying the supermarket or the service station. But when you *return* something to God it makes you remember His goodness in providing all the good things you have."

"I see what you mean. At least I think I do. I don't really own that money I earned. God has given it to me through the strength and health I have, and through helping me find a job. I return tithe to Him to show that I know who it is that has helped me."

"That's right, David. You will find as you return tithe that it is a pleasure to do it. Think about the blessing God has given you and be faithful to God in returning an honest tithe, just as He has been faithful to you in fulfilling His promises."

W.R.L.S.

A HOME FOR JESUS

The birds of the air have nests; but the Son of man hath not where to lay his head. Matthew 8:20.

Have you ever examined a bird's nest closely? If the only tool you could use was a beak, could you make such a strong, soft home for baby birds?

The oriole builds her nest from the top down, and as she nears the bottom she works from the inside, making a lovely gray basket that rocks from the tips of branches.

Another hanging nest is made by the baya bird of India, but this nest differs from the oriole's in several ways. The doorway is in the bottom and there are two baskets for each nest, with the bigger basket having two rooms. One room is the nursery and the other is the family room. But the second basket—that is for father only. Papa's study, if you please! But the queerest thing about the baya bird's nest is that around the walls are daubs of clay where the Indians insist the birds fasten lightning bugs to give light inside the nests!

Have you ever heard of bird's-nest soup? It is made from the nest of the Indochina swift. The entire nest is made from a solution which comes from glands under the mother's tongue, hardening in the air into a glasslike nest.

Another glasslike nest is made by the Oriental swift. It is so delicate that it holds only one egg, and the mother cannot sit upon it. She has to sit beside the nest and fluff her feathers over the egg.

The nest of the bowerbird of Australia is plain enough, but the male bird builds a bower when courting his mate. The bird surrounds it with moss and decorates the whole thing with bright fruit, colored flowers, and brilliant insects. As these fade, new ones are brought.

Mrs. Hornbill of Africa and Asia crawls into a hollow tree and lets Mr. Hornbill seal her in with mud until only her beak can reach out. Then she undresses in her snug room by pulling out nearly all her feathers to line the nest. She stays there for weeks while her husband brings her food.

When Jesus was here on earth He said that even the birds have nests of their own, "but the Son of man hath not where to lay his head."

Won't you give Him a home in your heart?

M.H.

181

MORE ABUNDANTLY

I am come that they might have life, and that they might have it more abundantly. John 10:10.

The story is told of a visit made by the artist Michelangelo to the artist Raphael.

Michelangelo admired the canvas Raphael was working on, but pointed out that it needed to be larger and greater. And Raphael, following the other man's advice, added a new dimension to his painting.

Jesus wants to add a new dimension to our lives. If we allow Him to take charge of our lives, we become more abundant persons. Our capabilities become larger, our horizons broader. We have deepened insight, greater hope, more vitality.

Bud was a young teen-ager who had been feeling very blue about things that didn't go as he had hoped or planned. Discouragement clouded his vision until he couldn't see any of the good and happy things in life. All he could see was a mass of problems that seemed to close in around him.

He thought of experimenting with some of the things that his friends used to drown out the world. He knew it wouldn't be hard to get drugs of one kind or another in his neighborhood. Yet he had read enough about drugs to know that he wouldn't really be helping anything. He would just have a greater low later on.

Down the street lived Bud's friend Gary. Sometimes Bud considered Gary a square. But when Gary noticed that Bud wasn't feeling too cheerful, he sat on the steps and visited with Bud, and brightened his outlook.

How did Gary do it? He pointed Bud to the wonderful love of Jesus who knows the answer to every problem and discouragement. He explained that it is when our feelings are at the lowest ebb that the angels are the closest, waiting to strengthen us if we but say Yes to His love.

Whatever problems face us, we should remember the twin texts "Without me ye can do nothing" (John 15:5, last part), and "With God all things are possible" (Matt. 19:26). Then turn to Him and let Him make our lives larger and greater.

R.E.

THE GREAT GRAIN ROBBERY

Wherefore do ye spend money for that which is not bread? and your labour for that which satisfieth not? hearken diligently unto me, and eat ye that which is good, and let your soul delight itself in fatness. Isaiah 55:2.

A holdup man thrusts a gun in your ribs. "Stick 'em up!" he demands brusquely. You get your hands over your head in a hurry. The bandit pulls the billfold out of your pocket, removes twenty dollars in various size bank notes, and takes off.

Suppose a few days later you receive in the mail a letter from the robber. It reads, "My conscience has been hurting me, and I'm sorry I took the twenty dollars from you. Enclosed is four dollars. Please forgive me!"

You would be glad to have at least four of your twenty dollars back, but you wouldn't feel that the holdup man had really done a complete job of making things right. Four dollars out of twenty really isn't a good return.

Now, stop and think what happens when you eat some of the enriched white bread you buy in the supermarket today. It's white, fluffy, appetizing. It tastes good. Then, too, the wrapper in bold letters declares the loaf is enriched with certain essential vitamins.

You see, as the kernel went through the various processes the best part of the grain of wheat was sifted out. The bran, the germ, and portions of the kernel that contain the best vitamins and other food nutrients were removed. White flour was left.

"But," you say, "the bread I eat is enriched. It has the vitamins put back in, so it's as good as it was originally."

Is it? Actually what happened was that some *twenty* vitamins and minerals were removed, and the bakers returned only *four* of these nutrients. It's like the bandit who took the money from you and returned only a portion.

We are very careful about the fuel we use in our automobiles. We would never mix kerosene or water with the gasoline. We think too much of the engines to do that. Yet, how many of us eat what we like and what tastes good instead of putting into our bodies, the most delicate mechanism there is, the very best food God has given us. This really doesn't make good sense, now, does it?

R.H.P.

OUT OF CONTROL

So the tongue is a little member and boasts of great things. How great a forest is set ablaze by a small fire! James 3:5, RSV.

Gus, an employee in a pet shop in New York City, noticed a monkey caught in the wire of a large cage. Gus knew he should always lock the door to the monkeys' cage when entering, but in his eagerness to help the animal, he forgot to be careful and left the cage door open as he untangled the little fellow. In an instant the freed monkey made a dash for the open door and was followed by nineteen other monkeys. Promptly those twenty opened the doors to four other cages. In seconds 100 monkeys were racing around the pet shop.

Frantically, Gus tried to trap them. Then one little fellow discovered a ladder leading to an open skylight. Without hesitation ninety-nine other monkeys followed him out to freedom and downtown New York.

Not far away a grocery clerk was working in a storeroom when forty monkeys entered through an open window. Half of the intruders began opening sacks and dumping out the contents while the rest enjoyed a feast of bananas.

Other monkeys visited a three-story firehouse, where they had a great time sliding down the pole and turning on all the showers. When the fire alarm rang they jumped on the hook-and-ladder truck for the ride. The call was from someone who needed help to get monkeys off a high building. When they arrived the policeman stared unbelievingly, shouting, "It isn't possible. They're bringing more."

Not far away in a church the choirmaster was practicing with a boys' choir when two monkeys jumped on the piano, swung from the curtain, and hung from the chandelier. The singing stopped while the choir leader organized the boys in the first monkey hunt in that church.

Three interesting months went by before all one hundred monkeys were returned to the pet shop. Just one careless act, but so much trouble! Still one hundred monkeys loose in New York City isn't as disastrous as one uncontrolled tongue. Unkind or cruel words can't be retrieved. Like setting a whole forest ablaze, the damage done is forever, destroying life, happiness, and beauty. Only as you let God control your tongue are you and those with you safe from words that can kill.

E.E.L. and J.H.L.

THE VALUE OF MONEY

But thou shalt remember the Lord thy God: for it is he that giveth thee power to get wealth. Deuteronomy 8:18.

Money is another wonderful gift of God. It is not *money* but the *love of money* that is said to be the root of all evil. "Money has great value, because it can do great good. In the hands of God's children it is food for the hungry, drink for the thirsty, and clothing for the naked. . . . But money is of no more value than sand, only as it is put to use in providing for the necessities of life, in blessing others, and advancing the cause of Christ."—*Christ's Object Lessons,* p. 351.

In the seventeenth verse of this chapter we are warned against pride when we get wealthy and then say in our hearts, "My power and the might of mine hand hath gotten me this wealth." It is dangerous to pamper our pride by taking credit for our successes. The wise man observed that "bread" is not always "to the wise, nor yet riches to men of understanding." We must never take the praise for our prosperity to ourselves.

It is God, we read, who gives us power to get wealth. What would we do if God did not water the earth with the refreshing rains and with the gentle dews from heaven? What would we do if He did not give us the sunlight that warms the soil and thus awakens to life the little seeds waiting in the earth? What would we do if the things of nature did not respond to the divine touch and grow and flourish and bear fruit? Where would our crops come from if God failed to uphold all things by the word of His power? Man still lives because seedtime and harvest come in their appointed time.

In view of all these providential blessings of God, humility is the best ornament of prosperity. Don't get lifted up with your success or your financial standing. Don't even say in your heart, "My hand hath gotten me this wealth." After all, "all we possess is the Lord's, and we are accountable to Him for the use we make of it. In the use of every penny, it will be seen whether we love God supremely and our neighbor as ourselves."—*ibid.*

Notice that phrase "every penny." Then God is interested in how we spend our nickels and dimes and dollars. Are we thinking only of chewing gum, soft drinks, and candy?

A.A.E.

YOUR MAKER KNOWS

Know ye that the Lord he is God: it is he that hath made us, and not we ourselves; we are his people, and the sheep of his pasture. Psalm 100:3.

The Lord who fashioned Adam out of the dust knows us much better than we can ever know ourselves. "He knoweth our frame; he remembereth that we are dust" (Ps. 103:14). Pastor E. E. Cleveland has given a forceful illustration of this spiritual truth.

A Pan American plane was heading out over San Francisco Bay when an engine caught fire. Suddenly one of the engines and a huge section of the wing dropped into the water. By all laws of aeronautics the plane should have gone out of balance. The pilot acknowledged that only a Higher person than himself kept them in flight. Sensing that the plane could still fly, he headed for an emergency landing at a nearby air base.

Suddenly a passenger rushed to the stewardess in excitement. "I must see the pilot! I must see the pilot now."

Contrary to her training—the young woman opened the door to the cockpit. The man asked the pilot, "How do you plan to set her down?"

"I have no choice—a belly landing."

"You have too much fuel for that," protested the stranger.

"But my hydraulic system is out; we cannot lower the landing gear."

"That's why I came in. I am an engineer from Boeing Company that makes these planes. Give me permission and I will hand crank your landing gear down."

Permission was given. Soon the man demonstrated his aeronautical know-how by tearing up the floor board. Then he had somebody hold him by his feet upside down. With his arms and head down in the undercarriage of the plane, he skillfully hand cranked the landing gear into position.

Passengers and crew all landed safely because in the providence of God one of the makers of that plane was aboard. He understood its inner workings. Two praying Seventh-day Adventists, ministers of the gospel, knew why this engineer was traveling with them that day.

Christ is your daily Companion. He is your Maker and, if you so choose, your King. Turn your perplexities and problems over to your Maker for solution.

L.C.W.

WITH GOD

Thy right hand shall hold me. Psalm 139:10.

This story is just for girls—little girls. But if the rest of you will read it through, I think you can learn a lesson from it too.

Judy and Patsy were busily playing with their dolls, Susie and Doris. They dressed them up and walked around the block, pretending they were going to town. Home again, the girls played it was time for supper. They thought it great fun to stir up "chocolate milk" by mixing mud with water, and flowers made a beautiful salad. After the dolls had been duly fed they were undressed and put into their pajamas, ready for bed.

"Let's rock Susie and Doris for a while before we put them to sleep," suggested Patsy, climbing up onto the porch swing and settling herself among the cushions.

"O.K.," agreed Judy. "And Susie likes me to sing to her while I rock too."

Pushing with her feet to get the swing started, Patsy asked, "What shall we sing?"

"Oh," hesitated Judy as she searched for a suitable song, "let's sing 'Safe in the Arms of Jesus'!" And soon the two little girls were singing softly to their dolls.

As the first stanza came to an end, Patsy, the younger of the two, asked thoughtfully, "Judy, how do you know you are safe?"

Judy thought for a few moments as the swing rocked back and forth slower and slower. Then she answered, "I'm safe because I'm holding Jesus tight with my two hands."

"Oh," scoffed Patsy, shaking her head knowingly, "that doesn't make you safe! Suppose Satan creeps up and cuts your two hands off? How safe would you be then?"

Judy looked troubled as she hitched herself into a more comfortable position, making poor Susie tumble to the floor. Judy didn't even notice her fall. Suddenly the little girl had an inspiration.

"I forgot," she cried. "I'm not holding Jesus' hands. He is holding mine and Satan can't cut His hands off. So you see, I am safe!"

And you will be too, if you let God's right hand hold you.

M.H.

187

BROKEN-WINGED PEOPLE

Inasmuch as ye have done it unto one of the least of these my brethren, ye have done it unto me. Matthew 25:40.

We are sometimes kinder to animals than we are to people. We will take in a lost cat, but we are too blind to help a lost soul.

All around us there are people who go through life with some defect that cripples them. They are like birds with broken wings and cannot fly fully into life. They are too helpless to mend their own bad habits, and so people abandon them and leave them alone. Perhaps we even call them repulsive.

But if we are willing to befriend a stray dog or cat, why can't we show the same compassion for a person who has strayed from being lovable?

Karen had a friend Sue who talked nonstop. Even though she lived on the same block, Karen would look for a dozen excuses not to walk to school with Sue. Many other children in school would not eat lunch with her or choose her for any team games. They didn't even say "Hello" to her because she would begin a long, rambling conversation that would go on and on and on.

At last Sue's parents took her to see a psychiatrist. He sent her home after one session. There was nothing wrong with her, he assured them. She just wanted someone to listen to her. She was so overanxious to make friends that she scared them off. She talked too much because she was unsure of herself and felt that nobody would pay attention to her.

A person like Sue can be annoying. There are many other persons who have faults that we don't like, and so we stay away from them instead of trying to help them.

Kenny was a borrower, which was only half of the fault. He borrowed and then forgot, quite honestly, to return a pen or a book. After a while, the boys refused to have anything to do with him. Was this the right way to handle it?

Of course, we should not encourage a person who has bad habits to continue them. But neither should we shut them out from our company and our companionship. The next time a friend of yours shows an annoying habit, try to help him.

R.E.

SKUNKS AREN'T BAD

Never pull each other to pieces. . . . If you are judging your brother and setting yourself up in place of God's Law. . . . How can you then be so silly as to imagine that you are your neighbor's judge? James 4:11, 12, Phillips.

Only small minds delight in criticism. Satan jeers when he hears Christians finding fault with others, for he knows this brings discouragement, envy, and strife. A beautiful little animal, often criticized and judged to be all bad because he uses a powerful, unpleasant odor for defense, proves that this is not true, even about a skunk.

One spring evening the Hoyt family were in their cabin eating supper, when through the open door stepped a black and white animal. Remembering his bad reputation, they hesitated but finally offered him some milk. Setting a bowl on the table, they pulled up a chair. Their guest, whom they named Little Corporal, accepted the invitation.

From that time on he came for dinner frequently, always displaying the best of manners. If the door was closed, he'd thump his feet or utter little noises. Then one day he disappeared. How they missed his evening visits! Weeks later they heard the familiar thump. Opening the door, they found he had brought Mrs. Corporal and six babies!

Assuring his timid family, he brought them into the cabin. Mrs. Corporal, worried, began thumping the floor and standing on her front feet. The little ones followed. Fearfully, the Hoyt family waited, but their bad thoughts about skunks were groundless. Little Corporal climbed up on the chair and pounded the table. The Hoyts quickly put bowls of milk on the floor for Mom and the kids while Dad ate in style.

Frequently the skunks came to visit and enjoy their milk. Not once did they break the confidence of friendship. These friendly animals had no desire to leave their sickening odor in the Hoyts' home. When autumn came the family left.

Don't condemn others. It is not for us to criticize or speak evil of anyone. When the accusers of the woman caught in sin walked away, the Lord Jesus said to her, "Neither do I condemn you."

Remember the friendly skunk family when you are tempted to believe the worst about others. Never spread hearsay or idle gossip. We have no right to judge anyone.

E.E.L. and J.H.L.

REFLECTORS

Arise, shine; for thy light is come, and the glory of the Lord is risen upon thee. Isaiah 60:1.

If a flashlight is pointed up into the sky at night, and there are no particles of dust in the air, you would not know the flashlight was on. It is obstacles in the path of a beam of light that let you know the light is shining.

So it is with Jesus' light. If you do not stand in His light and reflect it, the world will not know the light is there.

Another thing about light is that the higher the polish is on the reflecting surface the greater the amount of light reflected.

Mike's father once made a small telescope, for which he ground his own mirror. For hours at a time he worked away on the glass, and often commanded Mike's services to help with the grinding.

"Aw, Dad," he questioned many a time, "isn't this good enough?"

"No, son, it must be perfectly smooth to reflect properly."

The grinding went on and on and on. Finally Dad pronounced the job done and shipped the glass to a factory where a silver coating was painted on. Several times the coating flaked off and had to be redone. At last Dad decided to use a thin layer of aluminum.

"OK, I think we have that problem licked," he declared. "Let's install it."

Eagerly Mike helped fit the pieces together. He could scarcely wait until dark to try it out.

That night when his father put his eye to the eyepiece, Mike was right beside him. "Good," grunted Dad. "That reflector is doing a fine job!"

"What do you see?" inquired Mike impatiently.

Moving out of the way, Dad answered, "Look for yourself."

"Why," exclaimed Mike as he squinted into the telescope, "I can see the craters in the moon!"

The more you let Jesus polish your character, the better your neighbors will see Jesus in you. "Arise, shine; for thy light is come, and the glory of the Lord is risen upon thee."

M.H.

THE "WHY" OF NATHANIEL'S DEATH

He hath done all things well. Mark 7:37.

Nathaniel was dead. Seated in his rocking chair, dressed in overcoat, cap, and gloves, waiting for his sister Anna to bring him a tray of food before she took him riding, he leaned back and died, while the chair continued to rock.

Of course everybody knew that Nathaniel had tuberculosis. His brother and sister-in-law, James and Ellen White, had often met with the believers there in Rochester, New York, and prayed for him. They had anointed him, and each time he had received a rich blessing. The believers all hoped that the young man would recover.

In those days, part of the tuberculosis "cure" was for the patient to "ride out" every day. But that day, Nathaniel did not have his ride.

The word quickly spread. It was unbelievable. So many sick people had been healed through prayer in that house in Rochester that they had come to believe that God would always answer Yes. But this time He had said No. Some could not accept it, especially Sister Seely who thought that she was exercising great faith by crying out, "He is not dead! He cannot die, for we have prayed for him." "He is dead," she was told. "Well, then," she replied, "he will surely come to life again, for God has greatly blessed in his case in answer to prayer."

Through a vision given to Ellen White, God gave the answer: "The Lord has heard and answered prayer in Nathaniel's case. He has gently let him down to the grave in a manner that is no burden to anyone. He knows the future best, and the dangers to that ambitious young man. While in a well-prepared state of consecration he has let him fall asleep.

"It was presented to me like children asking a blessing of their earthly parents who love them," she continued. "They ask something that the parent knows will hurt them; the parent gives them the things that will be good and healthful for them in the place of that which they desired. I saw that every prayer which is sent up in faith from an honest heart, will be heard of God and answered, and the one that sent up the petition will have a blessing when he needs it most, and it will often exceed his expectations. Not a prayer of a true saint is lost if sent up in faith from an honest heart."

V.E.R.

I WISH EVERY DAY WAS SABBATH

Remember the sabbath day, to keep it holy. Exodus 20:8.

"Come and help me lift this big rock. It's just the right size to fill up the hole in our dam. The water will form a pool."

The three brothers were playing together in the stream, building a dam as the beavers do. Dad helped when he wasn't watching a bird through his binoculars. Mother, from a nearby rock, enjoyed the beauty of the woods and the joy of being with her family.

Suddenly the youngest boy smiled at his parents and said, "I wish every day was Sabbath. That's when you belong to us."

Yes, Sabbath has always been a happy day in our home. The reason is that whenever possible we enjoy God's out-of-doors. In the cold winter we may put on heavy clothes and boots and follow animal and bird tracks in the snow. In the spring we hunt for the first flowers, vying to see who can find the crocuses blooming from a snowbank. We stop to examine the shapes of the delicate leaf buds as they begin to open. In summer we sometimes take our lunch and our dog and hike many miles on the mountain trail. Autumn's lovely colors bring exclamations of joy and delight from mother as her boys gather huge bouquets of colorful leaves.

As missionaries in the tropics we spent many Sabbaths at the seashore. The boys had starfish races, turning the creatures upside down and timing them to see which would right itself first. They squirted each other with sea cucumbers, stuck their fingers into sea anemones and watched them close up, or found sea horses, jellyfish, sea urchins, and sand dollars.

Walks in the nearby jungle were made exciting when we found the gorgeous butterflies that mysteriously disappeared when they lit in the deep foliage, so well camouflaged that we could not see them. We hunted for the ventriloquist cicadas that seemed to call from everywhere. We caught huge ants an inch long, found a tarantula spider with hundreds of babies, and played with mille-pedes that rolled up tight like a marble.

You will never fear boredom in heaven if you have spent your Sabbath days with Jesus here, learning about Him through nature.

E.E.L. and J.H.L.

A BROTHER LIKE THAT

I have shewed you all things, how that so labouring ye ought to support the weak, and to remember the words of the Lord Jesus, how he said, It is more blessed to give than to receive. Acts 20:35.

Bill Haney's shiny, new Mercedes-Benz was parked across the street from his office in Mobile, Alabama. When he left his office at five-thirty and crossed the street to get his car he noticed a little urchin in ragged clothes, looking the Mercedes over admiringly.

"Is this your car?" the little fellow asked eagerly.

"Yes, it is," Haney replied as he opened the car door to get in.

"Where'd you get it?" the child pressed.

"As a matter of fact," Bill explained, surprised at this candid approach, "my brother gave it to me as a Christmas present."

The tiny moppet's eyes bugged wide. "You brother *gave* it to you?" he measured his words incredulously. "I wish I . . ."

Haney was sure the little fellow was going to say, "I wish I had a brother like that who would give me a car!"

But he didn't say that. Instead, he spoke thoughtfully—longingly: "I wish I could be a brother like that!"

Bill Haney was so impressed with the child's philosophy he invited him to take a drive in the shiny Mercedes. They drove by the boy's home on a back alley and picked up his little brother, who had been crippled by polio. Bill knew now why the big-eyed moppet wanted to be a brother who could give.

The apostle Paul, who spoke the words in our text today, left us a great truth that we as Christians should ever keep in mind: "It is more blessed to give than to receive."

Ellen White says: "The principle of worldlings is to get all they can of the perishable things of this life. But the purest joy is not found in riches nor where covetousness is always craving, but where contentment reigns and where self-sacrificing love is the ruling principle."—*Testimonies*, vol. 3, p. 382.

How is it with *you*? Do you have an unselfish heart? Are you willing to share with those who may be in need?

I hope every one of you can say, "I wish I could be a brother like that!"

R.H.P.

THE SAD-FACED BOY

A merry heart maketh a cheerful countenance, but by sorrow of the heart the spirit is broken. Proverbs 15:13.

Marvin Scott wished he had a close buddy—someone who would like him especially well and want to do the same things that he did. Perhaps he would find such a friend at the academy. He made himself look as sad and lonely as he possibly could, but no one cared. They didn't even *notice.*

His roommate, Virgil Drew, had friends at school from his own home-town. And if Marvin didn't want to go along when Virgil went out to play ball, then Virgil would go anyhow and play with the other fellows. He didn't offer to stay in the room and do what Marvin wanted to.

The boys in the room next door went around with each other. Marvin stopped in their room and talked to them a few times. he even told them that he had come to the academy in hopes of finding friends. He explained that back home he hadn't had any friends because he went to public school and was left out of all activities. But they didn't take any more interest in him than they had in the first place.

Were the fellows looking down on him because of his job? He had hoped to work in the broom shop or the book bindery, but students who had been there the year before, or who had worked there during summer vacation had those jobs. So Marvin was assigned to the menial task of janitor duty in the boys' dorm.

At Saturday night social events, Marvin stood sadly on the side lines waiting to be invited to join a group. As he stood in line at the cafeteria, Marvin assumed his most sorrowful expression. He thought surely someone would ask him what was the matter. Then he would know who was interested in him enough to become a good friend. But that never happened.

Marvin didn't go back to the academy a second year. He hadn't noticed one important thing about the students who *did* have a lot of friends. Those students were not the ones with the sad faces at all; they were the ones with the smiles—the people who were fun to be with.

Whether you feel happy or not, put on your merriest smile and spend a cheerful day. See how much better you feel at the end of it!

R.E.

HOLLY'S FIRST BIBLE STUDY

Lay up for yourselves treasures in heaven. Matthew 6:20.

En route to Florida the Sullivan family planned to stop overnight with Uncle Neal. Holly had never met this particular uncle. Daddy explained, "There are no boys or girls at your bachelor uncle's house, and no auntie. You may find the place a bit lonesome."

"Aren't there horses, chickens, and cows? I'm sure Uncle Neal will be fun to know, for he lives on a farm."

The next morning after breakfast Holly's parents went out to see some friends, and left their daughter with her uncle. "Holly, I have some important accounts to go over while your folks are away. Here is a picture book to make you happy. You can keep it." The eight-year-old girl felt disappointed, for she had hoped Uncle Neal would take her for a walk over the farm and let her ride a gentle horse. Instead he said, "Don't bother me while I'm busy."

After an hour the uncle shut up his account books and talked as if pleased with himself. "That's done. I've quite a sum laid up for a rainy day."

Holly asked, "You mean you laid it up in heaven?"

The farmer looked uncomfortable. This question reminded him of what his parents had said when they were alive. "No, Holly. I don't have my money up in heaven, but my cash is in banks, savings and loan companies, and in different investments. I could live on the interest I get."

"Money is safer up in heaven," Molly suggested, and she rushed to get her Bible and read Matthew 6:19-21. The niece could not tell if her uncle was pleased or not, but she asked, "Do you pay tithe, one tenth of any money you get?"

"Does the Bible tell us that we should pay tithe?" asked Uncle Neal.

Holly found Malachi 3:8-12 and asked her uncle to read; "Will a man rob God?" It had been years since Neal Sullivan had read those verses about the "curse" and the "blessing." When the Sullivans stopped overnight on their way home, Neal said, "Don, I've been going to church since you were here last. Also I turned in a sizable check for tithe. I feel happy once more."

"What made the change?" exclaimed Holly's father.

"Holly's Bible study about laying up treasure in heaven," said her uncle.

L.C.W.

THE LITTLE HAYMAKER

In whose hand is the soul of every living thing, and the breath of all mankind. Job 12:10.

Trail Ridge Road follows the high country in Colorado's Rocky Mountain National Park. The highway continues upward 11,000 feet, past timberline, where the trees abruptly stop growing, and on to the top of the mountain ridge.

Parking our car, we chose to follow a foot-trail. Suddenly I was attracted by a series of sharp, shrill whistles, the call of the pika, or cony, who lives just above timberline. Having seen these animals years before on Long's Peak, I wanted a closer view. Sitting on a rock pile from where the whistle came, I watched a crevice from which the sound was constantly repeated. Small bits of grass which the animal had carried down into his home were visible, but the cony, no doubt sensing my presence, was wary. I sat motionless, waiting. Finally he ventured upward, and I saw his nose. Cautiously he inched forward until all of him was visible just below my feet. About seven inches long, he wore a grayish-black coat. Although he is a relative of the rabbit, he had short ears and looked much like a guinea pig.

Even though winter is from late September till May at this altitude, these busy little creatures do not migrate or hibernate. Summer and autumn are used to cut grass and plants. The green color is preserved as well as the odor of hay, because they dry them in shaded, airy places. Each cony stores at least a bushel of material where it is well protected from snow or running water. By what knowledge does he leave nearby grass to select the best food for storage, which may be seventy-five feet away from his home?

When winter comes several congregate together, using their hay for a bed, as well as food. Why does the marmot, who also lives in the high mountains, hibernate, while the cony doesn't? Who teaches the cony to select certain foods? Where did he learn the correct method for drying hay so as to retain its full nutritional value and green color?

There is no explanation except that each animal is taught of the Lord. God planned his life, for the soul of every living thing is in His hand. God is the only answer to this wild wisdom or instinct. He's your only answer, too, for you are also in His hands.

E.E.L. and J.H.L.

TAKE YOUR STAND!

For the Lord God will help me; . . . therefore have I set my face like a flint. Isaiah 50:7.

John arrived at his induction center on Wednesday and the strenuous training program began immediately. After rising early in the morning the men were kept busy all day long running, jumping, digging, marching, and drilling, with only short periods allowed off for meals. Before he realized it, Sabbath had come, and John had not made arrangements with the sergeant to have the Sabbath off.

After breakfast next morning when the men went out onto the drill field, John took his Bible and sat in the great empty barracks alone. Seeing him sitting there, one of the soldiers reported him to the sergeant. In a few moments John heard the question echo through the hall, "Where is he?"

Laying down his Bible, he stepped out into the hall to face a very angry officer.

"What are you doing here?" he asked sharply.

"Reading my Bible, sir."

"You can't do that here. This is Saturday and you must go immediately to the drill field."

"I cannot go, sir."

"Why not?"

"My conscience will not permit it. I am a Seventh-day Adventist, and God's Word commands me to keep this day holy."

"Enough of that. Follow me," the sergeant ordered.

John followed the sergeant to the captain's office where he was asked, "Don't you realize that there can be no holy days in the Army?"

"I cannot do what God forbids, sir."

The captain turned over some papers on his desk. Then he smiled and turned to the private.

"Take your Bible and go back to the barracks. After lunch, return and stay in the barracks until sundown. My mother, God bless her, is an Adventist."

"Thank you, sir," said John, saluting smartly.

That young man had set his face like a flint and nothing could move him. God stands by those who stand up for Him.

V.E.R.

HOW NOT TO STEAL

Judge not, and ye shall not be judged: Condemn not, and ye shall not be condemned: forgive, and ye shall be forgiven. Luke 6:37.

Jerry had a good reputation. One day Clive saw him taking something out of Robert's locker. Instead of asking Jerry what he was doing, or checking with Robert, he began to whisper that Jerry stole things. But the real thief was Clive. He didn't think he was stealing, but he almost stole Jerry's good reputation. Only last-minute intervention by a teacher and Robert saved him.

Do you think Clive intended to be a thief?

Karen passed over the dollar bill and watched the clerk making change. For a moment her mind drifted to a delicious cake on the counter. Then the lady was counting money into her hand. But she did not stop when she had given her change for a dollar. She went right on and gave her change for five dollars! Karen pointed out the mistake and returned the excess change. She puzzled later why the clerk hadn't been more grateful, and was glad she hadn't stolen.

What would you have done if you had been Karen?

No one will ever know, thought Donald, as he pretended to head toward church. *I can miss church, and with mom and dad away, no one will ever know where I have gone, and I can have a good time.* So Donald robbed God of the time that was His.

How *not* to steal?

Be strictly honest in the way you handle money. Always use it in the way intended. Return promptly anything you have borrowed and make good any damage you have caused. Remember your words can steal someone's good name. Be careful what you say about others. Use your time and talents the way God wants you to use them.

If you said to Robert or Donald, "You're a robber!" they would probably say, "Me? Not me."

What do you think?

W.R.L.S.

THE BLACK THREAD

Now we see through a glass, darkly; but then face to face: now I know in part; but then shall I know even as also I am known. 1 Corinthians 13:12.

Everyone was buzzing around junior camp in a state of great excitement. That is, everyone except Lynette. She wasn't happy at all. Several weeks before, her daddy had been suddenly taken away from them by an accident and Lynette could not forget. She felt rebellious and couldn't understand why the Lord had to allow this to happen to her family. Why? Why? Why? Didn't God care?

As one of the counselors watched the sad little face, her heart was touched and she watched for an opportunity to speak to the girl. Her opportunity came one evening when she noticed that Lynette didn't come to supper. Leaving her own meal, she went to Lynette's cabin and found her lying on her bunk, crying her heart out.

"Lynette," spoke the counselor softly as she gently stroked the girl's back, "you feel sad because of your father, don't you?"

"Y-y-e-s-s," sobbed the heartbroken child.

"I know it is hard to understand," continued the woman. "We don't know why God allowed your daddy to be taken, but someday you will understand. We are told that if we could see the end from the beginning, we would not want one thing changed.

"You know, Lynette," she went on, "when rug weavers weave a certain kind of rug, they work from the underside. They cannot see the pattern. But the master weaver knows, and he tells them which threads to use—sometimes beautifully colored, and sometimes dark and ugly. When the rug is finished, and the weaver looks at it from the top, for the first time he can see the beautiful pattern. He discovers why he had to use the dark colors along with the bright. And he is satisfied. Those black threads were needed to make the rug beautiful.

"That is the way it is with you, Lynette. You are weaving a life. You do not know how God, the Master Weaver, is going to work a black thread into the pattern, but someday when you see the finished work from up in heaven, you will be satisfied. It is like the text says, 'Now we see through a glass, darkly; but then face to face: now I know in part; but then shall I know even as also I am known.'"

M.H.

YOU NEED THIS DOOR

I am the gate. Whoever comes in by me will be saved; he will come in and go out and find pasture. John 10:9, TEV.

A traveler in the Middle East happened upon a sheepfold one evening just as the shepherd was bringing in his flock for the night. The sheep pen was only a low wall that formed an enclosure. A single opening provided a way for the sheep to enter. There was no door or gate.

Pausing to take in the peaceful picture, the interested traveler approached the shepherd. "Do you have any wild beasts around here?" he asked.

"We do," answered the shepherd. "I have to be on guard constantly, watching for them."

"But don't you need a door here to protect your sheep?" the surprised traveler queried.

The old shepherd, his skin browned by many days in the open fields and wrinkled by sun and wind, thought for a moment and then replied slowly, "I am the 'door' and the 'gate.' When my sheep are all in for the night I lie down in the open space, and no sheep goes out except over my body. No animal can come in without first passing over me."

During His earthly ministry Jesus used the scenes of nature and the common people about Him to illustrate His sermons. No doubt, as a boy climbing the hills around Nazareth, He had watched shepherds bring in their sheep at night and then lie down as human doors.

It was natural, then, for Him to use this illustration of the sheep to show His love for us and to remind us how much He is willing to do for us. He explained to His people that He is the door or the gate to keep the evil one from destroying us. He said, "I am the good shepherd" (John 10:11), and "I am the gate."

Jesus said that thieves would come in to steal, kill, and destroy the sheep. How many thieves He wants to protect us from today —thieves that steal our time as we watch violence and crime on TV, thieves that would steal our health, thieves that would steal us and take us away from His fold—the Sabbath school and the church.

He is still the door, the gate of protection, for His sheep today.

R.H.P.

WHO GUIDES THIS GIANT MISSILE?

Canst thou guide Arcturus with his sons? Job 38:32.

Go outside on a starry night and get acquainted with one of the most magnificent stars in the sky. Here's how you find it. If you live north of the equator you can easily locate the Big Dipper, and this will aid you. Follow the curve of the Big Dipper's handle to a glorious, bright, orange-tinted star. You've found Arcturus in the constellation of Bootes, the fourth brightest star in the Northern Hemisphere.

Why do you think God asked Job the question in our text? He who made the stars wanted both Job and you to find an answer. In doing so you'll find out much about God. Job, without telescopes or the science of modern astronomy, could never know what you know. He knew nothing of rockets, missiles, or satellites. Surely he never guessed that this orange sphere was really a blazing sun 22 times larger than earth's sun with a diameter 30 times greater.

It is far away. Distance in the sky is not measured in miles but in light-years. A light year is nearly 6 billion miles, which is the distance light travels in a year. We know that Arcturus is 32.6 light-years distant. That means that if your parents are about 33 years old, the light you see tonight left Arcturus at the time they were born.

Did you notice that God asked whether Job could guide Arcturus? How fast is Arcturus moving? Astronomers tell us it is traveling about 70 miles every second. That's four times the speed of the earth. How would you like to be in control of a giant missile speeding through space, covering about 5,000 miles every minute. It would be a terrific steering feat to miss the billions of objects in space and still keep this enormous sun on course. But there's no need to be concerned. The One who created Arcturus will never lose control.

Now do you see the importance of this question? God wanted both Job and you to know that if He can easily guide such immensity through space, He can lead you in safe paths. You'll never face any situation that God can't handle. Then why do you have so many problems when it's so easy for God to solve them? Maybe it's because Arcturus lets God guide and you don't. Quit trying the impossible and turn yourself over to your wonderful Friend, the God of the universe.

E.E.L. and J.H.L.

YOU NEED PATIENCE

Patient endurance is what you need if, after doing God's will, you are to receive what he has promised. Hebrews 10:36 (Phillips).

Bobby was not his real name but we will call him that. As a farm boy he had to do all kinds of work. Some work on the farm he liked, and some other work he did not like. But Bobby soon learned that he needed patience to do his best at any kind of work. There were times when he was ready to quit, but he would remember his father's oft-repeated statement, "Steady, boy, steady."

Bobby had heard his father say that to the horses when they were not pulling together and the plowing was tough and the horses wanted to quit. Then Dad would say in a very calming voice, "Steady, now, steady." And the horses would buckle in and pull together and soon the job was done.

One day Bobby was having a hard day. Everything was going wrong. He got mad and no one knows what he would have done if it had not been for Dad's quiet voice, "Steady, boy, steady." Bobby took a deep breath and settled down to the job again and finished it.

After he left home to go to school and after working for some years, Bobby met some problems in his lifework that just about floored him. He wondered whether he should quit. Then there came back to him the echo of those wise words he had heard often when he was a boy, "Steady, son, steady." It helped to solve his problems.

Yes, Dr. Luke was right when he said, "In your patience possess ye your souls" (Luke 21:19).

There would not be so many dropouts in our schools if every student would listen to those wise words, "Steady, boy, steady!" And then settle down to finish the job—whatever it is.

All heaven is before us. Eternal life, eternal health, eternal happiness—all these wonderful blessings are promised us. But we have need of patience, so that after we have done the will of God we might receive the promise. So, whatever your problem, whatever your situation, don't quit or become a dropout, but listen to these wise, calming words, "Steady, son, steady."

A.A.E.

FAITHFULNESS

Moreover it is required in stewards, that a man be found faithful. 1 Corinthians 4:2.

What is a steward? Today we would call him a clerk. In the bank he would be a teller. Before he is given work in a bank, a man's record is carefully examined. If in that record there is found a single instance of dishonesty, he can never work there. It does not matter whether the man has repented and restored what he stole. Bank officials make no exceptions.

When you find a friend who is faithful, consider yourself fortunate. No matter what you may do, this friend sticks close. He knows all your strengths and weaknesses, yet he loves you just the same.

During World War II, when the Japanese armies invaded the South Pacific, all white missionaries on one island had to leave hastily. The native Christians couldn't go, for the island was their home.

Behind them, when they fled that island, the workers left one of the mission launches used on errands of mercy. When the local Christians knew the Japanese were near, they took the boat to pieces and carried it, plank by plank, pipe by pipe, into the jungle where they hid everything in caves. They were determined that the boat should not fall into the hands of the Japanese.

Years passed and the invaders were driven out; the war ended, and peace returned. The missionaries came back and looked at their ruined homes, and thought of the beautiful launch they had left behind.

But the Christian islanders had a wonderful surprise for them. They led the mission director to the cave, and showed him what they had done. Then they carried all those parts to the mission compound where they put them down in piles. The missionary engineer took the parts and put them all together. Not a single plank, board, nail, or spring was missing. Surely those islanders showed they understood what it meant to be faithful.

The Lord has given each of His children a particular work to do. And to each one He has given certain talents. No one can say he has no talent, because time is a talent, and everyone has that.

Are you a faithful servant? When He comes in the clouds of heaven, will Jesus look at you and say: "Well done, thou good and faithful servant, . . . enter thou into the joy of thy lord"?

V.E.R.

FORTY THOUSAND ROSES!

The Lord will perfect that which concerneth me. Psalm 138:8.

Without Jesus our lives are like a field of weeds and wild vines. These thistles, weeds, thorns, and briers are all the result of sin. They represent ugly words and evil habits of boys and girls who are not led by the Spirit of God.

But wait a minute, thank God, He can take just such lives and make them all over. The rude speech will become kind and thoughtful, careless manners become considerate behavior, and ugly frowns turn into pleasant smiles.

Perhaps we can better understand God's workmanship on our characters by thinking of the method used in making an expensive French perfume.

At the right time of the year the gardener takes tiny shoots of a rare variety of rose and very carefully plants them in well-prepared soil. Faithfully he watches over the baby plants. He covers them so they will not freeze and uncovers them in the mornings so they will be warmed by the sun. He waters, sprays, and prunes them.

When the harvest time comes and the beautiful roses are in full bloom, the gardener cuts the blossoms and takes them to a factory where the slow process of distillation begins. This collects the rare perfume. It is eventually sent to markets throughout the world.

It takes forty thousand blossoms to make one ounce of perfume! Eighty roses give but one drop of pure perfume. All this work and expense goes into the production of just one ounce of exquisite scent.

Think of all that our heavenly Father has done to help us to become truly loving Christians. It is a difficult process to bring some of us to the place that we reflect Jesus in our characters. God gives us His Holy Bible so that we may learn of Him and His way of life. He sent His only Son, Jesus, into this world to show us how to live the overcoming life. Then Jesus died for us that we might have a life that measures with His. He has given us Christian parents and Christian teachers to help us. He sends His Holy Spirit to speak to us and to guide us.

If we accept all that He has given for us we may become like that fragrant, choice perfume. All who come in contact with us will be blessed, for we have, indeed, been with Jesus.

R.H.P.

UNFRIENDLY MOTHERS

Flee also youthful lusts: but follow righteousness, faith, char-ity, peace, with them that call on the Lord out of a pure heart.
2 Timothy 2:22.

Joe laughed at the story Walter whispered to him, but his smile faded when Walter said, "I can come to your house after school for an hour."

"Why, uh . . ." Joe coughed a little. "I guess my mother doesn't want me to bring anybody home after school this week."

Walter called to another friend who was already heading home. "Hey, Rodney!" he shouted. "Wait up!"

When he caught up with Rodney, Walter said, "Maybe I'll walk home with you. Mom said I could play with someone after school if I wanted to."

"I don't think Mother would want me to bring anybody home with me today," Rodney said. Something in his manner reminded Walter of the way Joe had hedged.

Mrs. Wolcott had acted the same way that morning. He used to stay across the street with Wolcotts every time Mom had to be gone when school was out. Lately every time Mom called, Mrs. Wolcott had some reason why he shouldn't come.

"I declare," Mom had said this morning, "I don't think she wants to exchange with me on watching the children anymore."

It was true. Walter thought back. Mrs. Wolcott hadn't sent her children over or invited Walter there since the day Susie overheard him telling stories to the boys out behind the garage. Of course he wouldn't have told those jokes if he had known Susie was listening. They weren't the kind he would tell in front of a girl. Since Susie didn't understand the words he used, she had run right into the house and asked her mother what they meant.

Had Mrs. Wolcott told the other mothers? Even Father was touchy on the subject. When he found the joke magazine Walter had hidden away, he'd said, "Don't contaminate you mind with smut, son." He had thrown the jokes into the furnace.

Now as Walter reached his own house and let himself into its empty silence, he thought of what Father had told him and decided maybe he had better stop repeating those jokes.

R.E.

WHEN RICKY FOUND COURAGE

Be strong and of a good courage, fear not, nor be afraid of them for the Lord thy God, he it is that doth go with thee; he will not fail thee, nor forsake thee. Deuteronomy 31:6.

One thing Ricky prided himself on—his courage. Even if he was only twelve he would tackle almost anything. But one week he discovered that he was not as brave as he had supposed.

Baker's Nursery had hired him to work during Easter vacation and after school each day. He had to transplant flowers and vegetables from large flats into separate cans. Because he hoped to work during the summer, Ricky tried especially hard to do good work.

Now Ricky was bothered because he had not yet told Mr. Baker about his not working late Friday evening and never coming on Saturdays. Monday, Tuesday, Wednesday, and Thursday rushed by as if on wings. Mr. Baker gave the new boy many a smile as he saw him hard at work. He even remarked, "You do turn out a lot of work in a short time—good work too." Ricky always began to work ten or fifteen minutes early and did not lengthen out his breaks. He planned to make himself indispensable to Baker's Nursery.

Friday he had to face the Sabbath issue squarely. Before leaving home he had a little talk with himself and then a special prayer. He determined to march into his employer's office before he began work for the day.

"May I have a word with you before going to work, sir?"

"Sure. You want to get off to go camping or fishing this weekend?"

"No, sir. But, you see, I did not tell you on Monday that I am a Seventh-day Adventist and begin keeping God's Sabbath at sundown on Friday. I can't ever work on Saturday because then I attend Sabbath school and church. But I'll be sure to come Sundays, if you need me."

Mr. Baker looked Ricky full in the eyes. "I hired you because you are an Adventist. Your principal at the junior academy highly recommended you. Indeed you may work all day Sunday. If your sundown comes before quitting time, come in earlier in the morning, or cut your lunch period. I'll trust you."

Ricky thought, What a fool I was to suffer the first four days about my problem, when God had made it so easy for me! I'll know better next time.

L.C.W.

WINGS TO DEPEND ON

You have seen what I did to the Egyptians, and how I bore you on eagles' wings and brought you to myself. Exodus 19:4, RSV.

Do you know there are more than 300 Biblical references to birds? Surely God wants us to learn of Him through these beautiful winged creatures. No wonder Jesus told us to consider them.

Probably their ability to fly is what has most intrigued man for thousands of years. History tells us that Leonardo da Vinci began studying bird flight for his flying machine designs about 1500.

Hollow-stemmed feathers, hollow bones, and pockets of air in the bird's body give it lightness, strength, and buoyancy. The bird flies by pressing its wings down against the air. Its wing feathers are curved to catch more air. The tail, the bird's rudder, is spread out in flight.

No man-made airplane, glider, rocket, or satellite can match the incredible flight feats of birds. An African eagle can swoop down at a speed of more than 100 miles an hour, and then come to a dead halt in just twenty feet by spreading its wings and tail in an aerial braking maneuver.

How can it land with such speed and not break its legs? God cushions its landing by three single rigid bones that have joints that work in opposite directions. This is the most effective shock-absorbing mechanism in all of nature.

A big Cooper's hawk swooped down with terrific speed on a quail perched on a limb about five or six feet above the ground. Seeing it coming, the quail dropped into a clump of bushes. But in that instant, before its body hit the protective shelter, the hawk shot under it, flipped upside down in full flight, caught the falling bird, righted itself and zoomed upward with the heavy quail in its strong talons. And the hawk didn't even slacken its speed.

These marvelous wings enable some birds to soar for hours without any apparent motion. Several species of small birds hover in the air like helicopters, but what man-made flying machine can fly in reverse like the hummingbird?

God will guide your life just as He guides the flight of the birds.

E.E.L. and J.H.L.

BE COURAGEOUS

Only be thou strong and very courageous, ... that thou mayest prosper whithersoever thou goest. Joshua 1:7.

Moses was dead, and Joshua had been given the task of leading Israel into the land of Canaan and conquering the people living there. Forty years had gone by since he and Caleb, with the ten spies, had returned from an inspection trip. Now, of all the men living then, only Caleb and Joshua were still alive, ready to go forward at God's command.

We admire courageous people. The Bible tells of the brave deeds of Joshua, Gideon, Samson, and Elijah. David was just a youth when he stepped out to meet Goliath, the Philistine giant. Armed with sword and shield, Goliath wore heavy armor over his entire body. David had only his shepherd's staff and a sling. But he had something else that was of more value than anything the giant possessed. He had faith in God, and God gave him the victory.

Early one morning Jonathan slipped out of his father's camp with only his armor bearer to attack thirty thousand Philistine soldiers lying encamped on a cliff on the far side of a narrow valley. They were only two against thirty thousand! Where did Jonathan get his courage? Like David, he had faith in God. He told his armor bearer that God could as easily deliver by means of a few as by many. God sent an earthquake, and the Philistines fled in panic.

In 1927, Charles A. Lindbergh, known as the Lone Eagle, took off in his plane, the *Spirit of St. Louis,* from New York to fly the Atlantic Ocean. He was the first man ever to make this crossing alone. For more than twenty-four hours he sat in his plane, guiding it across the waste of waters, and finally landed it safely in Paris.

That took courage. But Lindbergh also showed another kind of courage. A large tobacco company in the United States offered him $25,000 if, on landing, he would ask for one of their particular brand of cigarettes. They knew he didn't smoke, and didn't expect him to smoke. But they hoped he would pose with a cigarette. Lindbergh refused their offer, saying that his good name was not for sale. He could have used that money, for he was in debt at the time.

We need courage also, the kind that comes when we realize that we are not alone, that the mighty God is with us.

V.E.R.

DO NOT BE AFRAID TO FAIL

I have laboured in vain, I have spent my strength for nought, and in vain: yet surely my judgment is with the Lord, and my work with my God. Isaiah 49:4.

"We have nothing to fear but fear itself," President Roosevelt said during the days of a great depression. These words are just as true during times of great prosperity. Our fears will often trip us up and defeat us before we get started.

John was afraid to apply for a job as a stock boy because he had no experience and was sure he could not get the job.

Bob was afraid to apply to college because his marks were not in the higher rank of his class.

Roberta was afraid to become a Sabbath school teacher because she had not been an Adventist very long.

Timothy was afraid to try out for the school orchestra because he did not think he could play well enough.

Jane did not answer the call for volunteers for the school yearbook because she was afraid there was too much competition for the job.

Bill was lonely because he was afraid to smile and speak to students in his new school.

But we lose so much more by *not* trying. The worst kind of failure is failure to try.

In *Life Sketches of Ellen G. White* is advice about how to handle failure. "They should not become discouraged, but should endeavor to learn by every apparent failure how to make a success of the next effort. And if they connect with the Source of wisdom, they will surely succeed."—Page 245.

Occasional failure, apparent failure, those are not new to our generation. Our Example, Jesus Christ, met apparent failure many times. There was much He longed to do for people, and all the forces Satan could muster were opposing Him. Yet He would not be discouraged.

No one likes to be turned down, but failure can be the goad that we need to succeed. If you let failure cause you to doubt yourself, that self-doubt will lead you to strike out.

When you are faced with a situation in which you are afraid, do the best you can and put your trust in God. It is a failure of the spirit that leads to other failures.

R.E.

GOD'S BEST PROMISE

I will be with thee: I will not fail thee, nor forsake thee. Joshua 1:5.

Some years ago an old lawn mower that had given me good service finally cut its last swath through the grass. One wheel came right off, not just from the axle, but from the frame itself, as a whole section gave way. A new mower took its place.

For some weeks the old machine stood in the shed. Then one day my son and I stood looking at it speculatively. "You know," I said, "I think we could turn that engine into a go-cart."

We tried the engine and it ran perfectly. In a few minutes we had it off the frame. Then I had second thoughts. I said nothing at that moment, but the more I thought about it, the less likely it seemed to me that I could do what I had promised. As a soapbox maker I performed fairly well, but taking tubular steel and shaping and welding it into a frame for a go-cart was another thing again.

One day I had a confession to make. I just could not make a go-cart. My son, who had visions of racing around the field at the back of our house, was most disappointed. I learned a lesson that day: "Be sure of performance before you promise."

The Bible speaks of something that is impossible for God! What is it that God cannot do? He cannot go back on His promises, for it is impossible for Him to lie.

God's best promise to us is His promise to be with us always. Joshua found this true when he faced the problems of taking possession of the land of Canaan. The author of hymn number 397 in the *Church Hymnal* says, "I will never, never leave thee, I will never thee forsake." Not under any circumstances will God turn away from us.

We have a word that we use for a man when we think highly of him. We say he has integrity. He is a man of his word. He can be trusted. Likewise we can say of God, He has integrity. You can take Him at His word. And more than that, behind His promises is His power, His knowledge, and His presence. As one author said, "What a God!"

W.R.L.S.

GLEAMING RINGS OF GLORY

O Lord, how manifold are thy works! in wisdom hast thou made them all: the earth is full of thy riches. Psalm 104:24.

Never before had this jungle clearing been the stage for such an exciting occasion. Members of the Pathfinder Club of Singapore stood waiting in small groups. Everyone was looking upward. The moonless jungle night was a perfect background for the magnificent spectacle that held our attention. All eyes were turned to the constellation Gemini, but we weren't looking at its brightest stars, Castor and Pollux.

Our interest was focused on the steadily gleaming orb shining brightly from that part of the sky. This was Saturn, the second largest planet in our solar system. Excited Pathfinders could hardly wait for a glimpse through the telescope that had been set up by those who were teaching star study. Every few minutes the telescope had to be reset because of the movements of our earth. Finally it was my turn.

Kneeling on the ground, I crooked my neck backward. Though we had been told Saturn was one of the most interesting objects in the solar system, I wasn't prepared for what I saw. Surrounding this planet are three thin, flat rings that always tilt at the same angle as its equator. Countless tiny particles, too small and too close together to be seen individually, make up the rings. Astronomers say they appear to be ice crystals or solid objects measuring about one tenth of an inch in diameter, covered with ice. Although the flat rings appear to be less than ten miles thick, the outer one is about 10,000 miles wide. The middle and brightest is about 16,000 miles wide.

As I looked at those gleaming rings of Saturn I felt goose pimples of excitement all over my body.

Someday soon aboard Jesus' "Cloud Spacecraft" en route to the New Jerusalem, you'll be privileged to speed past Saturn with its three rings and ten large moons. The wonder of it all will be that the One who made Saturn and all the glories you'll see in His universe, will be escorting you home to live with Him. Wonderful, wonderful Jesus, who died in your place that you might live eternally to enjoy the thrills He has planned for His beloved children.

E.E.L. and J.H.L.

IT TAKES TWO

I say unto you, That ye resist not evil: but whosoever shall smite thee on thy right cheek, turn to him the other also. Matthew 5:39.

The year 1901 saw many changes in the Seventh-day Adventist Church, the newly elected General Conference president, Elder A. G. Daniells, was trying to follow Sister White's counsels to reorganize and strengthen the work. In doing this, he could not avoid offending some people. But he resolved never to take sides in any personal quarrels. On May 31 of that year he wrote:

"Just as surely as I allow myself to be dragged into squabbles, I shall be ruined; so I have firmly resolved to pursue a straight course, and let the other fellow do the fighting—and by the way, this may save a good deal of fighting in the end.

"The other day, when I came home to dinner from the office, my little boy told me about some soldiers he had seen, and then proposed that we have a fight. I consented, and we had one good, stiff round. He enjoyed it so well that he wanted another; but I did not care for it, so I stood still and let him do the fighting.

"After a few wild rushes at me, he stopped, and said, 'Papa, why don't you fight?' I told him that I was tired, and would let him fight alone. Then he said, 'But it's no fun to fight alone.' I told him that he could make fun out of it; so he tried again; but he soon gave it up, saying that he couldn't fight alone, for he didn't know how.

"Perhaps if some of us Christians would let people fight alone, they would find so little 'fun' in it—yes, find it such hard work—that they would conclude they could not fight alone."

One sad night Peter became furious because of the rough way his Master was being handled. Swinging his sword, he cut off a man's ear. This could have started a free-for-all. But Jesus immediately "touched his ear, and healed him." Then he rebuked Peter, saying, "Put up thy sword into the sheath."

Jesus never struck back at those who wished to harm Him. His way was the way of peace.

The next time you see a hot argument coming up, step aside, say nothing, and watch it die.

"It takes two to make a quarrel, but only one to end it."

V.E.R.

"WHY ARE WE POOR?"

For I was an hungered, and ye gave me meat: I was thirsty, and ye gave me drink: I was a stranger, and ye took me in. Matthew 25:35.

With his arms plunged into soapy dishwater a small boy of six faced his mother. "Mother, why does God want us to be poor?" The Edwards family was in poverty, no doubt about it. While they were not actually starving, food was not abundant. Most of their nourishment came from cornmeal cooked in a variety of ways. The welfare helped them some. All the children waited for mother's answer to their small brother's question.

God inspired the mother with the right answer for her six children. "I think God wants us to be poor so that we'll know what it feels like. Our situation will no doubt improve. Then we must not forget other poor people, but do our best to help them." The children appeared satisfied with the explanation. Gradually the Edwards family climbed up in the financial scale. They had better food, new clothes, better housing, and finally a *new car.* To herself the mother wondered, Will my children still remember those who are unfortunate?

To her great satisfaction the children did remember. One day Cindy came home from school and asked, "May I give my extra pair of mittens to a girl in my grade who has no mittens?" Gladly the mother gave her permission.

Roderick wondered if a jacket could be provided for a schoolmate who was coming to school in the coldest weather with only a sweater. Mrs. Edwards enlisted the help of mothers in the PTA in getting a used-clothing and shoe bank upon which they and the teachers could draw for needy children. The boy got a well-lined jacket.

The oldest daughter, now in high school, became concerned over a classmate who came daily with tangled hair and unpressed dresses. June made friends with her, taught her how to care for her hair, and helped her with her clothes. June discovered that this girl's alcoholic parents took no interest in her.

Since their experience with poverty the Edwards children were always on the lookout for people to help. They ran errands for elderly and feeble neighbors.

Jesus tells us that when we help the unfortunate we are doing it for Him.

L.C.W.

HELP IN TIME OF NEED

God is our refuge and strength, a very present help in trouble.
Psalm 46:1.

It was midnight in the town of Plymouth, England. Two men stood before the town clock and heard it strike thirteen times. One of the men who heard this phenomenon was Captain Jarvis. The other man was a stranger in town.

Several months later Captain Jarvis awakened at midnight. He felt impressed to dress. After dressing, he went out his front door, and to his amazement found his groom standing there with his horse. He said, "What are you doing here?"

"I don't know. I just had to get up and here I am."

Captain Jarvis got on the horse, and of its own accord the animal headed straight to the ferry. And there, at one o'clock in the morning, the ferryman stood waiting. Normally the ferry stopped running at eleven. "What are you doing at this hour?" asked the captain.

"I don't know. I had to get up and here I am."

So Captain Jarvis and his horse crossed on the ferry. Again he gave the horse free rein and they traveled through the winding trails of Devonshire throughout the night.

Around ten o'clock the next morning he met a man in a village and asked, "Anything special happening here?"

The stranger answered, "A trial is on. The man has been found guilty and the judge is getting ready for his decision."

Captain Jarvis walked into the courtroom just in time to hear the judge announce his decision—death by hanging. Then he asked the man whether he had anything to say for himself.

"Only this," said the man. "I am innocent, and there is only one who knows I was not at the scene of the crime that midnight, and I don't even know his name."

Captain Jarvis arose. "I am that man," he said, and told about the strange incident when the clock struck thirteen times. He also told how he got there at that precise moment.

The man was saved from death. Only divine guidance and providential leading could have performed the many miracles involved in this experience.

A.A.E.

GOD'S WORD GIVES LIGHT

The entrance of thy words giveth light; it giveth understanding unto the simple. Psalm 119:130.

On April 28, 1789, the sailors on the British ship *Bounty* rebelled against their captain, William Bligh. Expelling him and his loyal followers, they turned them loose on the open ocean in a small boat. The mutineers then took the ship to the island of Tahiti, where they persuaded some of the women of the island to go with them to Pitcairn Island, a lonely spot in the South Pacific Ocean. Knowing they could never return to civilization, they burned the *Bounty* after stripping it of everything valuable.

Years went by. Some of the men learned to make strong drink and lived wicked lives. There was fighting and murder, and one by one the men were killed off or died of drink, leaving their wives and many children who had been born on the island.

At last only one man remained of the original mutineers, John Adams. As he looked at the many boys and girls growing up around him, he realized that not one of them knew anything about God. They had no church and no school.

One day as he was going through the old trunk that had been taken from the *Bounty* before it was burned, he found the Bible that had belonged to the leader of the mutineers. He read it for hours. As he did so, a great longing came over him. In his heart he wanted to live a better life so he might help his people.

Calling the women and children around him, he began to read to them out of that Bible. They agreed to live by the rules of that wonderful Book. John Adams taught the people to read. He taught them to be clean, and every Sunday he held services with them.

In 1808, eighteen years after the mutineers had landed on Pitcairn, an American vessel dropped anchor offshore. The captain came ashore and the great secret of what had become of the mutineers of the *Bounty* was at last revealed. The captain might have taken John Adams back to England to stand trial, but when he saw how the people of the island loved him and clung to him, he decided not to take their "father" away.

The same Bible that wrought such a transformation on Pitcairn Island is still changing the lives of boys and girls today.

V.E.R.

FOLLOWING BIG BROTHER

Who is he that will harm you, if ye be followers of that which is good? 1 Peter 3:13.

The morning Billy noticed the first snowfall, he shouted with delight. It meant snow fights and snow forts. Quickly he finished his chores and telephoned the Lance children. They promised to come over soon. Meanwhile Billy took his two-year-old brother outdoors so he could make a snow man. When the children arrived, yells and threats accompanied snowballs flying in all directions. The children's allotted hour to stay passed altogether too quickly.

Billy promised his departing guests, "I'll see if I can come over to your place after lunch so that we can build a snow fort in your pasture." His mother readily gave him permission. Billy decided that he would take the short cut along the railroad tracks, although his mother had told him never to go that way. Her reason? Once a small child had been killed while playing along the tracks. Because of the freeway noise it wasn't always easy to hear the train before it came around the bend. Billy felt that since he was eleven, almost a teenager, he no longer needed mother's warning.

Many children had come to the Lances' pasture to build forts, and the battle raged with real spirit on both sides. Finally they all agreed to sign an armistice and go home to get warm. As he started for the tracks again, Billy suddenly heard long shrill blasts of the train whistle. The engine screeched to a stop. Two men came running and picked up something red from the tracks. It was Teddy! His *brother*! Crying at the top of his lungs!

The engineer and fireman asked Billy, "Do you know this little guy? How did he find his way clear over here!"

Billy's heart pounded. "I think he must have sneaked out of the house while my mother was napping. He probably tried to follow me. He is only two."

"Your little brother followed your footprints in the snow. Thank God I was able to stop the train in time. Glad the baby wore something red."

As the train pulled away, Billy hugged baby brother close and poured out his prayer of thanksgiving: "Lord Jesus, thank You for saving Teddy's life when I did not follow mom's advice. Help me always to be a good example to Teddy so that it will be safe for him to follow me."

L.C.W.

STILL SHINING

The heavens declare the glory of God, the vault of heaven proclaims his handiwork. Psalm 19:1, Jerusalem.

Gaze upward and behold that the night sky is not just a black vault spangled with silver. Looking closely, you will see that the white star, Sirius, has a sapphire glint, Capella is yellow, and Arcturus a vivid orange. The constellation Orion has both red and blue stars, and telescopes reveal that Orion's Great Nebula is bluish-green and pink.

Yes, the heavens, God's great universe, is an exciting place. The great telescope that sweeps the sky from Palomar Observatory in California, is finding immense numbers of celestial bodies never known before. The astronomers have photographed objects whose light, traveling 186,000 miles a second, took 300 million years to reach our earth. It could be that many of those stars ceased to exist centuries or millenniums ago, but their light keeps traveling through space. Like them, our influence goes on even after we are gone. The words we say, the kind things we do will continue to light the way for others. You may move away from your friends, or even die, but your influence will always remain to bring joy to those who remember, or horrible memories to those who wish they could forget.

All of man's history is like the tick of a clock compared to the time this light has been speeding through space. What you say or do will continue on throughout all eternity. After 3 million centuries, these heavenly bodies may be entirely different now, or not be at all, but we see them as they were.

Truly, our human minds stagger as we try to think of the immensity of God's universe. We exclaim with Job: "Lo, these are but the outskirts of his ways: and how small a whisper do we hear of him! But the thunder of his power who can understand?" (Job 26:14, ARV).

Smoke and clouds may cover the glory of the heavens, but the stars shine on, though hidden from our view. The goodness of God lives on in spite of circumstances that may seem to hide Him from us. Have faith, for His love will shine out clearly again. He will keep your life pure so that your influence will declare His glory, as do the heavens, throughout all eternity.

E.E.L. and J.H.L.

SIN AGAINST THE HOLY SPIRIT

He that is not with me is against me: and he that gathereth not with me scattereth. Luke 11:23.

Jesus warned the religious leaders of His time that in resisting truth they were sinning against the Holy Spirit.

He compared their nation to a demon-possessed man. For a time it may seem that the man has repented and that the demon has departed. The demon wanders out in the desert finding no rest and finally decides to return to the man from which it came. The returning demon finds the man's heart clean—but empty. So with seven other spirits even more evil than itself, it takes over the man's mind again and the man is then worse off than before.

That is the condition in which we find ourselves if we do not surrender ourselves to Christ daily, so that He may live in our heart. We do not have to deliberately choose Satan in order to serve him; we have only to neglect to choose Christ.

But sometimes we live in fear because we do not properly understand what is meant by rejecting the Holy Spirit.

Ron, for instance, was moody, depressed, and withdrawn for several months, worrying about a wrong thing he had done. He had broken something, and fearing the punishment, he put the blame on another boy who was staying with his family at this time. The other boy got the spanking.

In his heart he felt convicted to confess, but he was afraid to. Then one Sabbath the preacher spoke about the sin against the Holy Spirit, and Ron was frightened. Perhaps he had already committed the unpardonable sin!

After supper one evening he sat down to talk it over with Mother, confessing what he had done and telling her his fear that he had sinned against the Holy Spirit.

Mother explained to him that when the Spirit withdraws from us, we have hardened our hearts and don't feel bothered or guilty.

The Desire of Ages puts it thus: "The most common manifestation of the sin against the Holy Spirit is in persistently slighting Heaven's invitation to repent. Every step in the rejection of Christ is a step toward the rejection of salvation, and toward the sin against the Holy Spirit."—page 324.

Let us keep our hearts open to His love.

R.E.

TRUE CHRISTIAN FORGIVENESS

Forgive us the wrongs we have done, as we forgive the wrongs that others have done to us. Matthew 6:12, TEV.

Some years ago J. M. Mershon quoted the following letters in the *Review and Herald*:

"My dear Madam:

"In the course of a commando raid on a French village, it became my duty to kill your son. My heart aches with sorrow in sharing with you the experience of loss that must be yours. I write earnestly to ask your forgiveness, for I am a Christian. I hope that after the war is over I may see you and talk with you face-to-face."

Months later the young officer received this reply from the compassionate woman:

"My dear Captain:

"I find in my heart to forgive you, even you who killed my son. I, too, am a Christian. If we are living when the war is over, I hope you will come to Germany to visit me, that you may take the place in my home, if only for a time, of my son whom you killed."

This is a miracle of God's grace in the human heart.

Only a real Christian can truly forgive after a great loss and while the hurt is deep. There is something very Christlike in forgiving those who wounded us.

> The sandal tree perfumes, when riven,
>> The ax that laid it low.
> Let him that hopes to be forgiven,
>> Forgive and bless his foe.
>> —Author unknown

"Nothing can justify an unforgiving spirit," Ellen White writes. "He who is unmerciful toward others shows that he himself is not a partaker of God's pardoning grace. In God's forgiveness the heart of the erring one is drawn close to the great heart of Infinite Love."—*Christ's Object Lessons*, p. 251.

How do you forgive, my son, my daughter? Do you forgive each other in the same way that the Lord Jesus has freely forgiven you?

R.H.P.

PREPARING FOR A JOURNEY

For this reason, then, you also must be always ready, because the Son of Man will come at an hour when you are not expecting him. Matthew 24:44 (TEV).

Since this is the last day of July, we have only a few weeks left before school begins in early September. Have you had your summer vacation yet? Only one long holiday weekend—Labor Day, the first part of September—is left this summer.

The story is told of what happened during the start of a long holiday weekend when the gas station was crowded. Eventually the attendant rushed up to the local minister whose car was in line.

"I'm so sorry about the delay, Pastor," he apologized. "It seems like everybody waits until the last minute to get ready for a trip that they know they are going to take."

The minister smiled as he said: "I know what you mean. I have the same problem in my business!"

Perhaps it is because of this human trait of procrastination that God warns of the danger of delay. Jesus said, "You also must be always ready, because the Son of Man will come at an hour when you are not expecting him."

How often we read that phrase in the Bible: *Prepare to meet thy God.* If we are really expecting to take this long and happy journey with Jesus on our way to heaven and to enter through that glorious corridor in Orion, we should be getting ready. Are we prepared? Our preparations must be complete before He comes. There is no second chance! And yet "it seems like everybody waits until the last minute to get ready for a trip that they know they are going to take."

"The righteous will take every grace, every precious, sanctified ability, into the courts above, and exchange earth for heaven. God knows who are the loyal and true subjects of His kingdom on earth, and those who do His will upon earth as it is done in heaven, will be made the members of the royal family above."—*Sons and Daughters of God,* p. 361.

A family reunion! What a journey that will be! We must be ready when Jesus comes for us. This is the most important journey of our life. Make all of your preparations now!

A.A.E.

CONFESSING WITHOUT SQUEALING

To him that soweth righteousness shall be a sure reward.
Proverbs 11:18.

The trouble started with Dick Brown. The ground under the apple tree where the four boys stood was covered with half-rotten apples. Dick threw an apple into the air and dared Johnny to throw one higher. Soon Mr. Holiday's barn became the target. When the culprits spied Mr. Holiday's car coming down the lane, they scurried into the woods for cover.

When Johnny and Frank finally walked toward home, John said, "I wish we had not spattered his barn with those rotten apples." Frank agreed. At dinner that evening Johnny's dad remarked, "Mr. Holiday just told me some boys messed up his barn by throwing rotten apples against it. I hope you were not one, my son."

Johnny had never lied to his father, and this time he merely kept silent. When Father Abbott went on to talk about something else, the boy felt relieved. Yet for two days he carried his guilt. Keeping still was like lying. Finally after dinner he followed his dad out on the porch and took the big plunge. "Dad, if I did something wrong, could I tell you about it and not involve anyone else? I don't want to get others into trouble."

"Yes, I guess so. I know how you feel about squealing on someone. I will not ask you who else was involved."

"You remember Mr. Holiday's barn? I was one of the boys."

After some minutes Mr. Abbott asked, "A son of mine had nothing better to do than to splatter up a neighbor's barn with rotten apples? Right after school tomorrow you will march over and tell Mr. Holiday. You will accept whatever punishment he would have given all of you. I'll telephone him not to ask you questions."

Johnny announced the verdict to his chum Frank, who protested, "That's not fair. I'll go too and we will both take the punishment."

First Mr. Holiday asked the boys to count the apple cores in a basket where flies were buzzing around. They counted 43. Then the man asked them to work one hour for every core—an hour each day after school and eight hours on Sunday.

After their time was all in, their stern master beamed. "You boys are such good workers I wonder if you would like part-time work now and several hours a day during the summer. I'll pay you well."

The right-doing of these lads really did lead to a "reward."

L.C.W.

221

WHO IS MY GOD?

I will take you to me for a people, and I will be to you a God:
and ye shall know that I am the Lord your God. Exodus 6:7.

What would you want to say about your God if someone asked you? Would you want to tell him that He lives up in heaven? Or would you try to say how big He is? Would you talk about the wonderful things He has made?

Perhaps the best thing you could say about your God is this: "He is my God. I know Him and He knows me."

When the ancient Israelites wanted to identify their God, they often did so by calling Him the God of Abraham, Isaac, and Jacob. This is just another way of saying that God knows us as individuals.

One of the tiniest instruments in an orchestra is the piccolo. Usually the sound of the piccolo is lost among the rest of the instruments, except to discerning ears. Sometimes it has a solo for a few bars, but not too often.

In one of the great orchestras the piccolo player decided that he was hardly needed. *He* never had important pieces to play. Besides, he felt tired. So he quit.

With a violent sweep of his arm, the conductor halted the orchestra. "Where is the piccolo?" he demanded. "I do not hear the piccolo. Why are you not playing, sir?"

Embarrassed, the player stammered, "I thought it would not matter if I stopped for a few minutes. You can hardly hear my instrument."

"You are as important as any other instrument. More important, in fact, because there is only one of you."

Perhaps you have thought about the millions of people who live in your city, or country; about the billions who fill the earth. And here you are—a tiny, insignificant grain of sand.

Does God know you? Yes, says the Bible. He knows you by name, just as He knew Abraham, Isaac, and Jacob. Isn't that a wonderful thought? Isn't it wonderful, too, that He wants you to live with Him forever?

W.R.L.S.

THE POWER OF GOD

Fear ye not me? saith the Lord: will ye not tremble at my presence, which have placed the sand for the bound of the sea by a perpetual decree, that it cannot pass it? Jeremiah 5:22.

It was junior camp time again, and this year it had been decided to hold the camp in a grove of trees at the seashore. How excited the campers were as they packed. It was said that some of them never slept a wink all night, they were so busy getting ready to leave early the next day. Even the trip to camp was fun, as there was a two-hour boat ride down the river and along a canal before they came to what they called the jumping-off place—where they had to start hiking the last six miles to the ocean. For this camp was in India.

When the young people arrived at their destination they found no cabins or even tents awaiting them. Only sand and trees. But they were prepared. Quickly they strung ropes between the trees, hung blankets over them, and presto, tents!

The place that intrigued each camper the most, however, was the beach. From the camp, though the water was hidden from view by a low sandy hill, the sound of the breakers rolling up to the shore could be heard continuously, and the first thing each camper did as soon as he dared was to make a beeline for the beach!

During the day the water was fun, but at night the roaring of the breakers frightened some of the girls. Suppose those waves should come rushing over that little hill? What if the water flooded the camp? What could they do? The trees were too small to climb.

But those girls did not need to be so worried! God Himself said He placed the sand for a boundary for the sea so it cannot pass. He asked Job, Who "shut up the sea"? (Job 38:8), and said, "Hitherto shalt thou come, but no further: and here shall thy proud waves be stayed" (verse 11).

The very fact that the ocean stays where it belongs is a proof of God's power.

The girls were afraid of the power of the waves, but it is God who controls them. He asks, "Will ye not tremble at my presence?" God wants us to respect and reverence Him, for He is more powerful than the breakers.

M.H.

SHORT CIRCUITS AND POWER

Both riches and honour come of thee, and thou reignest over all; and in thine hands is power and might; and in thine hand it is to make great, and to give strength unto all. 1 Chronicles 29:12.

Jennifer's friends would be along any minute. She gave a final flick of the brush to her shining hair. She was all ready to go.

"You don't want to go to the fair without shoes on," Mother said.

But nobody was wearing shoes that year; it simply was not "in" and Jennifer did want to go without them. Even the fact that the weather was cool and rainy didn't change her mind.

It was a small county fair. Most of the young people from the surrounding area were there on Saturday night, however, and Jennifer anticipated an evening of fun.

The group wandered down the midway looking everything over, deciding which rides to try first. The Tilt-a-Whirl ground to a halt and disgorged its passengers. Jennifer's group started to board, the boys' boots clanging as they went up the metal steps.

Jennifer had just started up the steps. All at once she stood rooted to the step, unable to move, electricity charging through her body.

"Go on, Jen," urged one of the kids behind her. But she could not move. She could not even speak.

One of the boys ahead of her turned to look back.

"Hey!" he shouted. "Something's wrong with Jen!"

The attendant taking tickets ran to throw the electric power switch, and friends then helped Jennifer down the stairs.

The attendant yelled, "Crazy kid, ought to know better than to go on rides without shoes, especially on a wet night like this."

Their evening of fun forgotten, the group drove Jennifer home, still frightened by the experience.

Harnessing electric power has made possible much of modern life as we know it. Take electricity out of your home right now and how many things would run?

Rightly used, electric power is one of our most efficient helpers. Yet the same power shorted-out can be responsible for injuries and deaths.

God's power is glorious and strengthens us. But there is a "shortened-out" power too. Colossians 1:13 calls it the "power of darkness." God is able to save us from the power of darkness. Today let us give thanks that He is stronger than any other power.

R.E.

THUNDER EGG BEAUTY

The king's daughter is all glorious within. Psalm 45:13.

Nestled close to the Rocky Mountains, near Loveland, Colorado, is a humble home filled with unusual treasures. The well-kept garden path, lined with choice flowers, led to a shed converted into a paradise of beauty that thrilled us.

Mr. Ross has had a lifetime hobby of collecting and studying rocks, minerals, and gems. Not only does he love each one, but he loves to share. When he was younger he traveled widely giving illustrated lectures. Through him we learned that the three main kinds of rocks are made largely of only eight elements. Demonstrating that rocks are a blend of many minerals, he showed us a chunk of granite that contained five types. We compared them with separate specimens of each. About 2,000 kinds of minerals are found in the earth, but only 100 are common. Most are harder to find than gold.

"You'll like my thunder eggs." He pointed to ugly round, rough, unpromising rocks. "With my diamond saw I've cut them in two."

As he opened the parts we gasped in wonder. Inside one was a beautiful display of quartz crystals. Another was a banded agate with multi-colored bands circling the core. Inside many were imaginary scenes of landscapes with mountains, valleys, ocean waves, or trees along a river.

From these masterpieces of nature he had cut thin slices from a cross section and mounted them as color slides. Slipping them into a projector, he thrilled us with the beauty of each. In many cases nature had supplied her own picture frame with a crystalline quartz border around the lovely scene.

Had I been choosing rock specimens, I'm sure I wouldn't have picked those ugly geodes or thunder eggs. I would have considered the outward appearance. But Mr. Ross knew; he found inward beauty where I saw ugliness.

When Jesus looks inside your heart, does He see a treasure of beauty or a mass of jealousy, envy, selfishness, or temper? Girls, are you all glorious within, filled with the beauty of kindness, helpfulness, love, courtesy, and reverence? Boys, do pure thoughts make you of great inward beauty? What does Jesus see in you?

E.E.L. and J.H.L.

NOT I, BUT CHRIST

I live; yet not I, but Christ liveth in me. Galatians 2:20, middle part.

I want to write a poem
  That will stand the test of time.
I want to sing a solo
  That will ring in every clime.
I want to preach a sermon
  That will match this solemn hour.
I want to pray a prayer
  That will move God's arm of power.
But sermons, prayers, and solos,
  And the best of poetry,
Are merely human phrases,
  And they fill all history.
But what this world is needing now
  Is more than lovely verse,
For prattling pretty platitudes
  Won't save men from the curse.
This old world needs the Saviour,
  Needs to feel His life of power.
Ah! Here's a living sermon
  That will match this tragic hour.
Christ's life was one grand poem
  Full of glorious melody,
His life a living prayer,
  And a hymn of harmony!
Lo! Christ makes life a poem
  Written well with loving deeds;
And life's a song of gladness
  Sung by serving human needs.
And prayer's a constant friendship
  With our Lord who makes life new.
And life's a living sermon,
  Preached in everything we do!

"When we submit ourselves to Christ, the heart is united to His heart . . . we live His life."—Christ's Object Lessons, *p. 312.*

A.A.E.

GOD WILL STILL HELP

Where is the Lord God of Elijah? 2 Kings 2:14.

Elisha watched fascinated as Elijah, his friend and teacher, disappeared into heaven in a fiery chariot. Down from the sky floated Elijah's mantle. Picking it up, Elisha walked back to the bank of Jordan, which he had crossed with Elijah a short time before.

Rolling up the mantle, Elisha smote the river. Would God hear and answer his prayer as He had for Elijah?

"Where is the Lord God of Elijah?" he asked, striking the water with the mantle. The river opened and Elisha crossed on dry ground. Now he knew that Elijah's God was not dead, but that He would be his God also.

Elder and Mrs. Berg were poor when they moved with their small son, George, to a town in Western Canada where Elder Berg would be the church pastor. Heavy medical expenses had used up most of the family savings. One evening while she was preparing to bake bread, Mrs. Berg found she had no flour. When she asked her husband to walk to the nearest store and get some, he replied that he had no money until his next check should arrive.

"What are we going to do?" asked Mrs. Berg anxiously. "We must have food."

"God has never failed us yet. Let us tell Him of our needs."

So father and mother and George, too, prayed that somehow God would send them flour. It was snowing hard when they went to bed, and there seemed no way for their prayers to be answered.

But they soon found that the God of Elijah is not dead. When they awoke in the morning they looked out on a world of white. Opening the back door, Mrs. Berg found a sack of flour leaning against the door. Any tracks made by the one bringing it had long since been covered by fresh snow. The Berg family never knew who brought that flour they needed so much, but they thanked God for it.

Do you have troubles at school, or at home? Do you sometimes wonder whether God will hear your prayers?

"Call unto me, and I will answer thee," is God's promise given through the prophet Jeremiah (Jeremiah 33:3). Repeat this promise, make your request, and prove for yourself that the God of Elijah still lives.

V.E.R.

THREE OR ONE

The Holy Ghost, whom the Father will send in my name, he shall teach you all things, and bring all things to your remembrance. John 14:26.

"Daddy, do we have three Gods or one?"

Startled, I stopped tying the tomato vines and looked down at my six-year-old girl. Why would she ask a question like that?

"Come and have a look at this lily," I said.

We bent over a beautiful white lily that was just beginning to come to full glory. "How many petals are there?" I asked.

Fingers flew over petals as she counted. "Three white ones and three green ones."

I explained that the three green ones were really covers for the more delicate petals so that they would not be injured while the bud was growing.

"Look inside the flower. How many of these yellow things can you see?"

"Three. Is this flower made up of threes?"

"Yes, even the seeds are in three parts and in rows of three. But it is still one flower. So we have God who is the Father, God who is the Son, Jesus Christ, and God who is the Holy Spirit. There are three persons in the Godhead but they are one God."

"Who is the Holy Spirit, Daddy?"

"He's the one who teaches us about God when we pray to Him. He helps us to understand the Bible. Through Him God is everywhere."

The Holy Spirit is a Person, a part of the Godhead. He teaches, He intercedes for us, He can be grieved, He reads and understands our hearts, He gives us good gifts.

We call the first person of the Godhead the Father because this is the best way we can understand Him. Jesus is the Son, because this is the way we understand best His relationship to the Trinity. The Father, Son, and Holy Spirit work in different ways for our salvation, but with the same purpose and plan. Like the flower—separate parts, but one flower.

W.R.L.S.

SUPER TREE, THE COCONUT PALM

The righteous shall flourish like the palm tree. Psalm 92:12.

Why did God choose the beautiful palm tree as a symbol for the growth and excellence of the righteous?

God made more than 1,500 kinds of palm trees but probably the most useful are the date, palmyra, and the coconut palm. In Southeast Asia, where I live, it is almost impossible to count the ways the coconut palm serves mankind. Not only does it provide the materials to build an entire house but also most of the furnishings— from beds and mattresses to soap and toothbrushes. Besides providing cooling shade and fans, palms give heat to cook food, oil for light, and even the lamp in which to put the light. From this tree the fisherman gets his boat, sails, ropes, fishing line, and nets, as well as clothes.

Like the tree of life, the coconut palm at any time has twelve different crops, from the opening flower to the ripe nut. The strength of the tree, as well as that of the righteous man, is in the condition of the heart. Located high at the tree's top, the heart is a bundle of tightly packed, yellow-white, cabbage-like leaves. If it is cut or slightly damaged the whole tree dies.

In most trees the bark carries the vital sap. But the coconut palm's sap rises throughout the whole trunk. God also uses the entire Christian as a channel through which His love and grace can flow.

Seldom are palm trees uprooted, for their roots are strong and deep. Their wood is made up of thousands of fibers that cross each other, binding them together. Youth bound by the promises of God and rooted in Jesus are trouble resistant.

If properly cultivated, the coconut palm will bear up to 120 nuts a year, but if let alone only from ten to forty nuts. Like the Christian, its fruit bearing is in direct proportion to the time and energy spent cultivating its growth.

When the nut is opened, it yields about two cups of clear, cool, sweet water containing minerals and vitamins. This water is so pure and sterile that doctors have used it in an emergency instead of sterile glucose solution to drip straight into patients' veins.

Won't you pray that you will flourish as the palm tree and be strong, pure, beautiful, and useful to both God and man?

E.E.L. and J.H.L.

DON'T BE STUPID

Forsake the foolish, and live; and go in the way of under-standing. Proverbs 9:6.

It started in Appleton, Wisconsin, as Art Linkletter talked to pupils in grades one, two, and three about drug abuse. Ever since Art's own eighteen-year-old daughter, Diane, went to her death under the influence of drugs, her father had dedicated his life to fighting drugs.

He found he had to approach small children in a special way. He first gave them a watchword or slogan to use as a guard, "Stupid."

He suggested that if anyone tried to get them to try a new kind of pill, a shot, or drugs, to say, "Stupid!" "How stupid can you get?" or "I'm not *that* stupid!"

Art Linkletter said that he believes in miracles. "I do not use the word loosely as we sometimes do when something unexpectedly wonderful happens, when I say I have seen miracles. I mean it in the Bible sense, miracles as great as restoring the blind to sight, or the crippled to walk, or to save the dying. I have seen habitual drug users withdraw from it 'cold turkey,' without the help of milder drugs or medicines to ease the agony, the vomiting, and all the horror that usually accompanies withdrawal. They did it by accepting Christ as their Saviour, putting all their trust in Him, and asking Him for help."

To this, Art Linkletter added his own personal testimony, "I am with Jesus Christ."

The same Jesus who can help young folks overcome drug habits, can help young folks to withstand the temptation to experiment with drugs in the first place.

He has promised, "When thou passest through the waters, I will be with thee; and through the rivers, they shall not overflow thee: when thou walkest through the fire, thou shalt not be burned; neither shall the flame kindle upon thee" (Isa. 42:2).

With His help, let's take up that watchword against drugs.

"Don't be stupid."

R.E.

ARE YOU AFRAID TO JUMP?

Then Moses stood in the gate of the camp, and said, Who is on the Lord's side? let him come unto me. And all the sons of Levi gathered themselves together unto him. Exodus 32:26.

The two-story frame house is in flames. Smoke billows out of the windows. Firemen arrive and pour water into the burning mass. Suddenly two small children appear in an upstairs window. One belongs to the family of the burning house. The other is a little neighbor boy.

The father and owner of the house spots the two children. He waves frantically. "Jump! Jump!" he cries. "I will catch you!"

The little son clambers up on the window ledge and without a moment's hesitation jumps into his father's outstretched arms. In a matter of moments the second little fellow jumps to safety.

The tiny son trusted his father. He did not hesitate. He knew his father always kept his word. He did not fear the fall, for he knew his father's arms would catch him and he would be all right. This was trust. This was faith in action.

We live today in a world going up in smoke. One of these days the whole earth *will* burn with real fire and smoke. There is no question about it. You and I need to be sure we have a way of escape. How will it be?

There are two pair of arms outstretched to us today. The voices are calling to us to jump. Both say that they will save us. Satan has his arms wide open, calling for us to let him catch us. He will take care of us, he promises. We can have all the pleasures of this world and heaven too, he assures us. No need for us to be concerned about how we live, where we go, what we do—everything is cared for.

Don't believe him! He is a liar, and has been from the beginning. If you jump at his bidding it will be the end, the bitter end. It will be an end in the lake of fire.

Jesus holds out His arms of love to you today. He has proved His love and concern for us by dying upon the cross of Calvary. There is no question about it. Trust Him. Respond. Let yourself fall into His waiting arms. He will save you.

R.H.P.

HOW MUCH ARE YOU SORRY?

Bear ye one another's burdens, and so fulfil the law of Christ. Galatians 6:2.

A beautiful thing happened on a San Diego pier one day. A ship had arrived and was unloading lumber and furniture. Contractors with their wagons were driving up and carrying the merchandise away. One man had a balky mule attached to his cart. People standing near watched as he tried to lead his animal over to a pile of furniture, but the mule refused to budge.

At last the mule began to move, not forward, but backward. The poor driver tried his best to stop the animal, but it continued to back up. Some of the spectators rushed to try and help, but it was too late. The cart and then the mule went over the pier and into the deep water.

The owner ran to the landing, borrowed a boat, and frantically rowed out to the spot where he had lost both animal and cart, but there was nothing there. The animal, hitched to the cart, had drowned.

"What a pity!" "Too bad!" "Poor man!" exclaimed the spectators. This did not satisfy an old German workman standing among them. Taking off his hat, he walked from one to another.

"Come on, boys," he said, "how much are you sorry?" To show what he meant he took out a ten-dollar bill and placed it in his hat.

"Dat man haf a vife and five children. Vat he do now? How much you sorry for him?" he repeated.

The people smiled, but they opened their wallets and dropped money into the hat. When all had given, the German took it over to the discouraged owner who was sitting sadly on a pile of lumber, wondering how to tell his wife about his loss. The German sat down beside him.

"Ve are sorry for you. Buy yourself another mule and vagon." With that he thrust a fistful of bank notes and some silver into the hand of the astonished drayman. Thanking the kind German, he hurried home to tell his wife that there were still many good-hearted people in the world.

We can show how sorry we are, and how much we care, by what we do. "Actions speak louder than words." Always remember the words of John: "Little children, let us not love in word, neither in tongue, but in deed and in truth" (1 John 3:18).

V.E.R.

REJOICING IN TODAY

This is the day which the Lord hath made; we will rejoice and be glad in it. Psalm 118:24.

Some days it is so easy to rejoice and be glad. Susan had that kind of day. It was vacation time and her doctor father and nurse mother were hers—hers for hiking the jungle mountain trails, for talking about the things Susan liked to talk about, not the sicknesses of the patients or the problems of the mission hospital that seemed to occupy every day at home. They had time to stop as she picked the wild flowers along the trail or looked at the many birds flitting in the bushes. They were interested in the huge dragonflies that hovered over the stream and the inch-long beetles that crawled on the leaf-covered paths. They sat with her on the moss-covered rocks and watched the water tumbling down the bank.

But not every day of Susan's life is as beautiful and carefree as this. How does a 12-year-old girl keep happy on days when mother and dad have to leave home at six-thirty in the morning for the hospital, and come home at night so tired they hardly have time for her?

Today's Bible verse is her answer. Young people who enjoy life don't worry about tomorrow or relive yesterday. They just live today with Jesus. Susan's today, no matter how beautiful, can easily be spoiled by thinking about the problems and difficulties coming tomorrow. Someone has said, "Satan tries to crush our spirit by getting us to bear tomorrow's problems with only today's grace."

So let's be happy today for God has promised to supply all our needs.

Be like Susan and be happy today in the beautiful things God has given you. Leave tomorrow with God, remembering that worry "does not empty tomorrow of its sorrow, but it empties today of its strength. It does not make you escape the evil; it makes you unfit to cope with it if it comes."

Rejoice and be glad today. If your happiness comes from the changeable, varying circumstances of life, it won't last. Joy and peace from Jesus is constant. It doesn't depend upon friends, possessions or circumstances. Lasting joy from Jesus makes each day beautiful.

E.E.L. and J.H.L.

WINNING SOULS

Will ye hunt the souls of my people? Ezekiel 13:18.

Perhaps you have thought it would be a wonderful thing if someday you could be an evangelist and preach the gospel. It would thrill you to see men and women, boys and girls, accepting Jesus as their Saviour. Once in a while we read of children who have not waited to grow up before starting to work for Jesus.

Maria, the daughter of a minister who was too sick to leave his house, went to the post office one day to get the mail.

"Are there any letters for my father? He is expecting some."

"What is your father's name?" asked the clerk.

"What! Don't you know my father?"

"Of course not," he replied carelessly. "How should I?"

"Everybody knows my father. Don't you go to church?"

"No, never!"

"You never go to meeting? That's why you don't know my father. He's the minister."

The next day she was back, but still there was no mail.

"You would like my father if you knew him. They say he is a nice preacher."

The day came when the expected letters arrived and the clerk handed them to her.

"I wish you knew my father; you would like him."

"No doubt I would, if he is like his daughter," the clerk smiled.

"Please come to church next Sunday night and hear him preach. I'll be there looking for you."

The man made no promises and didn't go. Maria asked him again and again. Finally he promised to go—once.

Sunday evening she stood at the entry to the church, watching for her friend from the post office. When he came she took him by the hand and led him to a seat near the front where she sat with him. At the close of the service he stayed, talked with the minister, and decided to join the church.

"Do you know what he told me, though?" asked Maria's father.

"No, what?"

"He said it was not my preaching that converted him, but the witness of my little girl."

V.E.R.

STANDING THE TEST

Thou therefore endure hardness, as a good soldier of Jesus Christ. 2 Timothy 2:3.

On August 15, 1907, Pedro Kalbermatter was inducted into the Argentine Army. He knew what he faced. Other Adventists who had preceded him, including two of his brothers, maintained that it was impossible to keep the Sabbath in the army if one wanted to live. Pedro was determined to prove them wrong or die for his faith.

Early in the week he called on his commander and told him that he could not work on Saturdays.

"The Bible is a good Book," replied the commander when Pedro quoted the fourth commandment, "but in the army you must forget your religion." He spoke to his orderly.

"Take this young man and teach him the military and penal codes." With a wave of his hand he dismissed them both. For four days the orderly tried to turn Pedro into a good soldier.

When he refused to work on Sabbath he was marched to the guardhouse where he spent the entire day facing a wall. The following week was a hard one, for there was scarcely a moment when the soldiers were not tormenting him, throwing things at him, tipping his bed over, or snatching his Bible out of his hand. The second Sabbath, Pedro was placed in irons in such a way that he could not bend his knees. He spent an agonizing day in the guardhouse.

During the week he tried unsuccessfully to see the commandant. When he refused to work the following Sabbath, the commandant had a tub of dirty clothes brought, and ordered Pedro to wash them in front of the regiment. A soldier with a whip stood near.

Pedro knelt by the tub and prayed God would give him strength. The soldier then began lashing him unmercifully as the officer shouted louder and louder: "Wash! Wash! Wash!" They tried holding his hands in the water, and rubbing them up and down on the clothes, but as soon as they let go the clothes dropped from his hands. This continued for two hours. After that, the officers, still furious, ordered him taken to the guardhouse for the remainder of the Sabbath.

After enduring hardships for a time and remaining steadfast, the Lord delivered Pedro from his persecutors. We shall see in following readings how God accomplished this.

V.E.R.

HIS GRACE IS SUFFICIENT

I can do all things through Christ which strengtheneth me. Philippians 4:13.

The next Friday night Pedro lay awake crying to God out of an anguished heart. An officer came to his room in the morning and told him to take his Bible and go with the other soldiers to the river. As soon as he arrived they grabbed his Bible and again commanded him to wash a pile of clothes.

"I cannot do it," replied the young man with tears in his eyes. "I cannot violate my conscience and break God's commandment."

They knocked him around until they were tired. Then an officer mounted a horse, took a whip, and drove Pedro all the way back to the barracks, lashing him all the way as if he were an animal. He was handed to the officer on guard who placed him on a stool with his legs stretched out and fastened in irons. For thirteen hours he sat thus, forbidden to make the slightest movement. The next day he was taken to the hospital and turned over to a physician.

"Doctor," said the officer, "take this man and examine him. We have reason to believe he is insane."

The doctor gave Pedro a thorough examination and sent him back to the barracks. "He is the sanest and most healthy man I have examined in a long time," he wrote.

Next Pedro was dragged before a judge from Buenos Aires, accused of disobedience and insubordination and sentence was passed.

"Put him in close confinement for seven months." Pedro was led away and place in the *calabozo*. The days dragged by. Never had liberty seemed so sweet to him as while lying in that tiny cell.

One day he heard his name called, and looking through the bars saw his father. The door was opened and father and son embraced.

"I have good news for you," said his father. "If you will only agree to work on Sabbath you will be immediately set at liberty."

"I cannot do it, Father," replied the young man firmly.

For two hours the father tried in vain to change Pedro's mind. "I shall never see you again," he sobbed as he left. The officers now despised Pedro more than ever for having rejected his father's counsel. But Pedro opened his Bible and read Psalm 27:10. "When my father and my mother forsake me, then the Lord will take me up."

V.E.R.

THE REWARD OF FAITHFULNESS

We went through fire and through water: but thou broughtest us out into a wealthy place. Psalm 66:12.

As the dark days passed in the loneliness of his cell Pedro had one friend—the Bible. Then one night a guard crept in while he was asleep and stole it. But two weeks later a good brother came and secretly slipped into his hands another copy of the Word of God.

When his seven months in solitary confinement were up Pedro was taken to Buenos Aires for final sentencing. The prosecutor asked for a five-year prison term. The judge admitted that never before had he sentenced a man for his religion. But the laws were strict, and reluctantly he sent Pedro to prison for one year.

He was taken to Martin Garcia, a lonely prison on an island in the river holding a large number of vicious prisoners. Here again he asked permission to keep the Sabbath. The commandant warned him that prisoners had no rights on Martin Garcia and pointed out that he had the power of life and death over every one.

"I suggest you drop all such ideas," warned the commandant. He sent the priest to try to convince the heretic that he was wrong. The two men talked for hours before the priest left, defeated.

When Sabbath came, Pedro once again asked permission to see the commandant.

"What for?" asked the guard.

"I wish to be relieved of Sabbath work."

"It is unnecessary. The priest saw the commandant, and we have orders not to ask you to work." The other prisoners whispered to one another, "God is helping the saint!"

Pedro was so happy he burst into song. His fellow prisoners were amazed. Later one of the convicts accepted Christ.

By order of the minister of war Pedro was transferred to another camp. Here the officer was surprised to learn why the young man had been in prison. He made Pedro his orderly, allowed him out of prison, and permitted him to live in his home.

The year ended and Pedro was set completely free. Shortly after this the Argentine minister of war issued an order exempting all Seventh-day Adventist young men from work on the Sabbath. Pedro had fought a good fight, he had kept the faith.

V.E.R.

LIVING LETTERS

You show that you are a letter from Christ delivered by me, written not in ink, but in the Spirit of the living God, and not on tablets of stone, but on the human heart. 2 Corinthians 3:3, Goodspeed.

You are a letter! Think of it—a letter from Christ. Every boy and girl in the church is to be a letter, a living letter, that everyone can read. A lady and her family to whom I have been giving Bible studies, told me that the young man who came to her home and sold her some Adventist books prayed for her. She thought it was the sweetest prayer she had ever heard. She wrote a beautiful letter to the publishing house about the call and what it has meant to her and her family. Now she is taking regular Bible studies. This young man was a letter—a living epistle for Christ.

"In every one of His children, Jesus sends a letter to the world. If you are Christ's follower, He sends in you a letter to the family, the village, the street, where you live. Jesus, dwelling in you, desires to speak to the hearts of those who are not acquainted with Him. Perhaps they do not read the Bible, or do not hear the voice that speaks to them in its pages; they do not see the love of God through His works. But if you are a true representative of Jesus, it may be that through you they will be led to understand something of His goodness and be won to love and serve Him." —*Steps to Christ*, p. 115.

In the post office there is a dead letter office. Thousands of letters are never delivered. The address may be inaccurate or the name misspelled or the people have moved and left no address. Whatever the reason, the person never received the letter that was intended for him. So all of those letters are sent to the dead letter office.

Many of those letters contain money intended for the people to whom the letter is addressed, but they never received that money. In fact, one year I called up the post office and inquired about this matter. I learned that in Washington, D.C., the dead letters that year contained nearly $300,000 that could not be delivered. Think of it—a treasure, but undelivered!

You are a letter! You have a treasure; the hope of heaven. Have you delivered the treasure? Or are you a "dead letter"?

A.A.E.

LOOK UP!

He determines the number of the stars, he gives to all of them their names. Great is our Lord, and abundant in power; his understanding is beyond measure. Psalm 147:4, 5, RSV.

Nobody knows how many stars there are. Though you can see only about 2,000 on a clear night, astronomers with their large telescopes have photographed more than 30 billion stars. There must be billions more beyond the reach of the most powerful telescopes. Yet your God not only knows the number but all their names. With all this measureless understanding, He is still concerned about every detail of your life.

For ages man has used the stars to guide him. Without them desert travelers would be lost, nor could sailors find their way across the trackless seas. Modern navigators use stars as guides as they pilot ships and airplanes. But the only safe guide in our mixed-up world is Jesus, the Bright and Morning Star. He alone can lead to happiness and heaven.

Nancy had lost her way. She had lost her peace, her happiness, her quiet, honest heart right in her own home. Hating this inward discontent and misery, life became a boring routine from one school day to the next.

One restless night she dreamed she had fallen into a deep pit with no steps, ladder, or rope. Fearful that she was doomed, she looked up into the deep blue of night and saw one star. As she gazed upward, she felt herself begin to rise. Feeling this strange sensation, she said aloud, "Who is lifting me?" and looked around to the sides of the pit. Instantly she fell to the bottom. Again she looked up, saw the bright star, and began to rise slowly. Again she looked around to see what was lifting her. Again she fell to the bottom. The third time she determined to look intently at that shining star. Slowly she felt herself rising. Keeping her eyes on its shining orb, she soon found herself out of the pit and in safety.

When she awoke she thought a long while. Then slipping to her knees, she prayed, "I see it all now, Jesus. You don't want me to look at myself nor at others. I'm just to look at You, the Bright and Morning Star." Won't you too, look up? You can trust in the infinite wisdom and power of God.

E.E.L. and J.H.L.

THE SYMPATHETIC JEWEL

Thus speaketh the Lord of hosts, saying, Execute true judgment, and shew mercy and compassions every man to his brother. Zechariah 7:9.

"Would you like to see some of the precious stones in my shop?" a jeweler asked his friend. Of course he would, so the jeweler unlocked the vault and brought out a number of beautiful gems.

"Oh, how lovely they are!" exclaimed the friend as he looked at first one and then another. "This diamond is magnificent!"

As the man examined and admired the many splendid stones, he noticed one that looked dim and pale beside the other shimmering gems. Pointing to it he asked, "Why is that one here with the other precious stones? It is not pretty at all."

The jeweler did not answer. Instead, he picked up the colorless stone and held it tightly in his hand for a few moments. When he opened his hand again, there on his palm lay a transformed gem. It glowed with every color in the rainbow! The friend was amazed. "What happened? What did you do?" he cried.

"This stone is an opal," explained the jeweler. "We call it the sympathetic jewel. It needs to be held in your hand to bring out its marvelous colors."

An old man had a son who had been a lot of trouble and caused him much sorrow. One day a neighbor asked how the boy was getting along.

"Not well at all," sighed the brokenhearted father. "He's been drinking again and causing more trouble."

"That's too bad," answered the neighbor. "If he were my boy I'd send him away from home. He's a disgrace to the family."

"Well, if he were your boy, I'd do the same. But he isn't yours—he's mine, and I can't do it."

Oh, yes, it is easy to be sympathetic and helpful to those you love. You'd do anything to encourage them. But how about the person who means nothing to you? What about that boy or girl who is the joke of the class, the dullest one there? Probably he feels lonesome, hurt, and terribly shy, and you might be surprised what a pleasing personality a little warmth from a sympathetic hand might bring out in him!

"Bear ye one another's burdens." Be sympathetic.

M.H.

THOSE TELLTALE NAIL MARKS

Because sentence against an evil work is not executed speedily, therefore the heart of the sons of men is fully set in them to do evil. Ecclesiastes 8:11.

Billy was struggling to be a Christian. It was so hard, it seemed. Before he realized it he spoke a bad or unkind word or did something he should not do.

"Maybe I can help you," his father offered. "Take this board, and every time you speak a bad word or do something wrong, drive a nail in the board. Then, every time you do something good, or when you ask God to forgive you, pull a nail out."

Bill decided to try his father's suggestion. But the boy was grieved as he saw the board filling with nails, reminding him of the many mistakes he was making.

Then, with the Lord's help, the nails started coming out. Some days more came out than went in. At last the day arrived when Billy could take the board to his dad and show it to him without a single nail in it. But Billy was still sad.

"Why are you sad, Bill? The nails are all gone," his father encouraged.

"Yes, Dad, I know the nails are gone," Billy replied, "but look at all the ugly holes that are left!" And he was right. The holes would always be there.

The devil gets us into sin, but even after we come to Jesus and ask forgiveness, the stain and the soil of sin may still be there. We can be forgiven and be right with God, but some deeds leave marks that can never be erased.

I've heard of boys and girls who think it is smart to do things that are not right. "I'll be a Christian someday," they say, "but now I want to have a good time. Someday I'll turn to God and have my sins forgiven, and everything will be all right."

Such young people fail to realize that sin leaves scars. We may find pardon, but ugly marks are left on the life. It is best to seek Jesus early and to let Him take over. He will spare us the ugly scars. You will do this, won't you? The fewer scars we have, the happier our lives will be.

R.H.P.

A SOFT ANSWER

A soft answer turneth away wrath: but grievous words stir up anger. Proverbs 15:1.

When John took the family car out of the garage to wash it he noticed the dented fender. He stormed into the kitchen where his wife was ironing.

"What's going on around here?" he stormed. "That's the third dent you have put in the car this year! I think it's about time you started paying for your blunders."

Helen looked at her husband's flushed face. There was no anger in her voice or eyes as she said, "I'm sorry, John, but I couldn't help it this time. If you will look in the glove compartment you will find the name and address of the man who bumped into me. He has promised to have it fixed."

John's face softened. "Oh, that's all right. I am sorry I spoke as I did."

There was no quarrel. A soft answer had killed John's anger.

When Gideon called for men to come and help him fight the Midianites, few came from the tribe of Ephraim. After he had won the victory, the Ephraimites began to feel sorry that they had taken so little part in the war. It was all Gideon's fault, they reasoned. They sent him an angry message.

"Why hast thou served us thus, that thou calledst us not, when thou wentest to fight with the Midianites?"

Gideon might have answered them sharply, pointing out that it was their own fault that they had not come since he had sent the call everywhere. He did not do so.

The Midianites had rushed defeated from the battlefield and the men of Ephraim had seized the fords of the Jordan. In this way they captured two of the princes of Midian, Oreb, and Zeeb.

Gideon sent a really soft answer to the men of Ephraim.

"What have I done now in comparison to you?" he asked humbly. "God hath delivered into your hands the princes of Midian, Oreb and Zeeb, and what was I able to do in comparison to you?"

It always takes two to make a quarrel. The next time someone says something to you in anger, try giving a soft answer. Praise him for something he has done. Then watch his anger evaporate.

V.E.R.

A SLOTHFUL KOEL

He also that is slothful in his work is brother to him that is a great waster. Proverbs 18:9.

"Look," gasped Donita. "See that big bird trying to get into that little nest?"

Donita was sitting in the open-air church at camp in India, but she couldn't keep her eyes from straying to the little hanging nest with the round hole in its side, swinging in the breeze hardly thirty feet away. She had seen the mother bird fly out a few minutes before, and now a large bird with a spotted tail was attempting to force its way into the nest.

"Oh," whispered Donita, trying to keep quiet, "I believe it is breaking the eggs! Look at its head banging up and down!"

"Where?" questioned Wanda who was sitting next to Donita.

"There in that tree just across the road."

"Oh, yes, now I see it. I wonder what kind of bird it is?"

"I don't know, but I'm going to ask Mr. Leston after meeting," Donita answered in a low voice. And then, because they were in meeting, both girls lapsed into silence, though neither one could keep her attention on the speaker. The goings on in the nest were far too interesting!

As soon as church was out, Donita and Wanda made a beeline for Mr. Leston. "What kind of bird has a spotted tail and tries to break other birds' eggs?" they demanded.

"Probably a female spotted koel. Koels use other birds' nests to lay their eggs in because they are too lazy to build their own or to hatch and feed the babies."

"Why, the big meanies!" declared Donita. "The poor little mother bird! Just think how sad she'll be! Her eggs are all wasted now and she won't have any babies except those big old koels!"

Later as Donita was thumbing through her Bible she read, "He also that is slothful in his work is brother to him that is a great waster."

"Well," she mused, "that certainly fits that old koel! It fits lazy people too. They are too lazy to work themselves, so they live off the work other people do. And usually they are not very thrifty either. They waste things, just like the text says."

M.H.

EXPERT FARMERS

Idler, go to the ant; ponder her ways and grow wise: no one gives her orders, no overseer, no master, yet all through the summer she makes sure of her food, and gathers her supplies at harvest time. Proverbs 6:6-9, Jerusalem.

While walking through the woods early one spring, Royal Dixon found a three-by-five-foot field of wild rice. The soil was loose, not a weed was in evidence. He looked around to find more rice growing, but there was none. Obviously, an expert farmer had planted that little field.

Stretching out on the ground, he determined to solve the mystery of the miniature field of wild rice. He noticed ants busily burrowing into the ground. Then it dawned on him. These busy insects were plowing. Others were weeding, clipping every bit of grass that showed above the ground. Another group was dragging the clippings away. More ants stood guard to fend off cutworms or insects that could ruin the crop.

All summer he watched the ants tend their little farm. By late August the ripe grain was twenty-four inches high. Now came the harvest. Steady lines of workers climbed the stalks. Each plucked one grain and carried it underground to their storeroom. Mr. Dixon marked the ants with different colors noting that the same ones stayed by the same stalk till the job was completed. One well organized crew climbed up, cut the grain, and dropped it to the ground. A waiting group picked up the kernels and took them to the storehouse.

Shortly after the field was harvested it rained for several days. When the storm cleared, the entrance to the ant city was alive with workers carrying grain to a sunny slope so it would dry. Evidently the storerooms had gotten damp. By evening the dry grain was carried back to the nest.

No lazy individuals lived in that ant city. Everyone did his work willingly without a boss. Not one shirked at his job. No wonder Solomon tells us to wisely live a life of service and patient industry like the ant. What kind of worker are you? Are you one who has to be watched and made to keep at your job, or are you willing to do your part even though no one is watching? Next time you feel lazy, go take a look at the ant.

E.E.L. and J.H.L.

WORTH IT?

For God so loved the world, that he gave his only begotten Son, that whosoever believeth in him should not perish, but have everlasting life. John 3:16.

Skippy was a delightful black kitten when sitting in the sun or skipping blithely about from room to room. But she had an annoying habit. She was willful. She could not adjust her time to coincide with her mistress' schedule. Mistress retired about eleven o'clock at night and wished to sleep until seven, which seemed reasonable to everyone but the kitten.

She woke at various times even at one o'clock in the morning. Her mistress crawled sleepily out of bed and opened the door to let her out. But Skippy did not want to go out; she wanted breakfast.

Surely Skip would learn that no breakfast would be forthcoming before seven. But one cannot reason with a frolicsome kitten. Children, though, are a different story.

Andy had been told by his parents that he was not to leave the yard without permission. But the new apartment building just a few doors away had a swimming pool. Andy could not resist. He sneaked over to the pool, dived in, and began swimming. Seeing how fast he could swim with his eyes shut, he crashed head-on into the side of the pool.

With a gash in his head, he ran home wailing, leaving a trail of blood. It could have been much worse. No one else was around, and he could have drowned.

Andy is smarter than a kitten. He could understand his parents' instructions.

Life is a school and every person has to learn some lessons. If we did not learn the first time, or the second time, the next one may be harder.

Sometimes God brought hard tests to His children in Bible times. Abraham failed to pass some of them, but at last he came to that tremendous test when God asked him to sacrifice his only son.

Skippy's mistress would not have tried to teach the kitten if she didn't think her pet was worth it. Andy's parents thought he was worth loving. God thinks we are worth His effort too, and He shows His love by giving His Son for us.

R.E.

THE DEVIL'S PRISON HOUSE

Is this the man . . . that made the world as a wilderness, and destroyed the cities thereof; that opened not the house of his prisoners? Isaiah 14:16, 17.

In the fourteenth chapter of Isaiah, from verse twelve on, you will see that this "man" is none other than Lucifer, or Satan. Our world is his prison house and no one can fly from it.

The astronauts may fly to the moon, but they have to return to this earth. Man knows of no way whereby he can permanently and safely escape from this planet. Jesus came to this world and died. Since He holds the keys, the time is near when He will come and set His children free. Then the tables will be turned, and Satan will be chained here on the desolate earth for a thousand years.

When World War II broke out Elder and Mrs. John Oss were taken to an internment camp by their Japanese conquerors. There they were shut up for nearly three years. There were not enough medicines for the sick people. Their food consisted of wormy oatmeal and a few stale vegetables.

Many of the prisoners became ill with dysentery, malaria, and other diseases. They became thin and weak, and many died.

Now and then a little news reached the prisoners. The American Army and Navy were slowly pushing the Japanese forces back in the Pacific. This news brought joy to their hearts, but would they be alive when the war ended? The food became worse.

One never-to-be-forgotten day they saw a woman standing outside the barbed wire surrounding the camp. She was shouting something and waving her hands.

"THE WAR IS OVER! THE WAR IS OVER!"

The prisoners could hardly believe it. Then they discovered that the Japanese guards were gone.

Then a fleet of planes swept over the camp. Out of the hatches came parcels of food and clothing for the prisoners. They knew then the war was truly over and they were free.

Someday soon the long war between Jesus and Satan will end with the complete defeat of the devil. The prison gates will be opened. God's children will be taken to heaven, free forevermore.

May that day soon come.

V.E.R.

BRIGHTEN THINGS

Let your light so shine before men, that they may see your good works, and glorify your Father which is in heaven. Matthew 5:16.

Maureen's classmates were making fun of Ellie. They teased and taunted until Ellie was about ready to burst into tears. Maureen didn't like to see anyone picked on, so she defended Ellie.

At that her classmates turned on Maureen and began teasing *her*. They called her a goody-goody.

Perhaps Ellie felt a little better, for the attention had been turned to someone else. But Maureen felt a whole lot worse. Why did her friends turn against her like that?

After school she was restless, and all through supper she was very quiet.

"Is something the matter?" Mother asked her. But Maureen made no reply.

That evening as Mother rocked on the veranda, watching the stars appear, Maureen went out to sit nearby. At last she took a deep breath and began to explain her trouble, hoping that Mother would have some comforting words for her.

She felt sure she had done the right thing, and told Mother so, concluding, "Why should you try to do right if it only makes you unpopular? Is it worth it?"

Mother listened quietly, but didn't answer for a moment. The only noise was the creaking of the rocking chair. Then she pointed to the dim light that illuminated the veranda.

"What does that light do?" she asked Maureen.

"Well, it makes it lighter for us."

"Do you see anything else?"

"Yes. It attracts moths and bugs and mosquitoes."

"That's the way it is with those people who try to be the light of this world," Mother said. "They not only brighten things for some people, but they also attract the pests who sting and bug us. We have the choice of either turning off our lights—then we will not do any good or be bugged by others—or of being used by God and ignoring the bugs."

R.E.

247

WITHOUT WAX

As newborn babes, desire the sincere milk of the word, that ye may grow thereby. 1 Peter 2:2.

Roman sculptors made many beautiful and lasting works. Marble was plentiful in Italy and skills inherited from the Greeks produced masterpieces still admired today. But there were many lesser craftsmen who were interested only in making money.

When they bought their marble they did not bother to check to see whether it was perfect. Later small cracks appeared. These they filled with a white wax. Only the most skilled could pick out these defects. The highest praise that could be given to a work of art were the words "sine cere"—without wax.

And the Bible is just that. It is complete and perfect. When we find Christ and begin to study the Bible it answers all our needs and helps us grow from babies to mature Christians.

Sooky came into the world weak and wobbly. When Jim found her he did not know whether to put her out of her suffering or try to rear her. Her mother gave plenty of milk and Jim thought that her calf might also be a good milker, so he decided to try.

"Come and see what I have," Jim called as he carried the weak calf from his pickup truck.

"Isn't she beautiful!" chorused Mary Lou and Lois. "Can we look after her?"

A lemonade bottle with a hard rubber tip proved the answer to her hunger needs and soon Sooky was sucking hungrily on the warmed milk. After a day or two she began to grow stronger.

"I don't think I have ever seen a calf who could drink that much milk," Jim told his two young sisters. "It looks as if she is trying to make up for lost time."

Babies, calves, puppies, and kittens drink milk to keep alive. No wonder Peter tells us to drink in God's Word. How else can we grow into strong Christians?

This morning as you drink your milk be glad you have the milk of God's Word.

W.R.L.S.

HE THAT KEEPETH HIS MOUTH KEEPETH HIS LIFE

He that keepeth his mouth keepeth his life: but he that openeth wide his lips shall have destruction. Proverbs 13:3.

Morris Frank, blind from age 16, proudly tells of experiences with his Seeing Eye dog, Buddy. He said, "She had very good judgment, and knew when to open her mouth and when to keep it closed much better than some people do."

Buddy was sleeping close by her master's side one night. Frank awakened to find his dog gone from her usual place by his side. Listening, he could hear someone cutting the screen in an attempt to reach the lock.

There was a tense moment of silence, then a scream of fright and pain, followed by running footsteps. Buddy calmly padded back to her bed.

The dog had heard the thief trying to break in, and without growling or barking had quietly waited beside the door until the thief's hand came in to unlock the latch. At that moment a pair of strong jaws with sharp teeth left a wound on his hand that would take some time to heal, and hopefully deter him from attempting to break into other homes.

On another occasion Morris Frank was with Buddy in a dark alley just back of their hotel. A thief came up behind him, stuck a gun in his back, and demanded his money and watch.

Buddy ordinarily would have fought for her master, as she had at other times, but now she came quietly to his side and stood very still. Evidently she had seen the gun and knew this was no time to attack.

As Morris handed over his wallet and watch he quietly explained that the watch would be of no use to the man since it was made for a blind person.

Ashamed, the thief handed back the things, then left.

Buddy led her master safely back into the hotel. She could have been lying dead with a bullet wound in her heart, and Frank could have been stumbling alone toward the hotel.

Buddy knew when to open her powerful jaws and when to keep them closed.

How much trouble we can save ourselves and others if we know when to keep still and when to speak!

R.H.P.

SAMMY'S SUMMER OF LOVE

Nothing will hurt or destroy in all my holy mountain, for as the waters fill the sea, so shall the earth be full of the knowledge of the Lord. Isaiah 11:9, TLB.

Sammy came to Chapman's Pool, a cove on the South Dorset coast of England, in May of 1961. No one could understand why this wild, gray seal, usually a shy animal, broke the barrier of fear to seek human companionship. Why did he choose to become a friend of this great enemy, man, who was mercilessly slaughtering gray seals?

Sammy wasn't beautiful on land. His shapeless four-and-one-half-foot-long body looked like a giant slug with a small flapping tail on one end. But his large black eyes were lovely. They expressed joy when meeting an old friend, or mischief as he played tricks on his human friends, who joined him in the sea. Tears of grief poured down his cheeks when evening came and his playmates climbed the cliff toward home.

Not interested in bribes of food offered him, Sammy loved the human voice and craved the society of people. Never did he use his inch-and-a-half-long razor-sharp teeth to hurt his human friends, although he often lovingly nuzzled their arms or legs with his wide-open jaws. His flippers, equipped with five sharp, black nails, could easily tear prey apart, yet he used them to caress and hug the children he loved.

The frolics began when a 4-year-old girl mistook him for a "doggie." Hugging his soft fur, she kissed his huge body as he clasped her with his flippers and moaned a love song. The two played for hours with the child receiving only tiny scratches.

In contrast to his land clumsiness this skillful swimmer received his greatest joy when his human friends joined him in deep water. With graceful speed he shot through the water, often stopping to express his joy of companionship by pressing his black nose against his human friend's cheek in a seal kiss.

All summer this fabulous seal expressed his love and trust in humans. Restraining his great strength, he even allowed Mrs. Nina Hooke the thrill of speeding through the ocean clinging to his back.

Sammy gave the world a glimpse of heaven where nothing will hurt or destroy in all God's holy mountain.

E.E.L. and J.H.L.

NEVER POSTPONE YOUR JOYS

Blessed is he that considereth the poor: the Lord will deliver him in time of trouble. Psalm 41:1.

Grace Carter was very unhappy that afternoon, for she hadn't found what she wanted at the store. Now she went into the park to sulk and wait until time for her appointment at the beauty parlor. She just had to look pretty that night, for she had a date with her boyfriend. But she didn't look pretty just now.

At the bench she chose there was only one person, an old man reading a newspaper. He immediately turned and glanced at her, folded his paper and said, "Good afternoon. And how are you?"

Oh, no! the girl thought, for she was in no mood to talk to anyone. However, she replied coolly, "I'm fine."

"Isn't this a beautiful day?" the man asked.

Without a bit of enthusiasm she replied, "Yes, it is."

"Let me introduce myself," the man continued; "I'm John Dawes. And what's your name, young lady?"

Slowly, grudgingly, the answer came, "My name is Grace Carter."

The man smiled, "Grace? That was my mother's name."

Just then a strong breeze blew a man's hat sailing past the bench. It landed on the cement and began to toss about in the wind. Mr. Dawes hurried to pick it up. Grace watched as the other man thanked him. The two shook hands. The man was very grateful and both men seemed so happy.

Then two small boys walked by. John Dawes talked to them and made paper airplanes out of his newspaper for them.

Grace smiled and said, "You made those boys very happy."

"Well," Mr. Dawes replied, "my mother often said to me, 'Never postpone your joys.' Of course, it was a while before I knew what she meant."

"What *did* she mean?" asked the puzzled Grace.

Then he explained that being kind and merciful to others brings you life's greatest joys—so never postpone your joys!

From her purse Grace took three candy bars, one for each of the boys and Mr. Dawes. She watched them smile their thanks.

When she left them, Grace thought: *Today my life has been enriched!*

A.A.E.

GOD HAS DRAWN A CIRCLE AROUND US

For thou art an holy people unto the Lord thy God: the Lord thy God hath chosen thee to be a special people unto himself, above all people that are upon the face of the earth. Deuteronomy 7:6.

Elder Mel Rees was visiting the Eskimo Adventists on St. Lawrence Island in the Bering Sea off Alaska. Jim Gaw asked Brother Rees to accompany him on a visit to an Eskimo village about five miles away. Elder Rees agreed, and off they went on a long, cold walk.

As the two men trudged along the beach Elder Rees spotted three heavy glass balls with rope-net covering. They were stray floats from nets used by a Japanese fishing fleet. He wanted them as decorations for his office.

"Where can I hide these glass balls?" Elder Rees asked.

"No need to hide," Brother Gaw replied. "Look, I show you."

Jim laid the glass balls close together on the beach in plain sight. Then with the tip of his heavy boot he drew a circle around the three floats.

"Everything all right. We go!" Jim announced with assurance.

Elder Rees was not so sure. "Let's hide them so that we'll be sure to get them when we return," he pressed.

"Everything all right. Everything all right," Jim assured. "Let's go. When Eskimo make circle around, no one take. They yours. No one touch. If they did, would be stealing."

That mark is the sign of ownership in that distant part of the world. The floats were still safe on the beach when the men returned that way later in the day.

Did you ever stop to think, boys and girls, that you and I belong to Jesus? He has purchased us "with his own blood" (Acts 20:28). In Eskimo parlance, Christ has drawn a circle around us. "Ye are not your own," He says (1 Cor. 6:19). We belong to Him.

What a wonderful thought: God has chosen you and me to be His in a very special way. He has drawn a circle around us. We are His. He will come back for us soon, and He expects to find us waiting for Him, because of that blood-red line He has drawn around us. We must not disappoint Him. That would be robbing Him of something that is His own.

R.H.P.

STRONG PEOPLE KNOW THEIR GOD

The people that do know their God shall be strong, and do exploits. Daniel 11:32.

In the seventeenth century the Waldenses suffered terrible persecution. They were banished from the valleys that had been their home for centuries and forced to live as exiles in Switzerland. After three years in that land they decided to return to their old homes.

With only six hundred soldiers, a brave captain by the name of Arnaud marched over the mountains and down into the valley of San Martin. Here they found refuge in a strong fort known as the Balsiglia. The kings of France and Piedmont determined to destroy the Waldenses who had returned.

Late in the fall of 1689 a powerful French army attacked the Balsiglia, but without success. The French general saw that he would need cannon to take the fort from the Waldenses. Winter was coming on, so the general sent word to Arnaud saying he would return in the spring and destroy them all.

During the winter the Waldenses made their fort as strong as possible. In May the French general returned with an army nearly fifty times as large as the one in the fort. The French set up their cannon and poured in shot and shell. By evening the walls of the fort were in ruins. In the morning the French could march in and capture the fort. To make sure the Waldenses did not escape, the enemy kept large fires burning all night and many soldiers stood on guard. The Waldenses could do nothing but wait and pray.

God answered as He had two centuries before. A dense fog settled over the entire valley. Arnaud found a man who could guide his soldiers past the camp of the enemy. In complete silence, sometimes on hands and knees, the soldiers slipped away from the fort, crossed the stream, and began climbing the side of a nearby mountain.

As soon as it was light, the French rushed forward to capture the Waldenses, whom they intended to hang. To their amazement they found the fort deserted.

The French general realized that his prey had escaped.

At the summit of the mountain pass Arnaud and his men knelt in the bright sunshine and thanked God for deliverance.

V.E.R.

THE PINK RIBBON

Blessed are they that mourn: for they shall be comforted.
Matthew 5:4.

Kitty Taylor's mother was dying in a crowded charity ward in a large impersonal city hospital. Kitty's father, an alcoholic, had left the family four years before.

So Kitty, at fourteen, had become the little mother in the family and cared for her three younger brothers after school. And now Dr. Gordon told Kitty that her mother had cancer.

"If your mother is lucky, she'll last three months," he said. "And if she is even luckier, she won't last three months."

Harsh as the words sounded, Kitty understood. The pain was so bad, and it would become much worse.

But Mrs. Taylor wanted to live. Each day that God granted her she felt was a blessing. She knew that as long as she remained alive, her children would not be placed in an orphanage or foster homes. So she prayed and clung to life. And Dr. Gordon who had given up hope for her long before, shook his head wonderingly as the months stretched on and on. "It's just a miracle," he said, moving on to the next patient. There was nothing more he could do for Mrs. Taylor.

And since he could not help her, Kitty's mother tried to help him. "When death comes swiftly, suddenly, one cannot prepare for it," she said. "But since I know that I am dying and each day may be my last, I can make it a day of beauty and blessedness."

Kitty was allowed to come to her mother's bedside, and each day she brushed her mother's long hair and pinned a pink ribbon in it.

Mrs. Taylor would send Kitty around to speak to other patients in the ward who had no company to cheer them. She asked Kitty to bake some cookies to bring in as a gift of appreciation to the nurses and doctors. She always thanked the nurses who came in to give her medicine. She bloomed with life as she lay dying with a pink ribbon in her hair.

At last, when there was no more strength left in her body, Mrs. Taylor passed away. But her day-by-day struggle to show how precious life was did not count for nothing. The doctor who had attended her adopted all four children so they could stay together.

"This woman taught me a great lesson," Dr. Gordon told the judge as he signed the adoption papers. "She showed me how to face death beautifully, and the pink ribbon was her badge of courage."

R.E.

YOUR BEHAVIOR

For ye were sometimes darkness, but now are ye light in the Lord: walk as children of light. Ephesians 5:8.

"By their fruits ye shall know them," is the way Jesus describes the behavior of people.

Even a little orphan boy saw there was something wonderful and "light" about the behavior of the matron and other Christians in the orphans' home to which he had just been brought from the slums. After he was given a bath he was led to a room where his bed was all made up with clean sheets. Puzzled, he asked, "Why do you want me to get in there?"

They explained that the bed was where he was to sleep. He had never slept in a bed before. He was amazed at the clean white sheets. When the matron tucked him in, she kissed him good night. He said, "What did you do that for?"

But the next morning he looked into the kind face of that lovely Christian matron and said, "Would you mind doing that again? I mean what you did to me last night?"

After a week or so, this little boy would come around several times a day and look up and say, "Would you love a fellow a little?" And the matron would kiss his little face.

Yes, even a 4-year-old orphan can tell that a Christian's behavior is something special and different—as different as light from darkness.

After a few weeks a woman came to the orphanage to adopt a boy. The matron brought this little boy out and the woman looked at him. She said, "Tommy, wouldn't you like to go home with me?"

But Tommy never took his eyes off the floor. Then the woman said, "I will give you a hobbyhorse and lots of playthings and there will be many nice things to do."

Finally, he looked up into her face and asked the all-important question to him: "Would you love a fellow?"

It seems the world is dying for love that the light heart of the Christian can bestow. What a privilege to be able to share God's love with a dark world.

A.A.E.

255

SAFETY FROM THE AVALANCHE

Beware that thou forget not the Lord thy God, in not keeping his commandments, and his judgments, and his statutes, which I command thee this day. Deuteronomy 8:11.

A mountaineer, hiking in the high, dangerous mountains above timberline, was crossing the snow crust of a glacier. A good hiker, he had often climbed in this rugged terrain. Using his ice ax and ropes, he carefully edged along the steep slope. Suddenly he noticed what appeared to be a puff of dust rising like smoke from the hanging wall just below him. Past experience indicated this was the first signal of an avalanche!

At the moment he saw the first sign of the avalanche, he noticed a mountain goat feeding on a nearby windy ridge. The animal stopped, tensed, and the big humpback quivered under his white fur. He too recognized danger. The signal was telling him to run. Instantly he bounced to an ice wall, sized it up, and sprinted out of sight. The mountaineer had learned long ago that the wild goats of the high country know their mountains. His only chance of safety was to follow this animal. If there was a way to escape, the goat would know it.

Running to the ice wall, he slammed his ax into the marks the goat had made with his hooves and heaved his body up the route. Ledges and hand grips he never guessed were there, appeared. Struggling, he rolled onto solid rock just as he heard the terrible roar of the avalanche covering the trail he had left a few moments before. The alert wisdom of the mountain goat had saved both their lives.

Do you feel that an avalanche of temptation is ready to sweep you away to Satan's ground? Though you want to do right, friends urge you to listen to bad music, see a late movie on TV, or read a sexy magazine. Like the climber, take a lesson from the mountain goat who had prepared himself for an emergency.

If you live by the Bible and its promises they will be yours for every emergency. God will send instant messages to help you escape. Know your Lord as the mountain goat knows his mountain; listen to the promises that will give you safety forever.

E.E.L. and J.H.L.

WHEN THE ANGELS REJOICE

There is joy in the presence of the angels of God over one sinner that repenteth. Luke 15:10.

Nancy saw something bright in the garden where Spot had been digging. As she picked it up she called to her friend Therese, "Look at this pretty little pin with the face of a lady on it—just the thing for my doll."

Therese had better thoughts. "Shouldn't you try to find out who the owner is? Some lady might be happy to get it back."

"It's mine; I found it." The girls went on playing with their dolls until Mrs. King came out with steaming cream of tomato soup and crackers. A little later she brought ice cream and cake because today was her daughter Therese's birthday. As both friends were just recovering from measles, no other guests were allowed.

The next day Nancy walked over to her friend's house to show the lovely dress she had made for her doll with mother's help. On a large bright red sash Nancy had fastened the pin unearthed by her dog.

Just then Grandma Farley came over to the Kings to borrow a lemon. With pride Nancy showed her doll, but it was the pin that attracted the older woman's attention. "Where did you get it?" she asked.

"Yesterday Spot dug it up when he was chasing a mole in our garden."

"Bless you. It is my heirloom, my mother's pin, that I lost three years ago when Mrs. Davis lived in your house. I was admiring her flowers in the backyard and dropped it off my dress. For hours we searched in vain for it. The pin means a great deal to me."

Quickly Nancy took it off the doll's sash and gave it to Grandma Farley. "I'm glad we found it. You can thank Spot for digging it up."

Later Nancy confided to Therese, "I was really glad to give up the pin when I saw how delighted Grandma was to get it back. You were right. I should have wanted to find the owner."

Jesus told a parable of a woman who after finding the silver coin she had lost in her house, called her neighbors and friends to rejoice with her good fortune. Thus "when one is brought back to God, all heaven is made glad; seraphs and cherubs touch their golden harps and sing praises to God and the Lamb for their mercy and loving kindness to the children of men."—*Christ's Object Lessons*, p. 197.

L.C.W.

HANDICAPPED HELEN

Whosoever doth not bear his cross, and come after me, cannot be my disciple. Luke 14:27.

Helen concentrated with all her might as her teacher tapped on her hand: W-A-T-E-R. Now her teacher had hold of her hand and was pouring water over it from a pump. She could feel the tingling cold as it raced through her fingers and splashed onto the ground.

Suddenly she realized what was happening. The cold fluid and the tapped letters on her hand went together. Things had a name! "There was a strange stir within me. . . . I understood that it was possible for me to communicate with other people by these signs," Helen later wrote.

Helen Keller came into the world in June, 1880. Following an illness at eighteen months she became blind, deaf, and mute. No one could seem to find a way to penetrate through to her senses and bring meaning to her life. Yet inside she was seething. Her active mind ran hither and thither, unable to organize itself.

Despite her limitations, her father tried to help her understand life. He let her feel animals on the farm. He took her to the zoo and she shook hands with a bear. Someone lifted her to fondle the ears of a giraffe. She gladly let an elephant twine its trunk around her and large pythons draped themselves over her.

When Anne Sullivan, her teacher, tried to associate in her mind words and objects it seemed impossible at first. She could not grasp that d-o-l-l meant the cuddly replica of herself that she took to bed. But once she learned that what gushed out of the pump was water, her curiosity became insatiable.

When Helen Keller died in 1968 she was world famous. Great statesmen paid tribute to her. During her life she traveled widely, working to help handicapped children. She wrote books, learned to speak, and gave lectures. Her example has inspired thousands to live above their difficulties.

What is a handicap? For some people it is a hurdle to be jumped.

W.R.L.S.

THE DOVE AND A WILDCAT

Then said Jesus, "Were not ten cleansed? Where are the nine? Was no one found to return and give praise to God except this foreigner?" Luke 17:17, 18, RSV.

How sad was the loving heart of Jesus when only one leper returned to say a grateful, "Thank You, Lord, for making me whole."

If only the nine healed men had been like the little mourning dove Alan Devoe found hurt and gasping beside the road. Frightened when he picked it up, the dove responded to the fresh water, seeds, and berries offered in the cage where Devoe cared for it. In eight days it was well, its wild eyes gleaming.

Taking the cage to the top of a wooded hill, Devoe opened the door. The dove darted out and flew into the woods. A week later when Devoe was sitting quietly on a stump watching a family of white mice, a bird suddenly flew to him and perched on his arm. The same mourning dove had stopped a few seconds, just long enough to say, "Thank you."

Phil Traband was hiking through a clearing of tall grass near an Oklahoma woods when he heard a sound like a crying baby. Turning, he was startled to see a wildcat coming toward him slowly. Knowing wildcats are usually mean, he was scared. Yet something about it made him stand still. As it came closer he noticed its mouth and muzzle were swollen.

Traband squatted, taking the animal's head in his hands. Gently he pried open the swollen mouth. The tongue, pierced by a sharp tooth, was held fast. The animal couldn't eat. The wound was infected. Carefully, though he knew it hurt terribly, he loosed the swollen tongue, ready to run if need be. The wildcat never moved. When he had finished it stood looking at him. Cautiously Triband stroked its fur, receiving a grateful "Meeow" in return. Then it disappeared into the woods.

If wild creatures can show their gratitude, why do we forget to praise God for our blessings? Have you thanked Him for keeping you well or for sending His angels to protect you from danger and calamity? God is listening for your grateful thanks. Today express your appreciation for the great gift of Jesus, which enables you to one day enjoy eternal life.

E.E.L. and J.H.L.

NOTHING BETWEEN

The Lord is my strength and song, and he is become my salvation. Exodus 15:2.

Vicky stopped by the public library on her way home from school every Monday afternoon. She liked to read better than anything else.

Stopping by the shelf labeled "Mystery—young adult," she scanned the titles looking for something really exciting.

She usually picked out five books. And she usually managed to read them before the week was over. Often her light burned far into the night as she lay awake reading. Sometimes she read so much that she didn't have time to get all of her school lessons done.

Another lesson she neglected more often than not was the Sabbath school lesson. It wasn't that she didn't have time to study it—she just didn't find the Sabbath school lesson very interesting.

One day someone new joined the Sabbath school class. Lucy Brown was one of the most attractive girls Vicky had ever seen, and Vicky decided to make friends with her if she could. Lucy certainly knew the Sabbath school lesson well. She must be a real brain.

Lucy and Vicky did become friends, and it was not too many weeks later that Vicky invited Lucy to stop by the library with her.

"Wouldn't you like to get some books?" Vicky said. "All you have to do to get a library card is fill out the application and get your mother or dad to sign it."

"Maybe I will," Lucy said. "But I can't take out many books."

"Don't you like to read?" Vicky asked.

"Yes, I do like to read," Lucy said. "That's just the trouble. I like to read so much that I have to watch myself. If I take out too many books from the library, my reading crowds out time to do other things—even studying the Sabbath school lesson. And when I read other things so much that I can't get interested in the Bible, then I know reading is becoming an idol for me."

Vicky thought about what Lucy had said. Was that one of her problems? How could she give up reading so many books?

Then she realized that if she cared more about reading than she did about pleasing God, that habit was an idol for her too. That week she took most of her stack of exciting stories back to the library unread.

Let us clear our lives, too, of anything that comes between us and the Saviour.

R.E.

THE STRAIGHT WAY

*Lead me, O Lord, in thy righteousness because of my enemies;
make thy way straight before me. Psalm 5:8, RSV.*

The Woods family, who lived on the West Coast of the United States, had been vacationing on the East Coast. Now they must return home.

"Where's Skippy?" asked Mr. Woods. He whistled and called, but their beautiful young collie dog didn't come. They searched for hours. With a deadline for arrival, they sadly drove away leaving their pet behind. They didn't know a pack of strange dogs had chased him into the woods.

Later, Skippy decided to return home by himself. At first he ran in great circles. Finally, tired, thin, and lame, he allowed a kind family to take him in. For several days they treated his sore paws and fed him. When he slipped away he didn't run in circles, but headed straight west.

It was winter by now and the ice and snow cut his paws. When he could go no farther he would stop with kind families, but when he regained his strength he'd slip away and head west. Coming to a big city, he had to cross a huge bridge that spanned a river filled with pieces of ice. Three men, dog catchers, followed him with their truck. Just as the men got their hands on him, he pulled away and jumped from the bridge to the icy water below. A boy saw him crawl out of the water and grabbed him by the neck. He rested a week with the boy, and then started off again. Just as he was leaving the city, the dog catchers saw him again. This time they caught him and put him in their truck. When they stopped at the dog pound, six men were waiting. He jumped right through their arms and was gone.

Somehow he caught enough game as he crossed the mountains to keep himself alive. Six months after his master left the East Coast, Skippy scratched on the door at home. No one can explain what guided the dog those 3,000 unknown miles, except a loving God.

You have a constant guide, your conscience. But it must be directed by the Holy Spirit or you will go in circles as Skippy did at first. Listening to an enlightened conscience will align you straight for heaven. When you run into troubles, interference, or problems, the Holy Spirit will say, "This is the way."

E.E.L. and J.H.L.

I WILL REMAIN STEADFAST

*I have set the Lord always before me: . . . I shall not be moved.
Psalm 16:8.*

Jerry lived in a small town along the rugged coast of Maine. He loved to sit on the shore, watching the huge waves roar in and dash against the rocks, throwing their spray high into the air. One day he noticed a limpet clinging to the side of a rock he often climbed. Wondering what was under the shell, he tried to pull it off with his fingers. The harder he pulled, the tighter the limpet clung to the rock. Jerry finally gave up and went home.

That evening during supper he thought about the limpet.

"Dad, why couldn't I pull the shellfish away from the rock?" he asked. "I was bigger than it was, and I knew I was much stronger."

Dad smiled. "The limpet holds onto the rock by suction. If you want to move the limpet, you must move the whole rock."

"Well, I could never do that," admitted Jerry. "That rock is half as big as this house."

So it was with David. He kept his eyes fixed on the Lord, and no mighty wave of temptation, no fierce trial, was able to move him, because he was fastened to the Rock.

The lighthouse stands firm and strong amidst fierce winter storms. Sometimes spray dashes right up over its windows. The keeper's family does not fear and tremble every time the wind howls and waves batter their house. They know that it is fastened to a solid rock; the mightiest ocean waves couldn't wash it away.

How can you know that you will be able to stand the great temptations that are coming? In your own strength it is impossible. But Jesus has made a promise, "They shall never perish, neither shall any man pluck them out of my hand" (John 10:28).

Daniel was fearless, even when threatened with a violent death. When they told him, "You must stop praying for a whole month or be thrown into a den of hungry lions," it made not the slightest difference in his daily prayer habits. He opened his windows as usual toward Jerusalem, and on his knees looked up through the blue sky and talked with his God. Nothing could move Daniel. God was his Rock. He had set the Lord always before him. God was present with him at all times, and he could not be moved.

V.E.R.

HOW TO OPEN A TURTLE

He is gracious and merciful, slow to anger, and of great kindness. Joel 2:13.

This is the way God deals with us. If we would only deal with others as graciously, showing the same love and kindness.

As he was going through the pasture, Mark learned how kindness brings results. In the grass he found a creature that carried his house with him wherever he went. Fascinated, he watched this well-protected turtle crawl through the grass and stones.

Grandfather had explained that the top part of the shell is really the turtle's backbone and ribs joined together in a solid mass by many bony plates. The bottom part is built around the breastbone and protects its belly. The shells are joined so there are openings for the turtle's head, legs, and tail.

Thinking he'd make a good pet, Mark decided to pick up this slow, clumsy land turtle. Immediately it drew in its head, legs, and tail, and shut itself very tightly. Mark took a stick and tried to pry open the shell. He wanted to play with his newfound friend. The more he tried the tighter the turtle shut itself.

Grandfather noticed what he was doing. "No, Mark, that's not the way."

Taking the turtle inside the house, he explained that it was a cold-blooded animal. Therefore, it can't live in cold climates unless it hibernates through the winter.

"Let's warm him up near the fire and see what happens."

As soon as the turtle began to get warm, it opened its shell, stuck out its head and feet, and started crawling toward Mark.

"People are like turtles in one way," Grandpa added. "When you try to make them do something, force them or put on pressure, they won't cooperate. But if you warm them up with a little kindness they will be glad to do whatever you want them to. Kindness and love accomplish wonders."

Many apparently hopeless hearts are melted by love. Acts of tender kindness do much to relieve the burdens and sorrows of others. Often the kindest act is to just listen to your friends who need someone who understands and cares. Then direct them to listen to Jesus.

E.E.L. and J.H.L.

THE COMPLAINT BOOK

I complained, and my spirit was overwhelmed. Psalm 77:3.

"Oh, dear! The railway gate is shut again. I wonder how long we'll have to wait this time," sighed Mother.

"You never can tell. Maybe five minutes, and maybe half an hour," answered Daddy as he parked the car in the hot Indian sunshine.

The twins leaned out the side windows trying to get a breath of fresh air. It *was* aggravating to have to wait and wait and wait for a train that seemed to take forever to arrive. What made it more unbearable was the fact that pedestrians and cyclists were crossing the tracks the whole time. Only vehicles that were too wide for the footpath, such as carts, trucks, and cars, were stopped.

Ten minutes went by. No train.

"Can't you open the gate?" someone asked the guard. "We could all be across and you could shut it again before that train arrives."

"No. Rules. I can't open the gate until after the train goes past."

Twenty minutes. "Surely you could get permission to open the gate. Just ask at the tower."

"No."

Half an hour. The man from the car ahead was exasperated. Getting out of his car he strode over to the gatekeeper. "Get me your complaint book!" he demanded. "I'm going to write a complaint! I've been here forty-five minutes and there is no earthly reason for making me wait this long at the crossing. Come, now, where is that book?"

Obediently the guard brought out the desired book, and as the irate man was writing his complaint the train roared past. With a triumphant grin the gatekeeper opened the crossing.

I wonder if God keeps a complaint book of all the times we moan and groan about our lot in life. Complaining really doesn't do much good. It didn't get the man across the railway tracks any faster, and it tends to make your disposition sour.

David figured it out well when he said, "I complained, and my spirit was overwhelmed."

M.H.

"TALK ABOUT WE LOVE ME"

Nor height, nor depth, nor any other creature, shall be able to separate us from the love of God, which is in Christ Jesus our Lord. Romans 8:39.

Three-year-old Jonathan loved to sit on Mother's lap and listen to stories. He usually asked for "little boy stories," his favorite tales concerning the doings of a boy named Jonny. He liked to have the stories begin by mentioning that Jonny's mother loved him, his daddy loved him, his sisters loved him, his grandmas and grandpas loved him, and most of all, Jesus loved him.

One morning everything went wrong for Jonathan. It was much too cold to go outdoors to play. Baby sister kept getting into his toys. Worst of all, he hurt his finger while trying to hitch the wagon to his little tractor.

Jonathan ran to his mother for comfort. Snuggling close he said plaintively, "Talk about we love me."

How comforting to a small child is the assurance that he is surrounded with love. As we grow older we may take the same comfort in the ever-present love of our heavenly Father. We have only to look around us to see evidence throughout nature of the all-encompassing love of God. If we want it written down in words, we turn to our Bibles, which are filled with assurances of His constant love and precious promises of His care for us.

Since God's character *is* love, we find that His whole Book speaks to us of that love. We find out about the constancy of His love as we read of the lives of some of the patriarchs, prophets, and kings and the very human mistakes they made. But God forgave them when they repented, and He loved them. He loves us when we are bad as much as when we are good, though His heart is grieved when we turn away from Him.

"Neither life nor death, height nor depth, can separate us from the love of God which is in Christ Jesus; not because we hold Him so firmly, but because He holds us so fast. If our salvation depended on our own efforts, we could not be saved; but it depends on the One who is behind all the promises. Our grasp on Him may seem feeble, but His love is that of an elder brother; so long as we maintain our union with Him, no one can pluck us out of His hand."—*The Acts of the Apostles,* p. 553.

R.E.

HOPE FOR THE BEST

Live in harmony with one another. Don't become snobbish but take a real interest in ordinary people. Romans 12:16, Phillips.

Sometimes we are inclined to lose hope for certain people. We see a careless boy or girl and we cry out, What hope is there for him? And yet there is always hope for anyone who gives God a chance. Someone has said, "Every child born into the world is a new thought of God, an ever fresh and radiant possibility."

Maybe that boy or girl has not made the most of his or her life. But still there is hope. Look at Field Marshall Jan Christian Smuts. He became South Africa's most distinguished citizen. He was Prime Minister of the South African Union for many years. Yet when he was a boy of 12 his father had no hope for him. He was a moping, ailing lad of whom his own father said: "He is a poor, unhealthy youngster, a queer fellow without much intelligence. It is best that he remain at home."

But that "queer" boy became the greatest citizen of South Africa. When he was prime minister he developed some strange methods of bringing harmony in his government. Sir Winston Churchill was impressed and wrote of this great statesman as follows: "When differences arose in the Union cabinet, General Smuts was wont to take the ministers responsible for a walk up Table Mountain [near Capetown], and if full agreement was not achieved by the time they reached the top, he would walk them down again. No divergent temperament could withstand the double dose."

In view of the tremendous possibility in every human being —even in as hopeless a boy as Jan Christian Smuts seemed to be—we are told in our text today that we should be interested in ordinary people. The very people whom we might call ordinary may become God's extraordinary people.

As a matter of fact, what hope was there for a boy named Joseph, hated by his brothers, sold into slavery, and carried down to Egypt? But God saw something in that boy that He could use. God may have great plans and great hopes for *you!*

So, take courage and be hopeful. And remember: Base your happiness on your hope in Christ and then go Straight Ahead.

A.A.E.

"ZEALS" IN CHURCH

For the zeal of thine house hath eaten me up. Psalm 69:9.

David, who wrote these words, had a deep love for God's house. His zeal was an eager desire, an enthusiastic diligence to build God's house.

When President Theodore Roosevelt was a boy, he wasn't as brave as when he hunted animals in Africa, explored the unknown, or fought as a soldier. No, he had a great fear of wild animals.

Near his home in New York City was the large church he attended. One afternoon he stood looking up at the steeple. The door was open. The sexton, cleaning the church, invited Teddy to come inside.

"Oh, no! I know what you've got in there. I'm not coming in."

Surprised, the kind man smiled. "Teddy, there's nothing in God's house that will hurt you. Please come inside and look around." He went down the stairs and took hold of Teddy's hand to lead him inside. Terrified, Teddy jerked away and ran home the three blocks as fast as he could. When his mother asked what had happened, he told her.

"But, Teddy, why don't you want to go in the church? You've been there many times. That's where we meet God."

"But, Mother, there's a 'zeal' in there." Teddy's eyes grew wide with fright as he imagined some dreadful animal, maybe a cross between a dragon and a crocodile, inside the church.

"I don't understand, Teddy. What do you mean?"

"Last week I heard the minister say the 'zeal' would eat people who came into the church." Then mother remembered the minister's text, "The zeal of thine house hath eaten me up."

Poor Teddy! He didn't understand that the psalmist was talking about Jesus who loved God's house so much that He drove away the irreverent folk who were buying, selling, and changing money. All week he had been afraid of an imaginary animal.

This zeal must be inside of us, like something we have eaten. If it's part of us, we will love God's house. We are quiet and reverent in God's presence. When God speaks to you through the minister, are you listening or whispering? Do you join in singing God's praises and take part in the Bible reading? Do you meet God there and hear Him speak to you?

E.E.L. and J.H.L.

GOD IS EVEN INTERESTED IN WHAT WE EAT

And God said, Behold, I have given you every herb bearing seed, which is upon the face of all the earth, and every tree, in the which is the fruit of a tree yielding seed; to you it shall be for meat. Genesis 1:29.

Red-headed Bill Walton, 21-year-old star center on the University of California, Los Angeles, basketball team a few years back, was different from most of his teammates. There was no meat in Bill's diet. He began each day with a good breakfast of yogurt, cottage cheese, nuts, cereal, raisins, seeds, and honey.

By the time he was a junior in college Walton had become the most successful college athlete of his generation. He had a personal won-lost record of 148 to 2.

Bill Walton was convinced that his health-care program and his nonflesh diet helped keep him in shape for one of the toughest games in sports. No doubt he was correct in his thinking. God has told us through His Word that fruit, nuts, grains, and vegetables provide us with the best possible diet.

In the beginning the Lord gave man his ideal diet: "And God said, Behold, I have given you every herb bearing seed, which is upon the face of all the earth, and every tree, in the which is the fruit of a tree yielding seed; to you it shall be for meat."

You see, the Lord knew that it was better for man to get his vitamins and minerals firsthand rather than secondhand from the cow or the sheep, which had eaten a rich, nutritious vegetarian diet and then been killed to provide steak or lamb chops.

God also foresaw the prevalence of disease among animals in these last days. He knew that many people would contract serious illnesses from eating their flesh, so He provided a better way—a better diet. Large numbers of people today, besides Seventh-day Adventists, have discovered this better way. Some of these people are outstanding scientists, nutritionists, and athletes, like Bill Walton.

Following God's way is still the best way—eating, drinking, playing, resting—doing all to the glory of God. We are always blessed when we follow His counsel.

R.H.P.

STRONG FOR THE BATTLE

It is good for a man that he bear the yoke in his youth.
Lamentations 3:27.

When Michael Dowling decided to attend school he arranged for his pony to stay on a farm. The day before leaving home he decided to pay a last visit to his pony. He found two farmers going that way willing to take him on the back of their lumber wagon.

Before the days of radio broadcasts, storms often took travelers by surprise. On that December morning a terrible blizzard swept over the Minnesota countryside. So thick was the snow that the driver could not see the heads of his horses. The driver whipped them up and soon they were galloping over the open prairie.

As they struck a ditch Michael was knocked over the side of the wagon. Stunned, he lay for a few moments then jumped up and tried to catch up with the wagon, but failed. He tried to follow the tracks, but before long the snow filled them in. In the bitter cold he stumbled along, vainly trying to find a railroad track, a fence, or a house.

Suddenly he came upon a woodpile. Knowing that there must be a house nearby, he began throwing sticks in various directions hoping to hit a wall, but in vain. He tried circling, then he lost the woodpile. He ran into a straw stack into which he tunneled to get out of the below-zero wind. There he lay all night keeping himself awake to avoid freezing to death.

In bright morning sunshine Michael looked around and saw a farmhouse. On legs that felt like sticks of wood he struggled to the door, where a farmer took him in and began the slow process of thawing him out.

When he could be moved, Michael was taken to the nearest hospital where doctors amputated both legs just above the knee, one arm at the elbow, and all the fingers on his other hand. He was fourteen years old!

He refused to give up. With the aid of artificial legs he went to school. By sheer determination he succeeded—learned to drive a car, married, reared a family, became a banker and State legislator.

Michael Dowling learned to endure hardships in his youth, and those hardships produced strength of character when he became a man.

V.E.R.

WON'T POWER

Blessed is the man that walketh not in the counsel of the ungodly, nor standeth in the way of sinners, nor sitteth in the seat of the scornful. Psalm 1:1.

You have all heard of willpower and determined to develop it. But there is another kind of power that is very useful. That is *won't* power.

Never heard of it? Well, the main thing you have to do to have won't power is to decide to do *nothing* wrong.

To keep out of some of the worst pitfalls that beset a young person's path, all that is necessary is *not* to walk into them.

For instance, to keep away from the tobacco habit, the best way is simply *not to smoke*. That's all. If someone offers you a cigarette, exercise won't power. Say to yourself, "I won't." To your friend, "No, thank you." Then don't smoke.

Or maybe the temptation doesn't come to you through a friend. Robbie walked along the edge of a country road on his way to school. He saw a crumpled cigarette pack in the ditch, apparently thrown from a car window. He picked it up, for he was saving bits of foil. As he tore the foil from the wrapper, he noticed that the pack was not empty after all. There was one cigarette left. He tucked the pack down into his pocket, cigarette and all.

He had often wondered what it would be like to smoke. Now he had a cigarette in his pocket and nobody knew it was there! He could try it if he wanted to!

He thought about it often during the day. He wouldn't tell even his best friend. He would only try it so he would know what smoking was like. He knew several of the other boys at school had tried it; they bragged about it. But he wouldn't brag.

And then another thought came to him. If it was something he was ashamed of—something he wouldn't want anyone to know he had done—why do it?

He didn't smoke the cigarette. He exercised won't power. That afternoon on the way home from school he crumpled up the cigarette and package and tossed them in a trash bin.

In the future whenever he wavered on a temptation he found one of his best defenses was to say right off, "I won't."

R.E.

THE LOST BLUE GLASS

But the tongue can no man tame; it is an unruly evil, full of deadly poison. James 3:8.

Only a match, but it can burn down acres and acres of timber.

Only a comma, but it cost the United States Government millions of dollars. A secretary merely typed a comma in the wrong place when copying a bill allowing certain fruit plants to enter the country duty free. She put a comma between the words *fruit* and *plants,* so that imported fruit such as oranges, lemons, and bananas, as well as plants, were free from duty until the Government could get the law changed. It was an expensive mistake!

Only a pencil eraser, but it saved a Catalina flying boat and the lives of those aboard. There was a bad gasoline leak and the plane had to land on the water in the midst of the Pacific Ocean for repairs. Time after time the machinist's mate tried to plug the leak, but nothing was successful until he discovered that the rubber on the end of a pencil fitted perfectly. The ship continued safely on its way.

Only a tiny piece of blue glass, but the picture was spoiled without it. An artist making a stained-glass window for a church was working on a delicate part of the picture when he became tired and decided to go for a walk. On his return he found that the janitor had cleaned his studio while he was out. Climbing the ladder, he began work again, but soon discovered that a piece of blue glass he had prepared before going for his walk was not where he had left it. Unable to locate it, he called the janitor.

"Did you see a tiny piece of blue glass?" he asked.

"A tiny piece of blue? Yes, I did, but it was so small I figured it couldn't possibly be of any use and I swept it up with the dirt."

"Oh, no," groaned the artist. "We *must* find it. I can't finish the picture without it."

Together the two men went to the trash bin and carefully sifted through the contents. When the janitor finally found the minute piece of blue, the relieved artist hurried back to his picture with the precious piece of glass. The janitor followed.

"There," said the artist as he fastened it in place. "See, that tiny bit of blue is the clear blue eye of Jesus!"

Oh, yes, little things such as studying your lessons every day or biting your tongue when you're dying to spread some gossip *are* important. Very!

M.H.

271

GATHER ROUND THE CAMPFIRE

Did not our heart burn within us? Luke 24:32.

"Everything about junior camp is fun, but the best is campfire."
"What's so great about campfire, Danny?"

"During the day we each go our own way, busy with all the fun activities—hiking, swimming, crafts, canoeing, or water skiing—but at campfire we are together. Sitting in a circle with the fire in the center draws us close. We aren't separate anymore. We become one by singing and listening together, watching the flames from the fire change color, seeing the sparks as the logs shift. Jesus is close to us. And we like one another better. I don't feel mad anymore at Leland for pushing me off the diving board, or at Bob for waking me up with a squirt from his water pistol."

Danny was right. The campfire unites hearts and people. The discouraged disciples on the way to Emmaus later said, "Didn't our heart burn within us?" That word *heart* is singular. Jesus' presence had burned its way inside, uniting their hearts into one. Wherever Jesus is, there are no differences, no racial prejudice, no separation. God's holy fire burns away selfishness, making us all one in His love.

It is like solder, the metal alloy that joins other metals. When heat from the soldering iron is applied, solder melts and fuses two metals' surfaces. Fire's uniting flame welds separate pieces of steel together as God's Spirit blends us in unity of faith and love.

Fire not only joins us together but makes the relationship permanent. Years ago I learned to make pottery. First we molded our vases from wet clay. After they had dried we painted them with an enamel glaze. Still looking dull, the vases were placed in a kiln. The fire burned hot and the temperature was high. Yet that heat melted the glaze on the vase until it was firmly fused to the clay. The vase came from the fire perfectly smooth with lovely colors, never to change. The fire of God's presence will make you steadfast, strong, and beautiful, permanently established in Him, no longer changeable. We can be true friends to others when we have become true to God.

E.E.L. and J.H.L.

LEARN TO STOP

I have written unto you, young men, because ye are strong, and the word of God abideth in you. 1 John 2:14.

There is a natural tendency for people to admire those who possess strong characters and look down on those who have weak ones. We look up to Joseph and Daniel, but especially to Jesus, who knew how to say No to temptation and make it stick. John points out here that the source of that strength is the Word of God. That Word in the heart enables the Christian to resist temptation.

Joe Thomas shifted into low gear as he gently eased his ten-ton tractor-trailer out onto the busy street in Parkersburg, West Virginia. Traffic was comparatively light as he followed the highway up the bridge and over the Ohio River. As he started down the far side, he put his foot gently on the brake. Something happened that had never happened before.

Instead of reducing the speed of the truck the pedal went clear to the floor. Joe realized instantly that he was face-to-face with total brake failure. Gradually the truck gathered momentum and the needle on the speedometer swung over farther and farther to the right. Thirty—forty—fifty—then sixty miles an hour.

Fortunately the road was straight and traffic not too heavy. Joe placed his hand on the horn and kept it there as the monster rolled down the bridge ramp and into a thickly populated area on the Ohio side of the river.

Then he saw a red light ahead and a car starting to cross directly in front of him. He tried to swerve, but hit the car broadside, hurling it with a loud crash to one side of the street. By this time he was going nearly seventy miles an hour. Overtaking cars, he tossed them right and left out of the path of his truck. Even pedestrians were struck and killed. By the time the truck finally came to rest, eleven persons had been killed and many more injured.

It is a serious thing when truck brakes fail. It is far more serious when the brakes of life no longer work.

Are your brakes in good order? Can you say No to strong temptations? Perhaps Joe's terrifying experience might have been avoided had he checked his brakes more often. How about checking your brakes? Let the Word of God abide in you, thus making you strong for God—strong to do right and to avoid evil.

V.E.R.

THE CHILD WAS GOD'S MAN

But the Lord said unto me, Say not, I am a child: for thou shalt go to all that I shall send thee, and whatsoever I command thee thou shalt speak. Jeremiah 1:7.

I was in North China when I met Liu. He looked like a boy in his early teens, for he was small, but how much enthusiasm was wrapped up in his young heart! He was actually 17 and had just accepted the truths proclaimed to the world by the church.

This earnest young man went to our college near Nanking. He was there for two years and was outstanding among the hundreds of students. At that time we wanted to open up a new section of North China. We had no churches or institutions in that area, so we looked around for a strong worker who could accept the challenge.

This news reached the college and when Liu heard about it, he was elated. He at once wanted to accept the challenge. So we called him!

When Liu arrived in the county seat he rented a room at a hotel. Then, on the telephone poles he tacked up posters that read: "Liu, the man with the message, has come." He also gave his address and invited everyone to come to talk with him. When the first man came to the hotel, the clerk sent him down to Liu's room. The stranger knocked on the door. When Liu opened it the man said, "I want to see Mr. Liu, the man with the message." Liu answered, "I am Mr. Liu. Come in." But the man said scornfully, as he pointed at him, "You—you are only a child," and walked away. Others came and had similar reactions.

After this humbling experience Brother Liu locked his door, fell on his knees, and earnestly sought the Lord for guidance. For three days he refused to see anyone. He fasted and prayed much. Finally he opened his Bible to Jeremiah 1:7. He found comfort and strength. Just then another knock sounded at his door. Answering it, he found a farmer from the country who said: "Three days ago I was in this town and saw a sign saying that you had a message. When I went home and reported to my village, they sent me back to bring you to give your message." Liu went. Three months later he sent for us to come. We went and seventy-nine converts were baptized. The "child" had become "God's man."

A.A.E.

THE LIVING THIEF

Thou shalt truly tithe all the increase of thy seed, that the field bringeth forth year by year. Deut. 14:22.

An evangelist presenting God's message night after night to a large audience came in due course to the subject of tithes and offerings.

After his presentation, one of the listeners wanted to talk to him. This man didn't think it was necessary to pay tithe. As proof of his point, he cited to the evangelist the story of the thief on the cross. He was sure that man had never paid tithe, and yet Jesus had assured the thief that he would be saved in God's kingdom.

It probably *is* true that the dying thief never paid tithe. For one who would make his livelihood by such dishonest means certainly was not likely to pay tithe on the gain!

"I don't pay tithe," the listener said to the evangelist, "and I don't think I need to. God can save me just as well as the thief on the cross."

"There is one big difference between the thief on the cross and you," the evangelist told the man.

"What's that?" the man wanted to know.

"He was a dying thief," the evangelist said. "But you, sir, are a living thief!"

We may think that is strong language, to call a man a thief just because he doesn't want to give a tenth of his income to God. But that is the exact language the Bible uses, for one who robs is a thief.

When we put our tithe in the envelope and put it into the collection plate at church, we are not giving something to God. That portion of our income doesn't belong to us in the first place; it is His. It is the part we return to show Him that we realize that everything we have comes from Him and belongs to Him. It is the part of our income that we don't even count on using for ourselves, for to do so would be to use God's money, money that He has designed for the support of His ministry.

This is why we do not simply divide up the one tenth of our income to distribute among various offerings. There is a difference between tithes and offerings.

Even though we are young and don't have much money, we should honor God by returning to Him His tenth. And then, if we love Him, we will want to give Him gifts, or offerings, as well.

R.E.

EVEN ELEPHANTS NEED UNDERSTANDING

And Jesus said, "Neither do I condemn you; go, and do not sin again." John 8:11, RSV.

Old Bozo, a well-loved circus elephant, enjoyed doing his tricks for all, but he especially loved the children. But one day a change came. He trumpeted angrily at the boys and girls; three times he attempted to kill his keeper. The circus manager decided he was dangerous and must die. Heartless and greedy for money, he sold tickets inviting the crowd to come to the circus and watch a squad of gunners turn their rifles on the mad elephant in his cage.

Bozo trudged in his never-ending circle, often lifting his trunk as he bellowed at the crowd. Outside the cage, the ringmaster waited to give the signal to fire, when a short man went up to the manager.

"Let me go into that cage. I can make your bad elephant well."

"Never! You'd be trampled to death in moments."

"I thought you'd say that so I brought along a legal paper to free you from all responsibility. All the risk is mine."

Assured that the paper was in order, the manager announced that an unarmed man would unbolt the steel door. As he entered, Bozo gave a warning squeal of anger. Then the man spoke a few words and Bozo grew quiet. The man kept talking. No one but Bozo understood what he was saying. Finally, with a small, childlike cry, the elephant began to wag his enormous head from side to side.

After a long while the man explained that Bozo wasn't bad, just homesick and frustrated. As an Indian elephant, he had grown up hearing Hindustani. His big elephant heart was at peace again as he heard the Hindustani words he knew and loved. The crowd cheered.

After the stranger had disappeared the manager noticed the signature of Rudyard Kipling, the famous writer on India, on the paper.

To understand those who act differently, you must be kind to them instead of condemning them. Then it's easy to forgive them for their actions.

E.E.L. and J.H.L.

276

REFINER'S FIRE

But who may abide the day of his coming? and who shall stand when he appeareth? for he is like a refiner's fire. Malachi 3:2.

In the silver-and-lead refinery a great pot of molten metal was being heated. Just a few hours before, it was dug out of the earth, crushed, and conveyed to the top of the smelting pot.

"Excuse me, sir," I asked, "but why do you heat the metal so hot?"

The smelter removed his asbestos gloves and leaned against a stack of pipes carrying cold water to a cooling rack. "We are separating silver from lead. Lead is heavier than silver and sinks to the bottom. Watch me now, I'm going to tap the metal for silver."

Putting his gloves on again, the smelter turned a spigot at the top of the large pot. Liquid fire began to run out and down a channel to cooling racks.

"What's that gray stuff that forms around the edges?"

"Slag!" he shouted against the noise of the furnace. "The fire burns it out."

In another part of the smelting works the silver is further refined and small amounts of gold are taken out of it. Huge dumps of slag outside the factory, processed years before by a less-efficient process, are being reprocessed to gather more silver and gold from them.

But everywhere there is the refiner's fire. That's the way you purify metal. Before gold or silver or even pure lead can be poured, every ounce of dross is taken out.

What does the Bible mean when it says that the King of kings is like a refiner's fire? It means that those who are ready when He comes will have to go through a special process of preparation. Sin is like dross, or slag. When God's love first takes hold of us many changes are needed.

When a goldsmith is looking for the top quality in gold he looks for one thing. If it says 24-carat gold he knows that it will stand any test. He can heat it, twist it, beat it, shape it.

What can you do to help develop a character that is pure 24-carat gold?

W.R.L.S.

HE IS MY ADVOCATE

For the Father judgeth no man, but hath committed all judgment unto the Son. John 5:22.

When Mel Barton, the local banker, died he left a large estate of stocks, bonds, and land. Mel had, he thought, carefully prepared his will so that his wife and other members of his family would be well provided for. His church and one or two charities in which he was interested would also receive help.

Unfortunately, the will was contested. Some who had been included in Mr. Barton's bequests were not happy. They felt that others were receiving too much and they were not receiving enough, so they employed lawyers to help them contest Mel's will in an effort to get more money and land.

John Miller, a local attorney and an acquaintance of the family, offered to help Mrs. Barton. The widow hesitated. She kept putting off the decision until she realized that she was about to lose the whole estate. Hurrying to John Miller's office, she agreed to accept his offer to handle the legal aspects of the case.

"I'm sorry, Mrs. Barton," the attorney said. "I was eager to help you. But you were not ready for me to handle your case. Now, since I talked with you I've been appointed a judge, and one of my first assignments is to handle the lawsuits in connection with your husband's will. I'm sorry, but now it's too late for me to help you."

Some of us may be very hesitant to accept Jesus as our Saviour. We have many things we want to do before we let ourselves become tied down with religion. We want to have a lot of fun. We want to make a lot of money. We are too busy now with big plans to bother with Jesus.

Did you ever stop to think, my young friend, that not only is Jesus our Saviour and our Advocate but He is also our Judge? "Christ has been made our Judge. The Father is not the Judge. The angels are not. He who took humanity upon Himself, and in this world lived a perfect life, is to judge us. He only can be our Judge."—*Testimonies*, vol. 9, p. 185.

Jesus, our Saviour, will also be our Judge. Let's be sure He is our Advocate now, as well.

R.H.P.

A SCRAPBOOK OF LIVING MEMORIES

A new commandment I give unto you, That ye love one another; as I have loved you, that ye also love one another. John 13:34.

You can make every day contain a treasure chest of memories for yourself. If you want to make a good year for yourself—a good life—do at least one good thing each day. Turn yourself into a living scrapbook so that you can look back upon each day with satisfaction. You can make a big thing out of your life by the little considerate acts you do for others.

It is so easy to take advantage of holidays and special occasions to remember someone. You don't have to spend money to send a fancy greeting card to your aunt who is having a birthday. You might drop her a note to show her that you remember, or make a card yourself. The personal touch will be treasured longer than a card from the store.

Is some friend sick? Drop off an interesting book or a magazine at his house on the way home from school.

If a neighbor child has left a bicycle in the middle of the street, why can't you be the one to put it to one side so that it does not get run over.

If some boy or girl thoughtlessly drops a candy wrapper on the ground, you could be the one who willingly picks it up—without thinking that it is none of your business.

When you see your mother struggling with packages as she comes in from grocery shopping, you could pull yourself away from the TV set, even if you are engrossed, and give her a hand.

These are trivial things that take only a minimum effort and yet can add up to a big difference in your life.

As you do this, you are following the example of Christ, who made His life a blessing to others. Everywhere He went—in the Temple, along the road, in the cities, by the seaside—He constantly did good things for people.

He never became weary of working for others. He never drew back from sacrifice or hardships.

As we look each day for some kind and loving ways to help someone else, we are following Christ's request that we love one another as He has loved us. Let us start now to turn our lives into scrapbooks of living memories.

R.E.

SON OF A KING

He that searcheth the hearts knoweth what is the mind of the Spirit, because he maketh intercession for the saints according to the will of God. Romans 8:27.

Even the teachers found that Phillip was different. Whenever other boys and girls shouted, fought, roughed up each other, teased or tormented, he would stand quietly by, ignoring what was going on. But if the teacher needed help, or someone had to do extra work, he always volunteered. What made him so different?

"Will you take me to see your mother?" his teacher asked one day. "She must be a wonderful person to have such a good son."

"My mother is dead. She died years ago."

"I'm sorry," his teacher apologized. "May I meet your father then?"

"He is also dead. But he was a good man." Phillip's eyes started to fill with tears. "If I tell you about them will you promise not to tell anyone else?"

He told her of his life in Europe and of the little school he attended near his home. "My mother and father were of royal blood. I am the son of a prince and a princess. When soldiers took my mother and father away, their last words were, 'Never forget that you are a prince. Do not do anything that would be unworthy of your rank.'"

Though others might be rough or rude, this boy was different. He was a prince!

And this is God's will for you. You are a prince, a princess, the son or daughter of the King of kings. When you accept Jesus, the Holy Spirit takes the message to the Father and things begin to happen. God begins to make your life more like Christ's. When you pray, your prayers help you change from your old ways to new ways.

Now you become part of the family of heaven. Think what that means! Besides your own mother and father, you have a heavenly Father who loves you and cares for you and wants you to be like His own Son.

Hold your head high! Live for the King, who is your Father!

W.R.L.S.

THE DOG KNEW THE MELODY

I have gone astray like a lost sheep; seek thy servant; for I do not forget thy commandments. Psalm 119:176.

Our story today concerns a lost dog, not a lost sheep; but the lesson is the same. When Mrs. Smith heard a snuffing noise, she went out to investigate and found a small Maltese terrier at the step, dirty and bedraggled! She decided to take him in until she could find the owner.

First she offered him a big drink of milk. He emptied two dishes. His bright little eyes shone with pleasure. Next she plunged him into warm water in the laundry tub. Then after he was dry, she gave his white, silky hair a good brushing. Now he could be a worthy member of their family until they could find the owner. She tried out several dog names, but he responded to none of them. Since he had been snuffing around the door, she decided to name him Snuffy. Before long he appeared quite settled in his new home. For several weeks the Smiths watched the lost-and-found column of the newspaper, but no one advertised for a white Maltese terrier. When six months had passed, Snuffy was considered as permanent as any other member of the family.

One evening the Smiths were entertaining some of their musical friends with a special musical event. Apparently Snuffy paid no attention to the guests, but went to bed in his basket. A pianist performed, then a violinist, but the dog slept on.

But when the bagpipes sounded, Snuffy was wide awake. His former master had made that weird squeezing tune that the dog loved. The pet tore through the door down the hall and into the living room. With a yelp of delight he jumped up on the player's lap and licked the surprised face behind the pipes.

"Mac! Mac!" exclaimed the piper as he gave his dog a big hug. "You have been lost for nine months. I advertised six weeks, but no one returned you." Then the Smiths explained that they had had him only six months.

Like Mac, children and youth wander from God to try the sinful pleasures of the world. Then one day something reminds them of their real Master. Once they get a glimpse of God, nothing else can take His place in their lives.

L.C.W.

NO SACRIFICE

Then he said, "Here I am, God, to do what you want me to do."
Hebrews 10:9, TEV.

If you live in a temperate climate, each year in October there are at least two weeks of brilliant autumn colors. Then most trees drop their leaves and expose the bare branches. Why must they sacrifice their beautiful foliage and stand naked and empty through the winter months? Is it a waste that trees spend so much energy making leaves only to have them a short time, and then they are forever gone?

When we understand the reason, we will understand why Jesus had to sacrifice His life to do God's will. There was no other way.

All summer long these handsome leaves refresh the earth by pouring water vapor into the air from water lifted from the ground. When the ground freezes, the water supply stops. If the leaves aren't shut off, they will waste vital sap that is in the tree, which cannot be replaced from the roots in the frozen ground. So to save the life of the tree, God devised a plan to completely strip it of its leaves.

As summer draws to a close special cells at the base of the stem of each leaf begin to loosen and dry out. Before they become so brittle that the leaves fall off, God prepares to heal the wound He has made. Special cells just below these brittle cells form a tough corky tissue that stops the pipelines that bring the sap into the leaf. When this happens the unstable chemical, chlorophyll, that makes the leaf green, is destroyed by the sun's rays. When the green color disappears, other pigments that have been in the leaf cause it to change color. If carotene predominates, the leaf turns yellow or orange. The red and bluish tones are from a sugar chemical. In God's glorious plan there is really no useless sacrifice.

Let's say like Jesus, "Here I am, God, to do what you want me to do." What Jesus asks us to surrender is only that which we are better off without. When we let go of the things of less worth, God always gives us that which is greater and more valuable. Hidden beauty emerges when, listening to His commands, we yield our all to Him.

E.E.L. and J.H.L.

SIGNS OF HIS COMING

The stars shall fall from heaven, and the powers of the heavens shall be shaken. Matthew 24:29.

When Elder J. N. Loughborough was holding meetings in Healdsburg, California, during the early days of our work there he was opposed by another minister who enjoyed making fun of Adventists and the message they preached. One night this man hired a hall and preached on the "follies of Adventism."

He began by making fun of the idea that the falling of the stars on November 13, 1833, fulfilled the prediction found in today's verse. He said, "This shower of meteors in 1833 happens every thirty-three years. I sat up all night to watch it in 1866."

In the audience sat an old gentleman, Brother Martin, who had seen the falling of the stars in Missouri in the year 1833, and who had regarded it at that time as a sign of the last great day. Brother Martin was an Adventist. He had gone to the meeting out of curiosity, and now expected to hear the minister give a wonderful description of the falling of the stars in 1866.

Instead, the minister said, "I took a position where I could view one part of the heavens, and my wife where she could see the other part. In a brief space I counted eighteen falling stars! My wife counted almost as many more!"

This description of the 1866 star shower so surprised old Brother Martin that he brought his cane down with a loud thump on the floor as he whistled his complete disgust at what the man had said. But the meeting continued in spite of this interruption. At the close the old man apologized to the minister.

"Elder," he said, "pardon me for that thump with my cane and for my whistle, but I couldn't help it. When you told about counting eighteen stars, I was so astonished that I forgot where I was. Man, I saw the real falling of the stars in 1833 when sixty thousand were falling each hour. You might as well have tried to count snowflakes in a heavy snowstorm as to count the stars that fell in 1833. You say you saw a similar sight in 1866? Nonsense!"

The old man walked out of the hall in disgust.

Now everywhere there are signs of Jesus' soon coming. Like Brother Martin and the stars, you will see them everywhere you look.

V.E.R.

THE GAME THE KING FORBADE

I press toward the mark for the prize of the high calling of God in Christ Jesus. Philippians 3:14.

About five hundred years ago in the country of Scotland, people began to play a new game. They called it "golfe." Archery was the favorite sport of Scotland at that time, and the king, James II, was furious when many people forsook the bow and arrow to go golfing.

So Parliament passed a law forbidding anyone to play the new game. The punishment was imprisonment.

One day a man who was very enthusiastic about the new game dared to speak to the king about it. "Sire," he said, "this new game is fit for a king like you."

The king decided to try his hand with a golfe club. He liked the new game. Soon the anti-golfing law was repealed and the people returned to the greens. The game continued to grow more popular.

A few years later the king's granddaughter, Mary, queen of Scots, became the first woman golfer in the world. Whenever she played, Mary employed a young boy to help her find the ball and carry her clubs. Mary had been educated in France, and she called the boy a "cadet," giving the French pronunciation. In time, the word became *caddie*, which golfers use today.

Golf was introduced into America in the eighteenth century. Its popularity grew more quickly in the United States than it had in Europe. Golf courses were laid out in many city parks. Many country clubs organized. Fans gathered to watch the players.

The popularity of the game still increases. The players number in the millions. Fans follow their favorite players in person and on television. The game is enjoyed by presidents, vice-presidents, businessmen, and housewives.

Back in the days of the Apostle Paul, the most popular games were gladiatorial games—where people fought each other or fought with beasts—and foot races or throwing contests, which took great physical stamina. The gladiators especially risked much, hoping to win the prize. But the prize Paul speaks of in today's verse is in the game of life, which we all play. In the earthly games Paul watched, there could be only one winner. But we may all be winners in the game of life. Let us ask God today to help us press toward the mark for that prize.

R.E.

SHREWD FOR GOD

The master of this dishonest manager praised him for doing such a shrewd thing; because the people of this world are much more shrewd in handling their affairs than the people who belong to the light. Luke 16:8, TEV.

The manager wasn't praised for his dishonesty, but he was admired for his thoroughness in carrying out a plan. Jesus here emphasized that sinners who live just for what they can get from this life often make better preparations than do Christians who are preparing for heaven. If only His children used the same zeal to serve God as do many who serve only themselves. Even animals are more clever for selfish reasons than some Christians are for the cause of God.

Whining loudly, a brown dachshund interrupted her master, Jack, as he was talking with his friend, Bob. Jack explained, "Sally wants a dime. Don't try giving her a penny, she knows the difference. She'll whine till she gets a dime." Curious, Bob gave Sally a dime and followed her to a nearby food store. She waited for Bob to open the door. Walking to the meat counter, she laid down her dime. The man at the counter saw her.

"Oh, ho, there's my good friend, Sally. And here's your food."

Wrapping two wieners in a package he gave them to her. Sally walked to the door, waited for Bob, and then went straight home. Laying her package down, she ripped it open and the wieners disappeared in two bites, and Sally was off, probably for more dimes.

Vicky, too, was clever. As a puppy she learned to watch for the mailman, who gave her all the letters, which she took to Mrs. Hunt. As a reward, she always received a dog biscuit.

One day Vicky came with just one letter, and wagged her tail as she got her biscuit. In about two minutes she was back with another letter, dancing happily as she received her reward. Thinking it strange, Mrs. Hunt assumed that the mailman had forgotten to give her both letters. But she followed Vicky to the room where she ate. The dog was chewing the biscuit with her paws on a third letter.

If animals can be shrewd for selfish reasons, why can't we create opportunities for sharing the precious things of God?

E.E.L. and J.H.L.

THE DESPISED DUSTING

Whatsoever ye do, do it heartily, as to the Lord, and not unto men. Colossians 3:23.

"I simply loathe dusting!" sighed Helen as the work whistle blew. "Why did they have to give me that old job of dusting the dining room, anyway? Chairs and more chairs, and all of them have rungs to be dusted!"

As she sauntered slowly down the hall toward the dining room, Helen passed the academy business office. The door was open and she could see Eileen working on the ledgers. "Now that looks like fun!" declared Helen. "I could enjoy work like that. Why did they have to give me that old dining room to do, anyway!"

However, as the girl started to work, her mood changed and she began to tell herself, "Look here, you old silly, don't you know that anything worth doing at all is worth doing well? You just go after each one of those chairs as if you expected Jesus Himself to sit on it! Maybe someday if you are a good worker you will be promoted out of the dirt-chasing department." So she set to dusting energetically, if not with a will. In fact, she became so engrossed with her job that she was surprised to look up and see Mr. Bradnor, the business manager, standing in the doorway watching her. However, he said nothing and soon went away.

A few days later as Helen was again lecturing herself about the necessity of doing a good job of the hated dusting, she looked up to see Mr. Bradnor once more watching her. She was getting used to seeing him around by now, so she merely kept on working. I suppose he is checking up on all the students, she thought.

Then one day Mr. Bradnor stopped her in the hallway. "Helen, we need another girl in the office. There is too much for Eileen to do by herself. How would you like to help her and take charge of the bookstore?

How would she? Helen nearly whooped for joy, but remembered her manners in time to exclaim, "I'd love to! But what about the dining room?"

Mr. Bradnor smiled. "We'll get someone else to dust."

How glad Helen was that whatsoever she had found to do, she had done it "heartily, as to the Lord"!

M.H.

UNITED WE STAND

Now you together are Christ's body; but each of you is a different part of it. In the Church, God has given the first place to apostles, the second to prophets, the third to teachers; after them, miracles, and after them the gift of healing; helpers, good leaders, those with many languages. 1 Corinthians 12:27, 28, Jerusalem.

Do you like honey? I like it so well that one time I bought the equipment necessary, ordered a package of bees, introduced them to their new home when they arrived, and set out to get lots of honey. But I had some things to learn.

I learned that I could do almost any kind of work with them or around them, if they were busy gathering nectar. But if there was no honey flow—much nectar being gathered—kindness and tolerance were just not in their vocabulary. They can be first-class warriors!

A joyful Christian who has a constant relationship with Jesus is so busy working for the Lord he has little time for criticism, gossip, or any other sin.

When the sun was hot, my bees maintained a constant cool hive temperature as thousands of little wings fanned to prevent the wax from melting. When it became freezing cold, they clustered together in an oval to keep the hive warm. Here they laid their eggs.

If I cut the honeycomb, an alarm spread and bees with the gift of repair arrived to fix it up so that scarcely a trace was evident. If broken, they repaired it also. A scar marred the original hexagonal pattern, but it was still very serviceable.

The healthy queen of my colony laid just the number of eggs needed for the bees' life and welfare. She laid many eggs just before a honey flow when nectar would be abundant, but only what was required for replacement if there wasn't much work to be done.

Like God's church, each bee had a specific gift or work. Some gathered nectar, others pollen, some made wax foundation, others produced the cells, some existed to mate with the queen, others defended the hive. But all worked together for the best good of the hive.

In God's church each one has tasks to perform to His glory. It matters not which gift is yours. The important question is, Are you using your gifts for God?

E.E.L. and J.H.L.

WHAT TO BE

Also I heard the voice of the Lord, saying, Whom shall I send, and who will go for us? Then said I, Here am I; send me. Isaiah 6:8.

Sally had a hard time making up her mind what she wanted to do as a career. Finally she took the problem to her college faculty adviser.

"What do you *want* to be?" the counselor asked.

"Well, my mother wants me to be a teacher," Sally said.

"But I asked what *you* want," the adviser said.

"Well, I think I might like teaching if Mom weren't so insistent on it," Sally admitted, "but I don't want to be pushed into something."

Her adviser gave Sally a series of aptitude tests that showed she had a very good chance of being successful as a teacher.

When she stopped to think seriously about the whole matter after the aptitude tests were over, Sally decided it was foolish to stay away from a career she really might enjoy—a career she could probably do a good job at—just because she didn't want to give in and do the thing that her mother wanted her to do.

Why *not* please her mother for a change? Why *not* go along with one of her mother's ideas if it would be to her own advantage? Why did she need to feel pushed into it if the decision was actually her own? Would it really make sense to choose another lifework for which she might be less suited, just to keep from feeling that she was being pushed into something by a parent?

Her adviser backed up that idea by suggesting that her mother's interest in Sally's plans actually stemmed from a deep desire to see Sally happy and useful, not from any particularly selfish purpose.

Sally sometimes saw her parents' interest as an attempt to run her life. She wanted to make her own decisions. But as she agreed to consider the whole problem in a more grown-up way, she saw that the choice of teaching as a career would benefit herself most, not her parents.

The instinct to make our own decisions, to grow up a little, has been put into us by a wise heavenly Father. It is a means of helping us learn to stand on our own two feet and not depend on our parents all our lives. But let's not cut off good choices merely for the sake of being independent.

R.E.

LIVING BY FAITH

The life which I now live in the flesh I live by the faith of the Son of God, who loved me, and gave himself for me. Galatians 2:20, last part.

The elderly rancher and his grandson stepped down the rows of the orderly kitchen garden. Summer had been kind with plentiful rains. Tomatoes blazed with color in a warm corner. Beans hung in clusters like long green fingers waiting to be grasped. Beets, carrots, and parsnips promised succulent roots.

But the little boy had a question on his mind. Right out of the blue it came.

"Grandpa," asked the six-year-old, "does it make God happy when we don't sin?"

"Why, yes, Jimmy, God is happy when we don't sin."

His fair little head bent as he hoed the soil and thought about that for a few minutes.

"Grandpa," he said, insistently, "is that *all* it takes to make God happy?"

What do you think? Is that all it takes to make God happy? What if you simply avoided doing anything wrong. Would that completely please your parents?

Besides not doing wrong things, we have a responsibility to do right things. Paul says that our bodies, our minds, our talents, are like tools in the hands of a craftsman. They can be used to make evil. When we come to Christ, this stops. We take them and yield them to Christ. They become tools in His hands to do good.

What kind of good should we do? Helping around the home, doing our share of the chores, making life pleasant for teachers and parents. These are necessary parts of doing good.

But goodness reaches within us and outside of us in other ways. Our thoughts, our private moments spent alone when no one is looking, should also show a change. Those in need, the poor, the suffering, those without Christ need our help. In this way we can make others happy, make ourselves happy, and perhaps even answer the question that six-year-old boy had for his grandpa.

W.R.L.S.

NO OTHER DOOR

I am the way, and the truth, and the life. John 14:6, RSV.

Jesus is the Door, the only door, that leads to heaven and God. From the earliest times all of God's children have found entrance through this Door. Those who have tried to come in by any other way of their own devising are thieves and robbers.

In Texas there is a species of ant that has a large stopper-shaped head that exactly fits the circular hole that forms the entrance to the nest. These soldier ants have only one purpose in life, to provide a movable front door to the nest. Always one soldier ant is on duty with its head pressed tightly against the door. When a worker ant wants to go out of the nest, she signals by stroking the soldier ant from the back. Immediately the "door" stands aside and lets her pass. When she returns from her duties, she strokes the soldier's forehead. Again the living door moves out of the way and allows her to enter. Should an enemy try to invade the nest, he must find another way. Then the soldier ants fight bravely, using their strong, powerful jaws to defend the colony.

All worker ants show a similar spirit of bravery, devotion, and self-sacrifice when their home is in danger. If a flood of water comes down into the nest, they begin to move with frantic haste, hurrying not away from the nest but back into it. Risking their lives, they return again and again for their young. Carrying both eggs and larvae to safety, they exhibit real courage as they save what they can, though they themselves may die. When a hungry or starving ant finds food she seldom eats it herself, but carries it to her sisters. Seldom will she take one mouthful. Instead she fills her crop and hastens home to share with others.

Though ants are governed by instinct, surely God implanted in them this unselfish and courageous behavior. For abundant living He bids you enter through the Way, Jesus. Surely this door of salvation will open to you since it "will open wide to the trembling touch of a little child"—*Christ's Object Lessons*, p. 404.

E.E.L. and J.H.L.

ALWAYS A WAY

What shall I render unto the Lord for all his benefits toward me? Psalm 116:12.

One of our workers came to a tropical island in Inter-America just after a hurricane had swept through the place leaving hundreds of homes demolished. Some of the islanders lost their lives. The banana and the coconut trees were either blown down or stripped. In one small town our Adventist church had been completely destroyed and many members had lost their homes.

How should they rebuild the church? When the leader asked the members if they should erect another church, everyone voted, "Yes."

One young man with a wife and two children had taken some of the timbers of their heavily damaged house and some corrugated roofing to make a temporary shelter. He told the visiting minister, "We were hit pretty hard, but our lives were spared. We have two goats left. We can salvage enough from the old house to build ourselves a shelter to protect us from the sun and the rain until we can build a more permanent home. My wife and I have decided to donate one of our two goats to buy material for our new church." This family gave a real thank offering for God's benefits toward them in sparing their lives.

Miracles in giving still occur in our day. One woman wrote to the Voice of Prophecy that she had accidentally thrown a $5 bill into the fire together with other things she planned to burn. When she successfully retrieved the bill she decided to mail it to them.

A family in San Diego, California, wrote that they try to keep their yard as neat as possible. But they live on a hill at the top of a street that dead-ends into theirs and trash and leaves do blow up their driveway. One morning the husband found a ten-dollar bill blown up against the garage. Since they could not find the owner, they sent the ten dollars to the Voice of Prophecy to blow the words of truth through the air waves.

Two years ago we began selling our raspberries for Investment. The first year we made $42. This year I told the Lord I was too busy writing this book to seek customers, but if He would impress folks to come to us, all the proceeds would be His. Telephone calls came in. Two customers wanted twelve boxes each, another twenty-four; still another thirty-six boxes. We could not supply the demand, and got $82 for Sabbath school Investment.

L.C.W.

MARYANNA'S PIE

To obey is better than sacrifice, and to hearken than the fat of rams. 1 Samuel 15:22.

Mother had worked hard to get the house clean for Sabbath, and when everything was ready, she had gone grocery shopping. Maryanna, who stayed at home, had some time on her hands, since everything was ready for Sabbath.

Looking around the sparkling kitchen, she had an idea. She would surprise Mother and bake a pie for Sabbath. She took Mother's cookbook, found the recipe, and began.

That pie crust sounded so easy. But was it ever rough to make it stick together. Maryanna's crust had holes everywhere, and she got so upset that she cried. But she patched it as best she could, put in the pie filling, and shoved it into the oven.

Just then Mother walked in. As she looked around she got the strangest expression on her face.

"What's the matter, Mom?" Maryanna asked with a smile. "You look so horrified. I am baking a pie for you."

Mother looked as if she tried to smile back but couldn't quite make it.

"Honey, would you look around for a moment please?"

Maryanna's smile froze. She had not thought of it because she had struggled so fiercely with the pie crust, but that whole kitchen was strewn with flour, pie dough bits, spilled blueberry pie filling, and dirty dishes.

Mom and Maryanna both worked fast and hard to clean up, but by the time Mom could come in without stepping into flour and put the groceries away, the sun was setting and the family was late for worship.

"I am so sorry, Mom, but I wanted to do something nice for you," Maryanna whispered in Mother's ear after worship. A tear escaped down her cheek.

"I know that, honey, but sometimes we act before we think, and you didn't remember that time flies, and we must plan."

There was one comfort. The pie was delicious and Dad took a second helping. The next week when Maryanna found some spilled flour in the sandwich-bag drawer, she could even laugh about it. Together she and Mom baked the next pie on a Thursday night.

R.E.

TROUBLE CAN'T BURY YOU

For who is God, but the Lord? And who is a rock, except our God? The God who girded me with strength and made my way safe. Psalm 18:31, 32, RSV.

Old Nell had been a good, hard-working horse. Now she was old, lame, and feeble. So the farmer turned her out to pasture for the rest of her days. Returning from the field one day, he missed the old horse.

Wonder where she could have gone, he thought. The gate's closed and she'd never leave even if it were open.

Could she have fallen into the deep unused cistern? Sure enough, he could see her skinny back. When he called her name, she whinnied.

"She probably broke a leg in the fall. If not, she's still no use to me. That hole is very deep. I'd have to get help to get her out and could waste most of a day. Besides," he reasoned, "I've been meaning to fill in that dry cistern for a long time. Old Nell looks half-starved. I might as well bury her and fill in the cistern at the same time."

While getting his shovel, the farmer remembered the years of faithful service Old Nell had given. Still, knowing her usefulness was gone, the hard-hearted man began to dig. Standing far enough back from the hole so he couldn't see her struggle, he hoped she wouldn't suffer long.

As the dirt began to fall Old Nell braced her back and shook it off. Her legs, though stiff and sore, weren't broken. As the earth settled around her, she wiggled and shook, constantly treading the soil under her feet. The farmer, hating himself and his job, worked feverishly and the cistern gradually filled in. Hungry and tired as she was, the determined horse used every bit of her strength to keep on top of the dirt. It rose higher and higher, and she kept tramping it down and shaking it off.

Suddenly the farmer, resting a few minutes, looked up in surprise. Old Nell stepped feebly out of the cistern and ambled slowly off to her favorite resting place under the shade tree.

Have you ever felt you were being buried with troubles large and small, that you haven't strength in yourself to get on top of them all? Jesus longs to give you all the help you need. His strength is all powerful. Take your troubles to Him, right now claiming this promise of God, our Rock.

E.E.L. and J.H.L.

AN ACT OF KINDNESS

Happy are those who show mercy to others: God will show mercy to them! Matthew 5:7.

A touching story is told of an act of kindness by Babe Ruth. The Babe had learned of a 13-year-old boy who had undergone a serious and apparently unsuccessful operation. The case looked quite hopeless. The "home run king" knew that he was the children's hero in those days. So he decided to visit this boy in a hospital in New Jersey.

It was quite a trip considering the limited time he had. But he went and found the boy. Babe Ruth sat on the edge of the bed and talked to the child as long as the doctors would let him. Then he told Johnny that he was going to hit a home run that afternoon especially for him. He did hit that home run for Johnny. The boy, with his interest in life revived, immediately began to improve.

It is unbelievable what an act of kindness or even just a kind word can do for the body, for the mind, and for the heart of a human being. Johnny is just one more example of how such an act can spark something in the human heart that tends to marshall new strength and new forces to help us in our struggles to survive.

Kindness is as rare, it seems,
As radium, in this world of selfish schemes;
And yet, its virtues, if applied with art,
Could heal the wounds of this world's broken heart.

Since God is love and since Christ came to reveal the love of God to lost man, we must receive more and more of Christ's spirit.

"Just as you received Christ Jesus the Lord, so go on living in him—in simple faith. Grow out of him as a plant grows out of the soil it is planted in, becoming more and more sure of the faith as you were taught it, and your lives will overflow with joy and thankfulness.

"Be careful that nobody spoils your faith through intellectualism or high-sounding nonsense. Such stuff is at best founded on men's ideas of the nature of the world, and disregards Christ" (Col. 2:6-8, Phillips).

A.A.E.

BLESS YOUR LEGS

Thou hast enlarged my steps under me; so that my feet did not slip. 2 Samuel 22:37.

The American army under General Andrew Jackson was camped on Mobile Bay when bad news reached the commander. The British general, Sir Edward Pakenham, had recently set sail from Ireland with a large force intending to attack and take New Orleans. The British general was confident of victory.

The only hope for the Americans, Jackson reasoned, was to contact General William Carroll in the Kentucky-Tennessee area and have him lead the long-rifle frontiersmen of those States to join Jackson's troops in meeting Pakenham in New Orleans. How could Jackson get word to Carroll fast enough? He was some six hundred wilderness miles away.

Holdfast Gaines, Jackson's personal Indian scout, was the answer. The General summoned the runner to his headquarters. Gaines was a huge tower of muscle and already a legend among frontiersmen when it came to athletics—particularly running.

"I'll give you ten days to get this message to General Carroll," Jackson commanded, "and may God bless your legs on this important mission."

For a few days the fate of America literally flew on the legs of the fleet Holdfast Gaines. He did not fail Andrew Jackson or his country. He covered the six hundred miles in six days and five nights —ceaseless running for sixteen hours out of every twenty-four. What a feat!

The needed frontiersmen were rallied in Kentucky and Tennessee. They met Jackson near New Orleans, and the Americans won a victory over General Pakenham on January 8, 1815. Surely America owes much to the untiring legs of Holdfast Gaines. Perhaps the Lord, with His hand over America in those dangerous days, made wide steps for Holdfast and kept his feet from slipping.

You and I will probably never be called on to make a historic race for our country, as was Holdfast Gaines. Surely in these days of motor cars, planes, trains, and buses we would not need to run six hundred miles. But your legs and mine are important to God. He has errands for us to run. May the Lord make wide steps for your feet, and keep them from slipping.

R.H.P.

THE BLESSED STRUGGLE

When we were actually with you we gave you this principle to work on: "If a man will not work, he shall not eat." 2 Thessalonians 3:10, Phillips.

How would you like to live under this rule? "Whoever doesn't want to work is not allowed to eat?" What is the reason behind such a principle? It this fair treatment? I learned the answer from the cecropia.

Ever since I was a small girl, I have loved to collect moths and butterflies. Pursuing these elusive winged beauties is real fun. Occasionally at night I would catch glimpses of the beautiful brown cecropia moth with its lovely eyespots and intricate design. How I wanted to catch this large North American species whose wing-spread is five and a half inches. Hatching into a one-fourth-inch black caterpillar, it changes color almost every time it molts. Eating its way to become a three-and-a-half-inch long ornamented bluish-green caterpillar as thick as a man's thumb, it has been orange, yellow, and blue.

So I kept hunting for a large cocoon whose outer wall was thick and paperlike. Have you ever watched the miracle that takes place as the moth emerges from the pupal stage? How hard the creature must work to get out of the cocoon! It struggles and rests, then struggles again and again. I always felt so sorry and wanted to help it until I read what happened when a boy who loved moths acted in sympathy.

He asked his mother to take a fine pair of scissors and cut away the outer wall of the cocoon, then carefully snip the inner wall. Pleased that she was helping the struggling moth, he watched the disheveled-looking creature crawl into freedom. Gradually the wet wings unfurled and the antennae stretched out. But before the wings could stiffen, the moth fell over dead.

In dismay he asked his mother what went wrong. She explained that the moth needs to work hard as it comes from the cocoon. The struggle drives from its body the waste that has accumulated during the long pupal months. If the waste isn't driven out, the moth will die.

People also need to work hard. The struggle makes us stronger and better. If life is too easy for you, you become weak. Something fine and good inside of you dies. Only through struggle can you grow. So, now do you understand the wisdom in this God-given principle?

E.E.L. and J.H.L.

STINGY FRIENDS

The borrower is servant to the lender. Proverbs 22:7.

Vera tapped on Patty's door and went in without waiting.

"May I borrow a stamp?" she asked. "I'm all out, and I have to write to my mother to send me some more. I can't do that without a stamp."

Patty handed her a postage stamp, and Vera pasted it on her letter, then wandered over to the closet.

"Do you have anything good to eat?" she asked, opening the closet door. Patty and Eloise usually kept a large tin box on the shelf with treats their mothers had sent from home. "Hey, where's the box?" she asked. It wasn't in its usual place.

"We moved it," Eloise said flatly. "The food wasn't keeping well there."

"Why, it would stay fresh anywhere in that tin box," Vera said.

"There's more than one way of not keeping," Patty put in. Then she changed the subject. "Did you finish your English yet?"

"I'm working on that theme now," she said. "Could you lend me enough paper to write it out for handing in?"

A few minutes later she went back to her own room, thoughtful. It wasn't like her friends to act so stingy. She had always gone to their room when they had a box from home, and they had shared their cookies and fudge and other goodies with her. Why had they now hidden the food?

Her roommate, Kathy, was just as stingy. This morning Vera had planned to wear Kathy's light-blue sweater, but when she went to get it out, Kathy had said, "I'm going to wear it myself."

Vera could tell that was just an excuse, for Kathy already had on a green skirt and had to change it before she put the blue sweater on.

Kathy was not in the room when Vera went back, so she reached under her bed for the box of food from home.

"They think they're so smart, hiding away their food," she said half aloud. "Well, I've got a box from home too." She ate some cake, and put the box away quickly before anyone might come in and catch her eating. She didn't have enough food left to share any. But what she had really been hungry for was some of Patty's fudge. And it was not until that moment that she realized a possible reason why Patty and Eloise didn't want to share their food any longer —especially with someone who never shared with others and never paid back what she borrowed.

R.E.

MEET IT, HEAD-ON

Fight the good fight of the faith and win for yourself the eternal life to which you were called. 1 Timothy 6:12, Jerusalem.

Next to fog, icebergs are the greatest natural danger to ships at sea. Towering as high as 400 feet above the ocean surface, these huge masses of frozen fresh water may be many miles long and weigh millions of tons. Unfortunately, only from one-eighths to one-tenth of the total mass is above the water. The submerged part is especially dangerous.

Like temptation, it is best to stay away from the area where they are, and that's just what most ships do. However, from April to June many icebergs, particularly smaller ones, drift south into the shipping lanes. Ellen G. White saw in vision a thrilling story of what happened when a ship and an iceberg met head-on.

"A vessel was upon the waters, in a heavy fog. Suddenly the lookout cried, 'Iceberg just ahead!' There, towering high above the ship, was a gigantic iceberg. An authoritative voice cried out, 'Meet it!' There was not a moment's hesitation. It was a time for instant action. The engineer put on full steam, and the man at the wheel steered the ship straight into the iceberg. With a crash she struck the ice. There was a fearful shock, and the iceberg broke into many pieces, falling with a noise like thunder to the deck. The passengers were violently shaken by the force of the collision, but no lives were lost. The vessel was injured, but not beyond repair. She rebounded from the contact, trembling from stem to stern, like a living creature. Then she moved on her way."—*Selected Messages*, book 1, pp. 205, 206.

Sometimes you too will find yourself in a place where you can't avoid temptation. You can't dodge or run away. The only thing you can do is meet it head-on. With God beside you, victory will come.

You know that if you don't overcome your fears and difficulties they will overcome you. Like the iceberg, there is more fear hidden than appears on the surface. It's too big for you to conquer. You shudder and shake like that old ship did. If you meet it head-on with Jesus through faith, you can be sure of victory. Fight the good fight of faith, and you'll have the eternal life to which you are called.

E.E.L. and J.H.L.

THE SECRET OF GOOD HEALTH

Then shall thy light break forth as the morning, and thine health shall spring forth speedily. Isaiah 58:8.

As Dr. Wolfe passed through his waiting room one morning, he spotted his good friend, William Stratford. He laid his hand on the man's shoulder and led him into his office, where he waved him to a chair.

"Something wrong, Bill?" he asked.

"Yes, but I don't know what it is. I don't feel well. I find it hard to sleep. Life seems to have lost its zest."

"Working too hard?" continued the doctor. The businessman laughed.

"Oh, no! I have turned over my business to my son and have retired."

The doctor looked at him keenly.

"Will you follow my prescription carefully?"

"Anything you say, doctor."

"Then go down to Grand Central Station tomorrow and find someone you can help. That shouldn't be too hard among all those people."

Mr. Stratford was surprised, but agreed to go. The next morning at the station he wandered for an hour among the rushing crowds of people. Then he saw a woman sitting alone on a bench, dabbing her eyes with a handkerchief. He went to her and asked if he might be of assistance. She told him she had come from the country to visit her daughter and had lost the address. After she had told Stratford her daughter's name, he looked up the address in a telephone book.

Calling a cab, he took her to the house, where he cheerfully paid the cabby his fare. The daughter was delighted to see her mother, and when she learned of the stranger's kindness she heaped blessings on him.

That night Stratford enjoyed supper and slept more soundly than he had slept for weeks. In the morning he was back at Dr. Wolfe's office.

"Doctor, I feel like a human being again!" he exclaimed.

A few weeks later he became the director of a boys' club. Life took on new meaning as he helped others. He had followed God's recipe for good health.

V.E.R.

DO YOU REALLY WANT TO GO HOME?

For he looked for a city which hath foundations, whose builder and maker is God. Hebrews 11:10.

Why did Abraham leave home to wander in a strange country? Being wealthy, he could have purchased land for a luxurious house. Instead, he looked for a better, more permanent home whose maker was God.

Tommy, a wise old cat, couldn't go with his master on a long trip. Friends, who lived five miles on the other side of the city, asked whether they might care for him. When the time came his master put Tom in a cloth bag, much to the cat's displeasure, as he drove across the city. Knowing the strong instinct animals have to go home, he felt the precaution would ensure that Tom wouldn't attempt to find his way back.

Arriving at his friends' home, he took the bag into the house. Although Tom was happy to get out, he didn't feel at ease. When the door was opened he darted out.

A few days later the neighbors in the home neighborhood noticed Tom trying to get into the locked house. He stayed around for several days and then disappeared. Going back across the city he had traveled in a sack, he returned to the place he had been for only a few hours, content to stay until his master returned. How did he find his way home and back again?

F. H. Sidney tells of a toad that lived in his garden. Fastening a tag on him he took him through the city of Boston to a spot ten miles away. It was almost 11:00 p.m. when he let the little fellow out of the box. The toad blinked his eyes a few times and started toward his home. The next evening at 6:15, when watering his garden, Mr. Sidney found the dusty little toad with the tag still attached to his hind leg. He had hopped ten miles through a strange city and arrived home in less than twenty hours.

God has given you more than an instinct to go home. You have the power of choice and can choose to accept a home so marvelous that words fail to describe it. Are you bending all your energies and desires to that end? Are you eagerly looking forward to that city whose builder and maker is God? The way home is to keep your eyes on Jesus only.

E.E.L. and J.H.L.

BEHOLD, HE COMETH

And he said unto me, Unto two thousand and three hundred days; then shall the sanctuary be cleansed. Daniel 8:14.

William Miller laid down the Bible he had been reading and looked up. He was a farmer living near Lake Champlain in New York State. For months he had been studying his Bible, especially the book of Daniel. As he read this verse again, he pondered over what it might mean.

"The sanctuary," he said to himself, "is the earth. What else in God's great universe needs cleansing? Sin is confined to our world and its inhabitants." He had learned that a day in Bible prophecy often meant a literal year.

He looked at the verse again. This statement evidently meant that there would be a period of two thousand and three hundred years before Jesus would come and cleanse the earth by fire. If only he could discover when that long time period began he would be able to figure out when Jesus would return the second time.

He continued to study the book of Daniel verse by verse. When he reached the last verses of the ninth chapter he found the key that helped him to locate the time when this prophecy began. In the year 457 B.C. the Persian king, Artaxerxes, made a final decree commanding that the city of Jerusalem be rebuilt. Using this point as the beginning of the period he traced down the 2300 years and found it would end between the spring of 1843 and the spring of 1844.

That would be the year, he concluded, when Jesus would come from heaven with all His holy angels, and take His waiting children home.

It was in 1819 that Miller became convinced of this. He checked and rechecked his figures. He investigated religious journals to see if anyone was writing about this subject. "Is it possible," he asked himself, "that Jesus is soon coming and no one knows it?"

"Go and tell the world of its danger," the impression came clear and strong.

"Lord, I can't do it," he always replied. "If You want this truth brought before the world, lay the burden on some talented preacher. I'm only a poor farmer." But God had work for him to do. After several years he clearly saw his duty, and the Lord opened the way for him to preach.

V.E.R.

301

GO AND TELL THE WORLD

Son of man, I have made thee a watchman unto the house of Israel. Ezekiel 3:17.

In Bible times every city was surrounded by a wall to keep enemies out. To make sure foes did not climb over, men were chosen to walk along the tops of these walls all night long. People could then sleep soundly, knowing the watchmen were on duty.

William Miller was called to be God's watchman. The more he thought about the discovery he had made that in 1843-1844 the sanctuary would be cleansed, the more uneasy he felt. As the years passed the impression grew stronger that it was his duty to tell the world that Jesus was soon coming. For twelve years he did not respond, claiming that he was only a farmer. He asked the Lord to call some powerful minister to give this message. Of course he did talk to his friends and neighbors when they visited him.

One morning in 1831 he awoke feeling under conviction more than ever. The words kept ringing in his ears: "Go and tell the world!" To quiet his conscience he fell on his knees and promised to go if someone invited him to preach. Immediately his burden left him. Surely, he thought, no one would come to his farm with such an invitation.

He was wrong. Before he had finished breakfast his nephew was at the door with the startling news that their local church pastor was away and the people wanted Miller to talk to them about the second coming of the Lord. Miller was dismayed and tried to go back on his promise, but found he could not.

Thus he began preaching, and during thirteen years he traveled all over New England and into other States preaching and telling the people that Jesus was coming soon. Many prominent preachers joined him in giving the message found in Revelation fourteen: "Fear God, and give glory to him; for the hour of his judgment is come."

It was a message that brought great joy to thousands of people. Can't you hear them counting to themselves: "Only four more years." "Only three years longer." "Only two years." "Only one more year to live in this wicked world"? Then came April, 1843, and they began to say: "Sometime during the next twelve months Jesus will come." Later a restudy of the prophecy of Daniel 8:14 convinced them that Jesus was coming on October 22, 1844.

V.E.R.

JOYFUL IN THE MORNING

Weeping may endure for a night, but joy cometh in the morning. Psalm 30:5.

Nearly everyone has suffered a bitter disappointment. Perhaps the prize for which you worked so hard was given to someone else whose work was really no better than your own. You may have set your heart on an interesting trip and then at the last minute your plan didn't work out. Perhaps you were so disappointed you went to bed and cried yourself to sleep. David must have had such an experience, judging by this verse. Of course it wasn't all sadness for him. He discovered that fresh joy comes at the beginning of each new day.

The disciples of Jesus also experienced this. On Sunday afternoon they walked beside Him as He rode on a donkey into Jerusalem while thousands shouted the glorious words, "Hosanna to the son of David: Blessed is he that cometh in the name of the Lord"—and they expected to see Him take the throne and rule as king.

On Friday afternoon, only five days later, they watched Him die on Calvary. That night and all through the Sabbath they wept. But the coming of the morning brought them joy as they received the wondrous news that Jesus had risen from the dead.

On October 22, 1844, thousands of fathers and mothers, boys and girls, watched the sky all day for the second coming of Jesus. When the day passed they were bitterly disappointed. There was weeping in many homes. Children went to their parents with the question, "Father, why didn't He come?" "Mother, is it true that He isn't coming?" The parents had no answer, for they had been disappointed too. All through the night they wept together.

One of those who wept was Hiram Edson, a farmer living in western New York. The next morning, with a friend, he went out to the barn to pray. Earnestly they asked the Lord to help them understand the reason for their disappointment. God heard and answered their prayer. While walking through the cornfield a few minutes later, Edson was suddenly impressed with the thought that instead of coming to this earth Jesus had entered the Most Holy Place in the heavenly sanctuary to begin a special work for His children. This explained the reason for their disappointment and brought them great joy when they realized that Jesus had not forsaken them.

V.E.R.

A BITTER DISAPPOINTMENT

Take it, and eat it up, and it shall make thy belly bitter, but it shall be in thy mouth sweet as honey. Revelation 10:9.

In Revelation 10 John saw an angel holding a little book in his hand, which he gave to the prophet to eat. This was the book of Daniel that was to be studied. William Miller fulfilled this prophecy, for in the book of Daniel he had found the message that Jesus was coming soon. To him and to the thousands who believed as he did, that was a message as "sweet as honey."

All through the spring and summer of 1844 the Adventists looked for Jesus to return. At first they did not know just when in the year to expect His return. In August some ministers came to the conclusion that it would be on the Jewish Day of Atonement, which in 1844 came on October 22.

The message took on new power as preachers went everywhere proclaiming the message: "Behold, the bridegroom cometh; go ye out to meet him. Get ready, get ready!" They fully expected that the world would end in a few weeks. Merchants opened their stores and invited customers to take whatever they wanted. Farmers refused to harvest their potatoes, thinking they would have no need for them. Sarah Farnsworth heard her husband singing as he went about his work: "I shall see my Lord a'coming in a few more days."

Adventist children went to school as usual that fall, but it was hard to concentrate on lessons. One by one the days passed until they could say, "Tomorrow He will come."

Some sat up waiting all that night. The children watched the sky the next morning. They were not interested in food. Why should they be when they expected to sit down in the kingdom of God and partake of the marriage supper of the Lamb in a few hours?

The sun went down and it was night. They were bitterly disappointed. Children cried and refused to be comforted.

"How can we go to school again?" they asked. "The teacher will laugh at us."

The sweet hope that Jesus was soon coming was replaced by bitter sadness. Had God forsaken them? No! He had another message for them to take to the world.

V.E.R.

COMFORT FROM HEAVEN

And he said unto me, Thou must prophesy again before many peoples, and nations, and tongues, and kings. Revelation 10:11.

The little book that John had eaten was sweet at first, but afterwards it tasted bitter. The Adventist people in 1844 had studied the book of Daniel and believed its sweet message that Jesus was coming soon. Then came the bitter disappointment of October 22 as they watched the skies all day in vain.

The Lord did not forsake His people in their hour of disappointment. Out in western New York the Holy Spirit impressed Hiram Edson, a farmer like Miller, that instead of coming to this earth to cleanse it by fire, Jesus had gone into the Most Holy Place in the sanctuary in heaven to begin the work of judgment.

Still more comfort came through the experience of a seventeen-year-old girl by the name of Ellen Harmon. Within a few weeks after the Disappointment God gave Ellen a vision of the coming of Jesus and showed her the wonders and glories of the heavenly home He was preparing for His children. God instructed Ellen to tell others what she had seen, and this she began to do.

How happy it made the Advent people to know God had not forgotten them, but had sent a special message to them! Today's verse indicates that there was yet another great prophetic movement that was to go to all the world. A few of the Adventist people began to keep the seventh day of the week as the Sabbath about this time.

If you would like to know just what Ellen saw in that first vision, turn to her book called *Early Writings* and read pages thirteen to twenty.

A father once carried his blind son on his shoulders downtown where he stood on a city street up which a circus parade was to pass. Peter couldn't see the animals, but he knew they were there. All about him the people were talking about the lions and tigers passing along in their cages.

"Tell me about it, Daddy, tell me about it. Let me see it through your eyes," he begged.

Today we cannot see the glories of heaven. But by reading Ellen's story we can catch a glimpse of the wonderful things she saw. As you do this, you will say to yourself, "I am going to be there."

V.E.R.

BETTER THAN EVER

Old things are passed away; behold, all things are become new. 2 Corinthians 5:17.

After the great Disappointment of the Advent believers in 1844 when Jesus did not come, there was great confusion. All kinds of false doctrines were brought in and it seemed as if the body of believers was being broken to pieces. William Miller felt very bad. To comfort him and bring him to an understanding of God's plans, the Lord gave him a remarkable dream.

It seemed that an angel placed in his hand a lovely box with a key in the lock. When he opened the box he was delighted to find it filled with all kinds of lovely jewels—diamonds, sapphires, rubies, pearls, and emeralds. Feeling that it was not right for him to enjoy this glittering sight alone, he placed the box on a table and went out to invite his friends to come and see it also.

At first only a few came, then more and more. Soon the room was filled. As they pushed and shoved, he was horrified to find that they were stealing the jewels and dropping in stones instead. Some tossed sand and gravel into the box, others handfuls of shavings.

Fearing he would be held responsible he tried to push the people out of the room, but while he was pushing two out four more entered. They grabbed the jewels, then scattered them all over the room. Finally they tore up the box and left Miller weeping amid the ruins.

Then he saw an angel enter. With a broom he began to sweep out the rubbish. Miller protested that some of the jewels might be lost, but the angel told him not to worry. Finally all the dirt was gone. The angel brought another box, much larger than the first, and into this he tossed all the jewels from the first box and many more. He then invited Miller to look. To his astonishment and joy, it was ten times more dazzling than it had been before. He gave a shout of joy and awoke wondering what his dream meant.

It is clear today. While his enemies brought in many false doctrines the Lord took care of the great truths Miller preached. Out of the confusion of those days arose the church to which you and I belong today. With ten times the power and glory of the Advent Movement in 1844, it has encircled the world.

V.E.R.

CANVAS TABERNACLES

How goodly are thy tents, O Jacob, and thy tabernacles, O Israel! Numbers 24:5.

Adventist history is full of interesting stories of pioneer preachers who traveled in many parts of the world, unfurled their canvas tabernacles, held evangelistic meetings and won many converts.

In 1880 a Mrs. Horton described the Battle Creek camp meeting. "It was a new experience for me, being the first camp meeting I had ever attended. The streets laid out in perfect order, the book tent, reception tent, a large tent for the children, and the general neat appearance of the grounds were greatly admired by me. Especially the large pavillion impressed me with reverence." Elder and Mrs. White were there. "Elder White took a leading part in the meetings and also won his way to our hearts," she wrote.

During this meeting Elder Horton decided to become a tent evangelist. Two friends helped him pitch the large tent near a small town. It was dark before they had the small living tent up and they forgot to fasten all the stakes. The men went home, leaving Elder Horton alone. "He had no time to purchase straw for his bed before dark," his wife wrote, "and being very weary from his hard day's work, he spread his bedding on the floor of his tent, thinking to get a little rest. . . . Near midnight . . . he was suddenly aroused by a terrific wind that snapped the ridgepole, allowing the rain to pour in on him in torrents. By the flashes of lightening he saw the large tent wrecked, lying flat on the ground."

He found shelter in a nearby barn and remained there, cold and dripping wet, the remainder of that long night. The next day friends helped him pitch both tents. This time they stayed up even though strong winds blew the next night also.

When the tents were taken down in September a faithful group of Adventists were meeting every Sabbath in a schoolhouse near that Michigan town.

"Go ye into all the world and preach," said Jesus. This command must still be obeyed. Though methods differ, all must help win souls for the kingdom.

All—that includes you and me.

V.E.R.

ANIMAL WISDOM

Faith is like that: if good works go not with it, it is quite dead.
James 2:17, Jerusalem.

Obviously the mouse liked cheese. For five nights the baited trap was sprung, the cheese gone, but no mouse was caught. Curious, Mr. Nelson decided to watch. Soon he saw a mouse approaching. Boldly, as if he had great faith in his accuracy, the mouse stood on the spring of the trap. Standing there, he carefully nudged the trigger with his nose. Snap! The mouse was thrown free into the air as the trap sprung. Immediately the smart little fellow, who combined faith in his ability with carefully planned works, ate his well-earned treat.

The Bible tells us it is impossible to separate faith from works. Yet foolish people say salvation consists only of faith—works are not needed. The devils believe, but they don't do anything about it, and remain devils. If even a mouse combines faith and works, certainly we need faith to make us act like God. But our faith must be in God, not ourselves. True faith leads us to obey God's laws.

A rabbit combined faith in nature's laws with works to save his life. Living in a desert area, he knew that the cactus plants had many long, sharp stickers on them. One day a coyote spotted the rabbit and determined to have him for dinner. The chase began. Fast as the rabbit was, the coyote was closing in. With a rush of speed the rabbit made for a certain tall cactus. Under it the ground was covered with many cactus stickers that had been placed in a wide ring around the cactus plant. He humped inside that ring, pressing his body against the portion of the cactus from which the stickers had been removed.

Round and round that ring of thorns ran the frustrated coyote. Every time he started to rush in, he felt the pain of those sharp cactus stickers on his tender paws. Each time he backed off. The rabbit, who evidently had worked hard to pull those stickers previously, sat safely watching the angry coyote.

Here was a perfect example of faith combined with works. If that rabbit had not combined both of them, he would have been dead. So will you be, if you don't unite genuine faith in God with the power He gives you to obey His laws and tell others what He has done for you.

E.E.L. and J.H.L.

THE FATHER'S COMPASSION

But while he was yet at a distance, his father saw him and had compassion, and ran and embraced him and kissed him. Luke 15:20, RSV.

The person who has not found himself tends to go whichever way circumstances turn him. He may jump from one job to another. He may choose friends at one time who have high standards; at another time, those who are worldly. In religion he may be carried away with many different doctrines.

This usually results in personal failure. James tells us that the man who is unstable is "double-minded."

The way to avoid unstable and insecure living is to bring the mind and heart together into one purpose: to do everything to glorify the Saviour.

The Bible characters who had the most happiness and through whom God achieved the most were persons who attained singleness of heart and mind. Abraham, Ruth, David, Paul, to name only a few, determined to have only one goal. The believers in the early church had one heart.

How is it possible to obtain singleness of heart and mind?

First of all, pray for it. Then trust in the Lord and believe that He gives it to you.

Grow in Christ by hearing and doing His Word. This brings a positive change in the character and makes one like the man whose rock-founded house could not be shaken.

Meditate on His instruction. Think about things that are true, honest, just, pure, lovely, of good report, virtuous, praiseworthy. This transforms the mind.

The prodigal son found himself when he arose and went to his father. Just so, we find stability, purpose, happiness—and ourselves—when we rise and go to our Father.

We will experience a new freedom as we stop trying to serve God and this world at the same time. Through Him we know what is best in this life and we leave the other alone.

With our interest in the things God offers, heaven is at the height of our upward look and we press on to that worthwhile goal.

Let us arise and go to our Father now.

R.E.

WHAT'S ON YOUR SHELF?

Whereby are given unto us exceeding great and precious promises. 2 Peter 1:4.

The shabby old man studied the object in his hand. He started toward the door of the Chicago jeweler's shop, then stopped. Fingering the rough-looking stone, he muttered to himself, "Won't hurt to ask. It's been lying around home so long. Might as well find out if it's worth anything."

Gathering up his courage, he stepped forward, hesitated, and finally opened the door. The expert jewel cutter smiled, "May I help you?"

"Yes, my father found this red pebble when he was a boy. When I came to the United States, my mother put it in my suitcase. Been lying around the house ever since. The kids played with it. The baby cut its teeth on it. A rat dragged it into a hole, but I found it. Things been mighty rough with us, real hard times. Been tempted to see if it had any value, but kinda hated to part with it. Been in the family so long. Think it might be worth cuttin' and polishin'?"

The expert craftsman studied the stone. It proved to be a flawless, perfect ruby, weighing nearly twenty-four carats, perfect in color and texture, beautiful, clear, full of red fire.

"Your pebble is a pigeon's blood ruby worth up to $250,000."

For years this old man and his family had struggled with poverty, had gone without, had suffered, when they had on their shelf that which could have changed everything, but they didn't realize its value.

You too have something very valuable in your home. God's promises are a wonderful simplifier of all the problems you'll ever face in life.

Open your Bible and read these promises right now. If you have difficulty getting along with others, follow the promise in Proverbs 16:7. You can overcome a bad habit with Hebrews 2:14, 15. Psalm 73:24 will give you guidance in making an important decision. God will do for your mouth and speech what you can't through Exodus 4:12. If you have fears of the dark, animals, or people, combine 1 John 4:18 with Psalm 34:4.

Don't be foolish like the old man and let the 3,573 great and precious promises lie unused when you need them so much.

E.E.L. and J.H.L.

UNCONDITIONAL GUARANTEE

Therefore being justified by faith, we have peace with God through our Lord Jesus Christ. Romans 5:1.

We see guarantees on nearly everything. Some blue jeans are guaranteed not to go through the knees before the rest of the pants give out. Men's socks may be guaranteed for a full year of wear. Some cars have a warranty for two years or 24,000 miles. Tires and batteries are guaranteed to last a certain number of months.

Some of the guarantees are worth something and some are not. Mr. Curtis bought a new car, and before he had driven it many miles he noticed a leak in the gas line somewhere. He took his car back and the dealer had it fixed at no expense to Mr. Curtis because the car was on warranty.

Mr. Deane bought a used car. It had a warranty too. "In writing," the dealer selling the car said. Across the front of the contract he wrote, "Standard GW warranty, twenty-four months." He gave Mr. Deane a warranty card to carry with him. But when the car developed trouble and he took it back to the dealer, he learned that the dealer's standard warranty meant a 15 percent discount on the labor required to do repairs. It wasn't much saving, either, for labor prices at that garage were 15 per cent higher than at others nearby.

Mrs. Brown buys records from a record club that guarantees satisfaction. Try their records for ten days, and if you are not satisfied, return them and owe nothing. She knows it works, for she has returned records that she didn't want to keep.

But the guarantee that I want to offer you today includes no repairs and no refund of money. For the thing I suggest you try does not cost money to begin with. I want to propose the idea that if you try Christ in your life for six months—give Him your heart and your will—your life will be changed. And I am so certain that this is true that I say the idea carries an unconditional guarantee.

Your life will be more peaceful, more happy, than it has ever been before. You will never be at a loss to know what to do next or how to handle a problem, for you may put all your problems into His lap. It's a guaranteed idea—a guarantee paid for you through Jesus' shed blood. Try it.

R.E.

REWARDED

The Son of man shall come in the glory of his Father with his angels; and then he shall reward every man according to his works. Matthew 16:27.

Fred and Grace spoke to the farmer early about picking raspberries. If they could start right at the beginning they would earn enough for new clothes and also help with their academy fees.

Picking raspberries can be hot, tiring work. After a while they don't even taste good anymore. But Fred and Grace tried hard to keep at the job. Down the long rows, pulling the bushes toward them and easing the berries off their white core they went.

"I'm tired," said Fred, sitting down. "I've been working all morning and have filled only two trays."

"But that's not too bad, Fred. Keep that up and you will have five trays by tonight," Grace encouraged her younger brother.

Fred stood up and went back to the job. Some of the other young people, tired of picking, began to throw raspberries at one another. Suddenly a whole tray of raspberries fell in a red scatter on the brown soil. Fred and Grace were wise enough not to join in the fight.

"You know, Fred, the next time we go through this row these raspberries will be so thick you can fill four or five trays easily in a morning." Grace was always optimistic.

The fight in the next row was just coming to a hilarious conclusion when the farmer strode angrily down the row. "You! You! and you! I will not have people spoiling my crop. Who spilled this tray of raspberries?" he demanded.

It was little use for the guilty ones to deny what they had been doing; raspberry stains soaked their dresses and shirts. "You're fired," he said. "Take what you have picked to the weighout stand and collect your money."

Fred and Grace kept working. As the farmer passed them, he said, "Glad you two are still at it. If you like you may take some raspberries home to your mother after you have weighed them in."

Rewards and punishments are often given out in this life. No one will be able to escape them when Jesus comes.

W.R.L.S.

A BEAR'S GRATITUDE

Your own soul is nourished when you are kind; it is destroyed when you are cruel. Proverbs 11:17, TLB.

The trees grew right up to the old dirt road. This was real wilderness in northern British Columbia, Canada. Two lumbermen were jolting along the rough road in their jeep when they heard screams coming from nearby.

"Couldn't be more than a few hundred yards away. Let's go down that dim, overgrown trail and investigate."

"But we don't have a gun, Fred. It might not be too safe."

"Listen, I couldn't sleep tonight wondering what's making those unearthly yells. Something is in trouble and I mean to find out."

Together they plunged down the trail. Near a huge spruce tree sat a half-grown bear, bawling, with a paw in the jaws of a steel trap.

"He must have been there a long time. Look, he's gnawed off all the underbrush, and even scratched the ground clean trying to find roots to eat. Poor thing is starving. Why can't those scoundrels who set traps at least come around often and check them?"

"Too bad we don't have a gun to put him out of his misery."

"I think we can help him without a gun. His screams and yells are not rage. That poor bear sounds to me like he's crying, pleading for help, and I aim to help him."

Fred got close to the bear. It took all his strength to depress the strong steel springs. The bear stopped crying. He remained motionless except that he leaned his furry body against the man. Finally the paw was free and Fred stepped back.

The two men watched, wondering whether the bear would turn on them in anger because of his pain. First, he lifted his paw, wiggled it back and forth, and looked it over carefully. Then he turned and looked at the two men. Never had they seen such a look in an animal's eyes. It just couldn't be interpreted in human language, for how can a bear express love, gratitude, joy at being free, and eagerness to quench his thirst and satisfy his hunger. Finally, after a long time the bear turned and hobbled off to the woods. As the men watched him go to his freedom their hearts were too full to speak.

Truly, it is your own soul that is nourished when you are kind.

E.E.L. and J.H.L.

SOLID COMFORT

Let us therefore come boldly unto the throne of grace, that we may obtain mercy, and find grace to help in time of need. Hebrews 4:16.

When Susie was small she fell on a rock and cut her forehead. Her mother took her immediately to the doctor, who said that a few stitches would be needed. He told Susie that he was going to have to stick her with a needle, and asked if she could sit very still without jumping.

"I can if Mother will hold my hand," Susie said confidently. Mother lifted Susie to her lap, and with arms around Susie's waist, held the two little hands. Susie's head was steady against Mother's shoulder. The doctor took the necessary stitches and Susie sat very still.

What good did it do to hold Mother's hand? Not one less stitch was taken. It didn't make the cut smaller at all. But Mother's arms provided the comfort Susie needed to accept what had to be done.

God's throne of grace is like that. Because Jesus died on the cross, we may take God's hand and know His mercy. The Christian's most solid comfort in time of need is God's grace. It's as though we say, "Yes, I can endure this if God will hold my hand."

We are told that one of Satan's most successful devices to ruin souls is to make people think prayer is unnecessary. He will try to prevent them from coming boldly to God.

We are also told that if we offer silent prayers throughout the day, those prayers will rise like incense before the throne and Satan's attempts to lead us astray will be thwarted.

"The Christian whose heart is thus stayed upon God cannot be overcome. No evil arts can destroy his peace. All the promises of God's Word, all the power of divine grace, all the resources of Jehovah, are pledged to secure his deliverance. . . .

"Prayer is the breath of the soul. It is the secret of spiritual power. No other means of grace can be substituted and the health of the soul be preserved."—*Messages to Young People*, p. 249.

Every day, every hour, is a time of need. For if we drop our guard even momentarily, that is when Satan will move in to see if he can overcome. But we can determine to accept the solid comfort of God's help through communion with Him.

R.E.

IS GOD DEAF?

Evening, and morning, and at noon, will I pray, and cry aloud: and he shall hear my voice. Psalm 55:17.

Some people say that God cannot hear them when they pray! Well, let me tell you that He *can* hear when we pray. And why not? About the only thing that makes Him turn a deaf ear is a favorite sin we refuse to give up. Then the only prayer He will listen to is one asking for forgiveness.

Do you know that biologists have listened to an earthworm calling its mate? The sound has been amplified so many times that it is easy to hear. Scientists can make a deafening noise out of the sound of petals opening, and a certain Professor Adrian, experimenting with his own muscles, found that he could magnify the sounds they made when they moved. He even made a record of them!

The other morning I turned on the radio in my home in India and heard the news broadcast from Montreal, Quebec, where I used to live in Canada, half a world away!

Airplanes use radio all the time to keep in touch with the airports, and even though the pilots cannot see a thing because of storms or fog, the men in the towers can direct the planes to safety.

Some ships at sea do not have doctors aboard. If someone falls seriously ill the captain uses the radio to get medical help.

I even read once of a man who sent a tape recording of the sound of his ailing washing machine to the manufacturer. They identified the trouble right away and told the owner how to fix it.

So why can't God hear you when you pray? If man can figure out how to hear things from so far away or such tiny sounds as a petal growing or muscles moving, don't you suppose God, who made all these things and the laws that make them work in the first place, would know even more ways to hear over great distances?

"Evening, and morning, and at noon, will I pray, and cry aloud: and he *shall* hear my voice."

M.H.

TEMPTATION

For the good that I would I do not: but the evil which I would not, that I do. Romans 7:19.

Many years ago, a well-attired man stopped in front of a little, poorly dressed urchin, put one hand in his pocket, and jingled some coins.

"I'll toss to see whether I pay for my paper or you give it to me for nothing," the man suggested to the newsboy. The child said nothing.

"I'll toss to see whether I pay double or you give it to me for nothing," pursued the customer. The boy seemed perturbed, but did not answer. Passersby stopped to listen.

"I'll toss you," the man persisted, "to see whether I pay you a dollar for the paper or you give it to me for nothing."

The boy's thin face clouded. Bystanders could see his troubled face as he thought of going to Mother without that important nickel or with all that extra money.

"I can't afford to lose, sir," he admitted as he turned away.

Do you have the pure willpower to resist a dare? Do you have the courage to turn away from a tempting situation?

The origin of the word *temptation* indicates a "test." And in a test no one likes to get an F for failure.

That little newsboy, back in the days when a dollar was a lot of money, had more strength than many of us have today. He was enticed, but he did not yield.

Even Paul, the great apostle, battled with temptation. J. B. Phillips translates today's text like this: "I often find that I have the will to do good, but not the power. That is, I don't accomplish the good I set out to do, and the evil I don't really want to do I find I am always doing."

The little newsboy surely went home with mixed emotions. It would have been wonderful to have been able to hand his widowed mother that extra dollar. However, he had not lost sight of the fact that he might have lost in the gamble. If he had lost, he would have been a nickel short. As it was, he went home weary, cold, and hungry, but with clear eyes and nothing to hide.

R.E.

BEAUTIFUL FEET

How beautiful on the mountains, are the feet of one who brings good news, who heralds peace, brings happiness, proclaims salvation, and tells Zion, "Your God is King." Isaiah 52:7, Jerusalem.

Do you know why Isaiah called human feet beautiful? Look at your feet and decide whether this is correct.

What would your life be like if you didn't have such a specially designed foot? It contains twenty-six bones. You can move it in all directions because God planned thirty-six different joints. Tough tendons tie the bones to a mass of about fifty muscles that act with split-second coordination.

The bones of your foot form three arches, two running lengthwise and one across the instep. These arches provide the natural elastic spring of your foot when you walk, run, or jump. God made your foot elastic so that although it constantly pounds on the ground, it absorbs each blow and prevents severe jolts to your spine or brain.

Most adults walk about eight miles a day. If you weigh 125 pounds, your feet absorb a total impact of 2,375,000 pounds, or more than 594 tons a day on each foot. Children weigh less than that, but take at least twice as many steps. Figure out how much punishment your feet have taken by multiplying 1,188 tons by 365 days by your age in years.

Could anyone but a wonderful God design such a marvelous transportation device? No other creature has a foot like yours. It takes both the front and back legs of four-footed creatures to accomplish the art of balancing that you do on one foot. While you are walking your hands are free, and your mind doesn't have to concentrate on taking steps.

Try walking very slowly. Imagine a line extending upward. Every time your body center passes that line you lose your balance and immediately throw out a foot to catch yourself. Almost all of your body moves as you take each step. Yet you learned all this as a baby.

Evolutionists suggest that human feet gradually changed, enabling people to walk on two instead of four feet. But no fossil remains show any such chain of events. No, God designed that your footprints would be like those of your Maker. The important question is Are your feet made beautiful by bringing to others the happy news of peace and salvation?

E.E.L. and J.H.L.

UNIQUE SALVATION

Whosoever shall confess that Jesus is the Son of God, God dwelleth in him, and he in God. 1 John 4:15.

Lake Michigan lies calm and placid most of the summer months. Great crowds flock there, enjoying the cooling breezes that sweep in across the beaches, and the swimming and boating.

Some years ago a group of people were on a small ferryboat touring along the edge of the water. Suddenly out of nowhere, and before they could make for shelter, a storm raced across the lake and engulfed them. Within minutes the pleasure party was in panic. Water pouring out of the sky and washing in with the high waves threatened to swamp the boat. Desperately they bailed, but it was useless. At the height of the storm the little boat foundered, and soon a score or more people were struggling for their lives.

On the shore a young man watched their plight. Seeing the peril of the passengers, he dived into the angry waves and swam toward the drowning people. He caught hold of one and dragged him in to shore until he could stand. A second he rescued from a broken mast, a third from a piece of drifting timber.

Time and again he went out into the angry water, until other small craft arrived and began pulling the survivors out of the water. In all, that young man rescued nineteen people from almost certain death. When it was over, he was exhausted. Hospitalized from exposure, he suffered a long bout with pneumonia before recovering.

On the anniversary of the tragedy and the gallant rescue, newspaper reporters came to the home of the youth. Among the questions they asked was this: "What is the thing you remember most about that day?" Can you ever forget his answer? "Not one of those nineteen people ever bothered to say Thank you!"

Are you thankful for the salvation God offers in Jesus Christ? Out of ten lepers whom He healed only one said Thank You. If you have made Christ your Saviour, you have found the unique salvation, the only way to eternal life. Accept this salvation and thank God for your rescue from sin.

W.R.L.S.

RESTORING A SEVERED HAND

O Lord my God, I cried unto thee, and thou has healed me.
Psalm 30:2.

At the annual meeting of the American Academy of Orthopedic Surgeons in San Francisco one year, Dr. William H. Harris, of Boston, told of a 27-year-old carpenter, Russell Stratton. Russell was using a radial saw one day when a piece of wood slipped through the saw at such speed that his hand too went through and was amputated at the left wrist.

With rare presence of mind Russell shut off his machine and picked up his hand from the scrap box. This severed hand he placed in the pocket of his carpenter's apron and walked to the construction job headquarters. The foreman promptly fainted. After Russell had revived his superior, he got the man to make a tourniquet from a necktie. When it broke, the foreman fainted again. After the carpenter revived him a second time, he suggested they use a belt for a tourniquet and drive him to the nearest medical help, which was a maternity hospital.

At the maternity hospital the staff was amazed to see him wave his bloody stump and show them his hand, but they gave him a sterile towel, called a police escort, and notified the Massachusetts General Hospital of the emergency. At once the general surgeon telephoned for Dr. Harris and his replantation team, asking, "Do you recall the method you devised for replacing a hand at the wrist?"

"Yes, I remember, and I'll bring along my drawings and come at once."

It took five hours for Dr. Harris and his surgical team to clean the tissues of the severed wrist and connect the bones of the hand to the wrist with heavy wires. They also stitched the severed veins together and attached the parted arteries. Three months later in another surgical procedure they joined the severed nerves and tendons. Russell Stratton still works as a skilled carpenter, hammering nails and carrying weights. He can write. In addition he has become a part-time minister.

When we hear about the wonders of surgery, should we be amazed at the character transformations the Lord can accomplish by the power of His Spirit?

L.C.W.

THE PEARL OF GREAT PRICE

The kingdom of heaven is like a merchant in search of fine pearls, who, on finding one pearl of great value, went and sold all that he had and bought it. Matthew 13:45, 46, RSV.

Before World War II the United States government sponsored an expedition to collect marine specimens off the Philippine Islands. Local people were hired as divers. A watch was kept so that none were down more than three minutes before another diver investigated to see what was wrong. One day an alarm sounded because a diver was down too long. When the diver who reached the trapped man surfaced, his fright was so great he couldn't talk. Two more divers went down and immediately returned with the news that the first diver had thrust his arm into a giant Tridacna clam that had closed on it. A cable was fastened around the shell, and a winch brought it and the diver to the surface, but the man was already dead.

Because so many divers are murdered for the sake of pearls, the dead man and the shell had to be brought to the local magistrate. The official ordered that the shell be cleaned in his presence. They found a huge, oblong, irregular pearl not weighing the usual fraction of an ounce, but 14 pounds and 1 ounce. The Muslim magistrate, claiming it looked like the head of the prophet Muhammad, declared it a sacred object that must remain with him.

About two years later the young man in charge of the scientific operations returned to the same place as a United States soldier. He learned that the magistrate's only son was ill with malaria, and given up by local medicine men to die. He offered to care for the boy if he could do so personally. The magistrate in desperation agreed. After several days, when the crisis had passed, the soldier told the chief his son would live. Immediately the magistrate went to his house and returned with the huge pearl that had been found at the time of the expedition. He gave it to the soldier for saving his son's life. Now that pearl is in a museum in America.

Like the merchant who sold all for the Pearl of Great Price, Jesus, pearl divers often give their lives for the jewels. How much better for you to give your life in service for Jesus now.

E.E.L. and J.H.L.

FOR HER CHILDREN

God commendeth his love toward us, in that, while we were yet sinners, Christ died for us. Romans 5:8.

When the hot northerly wind quickened to a mild gale, the farmer thought anxiously of the forest fire he knew was burning over the mountain. As long as the wind was from the south it could do him no damage, but the northerly wind would bring the fire his way.

Then looking up the valley, he saw the smoke thickening. Pieces of ash drifted down on his shoulders. Suddenly there was no time to lose. Cattle bunching in the shelter of the line of forest now found themselves driven into the center of a large field where they might survive.

The younger children and their mother jumped into the car and raced for a safe place. Father and the two older sons tried to hold the fire at the break they had plowed some weeks before, but it was hopeless. Within minutes they raced down the road in the truck to join their fleeing loved ones. Looking back, they saw smoke already rising from their home.

Within hours they returned, weeping at the sight of the smoking ruins of their farm. Could they ever start again? Would it be worthwhile to build once more?

Walking toward the chicken house, they came across the body of a hen. With his foot the farmer moved the body away. A rush of cheeping, golden feathers poured out from under the charred body of their mother, and out darted ten fluffy chicks!

"I guess we shall have to stay and raise these chickens, Mother!"

And so they began the long struggle back to a normal life and their former prosperity.

Life among the ruins. That's what God saw possible through the death of Jesus Christ. Satan might claim to have won the first round by leading man to sin. Disease and death might char His glorious creation, but God found the way out.

He did this that you might have the chance of new life. He clothed you with His righteousness; He makes you perfect in His sight.

W.R.L.S.

GOD WILL TAKE CARE OF YOU

On the day I called, thou didst answer me, my strength of soul thou didst increase. Psalm 138:3, RSV.

Little Virginia was visiting her grandmother. Suddenly the sky darkened, the whole world blazed with light, and the house reverberated with thunder. Torrents of rain pounded down on the earth and beat like fists against the windows. The roar was deafening.

Climbing into Grandma's lap, Virginia threw her arms around her. "Oh, Grandma, sing 'God Will Take Care of You!'"

Years ago Pastor W. S. Martin and his family visited friends in New York City. He had accepted an invitation to preach, but his wife became ill and he thought she grew worse. He decided not to leave her.

He went to the telephone, but his nine-year-old son interrupted. "Father, don't you think if God wants you to preach, He will take care of mother?"

Pastor Martin filled his preaching appointment, and God used him to stir the hearts of the people. Several accepted Jesus as their Saviour.

His heart warm with thanksgiving, he hurried home and was met by his son, holding out to him some lines scribbled on the back of an old envelope. They were the words of that comforting hymn, "God Will Take Care of You." Mrs. Martin, deeply touched by the faith of her young son, had written those words while her husband was gone.

The pastor too was inspired, and he went to the organ and composed the music.

Remember how terrified the disciples were in the storm on Galilee? And they had Jesus, His physical presence, right with them. He rebuked the wind, and the sea became calm. He saved his friends from the storm. And He is able to save now, too. "Wherefore he is able also to save them to the uttermost that come unto God by him, seeing he ever liveth to make intercession for them" (Heb. 7:25).

And if you find it hard to *feel* the presence of God, practice telling your troubles to Jesus. You can't stump Him. Jesus is God. The Holy Spirit is God. If your prayers are stammering and groping, He will send them on by the heavenly wireless, all beautiful and fragrant with your love. Whatever your problem or fear, God will take care of you.

R.E.

OBEDIENCE PAID

I will hear what God the Lord will speak. Psalm 85:8.

Harold Williams enjoyed his work at the St. Helena Sanitarium. He especially enjoyed driving the carriage that took patients to and from the railway station. Sometimes if there was a full load of guests he drove a stagecoach with six horses. Of them all, a gray stallion was his favorite, and a little brown mare he liked second best, even though she was slow.

One day Mr. Williams was asked to drive two women quickly to the station. He harnessed the mare, helped the women into the back seat of the buggy, jumped in, and started down the steep hill. He would have to drive carefully past the place where a road gang was working, trying to make the grade more gentle.

Drivers descending that long hill had to apply their brakes to keep the carriage from rolling faster than the horses could run. Harold was doing his best to hold the carriage back when he noticed that the bay mare was also holding back. Just when he was trying to decide what to do about his horse, a voice spoke to him. "Don't go!" The command was as clear as though someone had shouted it: "DON'T GO!"

At that instant another hospital worker was climbing the hill. Without stopping, but just slowing the horse to a walk, Harold jumped out of the buggy and asked, "Carl, will you drive these ladies to St. Helena?" Carl was happy to oblige. He climbed in and started off.

Just then there was a loud noise and a crashing sound. A huge rock had become loosened on the mountainside. It rolled, bounded, and landed on top of the brown mare, killing her instantly.

If Harold had not slowed for that brief minute to change drivers, the rock would have crushed the buggy and its occupants.

What voice was it that spoke to him? You might say that it was his guardian angel. Or you might call it the voice of the Holy Spirit. Because he obeyed that voice instantly, three lives were saved.

Although this happened in 1911, Harold Williams can never forget it. He says, "That experience has helped me many times not to hesitate when God, by the Holy Spirit, has spoken to me. The still small voice often speaks to us saying, 'Don't do that!' or 'You'd better do this.' Obey at once, and you will always be thankful."

V.E.R.

FORGIVE

Even as Christ forgave you, so also do ye. Colossians 3:13.

George had been swimming at the park. When the clock at the refreshment stand said 5:45, he picked up his shirt and his towel, got his bike from the rack, and started home. He was supposed to be there by six.

Just before he reached the place where he would turn off Park Road onto his own street, a car speeding out of control hit his bicycle.

A woman who had seen the accident from her window summoned an ambulance and George was rushed to the hospital. Since the boy was unconscious, it took some time to find out who he was and notify the family. Just about the time his parents and their pastor arrived at the hospital, George died.

His father and mother were stunned with shock and grief. The day, begun in the ordinary routine, had ended in the loss of one of the family.

A few days after George's funeral, the man who had been driving the car was placed on trial for manslaughter. George's father was present at the trial, and in the midst of a dramatic court scene, he walked across the room to the man whose automobile had hit his son.

The father extended his hand and said: "I want you to know that I do not hate you, that in my heart I have forgiven you." The newspaper headline the next day was "FATHER FORGIVES MAN WHO KILLED HIS SON."

Do you remember what Jesus said as He hung on the cross? He said, "Father, forgive them; for they know not what they do." George's father was following that example. In his deep sorrow, he did not lose sight of God, but forgave the one who had brought him heartache.

Most of the occasions we forgive someone will not be big and dramatic. We may never make the headlines for our forgiving spirit, but we will need one often.

Can you forgive the little brother who knocks over your glass of milk at the table when he is too small to clean up the mess and you have to do it yourself? Can you forgive the sister who breaks the dish and blames it on you? No matter how big or small the wrongs done to us, let us ask in Jesus' name for a forgiving spirit like His.

R.E.

SURE, CATS LOVE BIRDS

They shall not hurt or destroy in all my holy mountain, says the Lord. Isaiah 65:25, RSV.

Like all cats, Mittens loved birds, but not for dinner as is usually the case. Wandering about the stables, she came upon a white pigeon crouching in fear and pain behind some wood. Its broken wing trailed on the ground. Creeping quietly up to the wounded bird, Mittens gently stroked him with her paw, mewing softly. She shooed him from the stable through a hole into the barn where there was drinking water.

Leaving him in safety on the hay, she went to the house, returning with her own food. Remembering a sack of corn, she bit through the string by which it was tied, making a large opening. Now it was easy to use her paw to scoop out corn for her sick friend. For weeks Mittens cared for the pigeon until its wing healed.

Now it was time to invite in friends for a celebration. She scooped out a lot of corn on the barn floor, and enticed the whole flock of pigeons through the same hole for a feast. No one on the farm knew the pigeons could get into the barn, but one day the stable boy heard twittering noises. Investigating, he could hardly believe his eyes when he saw the large cat sitting on top of the corn sack deliberately scooping out the grain while the whole flock ate happily.

About this time Mittens reared three beautiful kittens in the barn. As soon as her special pigeon friend saw the little family he took over. If any danger threatened, he would fly about making alarm calls for Mittens to hear. As the kittens grew, the flock often joined in play. When the kittens got too rough, Mittens would spank them. One very naughty baby had to be punished by putting him on top of one of the corn sacks, where Mittens made him stay for a long time.

After the kittens were gone, Mittens still stayed near her friend, the white pigeon. Often she sat in the tree with the whole flock. When they were feeding on the ground below her, she'd drop playfully down on them. Knowing it was a game of fun, they'd scatter for a moment, then go back to eating with the purring cat in their midst.

Mittens' love for birds is only a foretaste of that happy day when all fear will be gone and nothing shall hurt or destroy in all God's holy mountain. Will you be there?

E.E.L. and J.H.L.

APPLES IN THE DARK

The Lord looketh from heaven; he beholdeth all the sons of men. Psalm 33:13.

"Look, fellows, that tree is simply loaded with apples. Let's take a few," suggested Pete. "There's not a soul around for miles."

"Why not," agreed Glen. "The place looks deserted all right. The glass is broken in the windows of the house, and the yard is full of weeds."

As they started through the gate into the old farm, Marty commented, "Sure doesn't look like anybody's been around for a long time, by the state of this gate. There's only one hinge holding the thing on."

But Ron wasn't so sure they ought to be taking the apples—at least not in broad daylight. "Er-r," he hesitated, "what if someone comes along the road while we are in here and sees us? We'd be in trouble."

Bob frowned. "You know," he said, "Ron just might be right. With that corner in the road there, someone could be on top of us before we had a chance to see him coming."

"Well, then," suggested Pete, not willing to give up the apples, "let's come back tonight and get them after dark."

And they did. They felt safe filling their bags in the darkness, so they were in no hurry to leave. As they were picking apples, chattering and munching, suddenly a horse and rider drew up before the gate. Jumping off the horse, the man hurried toward the boys, who were so intent on their fun that they didn't see him until he stood before them. Astonished, they stared at him openmouthed. How had he known they were there?

Unknown to the boys, seven miles away an astronomer, scanning the sky with his telescope, had seen them in the apple tree. He watched for a few moments and then ran to the telephone. The owner of that farm was a friend of his, and it didn't take long to inform the man of what was going on. Jumping onto his horse, the owner was soon facing the startled boys.

If an astronomer seven miles away can see boys picking apples in the dark from a tree in a deserted farmyard, don't you think it is easy for God to look from heaven and know what you are doing?

"The Lord looketh from heaven; he beholdeth all the sons of men."

M.H.

HE DIED FOR ME

For I made up my mind to forget everything while I was with you except Jesus Christ, and especially his death on the cross. 1 Corinthians 2:2, TEV.

One of the great stories to come out of World War II concerns two young merchant seamen. One was a Christian and the other was not. They worked closely together and so had plenty of opportunity to discuss various topics. However, when the Christian youth would bring the subject around to religion, the other boy would walk away. The Christian tried using tracts and other religious material, but he was met with rebuffs. Finally, he handed his Bible to his friend and asked him to read for himself, since he would not listen when the Bible was read aloud. Again he refused.

At last, in utter desperation our Christian hero decided just to live his religion. So he was especially kind and friendly. He did everything he could for his companion. But nothing seemed to make any impression.

Then came the supreme crisis and final opportunity to reveal Christ to his friend. The American ship was in dangerous waters. They sighted a Japanese submarine. Next they sighted a torpedo on its way toward their ship. The torpedo hit its mark amidships. Next came that awful cry "Abandon ship!" The two boys were together when the explosion took place. The Christian offered a silent prayer and took his life preserver from around his neck, handed it to the other boy, who did not have one, and said, "Jim, you take this. I am ready. Maybe God will give you a little more time to get ready."

His friend's life preserver kept Jim afloat for hours until a passing ship rescued him. As they lifted him up on the deck of the ship, he turned and looked back at the scene of the terrible disaster, and said softly to himself, "He died for me!"

Jesus once said, "Greater love hath no man than this, that a man lay down his life for his friends" (John 15:13).

After the war was over, Jim returned to America. One day he walked into a church in Chicago, told the pastor his story, and said, "He died for me. I want to be a Christian like my buddy was."

A.A.E.

ESCAPE FOR THY LIFE

Escape for thy life; look not behind thee. Genesis 19:17.

The night was quiet as the little company walked down the streets of Sodom. Day had not yet broken when they passed through the gate. One angel held the hands of Lot and his wife, while the other followed leading the two girls. The time came for the angels to leave them.

"Escape to the mountain," the heavenly messengers warned Lot and his family, "lest thou be consumed." When Lot protested his fears of what might happen in the mountain, he was allowed to go to Zoar, a nearby city that was spared just to make it a place of refuge for Lot. The fire fell and the cities of the plain perished.

The summer and fall of 1894 were extremely dry. In the last days of August great fires broke out that threatened numerous logging camps in Minnesota. On the first day of September the town of Hinckley was surrounded by fire. When a freight train pulled in, the desperate people crowded into the empty cars and begged the engineer to save them.

Seeing a great wall of fire beyond the edge of town, the engineer put the train into reverse and began to push the train back toward safety. They crossed bridges that were on fire, and in some places even the ties were burning.

The train left the burning woods and came to the town of Sandstone. The Hinckley people begged their Sandstone neighbors to flee with them on the train, but the latter felt secure and only a few climbed aboard the train, which pulled out and continued on its journey.

The people who had fled by train safely arrived in Duluth. Those who refused to flee when they had the opportunity discovered too late that they were in the pathway of the fire and the last train had gone. During those five days of fire more than five hundred persons lost their lives who might have escaped had they chosen to believe the word of their neighbors.

This world is going to be destroyed by fire. Today the invitation to escape is still being sounded far and near. But only those who place their faith and trust in Jesus will escape. Let us heed His words to the disciples: "Watch ye therefore, and pray always, that ye may be accounted worthy to escape all these things that shall come to pass, and to stand before the Son of man" (Luke 21:36).

V.E.R.

ENTERTAINING STRANGERS

Let brotherly love continue. Hebrews 13:1.

"But, Mom," Anne protested, "why does that woman from Nigeria have to come to our house? Couldn't someone else take her?"

"They probably could," Mother said, "but I wanted her to visit us. I'm counting on my family to be especially nice to her."

"We'll be nice," Anne promised, "but . . . I don't see . . ."

"Be very careful that she doesn't feel unwanted," Mother warned.

The women's club to which Mother belonged was preparing to entertain a convention. Members were making preparations to provide for the visiting speakers. Places for the other speakers had been volunteered quickly, but no one had volunteered for the foreign woman until Mrs. Walker spoke up.

"She can come to our house," Mrs. Walker said. "I'll be glad to have her. And Danny and Anne will meet her at the bus depot." Danny and Anne were not enthusiastic, but they met the bus.

"How lovely!" Miss Arouble exclaimed when they met her and told of their mission. "Nothing could be nicer."

By the time dinner was ready, the entire Walker family felt like Miss Arouble, a graduate student from Nigeria, West Africa, was an old friend.

"She's just folks like the rest of us," Anne whispered to Mom over the dishpan.

News of Miss Arouble's visit spread quickly. Some of Mother's church friends planned a backyard picnic with the visitor as guest of honor. Miss Arouble told of her own home and the changes that had come to her family after they accepted Christ as their Saviour.

Danny and Anne and some of their friends assisted in her part of the convention program by learning songs in her language. Many said that they had never seen anything like the enthusiasm Miss Arouble created. She even stayed an extra day and the juniors had a picnic with her.

"How about it?" Mother asked when she had gone. "Was entertaining a stranger so hard?"

"She wasn't a stranger, not ever!" Anne exclaimed. "She made me think of the verse in the Bible that says an angel may be among us unawares."

R.E.

ON DUTY

Keep on the watch then, for you never know what day your Lord will come. Matthew 24:42, Moffatt.

Stay awake. Watch constantly. You not only do not know the day Jesus is coming, but you don't know the hour, either. Animals do not go to sleep when they know there is a need to watch. Why are we not as wise? If only we could learn this from them.

Naturalist Archibald Rutledge watched two whitetail deer feeding in a meadow. He noticed that never did they both eat at once. While one was completely at ease enjoying the grass, the other stood with his head high, eyes alert, and sensitive nostrils constantly moving. Finally, the one who had been watching ate. Even when they rested, they lay back to back, facing opposite directions so that each could watch from all sides. When a herd is walking through the woods, the oldest buck always stays at the rear to protect the weaker ones, and to watch for enemies from behind.

Near our Boulder, Colorado, home was a prairie dog town. We tried to slip up quietly to see the animals feeding or scampering about. Always one prairie dog stood on a high spot watching while the others went about their business. He never failed them, for when he saw us, he gave a bark of alarm and all scurried immediately to their holes. It was very difficult to sneak up on them, for the watchman was always on duty.

Walking through the woods, I have often heard the loud cry of a bluejay or a crow. As soon as their watchful eyes spotted me, they gave the special alarm call to warn all the animals in the area. Squirrels too give loud barks of warning.

Right now we are living at the end of time. Almost all of the prophecies have been fulfilled. Three times in Matthew 24 Jesus repeated His urgent call to watch constantly and be ready, for no man knows the exact time of His return.

Why are we so absorbed in the unimportant minor things of life? No animal is so foolish as to enjoy the pleasure of eating, playing, visiting with friends, forgetting that he also must watch. If Jesus came today, would you be ready, waiting and watching for Him?

E.E.L. and J.H.L.

SNAP JUDGMENT

Judge not, that ye be not judged. Matthew 7:1.

A young man came out the back door of the lower left apartment across the alley with a heaped-up basket of wet clothes.

"Mamma, there's a man hanging out clothes!" My girls thought this was funny. I did too when I looked again. He had a whole basketful of sheets, and he draped them over the line one by one, tugging at the corners and pulling them smooth. When he had them all in place, he stepped back to see how they looked. Then he went solemnly along the line pegging on a clothespin here and there.

Just like a man, I thought. A typical bachelor.

Only he wasn't a bachelor. Mrs. Barton had told me that a young airman and his wife lived in that apartment. I had seen them driving in and out in their little green Volkswagen. The wife was dark-haired and had sort of a pixie quality about her. She was always neat.

But she must be a lazy wife, I thought, making him hang out all those sheets. She ought to wash them every week and not let them pile up. Furthermore, they were the dingiest sheets in any backyard along that alley.

A few weeks later I saw the pretty young wife out at the clothesline. In a small basket she had a few dish towels. She was struggling to hang up a couple of his blue uniform shirts. Then I noticed that she had only one arm.

It is easy to come to a hasty conclusion about someone's character or motives on the basis of some little thing we see. But Jesus warned against this in His Sermon on the Mount.

He can see into men's hearts. God can read the motives behind each action. God knows the circumstances of each person's life.

"All who are followers of Christ should deal with one another exactly as we wish the Lord to deal with us in our errors and weaknesses, for we are all erring and need His pity and forgiveness." —*Testimonies*, vol. 3, p. 93.

Let us ask God today to help us to examine our own hearts rather then jump to hasty conclusions about the doings of others.

R.E.

PILOTS, MAPS, AND GOD

I will instruct thee and teach thee in the way which thou shalt go: I will guide thee with mine eye. Psalm 32:8.

Little Edwin's eyes were wide with wonder as he clambered up the steps to the airplane. He was going to see his grandpa and grandma, and he was going on a plane! After he had been seated for some time and the plane was already flying through the clouds, the lad turned to his mother with the question, "Mamma, when are we going to go see Grandpa and Grandma?" He didn't even know they had left the ground, the plane was flying so smoothly!

Yes, airplanes are a comfortable way to travel. Recently we took a trip, and before we were through we had ridden on nineteen airplanes! They ranged all the way from big Boeing 707 jets to a little DC-3, but not one of those planes put down at the wrong airport. One ran into a snowstorm and another flew through lightning, but we still reached our destination.

"Of course," you say. "The pilots had radar, maps, and compasses. They can even set a plane on automatic pilot and it will fly on course by itself." That is true, but somebody had to chart the course in the first place. Someone had to know how to direct the radar and the automatic pilot. Someone had to make an accurate map of the route before it was safe to fly passengers from city to city, and the pilots have to be able to read those maps. They have to know the navigational aids, radio frequencies, and airport obstructions. These may change from time to time, and revised maps are issued. Government survey experts warn pilots of both airplanes and ships, "Don't use old maps!"

When we were on a freighter, the captain let us visit the chart room to see how they plotted the course of our ship. They showed us large maps of the ocean and pointed out where we were. Then they pointed to a place marked "uncharted." Our ship was staying away from that spot!

There are a lot of things in this old world that can turn a boy or girl off course, but God has given us a map to follow that is always up-to-date. He knows where the trouble spots are in life, and He will guide you around them if you will let Him.

He has promised, "I will instruct thee and teach thee in the way which thou shalt go: I will guide thee with mine eye."

M.H.

SALTY? I HOPE SO

You are the salt of the earth. Matthew 5:13, RSV.

What's so important about salt, a common mineral consisting of sodium and chloride? Every gallon of seawater contains more than one fourth of a pound of salt. In solid form it is found beneath the ground in almost every part of the world. Since the Bible mentions this substance more than thirty times, could it be that Jesus wants you to possess the properties found in salt?

When you put an egg in a glass of water, it will sink to the bottom. Dissolve a large quantity of salt in that water, and see what happens to the egg. It stays on top. Salt made the difference. It has lifting power. Thus Jesus challenges you, His salt of the earth, to use your influence to lift your friends to a higher spiritual level.

If you get a few grains of salt in a fresh cut, your nerves will tell you that salt has great penetrating power. Salt penetrates food, making it taste so much better. If you aren't convinced, try eating oatmeal or potatoes without salt. You'll understand why Jesus knew that His love in your heart, like salt, is a vital power toward bringing out a lovely flavor in your life.

When you have a sore throat, you may sometimes gargle with salt water because of its antiseptic qualities. Salt not only purifies, but preserves. Before men learned to can or freeze food, they kept it from spoiling by salting it. Like the saving knowledge of God, salt not only preserves us from the destroying influence of sin, but fills our lives with a vital power that will actually preserve the world from utter moral corruption. When Christ's love fills your heart, the Holy Spirit's penetrating power will use you to change lives.

By mixing salt with snow or ice, you form a solution that has a lower freezing point than water. That's why salt melts snow and ice. Could it be that Jesus has chosen you, His salt of the earth, to melt the cold, hard hearts of those who are bound by Satan?

There are more than 14,000 valuable ways to use salt. There are also many ways to use the vital power of Jesus' love and righteousness, which is represented by salt. When this power is in your heart, you can help penetrate the hardness of others, melt away the ice of sin, and kindle a love for God in their hearts.

E.E.L. and J.H.L.

HOW GREAT IS HIS BEAUTY!

And your renown went forth among the nations because of your beauty, for it was perfect through the splendor which I had bestowed upon you, says the Lord God. Ezekiel 16:14, RSV.

God is speaking to His people of Jerusalem. How different would have been their future had they trusted in Him who gave them their beauty instead of becoming proud of these God-given gifts.

To all things in nature God has given perfect beauty and design. Not content to make things merely useful, He planned beauty in all created things.

Note the graceful, curved lines of grass blades or waving grain. The S-curve necks of swans and herons show pleasing form. Marvel at the beauty and harmony seen in the spiral curve of snails and vines.

God loves to use geometric figures in nature. When you throw a rock in a pond you see widening circles in the rippling water. The wild ginger blossom is a triangle and the fringed gentian a cross. The five-pointed pentagon is seen in the starfish, the tropical starfruit, or the lovely design in the core when you cut an apple crosswise. Snowflakes in amazing varieties of intricate patterns are six-sided.

Innumerable solid geometric forms abound in nature. God used the sphere for oranges, grapefruit, and the moon. Cattail heads are cylinders. Many seashells are cones. A magnifying glass shows salt crystals as cubes. Polyhedrons, solid figures of many facets, are found in endless shapes in minerals such as lead and quartz.

Radial symmetry, like the spokes of wheels, is displayed by many flowers such as the daisy. The scallop shell shows one half of a radial design, and the sun-ray pattern at sunset is fan-shaped.

God used bilateral symmetry, left and right matching, when seen from above, below, front or back, but not from one side, in fish, birds, mammals, and man. He combined two S-curves in many leaves, and made softly blended masses in cumulus clouds or the foliage of trees.

Look for the natural loveliness near you. Talk of beauty as your mind is carried up through nature to the Author of all that is lovely.

E.E.L. and J.H.L.

AN UNUSUAL PARTY

He that hath mercy on the poor, happy is he. Proverbs 14:21.

When ten-year-old Lucy came to school, the girls her age began to whisper unkind remarks such as "What a faded and patched dress! Look at those odd shoes!" The newcomer felt sad to go into the fourth grade with younger children, but she applied herself and paid strict attention in class.

Only one girl opened her heart to Lucy—Norma Tidwell. Once when the two walked home together, Lucy slipped and spattered mud all over her dress. As she began to cry, the girls behind her began to titter, "Baby, baby!"

When the other girls were out of hearing and Norma had used her handkerchief to wipe off some of the mud, she asked her new friend, "You weren't hurt. Why did you cry?"

"If it can be our secret, I'll tell you. This is the only dress I have to wear to school. When Daddy worked on the railroad he got hurt, and for months he has not worked, but now he is back at his job again. Soon I can have a new dress. I asked mother if it could be my birthday present, but she says we need some other things first. Please, please, don't tell anyone."

Norma was doing some quick thinking. "When's your birthday?"

"Next Sunday, November 6. I will be eleven then."

"We're twins," shouted Norma excitedly. "I'll be eleven too."

That evening Norma and her mother laid some wonderful plans. On Friday pink invitations went to each girl in the room, telling her to come to Norma's home for a birthday party. The girls placed their gifts on the table decorated with flowers. Norma called out, "Surprise. The party is for Lucy, who is eleven today."

The little hostess announced, "All the gifts are for Lucy, for this is her first party." Norma's mother urged Lucy to tell the girls about her father's accident.

Then Mrs. Tidwell brought in dainty sandwiches, fruit salad, and ice cream. The guests oohed and aahed over the birthday cake with eleven candles on one half and eleven on the other, celebrating the double birthday.

Before many days had passed, Lucy owned a lovely wardrobe of dresses, shoes, sweaters, skirts, and a coat, given her by some transformed girls who were determined to make the new girl feel like one of them.

L.C.W.

ONLY ONE WAY

Jesus saith unto him, I am the way, the truth, and the life: no man cometh unto the Father, but by me. John 14:6.

Jane closed her eyes tightly and hung on to the seat as the roller coaster plunged downward. Going uphill wasn't so bad, but the downhill plunge took her breath away.

When she grew older, Jane had another experience that took her breath away and reminded her of the roller coaster with its sudden plunges.

Jane heard a young man witnessing for Jesus, and her heart was touched as she heard how he prayed for God to lead him to absolute truth. He pledged to follow that truth whether or not it agreed with what he had always previously believed.

Jane was a good Seventh-day Adventist. She was certain that she already *had* absolute truth. She loved the message so much that she often prayed for others to see it too, as clearly as she did. She prayed especially for her relatives. Some of their worldliness really grieved her.

But as she listened to the young man who prayed for truth, she felt moved to pray that same prayer. Perhaps God would send her a sign to show how right she was in her present belief.

Jane had grown up trying to be good so she could go to heaven. Her life was full of good works. She wanted her friends to believe the doctrines she cherished, and she knew how to prove every doctrine, too. She hoped to have stars in her crown when she got to heaven.

Soon after her prayer for truth, a Sabbath sermon startled her thinking. The minister said that all the good works one might do wouldn't guarantee the way to heaven. Jesus was the only way.

Jane knew that, but hearing it in a new way made her think. Was her own way of life an attempt to earn her way to heaven?

As Jane prayed for Christ to reveal Himself more clearly, she began to feel as if she were on a roller coaster. God's Spirit pointed out to her things she needed to change. She just came to the top of one thing, and another would be revealed.

She saw that some people whose ways she had longed to improve had more of Christ's love than she did—and a less critical spirit! As Christ's love began to shine through Jane, her work for others became more effective.

R.E.

HAVE FUN!

Happy is he who trusts in the Lord. Proverbs 16:20, RSV.

God intends for you to be cheerful and happy. He enjoys seeing you have good fun that helps and heals like a medicine. Not levity and giddy frivolity, but a glad heart that brings lasting joy.

Animals are happy and enjoy good fun. Did you know that a grizzly bear will eagerly climb the steepest hill over and over again just to slide down on the snow? Wouldn't you enjoy watching that huge animal laboriously climb to the top of the slope in order to whiz down like a small boy on a sled? Not just young animals but old ones also enjoy the thrill of speed. Gray otters join with the young ones as they delightedly take their turns on the mud slides.

Black and brown bears often roll themselves into a tight ball and roll end over end, tumbling and somersaulting down a hill. A naturalist told of a black bear cub in an American national park that climbed into an open barrel he found by a shack, lurched and rocked it until it was overturned, and then wiggled it toward a slope. Rolling wildly down the mountain, he had the time of his life.

Even birds enjoy good fun. A flock of rooks flew high into the air. After reaching a dizzying summit in the sky they closed their wings and zoomed straight down. They allowed themselves to come as close to the earth as they dared before opening their wings to break the fall. Then in group fun they flew high again to repeat the maneuver over and over.

You, as a child of God, can carry with you a spirit of cheerfulness and joy as you live each day, enjoying God's rich blessings. It is not what is around you, but what is in you; not what you have, but what you are, that makes you really happy. Life is filled with brightness and fun, but you have to gather the flowers, and let the briers and thistles alone. There is no sorrow in the blessings of God. With the heavenly peace of obedience and trust filling your life, you'll view everything in a happy, cheerful light.

Like the animals, take time to let your glad heart bring glory to God.

E.E.L. and J.H.L.

NOVEMBER BIRTHDAY

Thou crownest the year with thy goodness. Psalm 65:11.

I wish I knew how Ellen Harmon and her twin sister, Elizabeth, spent their birthdays so many years ago. I know one thing—they probably had their celebrations indoors, because they were born on November 26, 1827, and winter arrives early around Portland, Maine. Another thing is sure—their parents could not spend much money on birthday parties for the two little girls.

When Ellen and Elizabeth surprised the family by being twins, there were already six children in the home, and little Robert, born later, made a total of nine children. Mother Eunice and father Robert were faithful Christian parents, and during those early years "had the joy of seeing their children . . . all converted and gathered into the fold of Christ" (*Life Sketches*, p. 17). Father Robert was able to keep his children busy helping him in his trade as a hatmaker. And mother Eunice with such a large family set her girls to work knitting, sewing, doing housework, or helping with the little ones.

Such a busy family probably did not have much time for birthday celebrations. Ellen Harmon, who became Mrs. Ellen G. White, does not mention any during childhood. But during adult life she often described what she did on her special day. She never liked to have what she called "a big fuss" made of her birthday. She would rather have her friends give money to missions than to buy her expensive gifts. When November 26 came on Thanksgiving Day, she loved to express her thankfulness to God for His loving-kindness.

On her fifty-seventh birthday, in 1884, Sister White spoke for nearly an hour to a large audience in the Battle Creek Tabernacle. "I thank God for my life," she said. "I thank Him with all my heart; with all my voice will I praise the Most High. . . .

"Open the door of your hearts and let Him enter, and you will have such a Thanksgiving as you never experienced before" *(Review and Herald)*, Dec. 23, 1884.

On her seventy-eighth birthday she wrote, "At my age I have great reason to be thankful to the Lord for His goodness, His mercy, and His love . . . Through Him I shall be an overcomer" Ellen G. White manuscript 142, 1905.

When your next birthday arrives, take time to add up your blessings during the past year.

V.E.R.

NATURE'S WONDERS

Then Job answered the Lord: "I know that thou canst do all things, and that no purpose of thine can be thwarted. Job 42:1, 2, RSV.

Did you know that there are about fifteen thousand species of ants in the world, and that there are more than five thousand kinds of other creatures that depend upon the ants for their very lives? Well, there are. And among those five thousand is a spider. If something threatens his life, this spider makes himself look like an ant and he is left alone. He does this by holding an extra pair of legs high up over his head to look like antennae.

When a man once ran a mile in four minutes, it was thought to be a great accomplishment. But the swordfish can go sixty miles an hour, the bonito about fifty, the tuna forty-four, the dolphin thirty-seven, and the salmon, twenty-five.

Then there is the chinch bug. In winter it manufactures an antifreeze chemical so its insides won't turn into an icicle. Other insects keep from freezing by burying themselves below the frost line and going to sleep, and a silkworm moth spins a cocoon with double walls which trap air between the two layers, and so insulates itself.

Do you know how the lichen can grow on bare rocks? It is made up of a very small fungus and a tiny alga. The fungus oozes out acids onto the rock. These acids loosen the minerals, which the fungus takes up. Then the alga uses the minerals from the fungus to manufacture plant food. If it were not for this lichen, the caribou herds in the Arctic would starve to death, and along with them, the wolves and many birds, insects, and rodents.

A number of years ago someone discovered that no two finger-prints are the same, and out of that discovery grew a whole new method of identification. But did you know that no two zebras are marked the same either? You might say, their markings are like human fingerprints. Imagine an FBI file on zebras!

When a crayfish loses its eyes, new ones grow in their place, and of course you've heard about lizards. If something catches one of them by the tail, it simply lets go of it and grows another.

And so the list goes on and on. Things past our imagination God has built into nature around us. With Job, we can say, "I know that thou canst do all things."

M.H.

ANSWERING THE CALL

And this gospel of the kingdom will be preached throughout the whole world as a testimony to all nations; and then the end will come. Matthew 24:14, RSV.

Eric Warland was Ingathering along the streets of Southampton, England. Most of his donations were small. He was preparing to stop for the day when he saw a house set well back from the road. He almost let it go but decided to make one last call.

He knocked several times, and was turning to leave when the door opened and a little old lady stood before him. He showed her the paper and told her what he was doing. She seemed interested.

"How much would it cost to send a missionary to Africa?" she asked.

"I really don't know," Eric replied, "but I can find out."

"Please do; then come and see me again."

Warland was a ministerial student about to graduate from Stanborough College. He greatly desired to go to Africa as a missionary.

The young man wrote to the mission board and was told it would cost five hundred pounds to send a missionary to Africa. With this information Eric returned to the old lady's home. When he told her what he had learned, she laid her hand on his arm and said, "Will you go to Africa if I give you the money?"

Eric was stunned. "Well, you see," he finally managed to say, "I don't want to go to Africa alone."

The lady smiled and nodded her head.

"So you have someone you would like to take with you! What would it cost to send you both?"

Eric agreed to find out. A few days later he was back with the information that seven hundred and fifty pounds would be needed. The lady left him and went to another part of the house. Returning with a handful of bank notes, she slowly counted the full amount.

"The Lord is good! The Lord is good!" she kept repeating over and over again, as she placed the money in Eric's trembling hands.

Within a year Eric Warland and his wife went to Africa, where he spent more than twenty years in mission service. The woman who had made this possible continued to support his work, sending money with which he built a schoolhouse.

Do you dream of going someday to Africa, to South America, India? God has many ways of making those dreams come true.

V.E.R.

TED'S LETTER

For every one who asks receives, and he who seeks finds, and to him who knocks it will be opened. Matthew 7:8, RSV.

"Anything more?"

"No, that's all, thanks," replied Mr. Coombs as he buttoned up his jacket and put on his gloves. "It has been a hard winter."

The clerk tied the parcel of purchases and broke the string with a snap. "That it has," he agreed. "If spring doesn't come soon there's going to be more than one person suffering in this town."

Everyone, it seemed, was talking about the weather. But Mrs. Conner did more than talk. She worried. A widow with several small children, she found the severe winter had cost more than she could afford. Yesterday they had finished the last of the carefully doled-out food and she had no idea where she was to get more for her hungry children. A tear slipped silently down her cheek as she looked at the empty cupboard. "What are we going to do?" she worried. And more tears followed the first one.

Ted looked at his mother sympathetically. He was so hungry it was about all he could do to keep from giving way to tears himself, but manfully he tried to comfort her. "Mother, don't cry. I'll write a letter to Jesus."

Poor mother was feeling so miserable she never even heard what Ted said, and when she didn't answer, the boy decided she had no objections. So he found an old writing book, tore a page out of it, and began to write: "Dear Jesus, My mother and brothers and sisters haven't had any breakfast or dinner today. Please send us some food." After signing his name and adding his address, he ran to the post office and dropped the note into the mailbox.

When the postal clerk sorted the outgoing mail, he stared in surprise at the neatly folded paper addressed to "Jesus Christ." "How will I ever deliver this one?" he asked himself. Perplexed, he handed it to the postmaster, who opened it and read the short message. Just then one of the businessmen of the town came to pick up his mail and the postmaster showed him the letter. "What shall I do with this?" he asked. "Any suggestions?"

The newcomer took the sheet and read the few words. Then, tucking the note into his pocket and picking up his mail, he answered, "Don't you worry about it anymore. I'll look after it." And he did.

M.H.

GOD'S WORD IS TRUE

Whereby the world that then was, being overflowed with water, perished. 2 Peter 3:6.

George's father was not an Adventist and as a result the boy was sent to a public high school. When he brought home questions about the Bible raised by his teachers his mother, a strong Christian, did her best to answer them. One day he came in unusually perplexed.

"Mother, today our science teacher laughed at the idea of a universal flood. He says all the water in the world wouldn't cover Mount Everest. How can I make him admit that he's wrong?"

"I doubt very much that you could do that," replied his mother. "Peter had scoffers to meet in his day. He accused the men of his generation of being 'willingly ignorant' of the Flood. Like them, your teacher would rather not believe the Bible."

"Then how can we be sure that there really was such a thing as the Flood? Does it make any difference whether we believe that or not?"

"Yes, it makes a great deal of difference. If the Flood story never happened, how can we decide what to believe in the Bible? You ask how we can know? All we need to do is to examine the evidence."

"You mean there is proof in the world today?"

"Certainly. Before the Flood there were no lofty mountains like Everest. As a result of the upheaval caused by the Flood the mountains rose, and the water was gathered into the oceans. On the tops of mountains men have found fish fossils. How did they get there?"

"I suppose they were left there by the Flood."

"Of course. As scientists have traveled around the world they find scores of countries where people recite ancient legends of a great flood. Is it likely that so many different tribespeople speaking different languages, and living as far apart as Australia and Central America, would make up the same story?"

"No, it isn't."

"Then just look at the coal beds. Coal has been found as deep as four thousand feet beneath the surface of the earth. How did it get there if not by a worldwide flood?"

"Thanks, Mother. I guess Professor Hoxie should check his facts more carefully."

V.E.R.

UNDER HIS CONTROL

Under his control all the different parts of the body fit together, and the whole body is held together by every joint with which it is provided. When each separate part works as it should, the whole body grows and builds itself up through love. Ephesians 4:16, TEV.

Note that all the different parts of the body are to be under His control. Does that include the fingers? Does it include the feet? Does it include the eyes and the ears?

If our fingers are under His control then we won't be turning on the radio or television set to bad programs. If our eyes and ears are under His control, we won't want to see or hear the wrong kind of programs. We want our minds to think noble thoughts. So we reread that wonderful guideline for boys and girls and young and old: "Here is a last piece of advice. If you believe in goodness and if you value the approval of God, fix your minds on whatever is true and honorable and just and pure and lovely and praiseworthy. Model your conduct on what you have learned from me, on what I have told you and shown you, and you will find that the God of peace will be with you" (Phil. 4:8, 9, Phillips).

If our feet are under His control, then we will be eager to 'go on God's errands.' Our time is His and we are under obligation to use it to His glory. So as long as God sees fit to give us life, let us keep that life dedicated to His service.

Every day the world bombards us with sights and sounds that will overcome the power of the gospel in our hearts, unless we sincerely ask God to keep us true. The Sabbath day can do much to counteract the wicked influences of the world during the six preceding days. But it is not enough. We cannot eat enough potatoes Monday morning to last us all week. We need to eat our meals regularly every day to keep healthy and strong.

So it is with our spiritual natures. We must show the same common sense toward our spiritual needs that we do for our physical needs. "Consecrate yourself to God in the morning; make this your very first work. Let your prayer be, 'Take me, O Lord, as wholly Thine.'"—*Steps to Christ*, p. 70.

A.A.E.

CAN YOU TRUST YOUR CONSCIENCE?

Let us draw near with a true heart in full assurance of faith, having our hearts sprinkled from an evil conscience. Hebrews 10:22.

Giant men and women, with tremendous minds and great physical prowess, walked the earth before the Flood. Some of the strength that God gave Adam and Eve still lingered in the bodies of their descendants.

Some of these men, like Noah and Enoch, used this great strength of mind and body to glorify God. We call them the patriarchs. During lifetimes that lasted almost a thousand years they learned how to live for God.

But the majority of the people took no notice of the stories of Creation. They did not serve God. They mocked those who told of a better life, and urged sacrifices for sin. They kept this up week after week. Finally they came to believe lies instead of truth.

Then something strange happened to them. Instead of their conscience telling them to do good things and act in the right way, it began to tell them to do evil. Inside them a voice would say, "It is good to steal your neighbor's cows," and when another voice answered and said, "No, it is not good to steal," they actually believed that the second voice was telling them wrong!

It says in the Bible that God saw that "every imagination of the thoughts of his [man's] heart was only evil continually." They had an evil conscience. It prompted them to commit sin. Yes, you can have an evil conscience.

Your conscience may actually need educating. Missionaries face this problem when they come to places where sin has ruled for long centuries without any help from the gospel. It takes time to educate a conscience. How can you have that voice inside you saying the right thing at the right moment?

Check your conscience against the Bible. Educate it to respond to what the Bible says. Check it, too, by praying for guidance.

Now that you know how to educate a conscience, why not be your own teacher?

W.R.L.S.

DISOBEDIENT SQUIRREL

This is the love of God, that we keep his commandments: and his commandments are not grievous. 1 John 5:3.

Mother squirrel was having a wonderfully busy time. Acorns had to be gathered and stored. Trash cans had to be inspected for tidbits. And there was junior to be watched. Obviously junior had a right place to be, but he had his own ideas. With a scamper he was down the tree trunk and out into the wide world, tail held high, tiny eyes darting.

Just then mother heard his scurrying feet. Like a flash she dropped an acorn and darted after him. But he didn't want to be caught. Quick as a wink he fled to the other side of the tree. For a moment or two mother and son played tag around the tree, until mother reversed her track and met a startled junior head on.

Seizing the squirrel like a kitten, she darted up the trunk of the tree and deposited her young son at the entrance of their home. But he had other ideas. Dodging past his mother, he fled along a limb of the tree. Again he found himself dragged back to the nest. This time mother tried to push him in, but he refused to go. Clinging to the sides of the hole with his paws, he resisted her every effort and ignored her angry scolding.

Mother squirrel took the final and only solution. Seizing the young rebel she dragged him into the hole after her. From the squealings and protestations that went on inside that squirrel hole I can imagine that junior learned a very necessary lesson that day.

Does God love you when He says Do not kill, Do not steal, Remember My Sabbath? Yes, of course, because like the mother squirrel, He knows where disobedience can lead.

But what about us? Should we think only of the dangers that may lie in disobedience? No. Keeping the Sabbath, worshiping God, being pure, telling the truth, honoring our parents—these are part of a good life. They do not hurt us. They help us to be happy. When you love God you will find His commandments a delight, never grievous.

W.R.L.S.

STEADFAST UNDER PERSECUTION

If we suffer, we shall also reign with him. 2 Timothy 2:12.

Jack was a twelve-year-old slave boy, eager to learn. One of the household servants taught him to read. After he could read he was given a New Testament. The story of Jesus touched his heart.

"I've got to tell others about this wonderful Jesus," he said. So he gathered the slaves together on Sundays and preached to them. One day his master spoke to him.

"Jack, I hear you go preaching on Sunday. Is that true?"

"Yes, Massa, I must tell sinners how Jesus died for them."

"Jack, if you go preaching on Sunday, I'll flog you on Monday. Now I don't want to hear anything more about it."

But Jack went preaching just the same. He told the people that he would be whipped the next day, and asked them to pray for him.

Monday morning came, and true to his word his godless master flogged him before sending him into the cotton field. The next Sunday Jack could scarcely walk, but he was going to preach anyway.

"Massa 'most killed me last Monday; maybe he will tomorrow," he told his listeners the next Sunday. Sure enough, the next day he received a second whipping. When Jack went the following Sunday, he had to be lifted into the chair, he was so crippled. But again he preached about the love of Jesus.

The next morning the master called Jack and told him to bare his back. But as he looked at it, he saw only a mass of wounds.

"Why do you do it, Jack?"

"Oh, Massa, I love Jesus. He suffered so much for me that I am willing to suffer for Him. He died on the cross for you, too, Massa."

The whip dropped from the master's hand.

"Go down to the cotton field," he said.

In the afternoon a boy ran to the field, shouting for Jack.

"Come quick, Massa's dying."

When Jack got there he found his master crying to God for mercy. Jack prayed for him and pointed him to Jesus as the mighty Saviour, and before the sun went down he saw his master give his heart to God. Jack's master recovered.

A week later the master gave Jack his freedom papers, bidding him go and preach Jesus everywhere.

V.E.R.

A TIME TO LAUGH

To everything there is a season, a time to every purpose under the heaven. Ecclesiastes 3:1.

Following this verse in Ecclesiastes 3, Solomon gives a whole list of things people can find a proper time for—to be born, die, plant, harvest, kill, heal, weep, and laugh.

One set of statistics says that the average American who lives to be seventy years old will in his lifetime sleep twenty-three years; work nineteen years; take nine years for recreation and amusement, six years for eating; six years for traveling; be sick for four years; and use two years for dressing and one for religion.

A Swiss man who had lived for eighty years carefully figured out how he had spent his life. He decided he had slept for twenty-six years, worked for twenty-one, eaten for six, been angry nearly six years, wasted more than five waiting for people who were late, shaved for 288 days, scolded his children for twenty-six days, tied his necktie for eighteen days, blown his nose for twelve days, lighted his pipe for ten days, and laughed for only forty-six hours.

Imagine laughing for only forty-six hours in a whole eighty years of lifetime, and being angry for nearly six years! Especially when it takes less effort to smile than to frown. Smiles use fewer muscles.

There is a saying, "Laugh, and the world laughs with you. Weep, and you weep alone." People don't like to be around anyone who is gloomy.

But there is a big difference between laughing *with* people, and *at* people. While there is a time to laugh *with* people, there is never a time to laugh *at* them. Laughing at your friends is cruel.

Another time when it is not proper to laugh is in church. It distracts others who come for a blessing. Nor should you laugh at a dirty joke. Purity is sacred and not a reason for jesting.

However, sometimes it is a very good idea to laugh. If someone is angry, tell a little joke. Or if someone has blundered and is embarrassed, a few well-chosen words of humor will break the tension.

If you will keep your witty sayings clean, laugh *with* but not *at* others, and choose the proper time for your humor, you will attract friends as honey draws bees. There is a time for everything, even laughing.

M.H.

RICH IN KINDNESS

For you have tasted the kindness of the Lord. 1 Peter 2:3.

Many years ago Mary, who made a meager living selling butter and eggs, lived out these words. Most folks in town thought Mary the richest woman they knew, because although she gave freely of her kindness, she always had more to give.

Little Jerry, sobbing on the front steps, didn't see Mary when she stopped her wagon in front of the house, nor did he look up when she asked why he was crying. Major, his dog, usually romped and played with him, but now Major lay still, very still, and Jerry couldn't wake him up. Mary asked to see his mother.

As she handed Mother the butter and eggs, she suggested that Jerry could ride with her as she worked, maybe even have lunch with her, and come home before suppertime, adding, "It'll take his mind from his dog he loved so much."

Jerry was happy to ride in the wagon with the big red and yellow wheels. Soon he forgot to cry as she let him help her drive the horse. Soon she asked, "What made Major die?"

"I think I k-k-k-killed him. I was playing doctor. You see, I found a bottle of old medicine in the wastebasket, so I played Major was sick. I gave him the medicine to make him well. He liked it so much he drank the whole bottle. I don't think the medicine was good for him." Jerry started to cry again. But Mary had listened well.

Immediately she turned her horse around, making him trot back to Jerry's house, constantly urging him to go faster. As they neared the house Mary said, "Take me quickly to see your dog."

Major lay under the apple tree in the backyard where Jerry had left him. The empty bottle was on the grass. Mary laid her head on Major, listening for his heartbeat.

"I can hear it, Jerry. Your dog isn't dead. The medicine put him to sleep. Maybe I can help him wake up."

Rubbing the dog's body vigorously, Mary talked to him. Suddenly Major opened one eye, and soon he wagged his tail weakly. Yes, Mary's real business was giving out kindness. How much will you give today?

E.E.L. and J.H.L.

CHRISTMAS LISTS

Freely ye have received, freely give. Matthew 10:8.

Joe begins making Christmas lists early in the fall. He collects all the Christmas catalogs he can find and goes through them looking for things he would like to have. He sees so many things he wants that it would be impossible for any set of relatives to provide them all.

So Christmas isn't a very happy day for Joe. First, he feels disappointed that he didn't get everything on his list. Second, when he sees the things some of his friends have received for Christmas, he sees things that weren't even on his list that he wishes he had. Instead of being glad for his friends' good fortune, Joe feels miserable about what he didn't get.

Don also starts making Christmas lists early in the fall. But as he looks through the stores, Don doesn't write down what he wants for himself; he writes down what he would like to give to others. He usually has saved enough money that he can give a small remembrance to each of his parents, his brothers and sisters, and some of his friends and other relatives. He feels good all over when he thinks of something that will be just right for those to whom he wants to show love at Christmas time.

But Don does not stop with family and playmates. Each year he also remembers his best Friend, Jesus. Sometimes he does this by giving a special Christmas offering at church. Sometimes he does this by helping an older person, or by taking toys to a child who might not otherwise have gifts at Christmas time.

Don has read in his Bible that Jesus considers doing for unfortunate people the same as doing for Him. And he thinks the holiday season is one of the very nicest times to do something for Jesus by doing it for other people.

While Joe is making lists of what he wants for himself and making himself miserable because he can't possibly get it all, Don is finding Christmas the happiest time of the year.

Other people find Christmas happier too, because of Don!

If you have not experienced the warm glow that comes from making the season brighter for someone else—especially someone who does not expect it—try it this year. See how much happier *your* holidays are.

R.E.

HOW TO SYMPATHIZE

Rejoice with them that do rejoice, and weep with them that weep. Romans 12:15.

A mother sent her daughter to the grocery store with this admonition, "Now hurry. Dinner is almost ready." But the little girl did not return promptly. When her mother demanded an explanation, she said, "I met Mary, and she had dropped her doll and broken it. I stopped to help her."

"What do you mean, you helped her with the broken doll?"

The child lifted a tear-stained face to her mother. "I helped her cry."

Everywhere we may find opportunities to share burdens, express concern, and voice hope. Everywhere we may find an invitation to become involved. Too many are like the two boys on their way to school who met an old man having difficulty walking. His hat was blown off by the strong wind. "Please, boys, run after my hat. I can't hurry fast enough."

The boys just laughed. They thought it a joke to see the hat carried off. But Lucy, without being asked, ran after the hat, caught it, and wiped it off before returning it to its owner. The teacher had observed the episode from the schoolroom window. She told the children about it, and gave a pretty picture book to Lucy.

A Boston mayor decided to go to his ghetto slums to see "how the other half lives." In preparation he let his beard grow for days. Then he dressed himself in shabby clothes and walked through the slum streets searching for a cheap boarding house. There he was told to chop wood for his bed and a breakfast of thin oatmeal and skim milk.

But the "old" man had never used an ax in his life. He was having a hard time qualifying for board and room. Finally a young man insisted, "Give me that ax. You don't know how to use it."

When the mayor's job had been done, the older man said, "Here's my card, son; call me at four this afternoon and I'll see that you get a job."

"Poor man, he's crazy; he believes that he is the mayor," said the youth. But curiosity made him present himself at the mayor's office.

"I'll give you a job on one condition. Keep still about where you first met me; never tell anybody," cautioned the official. The young man promised, and smiled back his understanding at his benefactor.

L.C.W.

A UNIVERSAL ENEMY

Who hath woe? who hath sorrow? . . . They that tarry long at the wine. Proverbs 23:29, 30.

For six thousand years the devil has been inspiring man to invent things that bring him to ruin and destruction. At the same time God has been working to purify and save the wandering children of Adam. It was certainly a master stroke when Satan inspired man to create strong drink. Taking God's good gifts of fruit and grain, he learned how to turn them into poison. Perhaps only war has caused more suffering and misery on earth than has the use of strong drink.

Lee Tracy, a Hollywood star, told his story this way:

"I was just a kid—only eighteen—when I started drinking. To be completely frank, I instinctively liked the taste of whiskey. By the time I went on the stage in New York I was drinking pretty steadily.

"I came to Hollywood for the first time in 1930 under contract to Fox. I was getting $1,500 a week, and every time I thought of that salary I pinched myself to see whether I was dreaming or awake."

But his drinking became heavier and it wasn't long before producers were rejecting him. "Tracy's a good actor," they would say, "but you can't trust him to stay sober." A period of unemployment followed. Then one day he got to thinking.

"I looked around for my ambition and couldn't find it," he continued. "I tried to recall the great joy that I had once had in my work, and discovered that I had lost the ability to feel that joy. My nerves were shot; my energy was shot; I had lost interest in things. I lay there for thirty-six hours thinking it out.

"Over and over I kept telling myself, 'Tracy, from now on you've got to be terrified of liquor. It's the one thing on earth that's got you licked.' And then and there I made up my mind to quit."

Tracy quit. How does he feel about it now?

"I'm living again. I've acquired a new interest in my work. I quit for good. When I compare myself today with myself yesterday I have no urge to turn back the calendar. Tracy's been a fool, but he's through being a fool. He's scared to death of liquor."

Turn Solomon's statement around. Do you want to avoid woe, trouble, sorrow, grief? Then keep away from all forms of strong drink.

Never take the first glass.

V.E.R.

THE "NATION" NEXT DOOR

Go ye therefore, and teach all nations. Matthew 28:19.

Each Sabbath afternoon found Tim and Jerry bicycling to the farms near their academy to give out literature and enroll the farmers in a Bible course. Most of the farmers wanted nothing to do with the school or anything it represented, but the boys kept doggedly on.

When one farmer dismissed them with a curt "No!" after they had offered him a Bible, one of the boys asked, "Wouldn't you like to know why we are having so much war and trouble in the world? You can find out if you will study these lessons."

"Well, I guess there's no harm in looking at them," conceded the farmer as he took the Bible and the first two lessons.

"Who were those boys?" the farmer's wife asked as he came into the kitchen after the students had gone.

"Some fellows from the school."

"I hope you had nothing to do with them. What did they want?"

"Well, they left a Bible and a couple of lessons."

"They did? The nerve! Just you let me handle them the next time they show their faces. You go work in the field and I'll look after them!"

So the next time the boys came, the farmer disappeared, leaving his wife to greet them. She did, too, in no uncertain terms. Before they were even off their bicycles, she was outside ordering them, "Scat!"

The boys' mouths fell open, and they looked so disappointed that the woman changed her mind. "Well, all right. Seeing you are here, you might as well come on in." The boys lost no time in improving their opportunity.

Sometime later when he was sure Tim and Jerry must be gone, the farmer returned to the kitchen and stared in amazement at the sight of the two boys sitting at the kitchen table busily polishing off one of his wife's good pies.

"Why," he started, but his wife cut him short.

"We were just having a pleasant little conversation," she said.

Soon the farmer and his wife were attending church at the school.

You don't have to wait until you are a foreign missionary to "teach all nations." No, sir! Some of them might be right next door!

M.H.

RIPTIDE

Be not overcome of evil, but overcome evil with good. Romans 12:21.

Sunday crowds had flocked to the beach. Children splashed merrily in the breaking waves. Farther out a line of bodysurfers sized up the waves, waiting for the right one to ride in. Along the stretch of water, past the edge of the patrolled area, hundreds of board riders crouched on their surfboards, or rode weaving and twisting toward the shore.

Suddenly the bustling peace of the scene was broken with a cry of "Help! Help!" About twenty yards from shore a group of swimmers, a moment before enjoying the rise and swell of the waves, were struggling for their lives. Startled watchers saw them retreating from the shore faster than anyone could swim.

Instantly lifeguards sprang into action. Volunteers trained in the art of rescue seized lifelines. Donning light harnesses, they raced for the water while teammates payed out the line. Swimming with the riptide, they quickly overtook the imperiled swimmers.

Meanwhile minor dramas took place among the struggling groups. The more experienced swimmers urged the others to go with the riptide and concentrate on staying afloat. Some assisted the weaker swimmers. Help came none too soon. Taking life preservers first to the weaker ones, and with the help of their teammates pulling on the rope, the rescuers soon had the first gasping victims on shore. Within a matter of minutes all fiftythree swimmers had been rescued.

Afterward one of the lifeguards said, "You cannot blame those people. You just do not know when a riptide will develop and take you with it. Fortunately all of them could swim a little."

Rescue squads stand by to help you. God's promises are one such squad. The holy angels, another. Good companionship, a third. Finally Christ Himself will reach out to you as He did to Peter when he thought he would drown in Galilee.

W.R.L.S.

A LITTLE LIGHT SHONE ON HIM

You are the light of the world. Matthew 5:14, RSV.

"Man overboard!" What a bloodcurdling call to hear on a stormy night! The ship was crossing Lake Michigan, which, like the Sea of Galilee, is subject to heavy storms. People rushed to the side of the ship, but nothing could be seen in that darkness.

The ship began to turn around and the searchlights flashed on. But no sign of the passenger could be seen. It seemed hopeless to search in those turbulent waters.

When the announcement rang out over the public-address system, it roused one man who had already become seasick and had retired to his bunk. He rushed up on deck to see whether he could help spot the passenger struggling in the water. But he was so sick that he had to go back to his bunk. Still he was restless. How could he lie there when a man was drowning? Then he remembered his little flashlight. Grabbing it, he flashed it down through the porthole.

Suddenly the searchlight went out, and the ship continued on its journey. The sick man thought, How can they go on and let that man drown? All night he was unable to sleep, thinking about it.

In the morning he went on deck. Seeing one of the ship's officers, he inquired, "Why did you go on and let that man drown last night?"

The officer replied, "The man didn't drown. We saved him."

"How did you do it?" asked the amazed passenger.

"Well," said the officer, "our searchlight was too far above his head to help. But someone put a flashlight out a porthole window and it shone right on him. We threw a rope, which he grabbed. There he is in that deck chair."

The passenger rushed over and said, "Are you the one who nearly drowned last night?"

"Yes," answered the man, "and I would have, but for that little light that shone on me."

In heaven, how many will be there because of your little light?

A.A.E.

HOW GOOD A DETECTOR ARE YOU?

Now the Spirit speaketh expressly, that in the latter times
some shall depart from the faith, . . . speaking lies in hypocrisy;
having their conscience seared with a hot iron. 1 Timothy 4:1,
2.

A conscience is a sense of right and wrong both in conduct and motives. Just as burned flesh is incapable of feeling, so a conscience can be abused, blunted, deceived, guilty, weak, or dead. On the positive side it may be clear, educated, good, pure, quick, sensitive, and true. The spiritual condition of yours depends completely on the training and treatment you give it.

A conscience is a lot like Ben, a trained Labrador retriever, who worked with London's police. When Ben was just a year old he'd had three months' training on how to catch thieves. His master, Police Constable Shelton, patrolled an area of London that abounded in sneak thieves, the kind who slip off their shoes and quietly snatch purses.

Quickly Ben learned to detect the difference between right and wrong conduct in those he passed. As they strolled through a park, Ben would stop and growl deeply, his warning that trouble was near. With remarkable awareness he could sense the physical reaction of fear that a guilty person feels at the sight of a policeman and his dog. This ability to detect a guilty conscience was evident when a man, asked to be a witness about some crimes in his neighborhood, entered the car where Ben was. The dog growled deeply and was restless all the time the man was in police custody for questioning. When he left, Ben howled indignantly. Later they discovered this man had committed all the crimes.

Distracting influences didn't deter Ben from a command to find a criminal. Six houses had been burglarized, and about thirty policemen were looking for the thief. When Ben arrived and was given the scent, he dashed through the policemen and crowd of onlookers, and in a few minutes had the man cornered in an orchard just out of town.

In three years Ben captured more than 100 lawbreakers. How did he do it? By knowing the true, clear, pure, and honest, he could detect the false that leads to guilt and fear. What is the condition of your conscience; sharp and good, or seared so that you no longer hear God's voice? Better check up now.

E.E.L. and J.H.L.

ALL GOD'S CHILDREN

Of a truth I perceive that God is no respecter of persons: but in every nation he that feareth him . . . is accepted with him. Acts 10:34, 35.

It was a hard lesson Peter had to learn that day in Caesarea. He had always thought he belonged to God's chosen people and that all heathen were unworthy of God's mercies. Yet here he was in the home of a Gentile, having come at God's specific command. When the Holy Spirit fell on Cornelius and his family, Peter knew that God had given salvation to the Gentiles.

There are still people today who maintain that one race is superior to another. They refuse to make friends with someone whose skin is a different color from theirs. Yet often both profess to pray to the same God. Since God is the Father of the black, white, red, and yellow races, then all are His children, and brothers and sisters to one another.

Some people claim that their nationality, or race, or family, or church is superior to all others. Paul would ask such people a question: "What hast thou that thou didst not receive?" In other words, have you not received everything from someone else? Did you choose your parents? Did the Italian boy choose to be born in Italy? Did you decide to be born white or red or black?

A teacher once asked, "Johnny, who was the first man?"

"George Washington."

"No, of course not. Think again and tell me who was the first man."

"George Washington."

"Now, Johnny, you know that Adam was the first man."

"Aw, foreigners don't count," he remarked scornfully.

Too many people feel that way today. The really big man hasn't time to feel superior.

One morning a Negro man walked across the floor of the waiting room in New York's Grand Central Station burdened by two heavy suitcases. It was a hot day. Suddenly he felt himself being relieved of one suitcase. A stranger said, "Let me help you." The two men walked out to the taxicab stand, where they parted.

"And that," said Prof. Booker T. Washington, "was the first time I ever met Theodore Roosevelt."

Feelings of love for all on this earth will prepare us for living happily together in heaven.

V.E.R.

BILL OF RIGHTS

And if any man sin, we have an advocate with the Father, Jesus Christ the righteous. 1 John 2:1.

On December 15, 1791, the United States Congress ratified the first ten amendments to the Constitution, which we call the Bill of Rights.

Several of the early North American colonies had put lists of rights in their constitutions, so when this country was founded, some of these rights were written into the Federal Constitution.

Here are some of them: People have the right to say and write what they wish, to meet together peaceably, and to complain to the Government. Congress can not set up an official religion for the country or keep people from worshiping as they wish.

In peacetime people cannot be forced to take soldiers into their homes. An official cannot search a person or his home or take his property without a warrant.

No person can be put on trial unless a grand jury has decided that there is enough evidence for a trial. No person can be tried twice for the same crime. No person can be forced to give testimony against himself (this rule is to prevent the use of torture). No person can be executed, imprisoned, or fined except after a fair trial.

A person accused of crime must be tried quickly and in public. He must be able to see and hear the witnesses against him. If he cannot pay for a lawyer, the court must appoint one.

The Ninth Amendment even tells us that the rights listed here are not the only rights that people have. You can read the exact wording of the Bill of Rights by looking up the Constitution of the United States. Notice that many of these rights talk about what happens when a person is accused of a crime and has to go to court.

As Christians we have a "Bill of Rights" that tells us what happens when we go to "court." We have an Advocate, One who pleads for us, defends us—our court-appointed Lawyer, you might say.

When Satan accuses us as sinners and claims us as his subjects, Jesus pleads our case.

He doesn't excuse our sins as He defends us, but He covers our unworthiness with His righteousness.

To have our sins forgiven and covered by Him, we must repent and ask for forgiveness. Let us do that now.

R.E.

THE LOVING SHEPHERD

Surely he hath borne our griefs, and carried our sorrows. . . .
He was wounded for our transgressions, he was bruised for our
iniquities: the chastisement of our peace was upon him; and
with his stripes we are healed. Isaiah 53:4, 5.

R. A. Anderson, in his book *The Shepherd Evangelist*, tells of a tourist who, walking across the Scottish hills enjoying the beauties of the lake country, saw a shepherd with his sheep resting at noon.

The sheep were browsing. As he drew near to the shepherd he noticed one sheep lying down. It was evidently hurt, and the shepherd was speaking words of love and reassurance to the little thing.

"You have a sick one there?" asked the stranger.

"Well, not exactly sick. He has a broken leg."

"Oh, how did it happen? An accident, I suppose." But the old shepherd hesitated to say. Finally he told the story.

"This fellow is a good sheep. He has all the earmarks of a leader, but he was willful and wouldn't come when I called. He would always lead the flock the wrong way. I tried to teach him, but he was obstinate. He wouldn't trust me. I decided I'd have to do to him what I'd done to others before. It was hard, but I knew it would work. I prepared splints and bandages; then holding him down, I took the little fellow's leg in my hands and broke it over my own like this," and he showed how it was done. But his voice choked and his eyes were brimming.

"Then I set the leg," he continued, "and bound it up. That was weeks ago. Since then every mouthful of food and every drop of water this little fellow has had, he has taken from my own hands. Every day I carry him out to the field, and every night I take him back again. We have learned to love each other, for we have suffered together. In a few days I will remove the bandage, and he will be my leader, for he has learned in pain what I could teach him in no other way."

Discipline, always hard, was necessary because the sheep wouldn't listen to the shepherd. Before correction, Jesus makes preparation to bind up your wounds. In sympathy and love He shares your trials, sorrows, and afflictions. As your faithful, tender Friend, He only can bring comfort and relief. What a wonderful Saviour and marvelous God!

E.E.L. and J.H.L.

WORDS

Let the words of my mouth, and the meditation of my heart, be acceptable in thy sight, O Lord, my strength, and my redeemer. Psalm 19:14.

How powerful are words! They can make an enemy, or they can make a friend. Words can kill. Words can save a life. They can make you weep, or they can make you laugh. And the same word can have many meanings.

Several years ago Steve and Susie stayed at our home for a short time while their mother and father went for a trip. One Sabbath while they were with us we drove several miles to another church for services, and were invited to a member's home for supper. Little Stevie dallied with his food, not eating. Thinking to encourage him, I said, "Come on, Stevie, you'd better eat or I'll beat you!" Meaning that I would finish my food first and win the race.

One of the men at the table looked aghast. Then suddenly he caught my meaning and sheepishly said, "I thought you meant you were going to spank him if he didn't eat."

Beat to win, and beat to spank. I suppose it could be confusing. Maybe Stevie got the wrong idea too, for he ate his supper without any more fuss!

Dianne was the youngest girl in the dormitory, and the dean had given her a room with an older student. When the dean met Dianne one day she asked the girl how she liked her roommate.

Secretly Dianne wished she were rooming with someone her own age, but she realized the older girl was doing her best to make her feel at home. So she answered, "Oh, she's all right. She's doing the best she can." She meant that her roommate was doing all that could possibly be expected of her as a good roommate. But later Dianne learned that she had unwittingly been the cause of many tears. Her roommate had learned of the conversation and thought Dianne had meant, "The poor soul is doing the best she can and we get along, but there is sure room for lots of improvement!"

How careful we need to be of the words we use so that no one misunderstands us. We need to pray daily, "Let the words of my mouth, and the meditation of my heart, be acceptable in thy sight, O Lord, my strength, and my redeemer."

M.H.

SALVATION IS FREE

He that hath no money; come ye, buy, and eat . . . without money and without price. Isaiah 55:1.

A well-dressed man walking along a London street stopped to chat with a peddler trying to sell a basket of fish.

"Why can't I sell these fish, governor?" the peddler asked. "Aren't they cheap enough—three for a penny?"

"There are many poor people living here who don't have a penny in the house. Many of them are unemployed."

"In that case I'm wasting my time," muttered the fish peddler.

The stranger checked him. "How much will you take for your fish?"

"I have about four shillings' worth. Why do you ask?"

The stranger took out four shillings and handed them to the man, who appeared very pleased with his quick sale. "Where do you want 'em?" he asked.

"I don't want them. I want you to go down the street, calling out: 'Herrings for nothing.' Give three to each person until they are all gone."

The man did as he was told. Housewives heard the strange offer, came to the door, and looked at him.

"Want some fish, madam?" he asked one lady. "They're free," he added. The woman shook her head and returned to her work. When he reached the corner, he still hadn't disposed of one fish.

"Now let me try," said the stranger, taking the basket.

"Is there anyone who would like some herrings? They are yours if you want them." Recognizing the man's voice, they came, first a few, then more. Soon the basket was empty.

One woman pushed her way through the crowd. "Why can't I have any?" she demanded. "Aren't my children hungry too?"

The fish peddler pointed his finger at her.

"Governor, that's the first woman I offered them to, and she refused them."

"I didn't think you meant it," she protested.

"That's what you get for your unbelief," retorted the man.

Many people are going to miss heaven because God's offer to them seems too good to be true.

V.E.R.

BLACKIE'S SUICIDE

There is a way which seemeth right unto a man, but the end thereof are the ways of death. Proverbs 14:12.

No dog was ever loved more than Blackie, our handsome black Labrador pup. An affectionate nature, gentle ways, beautiful brown eyes, partnership in playful games and romps, and frequent hikes to the nearby mountains made Blackie an essential companion to the family's activities.

When he was about two years old we noticed a small cut on one toe. Possibly he had caught it in the back-yard wire fence. Knowing how difficult it is to bandage an animal's foot, my husband suggested, "Let him heal his wound by licking. All animals care for themselves that way."

Several days passed. Noticing Blackie licking his cut, I examined it. Surprised at the ugly sore that now covered his whole toe, I took him to a veterinarian for treatment.

The doctor explained that constant licking had caused an infection that had already affected the bone. To save Blackie's foot the toe must be amputated. I left him for the operation. Warning us that Blackie must not lick the paw till it was completely healed, the doctor fitted him with a large collar shield on his neck, designed to prevent him from reaching his foot. But he didn't know Blackie's determination.

We had to change the bandage every day. Using rolls and rolls of tape plus tight socks for covering, we spent hours trying to save Blackie's foot. But each morning we found that he had spent the night gnawing his hated collar, the sock, the tape, and the gauze. The bloody paw hung in shreds, with the surgical stitches broken by Blackie's sharp teeth. Bitter medicine smeared liberally, leather guards, tin cans fitted on his foot, much heavy tape, frequent calls to the veterinarian—nothing stopped Blackie from having his own way.

Discouraging months passed, but the infection spread. Finally, our once healthy young Labrador had to be put to sleep. Why? Blackie died because he insisted on having his own way.

Every person who will be eternally lost will have first chosen to have his own way. Because of his own self-deception the way may seem right to him, but the end is death. Don't commit spiritual suicide by following your own way. Listen to Jesus and follow His way.

E.E.L. and J.H.L.

GIFTS WITH LOVE

*For where your treasure is, there will your heart be also.
Matthew 6:21.*

In algebra we learn that if A equals B, then B also equals A. Or if A plus B equals C, then C minus B equals A. Using this same principle, we might turn today's text around and say, "Where your heart is, there will your treasure be also."

Jay didn't have much money, for he was working a large share of his way through academy. But he had quite a few people he wanted to remember at Christmas time. At the very top of the list was Cindy.

Cindy was the nicest girl in school, Jay thought. She had long blonde hair, and in his mind he called her "Cinderella." He liked her so much that he wanted to give her a very special gift.

Then there were Mom and Dad. He loved them too, of course, and wanted to remember them at Christmas time. And his roommate, who was so much fun to be with, should have a gift. Then the boys' club had exchanged names for the Christmas party, and that meant another gift.

Jay's experience is not uncommon, for we all have certain persons on our lists that we want especially to remember because we love them. But perhaps today would be a good day to check our lists for any name left off.

I've got my Christmas baking done;
I've trimmed a Christmas tree.
The house, all decked in evergreens,
Is filled with gaiety.
The Christmas cards are in the mail,
My shopping is all done.
I'll check my list once more to see
If I've missed anyone.
But when I check my list, I note
One detail I had missed.
The One whose birth we celebrate
Is not named on my list!
I'd thought my heart was generous;
I see my soul is small.
Forgive me, Lord! Your gift to me
By far surpasses all.

R.E.

SHINING FACE MEDICINE

In thy presence is fulness of joy. Psalm 16:11.

If a Christian is not happy, there is something wrong with him! Christianity is the only religion that has joy now and a hope for the future. Why shouldn't we be happy?

One Christmas Day in England a poor, ragged little girl was found sick on the street and taken to the hospital. While watching the celebrations she learned for the first time the story of Jesus' birth.

"But why did He come?" she asked.

"Because He loves you and wants you to live with Him."

The little girl was thrilled with the thought of being able to live in a lovely home forever and ever.

One day when the nurse came on her rounds, the child grabbed her hand and whispered, "I'm having such a good time here! I suppose, though, I'll have to go away as soon as I get well; but I'm going to take the good time with me—some of it, anyway. Do you know that Jesus was born?"

"Why, yes," answered the nurse. "Of course I do. But you just be quiet now and don't talk anymore."

The little girl's eyes opened wide. "You know about Jesus? I thought you looked like you didn't, and I was going to tell you."

It was the nurse's turn to look surprised and she forgot her orders to be quiet as she asked, "Why, how did I look?"

"Oh, like most people. Kind of sad. I didn't think you'd ever look sad if you knew that Jesus was born."

Mrs. White tells us, "Do not for a moment suppose that religion will make you sad and gloomy." It is Satan who likes to see long-faced Christians. They are the best argument he has for not becoming a Christian.

Some natives came to a missionary with the request, "Please give us some medicine to make our faces shine."

Puzzled, the missionary questioned, "What do you mean, 'medicine to make your faces shine'?"

"Your Christian boys look so happy and their faces are always shining," explained the natives. "We want some medicine to make ours shine too."

What medicine would *you* prescribe for shining faces?

Our text gives us the answer: "In thy presence is fulness of joy."

M.H.

363

FIRST PLACE IN ALL THINGS

He is the head of his body, the church; he is the source of the body's life. He is the first-born Son, who was raised from death, in order that he alone might have the first place in all things. Colossians 1:18.

Billy wanted a bright-red wheelbarrow for Christmas, and he began to pray several weeks before December 25, asking Jesus for it. Christmas morning when Billy awakened in his rural England home, sure enough, there was the red wheelbarrow. Pushing his pride and joy into his parents' bedroom, he cried excitedly, "Look what Jesus sent me! Look what Jesus sent me! I asked Him for it and He gave it to me!"

Quickly Billy dressed and told his parents he wanted to push his beautiful, red wheelbarrow around the square. On the corner of the square stood the church that Billy and his parents attended each Sunday. This morning the pastor came over to the church early to see whether everything was in readiness for the special Christmas service. Passing the Nativity scene, he noticed that the statue representing Baby Jesus was missing. Inquiring of the caretaker, he learned that a little boy with a red wheelbarrow had been in the church a short while before and had been sent away.

Hurrying out into the town square, the pastor soon found Billy pushing his new, red wheelbarrow with the statue of the baby Jesus in it. He was singing, "Away in a manger," at the top of his voice. The pastor stopped him.

"Why did you steal the baby Jesus from His crib?" he began sternly.

Billy looked up, surprised. "I didn't steal Baby Jesus," the boy replied with a hurt tone in his voice. "I prayed and asked Jesus to give me a new, red wheelbarrow for Christmas. I promised Him if He did I would give Him the first ride. That's what I'm doing."

The apostle Paul says that not only should Jesus be the head of the church but that He should "have the first place in all things' —that means everything in our lives.

Somehow I think little Billy understood what Paul was talking about. Even though Billy had a new, red wheelbarrow, Jesus was the center of his simple love and devotion. Christ must have first place in everything in *your* life too.

CHRISTMAS WITNESS

Grace be to you and peace from God the Father, and from our Lord Jesus Christ, who gave himself for our sins, that he might deliver us from this present evil world, according to the will of God and our Father. Galatians 1:3, 4.

Though she was only eleven, Beth loved Jesus and lived for Him. Her family had no interest in being Christians. Each day, morning and evening, Beth would go to her room and there read the Bible her grandmother had given her, and pray.

Beth didn't want Christmas to come. She knew that Father and Mother would drink and become noisy and perhaps quarrel with each other. How her parents could quarrel when they should be thinking about the birth of Jesus, she did not know. (Beth did not know then that December 25 is not the birth date of Jesus.)

When guests began to arrive for Christmas dinner, Father gave cigars to them. Soon the room was full of smoke. Then he said to Mother, "Get us something to drink." Drink followed drink, so that by the time dinner came, Beth and her grandmother were the only ones steady enough to serve dinner.

"Daddy, may I say the blessing?" Beth asked.

"Of course, my dear. She's a good girl, my Beth," he slurred to the relatives and friends.

"Dear Jesus," Beth began, "thank You for this food. Thank You for Your love in coming to save us. Help Father and Mother not to drink alcoholic drinks so that they may go to heaven. Amen."

Beth's blessing left everyone speechless. Suddenly sobered, her father said, "If it means so much to my little Beth, I'm not going to drink anymore."

Not long after this a series of meetings began in the Adventist church nearby. Beth asked her father and mother to take her to the meetings. By the end of the series the whole family joined in giving their lives to God.

But the best day of all came when, with her parents, Beth went down into the water in baptism. No wonder Beth whispered as she came up, "Thank You, Jesus, for letting me help my mother and father find You."

W.R.L.S.

THE REAL TREE

Heaven and earth shall pass away, but my words shall not pass away. Matthew 24:35.

Margy's earliest years were spent in the city. Each year at Christmas time she watched the man across the street string the colored lights around his front porch. She saw the wreath hanging in the next-door neighbor's window and the plastic Santa Claus on a roof down the street.

Sometime during the days before Christmas, Margy's daddy would go up to the attic and bring down the long box that held the Christmas tree. Margy's family used an artificial tree. Each year Daddy put the sections of tree trunk together, set it up in the Christmas-tree stand, and attached the branches. When it was finished it looked so real that Mother said that all it needed was scent to make it smell like an evergreen.

Then the family moved from the city to the country, where many evergreens grew in the woods. When Christmas came, the artificial tree stayed in its box in the attic. Daddy and big brother went into the woods to cut a tree.

To Margy the tree from the woods was nice, but it simply wasn't right. As she watched Daddy stringing lights on it, her expression became sad and she asked, "Why can't we have our *real* Christmas tree?"

In life we sometimes become so used to the unreal or artificial that we are confused as to what is actual reality. Our values become distorted. Our frame of reference isn't quite square with real life. We get out of kilter and sometimes don't even realize it.

There is one thing we can be sure of, and that is God's Word. If we truly want to discern the difference between the false and the real, we can turn to His Word and be certain of finding truth that is real—not just now, but eternally.

If we trust our own understanding, we will reap only sorrow and disappointment. But if we trust the reality of God, He will be our guide on the pathway to eternal life. Let us thank Him today for the reality of His love and His Word.

R.E.

THE DAY CHRIST WAS BORN

And she shall bring forth a son, and thou shalt call his name JESUS: for he shall save his people from their sins. Matthew 1:21.

We don't know what date it really happened, but December 25 is the date men have picked to celebrate the most important birth in all history.

Promised to Adam and Eve in the Garden of Eden, the Messiah was anticipated down through the years. Prophets foretold His mission and the manner and place of His birth. The morning and evening sacrifice pointed forward to Him. Yet when He came, the miracle met with unbelief and indifference.

Priests went about their duties in the Temple that day, performing the worship rituals and reciting their prayers. They knew the words so well they could say them without thinking.

Over in Bethlehem, business was bustling, for scores of visitors were in town to register for taxes. Inns were so full that the innkeepers began turning people away. There was no room.

Unseen angels hovered around Mary and Joseph as they journeyed toward Bethlehem. Heaven quivered with expectancy.

But on earth very few were even thinking about the Messiah. They had lived with the prophecies so long that they could recite them without letting the meaning touch their minds.

Joseph accepted shelter in the stable when he found no other place for a weary traveler to be squeezed in. There the greatest One to walk this earth was born.

Out on the nearby hills a group of shepherds talked together as they watched their sheep. They spoke of the promises and prophecies and prayed that the Deliverer might come. Yet they were startled when the bright light shone around them and the angels sang.

In an Eastern country, dedicated scholars who had studied Hebrew writings to learn more about astronomy realized from their studies that the advent of the Messiah was near. The night Jesus was born they saw a light in the heavens. As it faded, a bright star appeared.

Thus it was to shepherds and foreigners He was first made known, for their hearts were willing. Let us ask God today to give us willing hearts that He may be known to each of us in a more personal way.

R.E.

BEFORE WINTER

Do thy diligence to come before winter. 2 Timothy 4:21.

Paul was pleading with Timothy to come to him soon. His damp Roman cell was getting chilly. He also made two other requests: "The cloke that I left at Troas with Carpus, when thou comest, bring with thee, and the books, but especially the parchments." Warmth for his body and food for his mind were both urgent needs.

Paul had been pitifully abandoned by his friends. "At my first answer no man stood with me, but all men forsook me," he wrote. But he added, "Notwithstanding the Lord stood with me, and strengthened me . . . and I was delivered out of the mouth of the lion." Paul could not be sad very long, even though he was still under the power of Nero.

Please, please come before winter! To many people the winter of hardships comes all too soon. There is the winter of famine. Tonight half the people of this world will go to bed hungry. Especially from India and Africa comes this plea to every one of us. "Come before winter starves us," they beg. With their sunken eyes and shrunken bodies they cry, "Give us bread." If we do nothing to help such people in need, we begin to suffer from "hardening of the sympathies." To give is to live, and sharing is life's greatest joy. One of those small plastic loaves of bread with a slot through its crust, sometimes used to remind us of God's blessings, should be on every table. And it should be filled and refilled with money to be used for famine relief.

There is also the winter of loneliness. Visit any nursing home in your area. Elderly people are there, some in wheel chairs, some hobbling down corridors holding on to railings, others using canes and walkers. All of them have memories of life's summertime when they had homes, companions, children. Now their winter has come. But you can help turn it into spring. Watch their faces light up when you go out with your Singing Band next Sabbath.

If you have elderly grandparents, or loved ones in a far country, remember that they too suffer from loneliness. Write a cheerful letter. Hopefully it will reach them "before winter," and will fill their hearts with warmth and gladness.

"Come before winter." Every grief, every sadness, in this tired world is a kind of winter. Every day you can help turn someone's winter into a happy spring.

V.E.R.

OLD SAM'S TIN BOX

Who are thou that judgest another man's servant? to his own master he standeth or falleth. Romans 14:4.

Near a pioneer town, old Sam lived alone in a hillside shack, surrounded by a number of vicious dogs. These kept his neighbors from visiting him. On all sides of his land he had posted "no trespassing signs. People saw him mostly on his weekly trips for his provisions. Then he allowed himself the luxury of a warm meal at the town's one restaurant.

Shocked at his rough language and his unfriendly manners, people left him strictly alone. Old Sam appeared glad of it.

One day he died. Since he had no relatives or close friends, the mayor of the town called the mortician, asking him to arrange a funeral for the hermit.

"He has no known relatives and is not the member of any church, but he lived among us for a number of years and faithfully paid his taxes. For that reason I feel we must show him some respect and give him an honorable burial."

Then as an afterthought the mayor added, "Be prepared for a large funeral. He is so disliked in this community that many may be glad to hear that he is gone." The undertaker and the mayor asked a number of people if anyone knew something good about old Sam. The restaurant owner did. "I'm glad you asked me, for old Sam was not all bad. For years I have kept his secret faithfully. Every week when Sam ate here, he always left me some money to put in a small tin box. I was to pass it out to anyone in real need.

"Some money he wanted used for Christmas gifts for boys and girls, especially if their parents were poor. Look at these bills still in the box—more than $50. Really, Sam liked people, but he did not know how to show them any interest.

"I had to promise the recluse that I would not betray his generosity till he was gone. School ought to be dismissed so that the children may know about the old man who loved them, but who was misunderstood and misjudged."

At the service the minister showed the people Sam's tin box and what it had done for the needy. "We have had an example among us of the good Samaritan. God wants us to remember always to 'judge not.' He alone reads the heart."

L.C.W.

KEEP ALERT!

A man's gift maketh room for him, and bringeth him before great men. Proverbs 18:16.

There are several gifts to which Solomon may have been referring in this verse. Some are common, some very rare. It was the gift of prophecy that brought Joseph and Daniel before kings.

Some have the gift of eloquence, knowing how to use words well. The gift of friendliness often opens the door to success. Diligence, patience, honesty, and energy are all gifts worth cultivating. No one can sit at home and expect success to come knocking on the door. He must go in search of it. But first of all, he must be prepared.

A long line of boys waited in the office of a businessman, hoping for a job. John entered the room and took his place in line. He might have been discouraged when he saw so many ahead of him. Instead he took out a piece of paper, wrote a short message, folded it up, and handed it to the man's secretary.

A couple of minutes later the man stepped into the room.

"You may all go except John Williamson," he said.

"Where did he get his pull?" muttered the boys as they left the latecomer with the man.

On the businessman's desk lay the paper on which John had written his brief message. "Please don't hire anyone until you have seen me. I am number twenty-three." No wonder he got the job.

Another man advertised for a telegraph operator. Before his door also stood a line of young men, eager for the position. Busily chatting, they paid no attention to the dots and clicks coming over the telegraph. But Tom was not asleep. Suddenly he stepped out of line and marched straight into the office.

"How did he get ahead of us?" one asked. "We came before him."

"You might have had the job," said young Edison a little smugly as he came out of the office, contract in hand, "if you had listened to the message."

"What message?" they asked.

"Why, it came over the telegraph in Morse code—'The first applicant to come into my office gets the job.' I was listening, you weren't."

Be alert, be energetic, and your gift will open the door.

V.E.R.

WHEN THE CLOCK STRUCK SEVENTEEN

In the same way, when you see these things happening, you will know that the Kingdom of God is about to come. Luke 21:31, TEV.

Little Peggy was playing in the living room one day when the big grandfather clock began striking: bong! bong! bong!

Now Peggy had heard this big clock strike many times before, but she counted every bong this time. Bong ten, bong eleven, bong twelve, the clock struck. But then a strange thing happened. The clock didn't stop striking with twelve bongs as it should have. It went right on: Bong thirteen! Bong fourteen! Bong fifteen! Bong sixteen! Bong seventeen!

Startled, little Peggy fled into the kitchen, where her mother was preparing dinner.

"Mother! Mother!" she cried in alarm. "It's later than it's ever been before!"

Peggy decided that it was later than it had ever been by the number of times the old grandfather clock struck. If she had been a little older, she might have reached the same conclusion from what she read in the newspaper, heard on the radio, or watched on television. For all of this news reminds us that *it is, indeed, later than it's ever been before.*

What do you see on television? War. Violence. Murder. Robbery. Fighting. Cheating. Impurity. Shady dealing. Dishonesty. The newspapers and the airwaves are full of this kind of news. Isn't this the kind of thing you see or hear every time you watch television or listen to the radio?

On several occasions Jesus talked to His disciples about these very things that are happening today. He said: "When you see the events taking place that I've described you can be just as sure that the Kingdom of God is near" (TLB).

Aren't you glad that Jesus has told us in the Bible what all these things mean? Many people are worried to death today because of the terrible things that are happening all about them. They don't know what it all means. As Seventh-day Adventist Christians we know. Jesus told us in His Word many years ago. All of these terrible happenings tell us that it is time for Jesus to come back. What a wonderful thing to look forward to! Jesus will soon come, and we believe and hope that He will come while we are living. Let us be ready!

R.H.P.

A SPECIAL THANK YOU

Thanks be unto God for his unspeakable gift. 2 Corinthians 9:15.

Have you thanked God today that He gave you Jesus? If not, why are you so sparing in giving Him thanks? How happy God would be if you would cultivate a thankful disposition. He loves to hear you tell Him often how much you appreciate the blessings He gives.

A little girl whose daddy was a bus driver was playing alone by the river when she slipped and fell in. Unable to swim, she began to go under the water when a big brown dog spotted her. Instantly he plunged in and was soon pulling her to shore by her clothing. Friends who saw what happened took the girl home and related the story. Her happy father shared his joy by telling all his fellow bus drivers of the big brown dog that saved his daughter's life.

The next day, seeing the dog at the bus stop, he braked the bus, opened the door, and invited the dog to go for a ride. For a long while the dog sat on the back seat enjoying himself. When he stood by the door, the driver let him off. Other bus drivers, hearing of the dog's ride, said, "Let's make him a very special passenger. He can ride anywhere on any bus without paying. In this way we can show our thankfulness for his saving the life of the little girl." And how the dog did enjoy this treatment.

Every day the brown dog waited at the bus stop on Fifth and West streets. When the bus stopped, he walked to the back seat and sat down. His loving act had earned those rides. Now he was thanked every day by being a very special passenger.

Have you given God a thank offering for your comfortable home, good clothes, health, and the delicious food you ate today? He has poured out uncounted blessings on you, given you of His great bounties, cared for you constantly, and forgiven all your sins. Your life is a gift from Him. Have you thanked Him for answered prayers? Best of all, He gave all heaven in giving you the unspeakable gift of Jesus. Not only this day but every day, thrill your listening Lord with a heartfelt, simple "Thank You, God, for Your love."

E.E.L. and J.H.L.

THE KEY TO EVERYTHING

If ye know these things, happy are ye if ye do them. John 13:17.

People you know are searching for keys. Some look for the key to success. Some search for the key to peace. Some are not even sure what they seek. But perhaps the most universal search is for the key to happiness. If you find that key, you have the key to everything. Yet that key is so simple it can be summed up in nine words.

"The way to be happy is to be good."

I was ten when I first saw those words in a book I found on my mother's bookshelves. The author had dedicated the book to her beloved older brother who had drowned in his teens. She quoted this aphorism on the dedication page. Perhaps it was something her brother had often said to her.

Had you asked me at that age what *I* thought was the way to be happy, I might have answered, "The way to be happy is to have my own way."

Yet, even then, I was finding that it was not true. One day, for instance, when I wanted to play in the creek, my mother said No. But I begged until she gave in. Nothing spectacular happened that day. I didn't hurt; I hardly even got wet. It just wasn't fun. I had my own way, but it didn't satisfy me. I soon went back to the house.

If you had asked me in my teens for the way to happiness, I might have said, "The way to be happy is to belong to the 'in' crowd and do things that are fun." But as I tried to find happiness in that way, I discovered that there is more to happiness than having a good time.

I did learn the truth of the opposite of that quotation. The way to be *un*happy is not to be good. Having learned that Jesus expects certain things of His children, one feels uncomfortable inside not doing them. Peace cannot live in the same heart with a guilty conscience.

When I decided to love Jesus with all my life, I discovered the truth buried in that old quotation, "The way to be happy is to be good."

Through this year we have learned helpful verses, precious promises, affirmations of hope and trust. We have learned some verses that contain ground rules for victorious daily living. We have stored these scriptures in our hearts, and they are a treasure chest to us—something no one can take away.

Today's verse is the key to that treasure chest. "If ye know these things, happy are ye if ye do them."

R.E.

373

These last few pages
are just for you.
Maybe you will want to
jot down special thoughts
that come as you
read these daily devotionals.
Maybe you will
want to record your prayer
requests and note the way
that each was answered.
Whatever way you decide to
use these pages, it is
our prayer that this
devotional book has
enabled you to come
closer to God.